Masachiyo Amano/Michiko Ogura/
Masayuki Ohkado
(eds.)

Historical Englishes in Varieties of Texts and Contexts

The Global COE Programme,
International Conference 2007

PETER LANG
Internationaler Verlag der Wissenschaften

Bibliographic Information published by the Deutsche Nationalbibliothek
The Deutsche Nationalbibliothek lists this publication in the Deutsche Nationalbibliografie; detailed bibliographic data is available in the internet at <http://www.d-nb.de>.

This publication was supported by
The Global COE Program:
Hermeneutic Study and Education of Textual Configuration.

ISSN 1436-7521
ISBN 978-3-631-58190-2
© Peter Lang GmbH
Internationaler Verlag der Wissenschaften
Frankfurt am Main 2008
All rights reserved.

All parts of this publication are protected by copyright. Any utilisation outside the strict limits of the copyright law, without the permission of the publisher, is forbidden and liable to prosecution. This applies in particular to reproductions, translations, microfilming, and storage and processing in electronic retrieval systems.

Printed in Germany 1 2 3 4 5   7

www.peterlang.de

Historical Englishes in Varieties of Texts and Contexts

STUDIES IN ENGLISH MEDIEVAL LANGUAGE AND LITERATURE

Edited by Jacek Fisiak

Advisory Board:

John Anderson (Methoni, Greece), Ulrich Busse (Halle),
Olga Fischer (Amsterdam), Dieter Kastovsky (Vienna),
Marcin Krygier (Poznań), Roger Lass (Cape Town),
Peter Lucas (Cambridge), Donka Minkova (Los Angeles),
Ruta Nagucka (Cracow), Akio Oizumi (Kyoto),
Katherine O'Brien O'Keeffe (Notre Dame, USA),
Matti Rissanen (Helsinki), Hans Sauer (Munich),
Liliana Sikorska (Poznań), Jeremy Smith (Glasgow),
Jerzy Wełna (Warsaw)

Vol. 22

Frankfurt am Main · Berlin · Bern · Bruxelles · New York · Oxford · Wien

Preface

This volume is a selection of papers read at the second international conference of the Society of Historical English Language and Linguistics (SHELL) held at Nagoya University on 7-9 September 2007, under the auspices of the Graduate School of Letters, Nagoya University. The Society started its activity back in 1997 by exchanging papers twice a year on the computer screen so that every member could join the discussion and make comments on the papers. At the very first stage, members consisted of young theoretical linguists who had less chance for reading their papers in large conferences. Then the number increased by inviting philologists, and in 2001 the first preparatory meeting was held at Nihon University, where an introductory course of medieval palaeography is organised for linguists, as well as paper sessions on theoretical linguistics. In 2003 twelve members of the Society met at a hotel in Tokyo to declare the formal establishment of the Society, inviting Prof. Jacek Fisiak, then President of Adam Mickiewicz University, Prof. Yoshio Terasawa, Professor Emeritus at Tokyo University, and Prof. Masatomo Ukaji, Professor Emeritus at Tokyo Gakugei University, as counsellors. The first international conference of SHELL was held at Chiba University on 1-3 September 2005. At that time thirty people attended, and he proceedings published in the same series as this in 2006 included thirteen papers. This time more than eighty people came from eleven countries all over the world, and twenty-eight papers were submitted to this volume. The success of the conference was achieved by unsparing efforts of Prof. Masachiyo Amano, Nagoya University, by the organising committee led by Prof. Masayuki Ohkado, Chubu University, and by the governmental fund of the Center of Excellence (COE) Program called "Hermeneutic Study and Education of Textual Configuration", which has been proceeded by Prof. Shoichi Sato, Nagoya University. The publication of the proceedings was also supported by the COE Program, by the generous donations from Prof. Young-Bae Park, Kookmin University, Seoul, and from Prof. Yuji Nakao, Professor Emeritus at Nagoya University. We express our cordial thanks to Mr Tadashi Kotake, graduate student at Keio University, now staying in King's College, London, for his technical advice in the process of editing this volume. Our aim is to encourage younger scholars to read and publish their papers internationally so as to keep the reunion between linguists and philologists working on every subject of the history of the English language.

Editors
January 2008

The Opening Address by Professor Shoichi Sato (Nagoya University)

Dear Colleagues,
Ladies and gentlemen, it is a great honour for me to give an opening address for International Meeting of The Society of Historical English Language and Linguistics, SHELL. A few months ago, my colleague Professor Amano most kindly proposed to co-host the SHELL international conference. I agreed without any hesitation. Then we were just informed that our program for the Global COE, which we planed out to reply to an invitation from Japan's Ministry of Education and Research, was successfully chosen as one of those that survived the very selective screening process. The title of our program is "Hermeneutic Study and Education of Text Configuration." You can call it "HERSETEC" for convenience sake.

This program, which inherits our achievements through the 21st Century COE Program, aims at forming an education hub, which will efficiently rear a younger generation of researchers by developing a core theory that will reveal the overall configuration of an array of linguistic texts. The 21st Century COE Program, "Studies for the Integrated Text Science," involving history, literature, thought, image, gesture, and so on, has been very successful in synthetically explaining different types of text existing in human societies. Since our main purpose is to form an education hub, we will attempt to establish a teaching methodology that will deepen and renovate hermeneutic studies of linguistic texts and 'interpretation' as human intellectual activities.

One of the findings by the 21st Century COE Program during the past five years was that texts constitute their own special configuration. In general, texts consist of pre-texts, which are prerequisites for their existence, other related texts, which realise inter-textuality through cross-references among them, meta-texts, which are annotations or interpretations assigned to them, and para-texts, which are titles indicating genres of texts or categories they belong to, as well as their forms and structures. A particular text exists as the close-knotted gathering of all these constituent texts, and their overall configuration is characterised as text in a broad sense.

The reason we have decided to foreground linguistic texts out of the fruits of the 21st Century COE Program is that since the present program is primarily educational, its main purpose should be to build up an education research hub, and thus we should utilise for our education plan all the achievements which have been accumulated in the linguistic-graphic section of the 21st Century COE Program that achieved the most outstanding results of all its sections involved. On all these achievements we will reconstruct the results obtained through Hans-Georg Gadamer's text theory, which is a compilation of previous hermeneutic studies, and a refined methodology developed through post-Saussure modern linguistic theory. This will allow us to bring up young researchers with the ability and grounding that enable them to develop an up-to-date academic perspective. Alongside the development of the ability to construe texts spoken or written in various languages, we will build up an educational system for training of young researchers who tackle textual phenomena with a profound understanding that texts have a configuration. Our program involves a couple of promoting members invited from other graduate schools of Nagoya University, because it has law and economy texts within its range of research and education as types of linguistic-graphic text. Studies of law texts, for example, based on a textual theory, have practical importance as well, since Japan has already decided to have private citizens as members of a jury after reforming its judicial system. Semantic studies of law texts are of special significance in both jurisprudence and text science.

I am afraid I have talked too long about our COE program to celebrate the opening of international conference of SHELL. Nevertheless, I hope that my explanation of our program has not bored the members of SHELL who have gathered here from all over the world. I am sure that the members of SHELL and those of HERSETEC share the same academic and scientific interests. Neither group can be indifferent to studies that the other will carry out on any topic on language activities by human beings.

If I remember correctly, the members of SHELL gathered here as lecturers or speakers are from nine different countries except Japan, namely, New-Zeeland, France, South Korea, Taiwan, United States, Poland, Germany, Austria and England. I am deeply impressed because so many eminent scholars with such a wide variety of nationalities have gathered in Nagoya to acquire new knowledge and new contacts without public financial support. As a medieval historian of Europe, I cannot help thinking of the monk scholars in medieval Europe, who lived on the desire to acquire sacred knowledge and wisdom. So I would like to sincerely admire your pure and precious academic passions, which have become very rare nowadays. I wish the Goddess of Musa should reward this three-day conference with enormous academic discoveries.

Last but not least I would like to thank Professors Michiko OGURA and Masachiyo AMANO who contributed greatly to create this opportunity which must have the academic Holy Grail.

Thank you very much.

Shoichi SATO
Leader of the Global COE Program,
Hermeneutic Study and Education of Text Configuration,
at Nagoya University, Japan

Table of Contents

Part I   Old English   1

1. **Isao Hashimoto** (Shinshu University)
   Hebraisms in English Bibles   3

2. **Caroline Imbert** (CNRS – University of Lyon 2)
   Path Coding in Old English: Functional Story of a Typological Shift   17

3. **Kousuke Kaita** (Chiba University, Graduate School)
   Distribution of OE *mid rihte* as an Adverbial of Propriety —
   with Special Reference to the Textual Variation   33

4. **Yookang Kim** (Hankuk University of Foreign Studies)
   The Prenominal Prefix *ge-* in *Beowulf*   49

5. **Tadashi Kotake** (Keio University, Graduate School)
   Differences in Element Order
   between *Lindisfarne* and *Rushworth Two*   63

6. **Yoshitaka Kozuka** (Aichi University of Education)
   An Aspect of OV Order in the *West Saxon Gospels*
   with Special Reference to the Collocation 'Verb + *God/Gode*'   79

7. **Mitsuru Maeda** (Yamaguchi University)
   Insubordination in Old English   93

8. **Michiko Ogura** (Chiba University)
   Variant Readings in the Two Manuscripts of the West Saxon Gospels:
   MSS CCCC 140 and CUL Ii.2.11   109

9. **Masayuki Ohkado** (Chubu University)
   Stylistic Fronting in Old English Prose   121

10. **Aurelijus Vijunas** (National Kaohsiung Normal University)
    The Old English Adjective *sīht*   135

11. **Hideki Watanabe** (Osaka University)
    The Ambiguous or Polysemous Compounds
    in *Beowulf* Revisited: *æscholt* and *garholt*   143

12. **Tomonori Yamamoto** (Keio University, Graduate School)
    A Reconsideration of the Reliability of Alliterative Evidence
    for the Sound System of Old English:
    Does Old English Poetry Work Aurally or Visually? ... 157

13. **Tomohiro Yanagi** (Chubu University)
    Object Movement in Old English Subordinate Clauses ... 169

Part II Middle English ... 185

14. **Ayumi Miura** (University of Tokyo, Graduate School)
    New Impersonal Verbs in Some Late Fourteenth-Century
    English Texts ... 187

15. **Rafał Molencki** (University of Silesia, Poland)
    The Rise of *because* in Middle English ... 201

16. **Akinobu Tani** (Hyogo University of Teacher Education)
    The Word Pairs in *The Paston Letters and Papers*
    with Special Reference to Text Type, Gender and Generation ... 217

17. **Fumiko Yoshikawa** (Hiroshima Shudo University)
    Discourse Strategies in Late Middle English
    Women's Mystical Writing ... 233

Part III Modern English and the History of English ... 245

18. **Masachiyo Amano** (Nagoya University)
    A Broader and Sharper Characterisation of Grammaticalisation ... 247

19. **Magdalena Bator** (Adam Mickiewicz University)
    'Parts of the Body' and 'Parts of Clothing' — A Semantic Analysis ... 259

20. **Charles Elerick** (The University of Texas at El Paso)
    The Evolution of English Ordinals:
    Integrative Explanation in Historical Linguistics ... 269

21. **Sylvie Hancil** (University of Rouen)
    Aspect and Modality: The Blurring of Categories ... 281

22. **Yoko Iyeiri** (Kyoto University)
    The Verb *prevent* and its Changing Patterns of Complementation
    in the History of English ... 297

Table of Contents

23. **Namiko Kikusawa** (Kyoto University, Graduate School)
    The Subjunctive in Nineteenth-Century English Dramas ... 311

24. **Ji Won Lee** (Seoul National University, Graduate School)
    On the Development of *because*: A Corpus-Based Study ... 325

25. **Manfred Markus** (University of Innsbruck)
    Joseph Wright's *English Dialect Dictionary* Computerised:
    a Platform for a New Historical English Dialect Geography ... 335

26. **Fuyo Osawa** (Tokai University)
    Recursion in Language Change ... 355

27. **Young-Bae Park** (Kookmin University, Seoul)
    Multilingualism in English Literature:
    Applicable to the Study of the History of English? ... 371

28. **Hans Sauer** (University of Munich)
    Emotion, Interjection and Grammar ... 387

Part I
Old English

1 Hebraisms in English Bibles

Isao Hashimoto, Shinshu University

1. Hebraisms[1]

English Bibles are translated versions of the Bible. The original version of the Old Testament (hereafter, OT) was written in Hebrew and that of the New Testament (hereafter, NT) in Greek. English Bibles made in the OE and ME periods were not direct translations from these languages but indirect translations made from the Latin of the Vulgate (hereafter, VUL). Therefore, while it is a simple matter to examine the possibility of the influence of Latin on OE and ME versions of the Bible, the question of whether the languages of the original Bible exerted any linguistic influence upon the indirect translations of the OE and ME versions is considerably less straightforward. Still more problematic is the question of how to define the influence of a source language on a translation in the target language. This is because expressions perceived as alien by users of the target language are likely to be rejected, while expressions which are deemed acceptable are regarded as such only because there are specific receptors in the target language to which they can readily be seen to correspond. Such receptors are generally those expressions in the target language which are syntactically or grammatically similar to the formulations of the source language.

The following is a case in which a typical grammatical phenomenon in Hebrew is imported into an OE translation, but results nevertheless in natural English.

(1) OEH[2]: ON angynne gesceop God heofonan ⁊ eorðan   (*Gen.* 1:1)

This famous opening sentence from *Genesis* begins with an adverbial, which causes subject-verb inversion. This word-order is acceptable in OE and hence the translation does not appear foreign. However, if we trace the translation process back to the Hebrew sentence, we discover another reason for the inversion. The following is a Latin sentence in VUL[3] corresponding to (1).

(2) VUL: In principio creavit Deus caelum et terram   (*Gen.* 1:1)

---

1 Some grammarians of New Testament Greek, e.g., Moule (1959: 171), Jay (1987: 265-69), use the term 'Semitism' for 'Hebraism', as the former includes Aramaic influence. 'Hebraism' is used here as a term to indicate the influence of Old Testament Hebrew on target languages.
2 OEH = *The Old English Version of the Heptateuch*
3 Controversy still surrounds attempts to identify the Latin version from which OEH was translated. The Latin translation given by Crawford (1922) will be used here.

It is clear that the word-order in the English version resulted from a faithful translation of the Latin sentence (2). This Latin sentence is a translation of the following Hebrew sentence.

(3)   OBJECT   SUBJECT VERB   ADVERBIAL

HB[4]: הארץ   ואת   השמים   את   אלהים   ברא   בראשית

earth-the   AM[5]-and   heavens[6]-the   AM[5]   gods[7]   created   beginning-in

(= In beginning created gods the heaves and the earth)   (*Gen.* 1:1)

The Hebrew sentence (3) shows that the Latin word-order in (2) is a faithful reproduction of the Hebrew word-order. It is interesting that the normal word-order of Hebrew is V-S-O. This normal word-order in Hebrew is replicated in the Old English Bible as a consequence of successive faithful translations. An adverbial in the front position often produces an inversion of subject and verb in English. This might become a receptor corresponding to the Latin word-order 'adverbial-verb-subject', which originated from the normal word-order of Hebrew.

This demonstrates the possibility that different explanations may be adduced even for unmarked linguistic phenomena in Biblical English, if such phenomena are analyzed from the perspective of the original language and its translations. This shows also the difficulty of defining a foreign influence. Only when expressions in a source language have linguistic receptors in a target language, can they have any chance of being assimilated by the target language. In view of this, the Hebraisms found in English Bibles can be roughly categorised as follows: 1) expressions which occur with a high frequency; 2) syntactical hybrids and 3) hapax legomena. The first two will be discussed here.

2. High Frequency
2.1. AND
One typical example of the high frequency category is that of sentences beginning with AND both in OT and NT. In (4) are cited verses 10 to 14 from Chapter 1 of *Genesis* in OEH. Of these five verses, only verse 14 does not begin with AND (= ן). This phenomenon can be explained by closely examining the source texts and their translations.

---

4   HB = The Hebrew Bible. Vowel points and accentual or cantillation marks will be deleted here.
5   AM = Accusative marker in Hebrew
6   השמים (= heavens) is in a plural form to express 'width', but semantically singular.
7   אלהים (= gods) is also in a plural form to express 'respect', but semantically singular.

(4) OE Translation   [Genesis 1]
10. ⁊ God gecygde ða drignysse eorðan ...
11. ⁊ he cwæð: Sprytte seo eorðe growende gærs ...
12. ⁊ seo eor ðe forðteah growende wyrta ...
13. ⁊ wæs geworden æfen ⁊ mergen se ðridda dæg.
14. God cwæð ða soðlice ...

(5) Latin Translation   [Genesis 1]   (6) Hebrew Bible

10. et vocavit Deus aridam terram ...

                                            land dry-to God calls-AND$_8$
10. ויקרא   אלהים ליבשה ארץ ...

11. et ait: germinet terra herbam ...

                       grass earth-the will-bring God says-AND
11. ויאמר   אלהים תדשא הארץ דשא

12. et protulit terra herbam ......

                                 grass earth-the brings-AND
12. ותוצא   הארץ דשא ...

13. et^9 factumque est vespere ......

                                                evening— is-AND
13. ויהי   - ערב ...

14. dixit <u>autem</u> Deus, fiant luminaria ...

                                   light will-be God says-AND
14. ויאמר   אלהים יהי מארת ...

In (5) is the source text of the OE translation. A comparison between the ANDs positioned at the beginning of the sentences in (4) and the corresponding Latin expressions in (5) reveals that these ANDs are translations of the Latin conjunction ET, and that the nonoccurrence of AND at the beginning of verse 14 is caused by the non-use of ET in the corresponding Latin verse. The Latin sentences are translated from Hebrew sentences in (6).

The Hebrew sentences are written from right to left. The Hebrew sentences corresponding to the Latin sentences begin with the letter ו (waw). Hereafter this letter will be referred to as WAW. WAW is a prefix and it functions mainly as a conjunction. It is this Hebrew prefix that causes the frequent occurrence of the conjunction ET in VUL and AND in English Bibles. The question of why the WAW in verse 14 is not translated in VUL will be dealt with later in § 2.2.

The conjunctive prefix WAW can be used to connect any two units, from other prefixes to entire discourses. If any logical and/or temporal relation exists between any two given units, WAW is used to signal this relation. Generally, sen-

---

[8] The beginning of the Hebrew sentences in (6) consists of ו (= WAW)-*imperfect* verb, which expresses the *perfect* aspect. However, in the word-for-word translations put on the Hebrew words, WAW is replaced by AND, and the *imperfect* verbs by English verbs in the present tense.

[9] According to Weber (1969: 5), a version exists where the conjunction *et* is not used.

tences which precede and follow WAW have a more or less logical and/or temporal relation. Accordingly, Hebrew sentences usually begin with WAW, even in cases where no conjunction would be used in English. The function of WAW as a conjunction is highly abstractive and its semantic scope is very wide. Hebrew has a few other conjunctions, though none are as commonly used as WAW.[10]

WAW also functions as an aspect convertor while retaining its function as a conjunction[11]. Hebrew has no tense system and verbs express one of two aspects: the perfect or the imperfect. When WAW is prefixed to a verb, the aspect of the verb is converted to the other aspect. The parts underlined in (6) are all consist of 'WAW + verb in the imperfect form'. As WAW is prefixed to each of these imperfect verbs, the aspect of the verb is converted to the perfect aspect here. This function of WAW to effect aspect conversion is one of the distinctive characteristics of the Hebrew language. This is another reason for the frequent occurrence of the use of WAW in the Hebrew OT, which is in turn directly related to the frequent use of ET in VUL and AND in English Bibles. WAW is translated by ET in most cases. These ETs are replaced rather automatically by AND in OE and ME versions of the Bible. This is the reason why AND occurs so frequently in English Bibles.

2.2. *Waw, Et, Autem* and *Ða soðlice*

The WAW in verse 14, one among a sequence of five WAWs, is not translated by ET in VUL. But if the translation process is examined closely, it becomes clear that the WAW is replaced by AUTEM in VUL and moved after the verb, according to the grammatical rules governing its use[12]. AUTEM in VUL is generally translated by *ða, ðus* or *ða soðlice* in OE Bibles. In the case of verse 14, it is reproduced as *ða soðlice* in the same position as AUTEM. This is why verse 14 does not begin with AND and, instead, *ða soðlice* appears after the verb.

2.3. Redundant Verbs of Speaking

It is easy to find examples in OE and ME Bibles where the present participle or a finite form of the verb *cweðan* in OE and *seien* in ME occurs after a verb of speaking, as is shown in (7).

(7) 1. OEH: God ða spræc to Noe, ðus *cweðende* ... (*Gen.* 8:15)
     2. OEH: ÞA andswarode Moyses ⁊ *cwæð* ... (*Ex.* 4:1)
     3. EWB[13]: þese thingis seiþ þe lord ... *seiende* ... (*Jer.* 44:25)
     4. EWB: & Moises clepe al Irael: & *seide* to hem/... (*Deut.* 29:2)

---

10 See: Waltke and O'Connor (1990: 634-36)
11 See: Lambdin (1980: 107-8)
12 See: Mountford (1962: 171)
13 EWB = The Early Wycliffite Bible

(8) 1. VUL: <u>locutus est</u> autem Deus ad Noe *dicens* ...   (*Gen.* 8:15)
    2. VUL: <u>respondens</u> Moses *ait* ...   (*Ex.* 4:1)
    3. VUL: haec <u>inquit</u> Dominus ... *dicens* vos ...   (*Jer.* 44:25)
    4. VUL: <u>vocavitque</u> Moses omnem Israhelem *et dixit* ad eos ...   (*Deut.* 29:2)

The examples in (7)1-4 appear in the OE or ME Bibles as translations of the Latin in (8)1-4. The second verbs of speaking in VUL are faithfully reproduced in the OE or ME Bibles. As a result, the following collocations appear in the OE and ME Bibles.

[OE and ME Translations]   [Latin Translations]
Type i: verb of speaking – *(and) cwæð / (and) seide*   <   verb of speaking – *(et) ait/dixit*
Type ii: verb of speaking – *cweðende / seiende*   <   verb of speaking – *dicens*

Hebrew expressions corresponding to the Latin collocations used with 'verbs of speaking – *et dixit/ait/dicens*' are לאמר = *to-say* (preposition + infinitive) as illustrated in (9)1-2, and ויֹּאמר = *and-said* (WAW + finite) as illustrated in (9)3-4.

(9) 1.   SAY-TO Noah-to God SPOKE-and
         לאמר   אל־נח   אלהים   וידבר   (*Gen.* 8:15)

    2.   SAY-TO Israel of-Lord hosts of-God SAID thus
         לאמר   ישראל   אלהי   יהוה־צבאות   כה ־ אמר   (*Jer.* 44:25)

    3.   SAID-AND Isarel of-all-to Moses ANNOUNCED-and
         וַיֹּאמר   אל־כל־ישראל   משה   ויקרא   (*Deut.* 29:2)

    4.   SAID-AND Moses ANSWERED-and
         וַיֹּאמר   משה   ויען   (*Ex.* 4:1)

Both the infinitive and the finite form of the Hebrew verb אמר = *say* have the function of introducing direct speech[14]. The Bible contains so many examples of direct speech that the infinitive or the finite form of the verb אמר = *say* appears frequently. לאמר = *to-say* is generally translated by the present participle *dicens* and ויֹּאמר = *and-said* is generally translated by *et ait / dixi* or *ait / dixi* without being preceded by the conjunction ET in the case where a preceding verb of speaking is translated by the present participle, as exemplified in (8)2.

These Latin verbs in the participle or in the finite are reproduced rather faithfully by *cweðende* and *(and) cwæð* in the OE translations and *seiende* and *(and) seide* in the ME translations. This is a reason why a redundant verb of speaking appears so frequently after another verb of speaking in English Bibles.

---

14   See: Waltke and O'Connor (1990: 608)

3. Syntactical Hybrid: cognate objects without a modifier

Cognate objects in English are generally modified by an adjectival, like "they ... sleepe a *perpetuall* sleepe." (AV, *Jer.* 51:39[15]) in order to add new information to an intransitive verb. However, it is not difficult to find cognate objects without a modifier in English Bibles. Typical examples are cited in (10)1a-3a. The example in (10)3a is a citation from literature other than the Bible and the cognate object appears in a citation from OT. Strictly speaking, *deaðe* in (10)1a is not a cognate object of the verb *sweltan*, a common verb for *die* in OE. However, *deaðe* can be regarded as a quasi-cognate object of the verb *sweltan* and will be treated as an example of a cognate object here.

(10) 1a. OEH: ðu scealt   DATIVE *deaðe*   sweltan.   <   1b. VUL: ABLATIVE *morte*   morieris

1c. AV[16]: thou shalt *surely* die.   (*Gen.* 2:17)

2a. EWB: *deþ* he schall dye/   <   2b. VUL: ABLATIVE *morte*   morietur

2c. AV: Hee ... shall *surely* bee put to death.   (*Gen.* 26:11)

3a. PE[17]:   DATIVE *life*   he lýfað   <   3b. VUL: ABLATIVE *vita*   vivet

3c. AV: he shall *surely* liue   (*Ezek.* 18:21)

The cognate objects in (10)1a-3a appear in the English Bibles as translations of *morte* or *vita*, Latin cognate objects in the ablative case. A corresponding Hebrew expression is the infinitive of the same verb as a finite verb of the predicate, as shown in (11)1-3. This Hebrew infinitive is called the infinitive absolute and functions as an intensifier, an adverb to emphasise "the verbal idea"[18]. This is the reason why infinite absolutes are often translated by intensifiers like *surely, indeede*, as shown in (14)1-4 in AV. The infinitive absolute with this function co-occurs with transitive verbs as well as with intransitive verbs, though the English cognate object co-occurs only with intransitive verbs.

(11) 1.   you-shall-die = FINITE[19]   die = INF[20]
        תמות   מות   (*Gen.* 2:17)

---

15   This originates from a Hebrew sentence: וישנו שנת־עולם (= and-they-will-sleep *sleep* long.)
16   AV = The Authorized Version of the English Bible
17   PE = *Pœnitentiale Ecgberti*, p. 363.
18   Lambdin (1973: 158)
19   FINITE = Finite verb
20   INF = Infinitive absolute

```
        he-shall-die = FINITE    die = INF
2.           יומת                  מוֹת                    (Gen. 26:11)


        he-shall-live = FINITE   live = INF
3.           יחיה                  חיה                    (Ezek. 18:21)
```

The Hebrew infinitive absolute is replaced by the cognate object in the ablative case in VUL. This translation method seems to have been adopted, probably because this provided a satisfactory means of preserving the original form without sacrificing the acceptability in Latin. Latin generally has the cognate object with a modifier, which might be a receptor for the Hebrew infinitive absolute. This is a kind of syntactical merger or hybrid. The same method was to be adopted in the English translations. The Latin cognate objects in the ablative case are also translated by the following prepositional phrases in EWB to reproduce a grammatical function of the ablative case.

(12) 1. EWB: *with deþ þou schalt dye/...* (Gen. 2:17)
    2. EWB: *with deed dye he/... with deþ dye he/...* (Ex. 21:17-18)
    3. EWB: *In lyf he shal liue ... he shal die bi deþ ... in lyf he shal liue ... in lyf he shal liuen ...*
       in lyf he shal lyue ... he shal liue in lyf ... (Ezek. 18:2, 13, 18, 19, 21 and 28)

Evidence can be found in VUL to show that there was some hesitation with respect to the translation of the Hebrew infinitive absolute. In (13)1 are two Hebrew sentences, each of which contains an infinitive absolute which functions to intensify the finite verb. The infinitive absolute in the first sentence is shown by a single bar underline and that in the second sentence by a double bar underline. The first infinitive absolute is translated by the present participle and the second infinitive absolute by the cognate object in the accusative case in VUL as shown in (13)2. In EWB, the Latin present participle is faithfully reproduced and the Latin cognate object is replaced by a noun which is not cognate with the finite verb, as shown in (13)3. This confused translation produced the sentence construction 'finite verb + present participle of the finite verb' in EWB, as shown in (13)3.

```
              see = INF   you-see = FINITE-and    hear = INF   you-hear = FINITE
(13) 1. HB:      ראֹ         וּראוּ              ...    שָׁמוֹעַ       שִׁמְעוּ          (Isa. 6:9)

              PARTICIPLE                    ACCUSATIVE
     2. VUL: audite    audientes   ···   et videte   visionem

     3. EWB: herith heringe, ... & seeþ a viseon,
     4. AV: Heare yee indeede, ... and see yee indeed,
```

(14) 1. EWB: *buriounyng* it shal buriownen: ... (AV: *abundantly*) (*Isa.* 35.2)
    2. EWB: *wepinge* þou shalt not wepen/ ... (AV: *no more*) (*Isa.* 30.19)
    3. EWB: *spekynge* I hafe spokyn, þat ... (AV: *indeede*) (*I Sam.* 2:30)
    4. EWB: he *doende* shal do to hym ... (AV: *surely*) (*Ezek.* 31:11)

The same collocation appears also in (14)1-4 by the same translation process as the second infinitive absolute in (13)1.

One can also find examples in which the Latin collocation of 'present participle of finite verb + finite verb' was avoided in OEH and the finite verb was changed into a verb which is not cognate with the verb of the participle, as is shown in (15)3. As a result, a construction similar to the progressive form appeared in OEH, though the Latin collocation is kept in EWB.

(15) 1. HB: you-AM   I-visited = FINITE   visit = INF
             אתכם   פקדתי   פקד   (*Ex.* 3:16)
    2. VUL: *visitans* visitavi vos ...
    3. OEH: *Cumende* ic eom to eow ...
    4. EWB: *visityng* I haue visited ȝou ...

Hebrew has cognate objects both with and without modifiers. The Hebrew cognate object without a modifier has the same function as the infinitive absolute treated above[21], though the infinitive absolute is used much more frequently than the cognate object in HB. Some of the Hebrew cognate objects are reproduced faithfully in English Bibles, as shown in (16) 3-4 and (17)3, and some of them are translated by an adverb as shown in (17)4.

(16) 1. HB: say-to   vow = NOUN   Jakob   vowed-and
             לאמר   נדר   יעקב   וידר   (*Gen.* 28:20)
    2. VUL: vovit etiam *votum* dicens
    3. OEH: he behet *behat*, ꝥ cwæð:
    4. AV: And Iacob vowed *a vow*, saying,

(17) 1. HB: Jerusalem   sinned   sin = NOUN
             ירושלם   חטאה   חטא   (*Lam.* 1:8)
    2. VUL: *peccatum* peccavit Hierusalem
    3. EWB: *a synne* synnede ierusalem:
    4. AV: Ierusalem hath *grieuously* sinned,

---

21 See: Waltke and O'Connor (1990: 166-67).

(18) 1. HB: we-dreamed dream = NOUN
              חלמנו   חלום   (*Gen.* 40:8)

2. VUL: *somnium* vidimus ...
3. OEH: Wit gesawon *swefn*, ...
4. EWB: *a sweuen* we han (y)seeyn ...,
5. AV: we haue dreamed *a dreame*, ...

Some of the Hebrew cognate objects were translated by nouns which were not cognate with a finite verb in VUL, as shown in (18)2, so that they were not rendered as a cognate object in English Bibles, which were translated from VUL. However, there are cases where they are reproduced faithfully, as is shown in (18)5, which is translated directly from HB. "Dream *a dreame*" occurring in AV (*exx., Gen.* 37:9, 40:5, 40:8, *Judge* 7:13, *Joel* 2:28, *Daniel* 2:3) originates in a Hebrew cognate object used as an intensifier.

4. Hebrew influence on the New Testament

Hebraisms in the Greek NT occur mainly in citations from OT and in passages where Hebrew words, phrases, and styles have been borrowed from OT.

4.1. Frequent Use of AND

Sentences frequently begin with AND in the English OT as stated at § 2.1. This is the case even in the English Gospels. In (19) are cited seven verses from the OE Gospels, and the corresponding verses of the Latin and Greek Gospels. The OE Gospels were translated from the Latin Gospels[22], which were translated from the Greek Gospels.

(19)   [*Mark* I]
  1. OE Gospels]   2. Latin Gospels   3. Greek Gospels
  [17] And þa cwæð ...   < [17] et dixit ...   < [17] καὶ εἶπεν αὐτοῖς...
  [18] And hi þa hrædlice ... < [18] et protinus ...   < [18] καὶ εὐθέως ἀφέντες...
  [19] And ðanon hwon ...   < [19] et progressus ...   < [19] καὶ προβὰς ἐκεῖθεν...
  [20] And he hi sona ...   < [20] et statim ...   < [20] καὶ εὐθέως ἐκάλεσεν...
  [21] And ferdon to ...   < [21] et ingrediuntur ...   < [21] Καὶ εἰσπορεύονται ...
  [22] And hi wundredon ... < [22] et stupebant ...   < [22] καὶ ἐξεπλήσσοντο...
  [23] And on heora ...   < [23] et erat in ...   < [23] Καὶ ἦν ἐν τῇ...

An examination of the successive stages of the translation process from Greek to OE suggests that the ANDs in the OE Gospels originate in the Greek

---

22 The question of which Latin version formed the basis of the Anglo-Saxon translation of the Gospels remains controversial. Cf. Bosworth (1865: viii-ix), Liuzza (2000: 1-26) and Kedar (2004: 299-338). Fisher, *et al* (1969), is used as the text of the Vulgate here. Cf. Note 1.

conjunction καί. Grammarians[23] of New Testament Greek agree that the use of this redundant conjunction in the Greek Gospels is a typical example of the influence of the Hebrew prose style.

4.2. Redundant Verb of Speaking

'AND + the present participle of *cweðan / seien* ' or 'AND + *cwæð / seid*' after a verb of speaking is also possible in OE and ME as shown in (20)1-2 and (21)1-2, though the reason for the frequent use of this formula has to be sought in the Greek NT. This is also an example of the assimilation of a style occurring frequently in the Hebrew OT, through Greek translations[24] of LXX[25]. This is how Hebrew grammar introduces direct speech, as we saw in § 2.1.

(20) 1. OEG[26]: hig <u>andswaredon</u> *and cwædon* to him;   (*John* 18:30)
    2. EWB: Thei <u>answeriden</u>, *and seiden* to hym,
    3. VUL: <u>responderunt</u> *et dixerunt* ei
    4. GNT[27]: ἀπεκρίθησαν καὶ εἶπαν αὐτῷ

(21) 1.OEG: <u>andswarude</u> iohannes him eallum *secgende;*   (*Luke* 3:16)
    2.EWB: John <u>answeride</u>, *seyinge* to alle men,
    3. VOL: <u>respondit</u> Iohannes *dicens* omnibus
    4. GNT: <u>ἀπεκρίνατο</u> λέγων πᾶσιν ὁ Ἰωάννης

4.3. Cognate Objects and the Relevant Expressions

The Hebrew infinitive absolute dealt with in § 3 is translated as a Greek cognate object in the dative case in OT quotations in NT. This Greek cognate object is translated by the ablative case in VUL. The ablative cognate object is replaced by the English cognate object in the dative case or by the prepositional phrases referred to in § 3.

The OE examples in (22)1-4 are translations of the ablative cognate object *morte* in (23), which is a translation of the Greek cognate object in the dative case in NT in (24). This Greek dative cognate object appears as a translation of the Hebrew infinitive absolute in (25).

---

23   For example, Thackeray (1911: 4), Jay (1958: 265-70), Moule (1959: 172-74), Blass and Debrunner (1961: 227), Moulton (1979: 411-86).
24   See: Moule (1959: 184), Blass and Debrunner (1961:273), *etc.*
25   LXX = The Septuagint
26   OEG = The Old English Gospels
27   GNT = The Greek New Testament

(22) 1. OEG :   swelte se *deaþe;* (*Matt.* 15:4, *Mark* 7:10)
     2. RWG²⁸: seþe ... *deaða* swælteþ (*Matt.* 15:4)
     3. LFG²⁹: *mið deaðe* ge-deðed se (*Mark* 7:10)
     4. RWG : seðe ... *mið deaðe* gideðed bið (*Mark* 7:10)

         ABLATIVE
(23) VUL: *morte*   morieris / moriatur / moriature /
                   (*Gen.* 2:17, *Lev.* 20:9) >   (*Matt.* 15:4, *Mark* 7:10)

              DATIVE
(24) LXX and GNT: θανα 'τῳ ἀποθανεῖσθε θανατούσθῶ τελευτάτω

                   (*Gen.* 2:17, *Lev.* 20:9) >   (*Matt.* 15:4, *Mark* 7:10)

                       he-shall-die = FINITE   you-shall die = FINITE   die = INF
(25)= (11)1   HB: יומת   /   תמות   מות

                   (*Gen.* 2:17, *Lev.* 20:9)

The Greek cognate object without a modifier appears even in passages which are not quoted from OT, as shown in (26)1, though such examples are not plentiful. This might be an imitation of other Greek cognate objects which appear frequently as a translation of the Hebrew infinitive absolute functioning as an intensifier³⁰. The prepositional phrases in (26)3-5 are translation methods devised to retain the function of the Greek dative case.

              DATIVE
(26)   1. GNT: ἐπιθυμι'ᾳ ἐπεθύμησα τοῦτο τὸ πάσχα φαγεῖν   (*Luke* 22:15)

         ABLATIVE
     2. VUL: *desiderio*   desideravi hoc pascha

     3. OEG: *Of gewilnunge* ic gewilnude etan mid eow þas eastron
     4. EWB: *With desyr* I haue desyrid to ete with ȝou this pask,
     5. AV: *With desire* I haue desired to eate this Passeouer with you

5. Biblical Material as Linguistic Data
The examples which I have introduced so far might be explained in different ways, if translation processes were not taken into account. For example, Visser (1970: 415-17) cites many examples of the cognate object without a modifier in order to explain its origin and development with no explanation about biblical translations. So we should be careful when we use biblical texts as data for linguistic analysis.

---

28 RWG =The Rushworth Gospels
29 LFG = The Lindisfarne Gospels
30 Moulton and Howard (1979: 443) points out many examples of this case.

References

Bosworth, Joseph (arr. with preface and notes)
    1865   *Anglo-Saxon Gospels in Parallel Columns with the Versions of Wycliffe and Tyndale*. London: John Russell Smith.

Blass, F — A. Debrunner
    1961   *A Greek Grammar of the New Testament and Other Early Literature*. Chicago: University of Chicago Press

Jay, Eric G.
    1987   *New Testament Greek: An Introductory Grammar*. Cambridge: Cambridge University Press.

Kedar, Benjamin
    2004   "The Latin Translations" in: *Mikra,* Martin Jan Mulder and Harry Sysking (eds.). Massachusetts: Hendrickson Publishers. 299-338.

Lambdin, Thomas O.
    1976   *Introduction to Biblical Hebrew*. London: Darton, Longman and Todd

Liuzza, Roy M.
    2000   *The Old English Version of the Gospels*. EETS No. 314. Oxford: Oxford University Press.

Moule, Charles Francis D.
    1959   *An Idiom Book of New Testament Greek*. Cambridge: Cambridge University Press.

Moulton, Hope J. — Wilbert F. Howard
    1979   *A Grammar of New Testament Greek*. Vol. II. Edinburgh: T & T Clark.

Mountford, James (ed. and rev.)
    1962   *Kennedy's Revised Latin Primer*. Essex: Longman House.

Visser, F. Th.
    1970   *An Historical Syntax of the English Language: Part One Syntactical Units with One Verb*. Leiden: E. J. Brill

Waltke, Bruce K. — Michael P. O'Connor
    1990   *An Introduction to Biblical Hebrew Syntax*. Indiana: Eisenbrauns.

Editions and Abbreviations

Crawford, Suzanne J. (ed.)
    1922   OEH = *The Old English Version of the Heptateuch*. EETS OS. No. 160. Oxford: Oxford University Press. (repr. 1969).

Elliger, Karl — Willhelm Rudolph (edd.)
    1977   HB = *Biblia Hebraica Stuttgartensia*. Stuttgart: Deutsche Bibelstiftung

Forshall, Josiah — Frederic Madden (edd.)
    1850   EWB (NT) = *The Holy Bible, Containing the Old and New Testaments*. Oxford: at the University Press.

Lindberg, Conrad (ed.)
    1959-73 EWB (OT) = *MS. Bodley 959. Genesis-Baruch 3.20 in the Earlier Version of the Wycliffite Bible*. 6 vols. Stockholm: Almqvist & Wiksell.

Liuzza, Roy M. (ed.)
    1994   OEG = *The Old English Version of the Gospels*. EETS No. 304. Oxford: Oxford University Press.

Pollard, Alfred W. (ed.)
    1911   AV = *The Holy Bible: A Facsimile in a Reduced Size of the Authorized Version Published in the Year 1611*. Oxford: Oxford University Press.

Rahlfs, Alfred (ed.)
    1935   LXX = The Septuagint = *Septuaginta*. 2 vols. Suttgart: Württembergische Bibelanstalt.

Scholz, J. Martin Augustin (ed.)
    1848   GNT = The Greek New Testament in: *The English Hexapla*. London: Samuel Bagster. (repr. 1975)

Thorpe, Benjamin (ed.)
    1840   PE = *Pœnitentiale Ecgberti, Archiepiscopi Eboracensis* in: *The Ancient Laws and Institutes of England*. London: The Commissioners on the Public Records of the Kingdom. 362-92.

Skeat, Walter W. (ed.)
    1871-87 RWG = Rushworth Gospels; LFG = Lindisfarne Gospels. *Gospels according to St. Matthew, St. Mark, St. Luke, and St. John*. Cambridge: Cambridge University Press.

Weber, Robertus (ed.)
    1969   VUL = *Biblia Sacra Iuxta Vulgatam Versionem*. Suttgart: Württembergische Bibelanstalt.

2 Path Coding in Old English: Functional Story of a Typological Shift[1]

Caroline Imbert, CNRS – University of Lyon 2

1. Introduction

This paper is to be considered through the frame of recent functional linguistics and studies on grammaticalisation and consists of a typological perspective on Ælfric's 10th-century Old English[2]. It examines the coding strategies of Path attested in that language and explores the gradual "typological shift" that occurred from the prevalence of strongly verb-prefixing patterns to the prevalence of verb-particle patterns. For example, when a Modern English speaker wants to express the Path followed by an entity in a spatial situation, he may say something like "*he went out to the garden*". In early Old English texts, one rather finds sentences such as "*he outwent to the garden*". However, especially when one looks at late Old English, such as Ælfric's language, things are far from being so clear-cut. When Ælfric wants to express the same spatial situation, he does not really use a "prevalent" pattern, but uses a typologically puzzling wide range of patterns, such as : *he outwent to the garden, he went out to the garden, he outwent the garden to, he towent the garden out, he tooutwent the garden.*

This paper thus attempts to shed a new light on this "typological shift" from prefix-verb to verb-particle patterns. Firstly, it aims at analysing the multiplicity of patterns available for the expression of Path in Ælfric's language; but also at demonstrating how and above all why this shift from prefix-verb to verb-particle patterns only affected at first the domain of spatial relations.

Some preliminary remarks are required here to delimit the scope and implications of the present paper:

- All the data in the examples and tables of this paper refer to Ælfric's 10th-century Old English *only*. A larger corpus would be a second step for a larger study.
- As we will see, this paper does not deal with stylistics, metrics and syntactic word order issues. It strictly focuses its scope on the *functional motivations* for the typological shift. However and as rightly underlined by Ogura (2002) and Hiltunen (1983), it is obvious that this shift is a multi-dimensional phenomenon; issues such as metrics and word order are fully part of it and have been

---

1 I would like to thank for their collaboration, support, comments and criticisms: James Earl, Scott deLancey and Eric Pederson (University of Oregon); as well as Diana Lewis and Colette Grinevald Craig (University of Lyon 2)
2 The study is based on the full text and an OEC electronic corpus (http://ets.umdl.umich.edu/o/oec/) of Ælfric's *Lives of the Saints* (ÆLS), and to a lesser extent Ælfric's *Catholic Homilies* (ÆCHom).

extensively studied in the philological literature. The reader is thus referred to these studies for a complete account of the phenomenon under examination.
- For the sake of clarity, the general term *adposition* is used in this paper both for *preposition* and *postposition*, unless only one of the two possibilities is discussed.

Section 2 below is a short overview of the theoretical background used in this paper. Section 3 focuses on the morphosyntactic tools involved in Path coding and in the typological shift from prefix-verb to verb-particle patterns in Old English. Section 4 argues in favour of a central role of Path coding in the shift; it shows how and why this shift was functionally motivated and functionally-driven.

2. Theoretical background

This paper consists of a functional-typological linguistic approach. This is a functional approach in that it apprehends language as a system of communication based on experience and analyses the strategies of expression of *functional domains*. In this paper, the functional domain selected is that of space. This approach underlines the interaction between the semantic, syntactic and discursive levels. It is founded on the use that the speakers make of languages. It does not formally distinguish between synchrony and diachrony and incorporates the grammaticalisation axis. Linguistic structures and linguistic changes are considered to be functionally motivated and functionally-driven.

This approach is also intrinsically typological, in that it aims at identifying translinguistically the different and recurrent strategies used by various languages to express the selected functional domains, in view of proposing a typology.

More specifically, this paper is founded on Talmy's typology of *Motion event* (Talmy: 1985, 2000). A Motion event is a spatial situation which may imply Movement as well as Localisation (e.g. 'the man goes / is out of the house'), and which contains four basic semantic elements[3]:

- *the Figure*: Moving or localised entity (*the man*);
- *the Ground*: Reference entity with respect to which the Figure is moving or localised (*the house*);
- *Movement / Localisation*: Presence of Movement or Localisation (*goes / is*);
- *Path*: Path followed or site occupied by the Figure (*out of*)[4].

---

3   Beyond these four basic elements, a Motion event can be associated with a *Co-event*, which includes Manner of Motion (e.g. 'he ran') and Cause of Motion (e.g. 'he pushed').
4   In this study, only Movement expressions will be examined. The term "Path" will thus only refer to *the Path followed by the Figure*.

Talmy's typology aims at discerning the differences that exist between languages in the way they conceptually organise a Motion event. The typology considers what semantic element associated with the Motion event is coded in what surface element. To build his typology, Talmy focuses on the semantic element of Path, which he considers to be the most fundamental semantic element of a Motion event. He observes for each language where Path is coded and eventually proposes to divide the languages of the world into two main types. *the verb-framed type*, i.e. languages that code Path in the verb stem, and *the satellite-framed type*, i.e. languages that basically do not code Path in the verb stem, but rather in a "satellite" item.

Since Talmy's seminal proposal of such a typology, much research and discussion have taken place, in particular about the need to review his clear-cut bipartite distinction, when one considers serializing and compound-verb languages such as Mandarin Chinese and Japanese (Matsumoto, 2003 ; Ishibashi, 2006; to appear).

Finally, this paper is part of my PhD research and of an international research program of the French "Fédération de Typologie[5]" (CNRS), on the typology of Path in the languages of the world[6]. The results presented in this paper are thus to be referred as part of the Project's results.

This "Trajectory Project" paper therefore focuses, through Old English, on one type of *satellite-framed* language, and examines how its coding strategies of Path adapted the major typological change that affected it, from prefix-verb to verb-particle patterns.

3. Typological change and Path coding: something is going wrong

In Modern English, Path is mostly distributed into particles and prepositions. In contrast, early Old English mostly distributes Path into prefixes and prepositions. In between, Ælfric's Old English attests a much more diversified morphosyntactic toolbox, including the very productive prepositions (1), prefixes (2), particles (3) and directional adverbs (4); in parallel it also attests the very constrained multiple-prefixes constructions and postpositions – the length of this paper does not leaves space for the latter group to be addressed in this paper.

---

[5] Fédération de Recherche "Typologie et Universaux Linguistiques"; http://www.typologie.cnrs.fr/index.php.

[6] The project is coordinated by Colette Grinevald Craig (DDL CNRS/Lyon2, France), Anetta Kopecka (MPI Nijmegen, Netherlands) and Jean-Michel Fortis (HTL/Paris 7, France). Among its methodological and conceptual tools, the project is building an inventory of the linguistic elements that can code Path in the languages of the world. Each language has its own morphosyntactic toolbox; the project studies the diversity of strategies at work in languages to use this toolbox for the coding of Path. The project aims at providing descriptions of genetically and typologically varied languages and at proposing a typology of the expression of Path.

(1) V + adposition (ÆLS, III : 138-139)
...and feollan to his fotum
'...and fell at his feet'

and	feollan	to	his fotum
and	fall.INF	to	POSS.3SG foot.DAT.PL

[VERB]   [ADP]   [OBLIQUE]
  | | |
[MNR+MVT]   [PATH]   [GROUND]

(2) Prefix + V (± adposition) (ÆLS, II : 55)
hi becoman to ðære cristenra wununge
'They arrived at the Christian's abode'

Hi	becoman	to	ðære cristenra wununge
3PL.NOM	arrive.INF	to	ART.DAT Christian.GEN abode.DAT

[SUBJECT]   [PREV]-[VERB]   [ADP]   [OBLIQUE]
   | | | | |
[FIGURE]   [PATH]-[MVT]   [PATH]   [GROUND]

(3) V + particle[7] (± adposition):
fleah siþþan upp . forðrihte to heofonum
'And afterward flew up straightway to Heaven'

fleah	siþþan	upp .	forðrihte	to	heofonum
fly.PAST.3SG	after	up	straightway	to	heaven.DAT

[VERB]   [PTC]   [ADP]   [OBLIQUE]
  | | | |
[MNR+MVT]   [PATH]   [PATH]   [GROUND]

(4) V + directional adverb (± adposition):
beo þonne se soð god þe asent þæt fyr ufan
'And let Him be the true God that sendeth fire from above'

se soð god	þe	asent	þæt fyr	ufan
ART.NOM true.NOM God.NOM	REL	send.PRES.3SG	ART.ACC fire.ACC	from.above

---

7 Although the particle is postposed to the verb in (3), it may also be preposed (ÆLS, VI : 165-166).

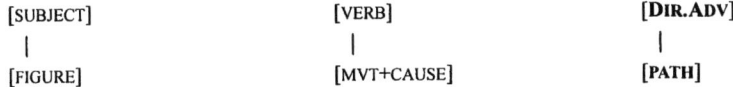

These static templates do not reflect the dynamics and complexity of the changes at work in Old English syntax at the time, especially the progressive typological change from prefix-verb to verb-particle patterns. Again, the latter occurs in the context of a multi-dimensional syntactic transition in the language. It will be shown in this section how and why the functional domain of space is at the core of this transition.

I will treat here, from the perspective of Path coding, three aspects of the transition: the increasing semantic and functional variety in the use of the prefixes, the disappearance of ancient "directional adverbs", in parallel with the increasing use of verb-particle patterns.

3.1. The Path prefixes have become multi-purpose

Even since early Old English, the language attests prefixes and adpositions that do not have a purely spatial meaning. However, two facts have become particularly salient in Ælfric's time:

- The inventory of items exclusively or mainly dedicated to the coding of Path decreases;
- The functional boundary between prefixes and adpositions tends to be increasingly blurred.

Table 1 is an inventory of the Path prefixes examined in this study, classified along two features: first, the prevalence of spatial uses when they are used as prefixes; second, the possibility of an adpositional use of these items.

A static reading of *Table 1* reveals some regularities in the system. First, one can observe that only 25% (i.e. 5 prefixes out of 20) of these "Path prefixes" are still dedicated to Path coding and exclusively used as prefixes in Ælfric. Second, a semantic and functional shift clearly appears as one goes down in the table, with the coincidence of two continuums: from more spatial to less spatial and from 'strictly prefixal' to adpositional:
- 25% of the prefixes (5 out of 20) have kept the prevalence of their spatial meaning and attest an adpositional equivalent in the language.

Table 1: Inventory of Path prefixes:
an increasing semantic and functional versatility

Prefixed item	Spatial meaning	Spatial meaning prevalent	Adpositional use
forð-	'forth'	+	-
in(n)-	'in'	+	[8]
niðer-	'down'	+	-
up-	'up'	+	-
ut-	'out'	+	-
geond-	'beyond'	+	+
neah/near-	'near'	+	+
ofer-	'over'	+	+
þurh-	'through'	+	+
to-1	'to'	+	+
æt-	'at'	-	+
be-	'by'	-	+
for-	'in front'	-	+
fore-	'in front'	-	+
of/af-	'off'	-	+
on-	'on'	-	+
under-	'under'	-	+
wið-	'away'	-	+
ymb(e)-	'about'	-	+
to-2	'away'	-	-

- 45% of the prefixes (9 out of 20) have lost the prevalence of their spatial meaning and attest an adpositional equivalent in the language.[9]

This means that a total of 70% of the prefixes (14 out of 20) attest in Ælfric an adpositional equivalent, and in a large majority of case this adpositional use coincides with the loss of spatial meaning.

Now a more dynamic reading of *Table 1* leads to further observations, developed below in 3.1.1 and 3.1.2.

---

8   Cf. Mitchell (1985:503) about how *in* progressively disappeared as an adposition in Old English, to the advantage of *on*. In my corpus, I have only 1 occurrence of *in* used as an adposition (ÆLS, XI : 180) – excluding of course the few occurrences of the compound adposition *into*.

9   The only case of a reverse situation (loss of spatial meaning with no adpositional equivalent) is the prefix *to*-2 'away'. Interestingly, *to*-2 is also the only Path prefix that did not survive in the language under any form and that was not replaced (as opposed for example to *niðer*, which was replaced by *adune*).

3.1.1. Prefix-verb fusion and decreased dedication to Path coding

At this stage of the language, several degrees of prefix-verb syntactic relation and semantic fusion co-exist in synchrony. Examples (5) to (7) below show how this "fusion gradient[10]" relates, first, to the lesser prevalence of spatial meaning among Path prefixes in Ælfric; and second, how it relates to the syntactic transition from prefix-verb to verb-particle patterns at work in the language.

Examples (5) to (7) select three prefixed verbs that represent three different degrees of fusion, from less fused to more fused:

- *utgan* 'go out',
- *becuman* 'arrive',
- *forgan* 'abstain of'.

For these three prefixed verbs, each example mentions the plain verb form (i.e. the form without prefix nor particle), the prefix-verb form and the verb-particle form. The forms marked with a * symbol are not attested in the corpus.

- In (5), the verb *utgan* 'go out' can be semantically identified with the plain form *gan* 'go' (a). The prefix *ut-* can be detached to be a particle, when the syntax allows it: *ut gan* or *gan ut* (c).
- In (6), the verb *becuman* 'arrive' can still be semantically identified as the plain form of *cuman* 'come' (a) (even if *becuman* does not literally mean 'to come by' any more). However this time, the prefix *be-* cannot be detached to be a particle, in any circumstances (*c).
- In (7), the verb *forgan* 'abstain of' is completely fused. The original verb *gan* 'go' cannot be semantically identified any more as its plain form[11]: they have derived into two different lexical verbs. Again here, the prefix *for-* cannot be detached to be a particle, in any circumstances.

(5) Utgan

a. Plain verb	b. Prefix-verb	c. Verb-particle
gan 'go'	**utgan** 'go out'	**ut gan** / **gan ut** 'go out'

---

10 The term "gradient" refers here to the fact that the fusion between the prefix and the verb is a continuum over time; the three stages selected here thus do not represent "abrupt" changes in the language.

11 It ought to be noticed that *forgan* 'abstain of' co-exists in synchrony with a less fused version of himself: *foregan* or *fórgan* (with a stress on *fór*), which means 'go before, in front, past'.

(6) Becuman

    a. Plain verb   b. Prefix-verb   c. Verb-particle
    cuman 'come'   **becuman** 'arrive'   *be cuman / *cuman be

(7) Forgan

    a. Plain verb   b. Prefix-verb   c. Verb-particle
    ***   **forgan** 'abstain of'   *for gan / *gan for

This paradigm shows two important correlations:

- a correlation between a higher degree of fusion with the impossibility of verb-particle patterns, as in (6) and (7);
- a correlation between a higher degree of fusion with the loss of spatial meaning – in other words, with a loss of Path-coding capacity, as is most clear in (7).

This case is representative of the phenomenon affecting the whole set of Old English prefixes. Over time and through processes of fusion and grammaticalisation, fewer "Path" prefixes are dedicated to the coding of Path, while more attest non-spatial uses.

3.1.2. Decreased dedication of the prefixes to the verb

As mentioned earlier, there are highly constrained occurrences of *post*positions in Old English[12]. What is relevant about this fact to the analysis of the prefixes is that these postpositions sometimes attach to the verb, when the verb directly follows them. This leads to the presence of "adpositional prefixes", that are morphologically prefixes but also functionally adpositions by introducing the oblique complement[13]. Examples (8) and (9) compare prefixes – which function adverbially, as a preposition is needed to introduce the oblique complement (8b) – with adpositional prefixes – which introduce the oblique complement by themselves:

---

[12] As mentioned by Mitchell (1985), postpositions in Old English are restricted to occurrences with the place adverbs 'here' and 'there' (*her – þær*), some relative pronouns, and personal pronouns (i.e. they never appear after full NPs; one can go further and point out that they are restricted to 3rd person pronouns, at least in Mitchell's examples and in my corpus).

[13] Equivalent phenomena are typologically attested in a variety of languages; for example in Rama (Chibchan, Nicaragua), postpositions attaching to the verb stem as prefixes are called Relational Preverbs (Grinevald Craig & Hale, 1988); a similar situation gave rise to multiple prefixation of verbs in Homeric Greek (as demonstrated in Imbert, 2007). The latter case may be comparable to the constrained occurrences of multiple prefixation in Old English.

(8) Prefixes

a. (ÆLS, XXXI : 247)
Martinus þa **inn**-eode
Martin then in-go.PAST.3SG
'Martin then entered' (*lit.* 'went **in**')

b. (ÆLS, VI:278-280)
wæter **ut**-teah . of
water:ACC out-draw.PAST.3SG from
heardum stanclude
hard.DAT stone.cliff.DAT
'...drew **out** water from the hard stone-cliff'

(9) Adpositional prefixes

a. (ÆLS, I : 124-125)
land and burga **geond**-færð
land and city beyond-fare.PRES.3SG
'...goes **beyond** countries and cities'

b. (Bosworth & Toller; ÆCHom, I:9)
His swurd sceal **þurh**-gan
3SG.GEN sword.NOM shall through-go.INF
þine saule
2SG.GEN soul.DAT
'His sword shall go **through** your soul'

This phenomenon, interestingly, is functionally constrained: it depends on the functions that the involved items can assume in the language:

- If the Path prefix does not have a spatial adpositional equivalent in the language, as *inn-* and *ut-* in (8), then it cannot function as an adpositional prefix, and an adposition is required to introduce the oblique complement (*of* in (8b));
- If the spatial prefix has a spatial adpositional equivalent in the language, as *geond(-)* and *þurh(-)* in (9), then it can function as an adpositional prefix and directly introduce the oblique complement.

Thus in Ælfric, the Path prefixes are not clearly distinguished from adpositions any more.

3.2. Disappearance of the directional adverbs

Meantime, the language is progressively losing a set of ancient "directional adverbs", also called "adverbs of place" in the reference grammars. They consist of paradigmatic sets inherited from the Germanic system. These adverbs each have one ablative, one locative and one allative form, which allow them to code different directions by themselves. This tripartite system is already decaying in Ælfric's language.

Table 2 presents an inventory of the directional adverbs attested at this stage of the language and that are relevant to this paper; the = symbol signals forms that are in a process of semantic merge (for example *inne* in (10b): to say 'he is *inside*', one could use indifferently the locative *inne* or the ablative *innan*).

Table 2: Directional adverbs in Ælfric's

(10a) Ablative		(10b) Locative		(10c) Allative	
heonan	'from here'	*her*	'here'	*hider*	'to here'
Ø		*þær*	'there'	*þider*	'to there'
Ø		*hwær*	'where'	*hwider*	'to where'
innan	'from in'	*inne* =innan	'in(side)'	*in, inn*	'(to) in'
utan	'from out'	*ute* =utan	'out(side)'	*ut*	'(to) out'
uppan,	'from up'	*uppe*	'up'	*up, upp*	'(to) up'
ufan	'from down'	Ø =neoðan	'down'	*niðer*	'(to) down'
neoðan	'from in front'	*fore*	'in front'	*forþ*	'forth'
foran	'from near'	*neah*	'near'	*near*	'(to) near'
nean					

A quick static reading of *Table 2* allows two simple observations:

- The ablative and locative forms are merging and tend to disappear (Ø slots);
- while all the allative forms are preserved unchanged.

A more dynamic reading reveals a much more interesting situation:

- The ablative forms that are formally present in the language (column (10a)) have more and more difficulties to convey an ablative *meaning*. They tend to convey a locative meaning, hence their presence in the locative set (10b). The ablative forms are progressively disappearing from the language, most of them occurring less than 10 times in the whole corpus selected for this study; and their "attempt" at formal survival in the locative set will not maintain them much longer in the language.
- This attempted ablative-locative merge will be short-lived, since the locative forms themselves are in turn merging with the allative forms. The locative forms have been lost later in the language, but the merge was successful at least *semantically*: today, *in*, *out* or *up* may have an allative or locative meaning, depending on the context and the verbs they associate with (*go out* vs. *be out*) – conversely, since after the disappearance of the ablative forms, an ablative meaning requires more complex constructions such as '*from inside, from outside, from above*'.

In a word, the ablative forms have disappeared over time, and all that is left today is a locative-allative set.

These changes in the sets of directional adverbs are relevant here in two ways. First, they are part of the progressive decay of the strategies traditionally dedicated to the coding of Path in Old English, as observed above with the prefixes. Second, the surviving allative forms happen to match the inventory of "emergent" particles at the time – except for *near*, as will be discussed at the end of this paper:

Table 3: The emergent set of particles in Ælfric

forð	'forward'
in(n)	'in(to)'
niðer	'down'
up(p)	'up'
ut	'out'

3.3. The spread of the verb-particle pattern

As mentioned earlier, the particles in Old English could be preposed or postposed. The preposed construction appears more frequently in older texts and is sometimes analysed as a "detached prefix" or "half-prefix half-particle" construction.

In terms of frequency, this preposed construction seems to be overtaken by the postposed construction in Ælfric – namely the verb-particle patterns. Two interesting remarks about that fact can be briefly mentioned here, from the perspective of Path coding and in relation to the phenomena previously examined in this paper:

- Overtime, the more the sets of directional adverbs decay and merge into single allative forms, the more the postposed construction takes over the preposed construction;
- Simultaneously, the more the Path prefixes fuse with the verb stem and develop adpositional uses, the more the postposed construction takes over the preposed construction.

Therefore, it seems that both the changes affecting the Path prefixes and the directional adverbs work in a way that promotes the spread of verb-particle patterns. The latter finally takes over in terms of Path coding and gives birth to the phrasal verb constructions that we know of Middle and Modern English.

4. Solving the puzzle: Function as key

This section proposes a functional insight to this complex situation, in order to clarify the dynamics and motivation of the typological shift that occurs in Old English. *Table 4* below presents a list of items that are involved[14] in the typological shift from prefix-verb to verb-particle patterns, each with their spatial translation. The table shows their repartition in the language into the different functions of prefix, adposition, directional adverb, and particle. The "directional adverb"

---

14 The list thus excludes compound adpositions such as *beforan* and *into*.

column, for the sake of relevance, only contains the surviving allative forms (cf. *Table 2* for a more complete account). Finally, in the "prefix" column, the * symbol is used in the *translation* when the non-spatial uses of the prefix have become clearly prevalent (as examined in *Table 1*).

A static reading of the table works as a clear reminder of what has been observed throughout this paper:

- The prefixes have become multi-purpose. They can code Path, but also non-spatial meanings (10 out of 20 Path prefixes);
- Most of them (14 out of 20) can also function as spatial adpositions.
- The whole "emerging" particle set corresponds to the allative set of directional adverbs, except for *near* plus two later compound adverbs (*adune, aweg*).

Reading through the dynamics of *Table 4* leads these observations further. It appears that the items present in the particle set are the produce of a careful selection. This selection actually obeys three parameters, two of which can be developed in this section:

- It excludes all the items that attest an adpositional use (e.g. *neah, þurh, fore*). Thus, as if to make the emergent particles distinct from the prefixes that have become multi-purpose and unspecific, the language seems to operate a functional "sharpening" on the particles: the items that can function adpositionally (i.e. that do not have an exclusive relation with the verb) are dismissed.
- It excludes all the items that attest at least one non-spatial meaning (e.g. *on, æt, to*-2). The new set of particles, at that time, consists of items that are fully dedicated to Path coding. Thus, the typological shift has only affected the functional domain of space. This means that the typological shift was functionally-driven and not *only* syntactically-driven: indeed, the prefix system did not disappear when it was overtaken by the particle system; English actually kept a productive set of prefixes (*undertake, outlive, overdo*...) until today. But the *Path-coding function* has been fully transferred to the particles, as it still is the case today. The particles have in turn known further changes, as is addressed in the concluding section.

5. Conclusion: an intriguing question of Source/Goal asymmetry

Therefore, this paper argued that the typological shift from prefix-verb to verb-particle patterns that occurred in Old English has been strongly functionally-driven, through the progressive losses and changes in the coding strategies of Path available in the language. It was demonstrated that the emerging set of particles was carefully selected. It excluded all the items that had lost their Path-coding

Table 4: Functional distribution of the spatial items involved in the Old English typological shift

PREFIX	ADPOSITION		DIRECTIONAL ADVERB (surviving allatives)		PARTICLE (locative/allative meaning)	
					adune	'down'
					aweg	'away'
forð	'forth'	-	-	*forð*	'forth'	*forð*	'forth'
in(n)	'in'[15]	-	-	*in(n)*	'in'	*in(n)*	'in'
niðer	'down'	-	-	*niðer*	'down'	*niðer*	'down'
up	'up'	-	-	*up(p)*	'up'	*up(p)*	'up'
ut	'out'	-	-	*ut*	'out'	*ut*	'out'
neah/near	'near'	*neah/near*	'near'	*near*	'near'	-	-
geond	'beyond'	*geond*	'beyond'	-	-	-	-
ofer	'over'	*ofer*	'over'	-	-	-	-
þurh	'through'	*þurh*	'through'	-	-	-	-
to-1	'to'	*to*1	'to'	-	-	-	-
æt	* 'at'	*æt*	'at'	-	-	-	-
be	* 'by'	*be*	'by'	-	-	-	-
for	* 'in front'	*for*	'in front'	-	-	-	-
fore	* 'in front'	*fore*	'in front'	-	-	-	-
of/af	* 'off'	*of*	'from'	-	-	-	-
on	* 'on'	*on*	'at, in'	-	-	-	-
under	* 'under'	*under*	'under'	-	-	-	-
wið	* 'away'	*wið*	'toward'	-	-	-	-
ymb	* 'around'	*ymb(e)*	'around'	-	-	-	-
to-2	* 'away'	-	-	-	-	-	-

capacity and verb-related specificities, namely the items that could function as adpositions and the items that were not strictly dedicated to the coding of Path.

There might be a third parameter to this selection, that there is not time to present in this paper, but that is worth mentioning as an open conclusion, since it confirms the analysis presented here of a functional motivation for the typological shift that affected Old English. It happens that the selection operated by the language makes further distinctions *within* the functional domain of space. One can observe that only items coding Orientation of the Figure (*in, out, up, down, forth*) and Source (*away*[16]) have been selected, while the items coding Goal-related notions (*to, at,* allative *near*) have all been dismissed.

---

15 Cf. *Table 1* and the footnote on *in*.
16 Later reinforced by the appearance of the form *off*.

Two possible fields for further research lies in what became of this careful selection of particles.

First, from the point of view of English itself, one notices that the particles have in turn become multi-purpose over time; the situation of Path coding in Modern English is as puzzling as the situation that Old English had to face with its prefixes over ten centuries ago. For instance, in 'the climate change turned out to be the real threat', what has become of the Path-coding function of the particle *out*? In 'I will see to it' or 'he aimed at the deer', are the Goal items *to* and *at* merely adpositional items or actual *Goal* items that were finally accepted as particles? And in 'he looked after the kids', is *after* a particle or an adposition, or both?

Second, the third parameter mentioned above – the one that seems to distinguish between Goal and the other notions – can be ground for further research, since it links the data to a phenomenon of Source/Goal asymmetry recurrently attested in language typology (Bourdin, 1996; Ikegami, 1987; Stefanowitch & Rohde, 2004). One could revisit this phenomenon in the light of the new typological and diachronic data of ancient languages (Imbert, 2007). Old English clearly shows a Source/Goal asymmetry in its selection of particles, and Modern English – despite the recent evolutions that were just mentioned – still does not attest Goal particles. As opposed to *out, off, away* or even *on, in, through*, the items like *to, at, toward, for, after* are either exclusively adpositions or at most adpositional particles, but they could not become actual verbal particles. It is clear that these semantic constraints deserve full attention in further typological and diachronic studies.

In a broader perspective, this study demonstrates how Old English can add interesting data to a modern linguistic description of space and to current issues in typology, when revisited in the perspective of a functional-typological approach.

Abbreviations and glosses

1	1st person	MVT	movement
2	2nd person	MNR	manner of motion
3	3rd person	MID	middle
ADP	adposition	NOM	nominative
ALL	allative	PART	participle
AOR	aorist	PASS	passive
ART	article	PAST	past
DAT	dative	PRES	present
DEM	demonstrative	PL	plural
FEM	feminine	POSS	possessive
GEN	genitive	PRES	present
INF	infinitive	SG	singular
LOC	locative	V	verb

References

Bosworth, Joseph — T. Northcote Toller (comp.)
1898   *An Anglo-Saxon Dictionary*. [Electronic online version: http://beowulf.engl.uky.edu/~kiernan/BT/Bosworth-Toller.htm].

Bourdin, P.
1997   "On goal-bias across languages: modal, configurational and orientational parameters", in: Bohumil Palek (ed.), 185-218.

Chiba, Shuji (ed.)
2003   *Empirical and theoretical investigations into language: A Festschrift for Masaru Kajita*. Tokyo: Kaitakusha.

Dirven, René — Günter Radden (edd.)
1983   *Concepts of Case*. Tübingen: Narr.

Grinevald Craig, Colette and Ken Hale
1988   "Relational preverbs in some languages of the Americas: Typological and historical perspectives". *Language* 64-2:312-344.

Healy, Antonette Di Paolo
1998   *Dictionary of Old English corpus*. 1998 TEI-P3 conformant version [Ann Arbor: University of Michigan Press].

Hiltunen, Risto
1983   *The decline of the prefixes and the beginnings of the English phrasal verb*. Turku: Turku University Press.

Ikegami, Yoshihiko
1987   "Source vs Goal : A Case of Linguistic Dissymmetry", in: René Dirven and G.ünter Radden (edd.), 122-146.

Imbert, Caroline
2007   "Path coding and Relational Preverbs in Homeric Greek. A Native American story". *7th Biennial Meeting of the Association for Linguistic Typology (ALT VII)*, 25-28 September 2007, Paris.

Ishibashi, Miyuki
to appear   "Expression of 'putting' and 'taking' events in Japanese: 'Asymmetry of Source and Goal' revisited", in: Anetta Kopecka and Bhuvana Narasimhan (edd.).

Ishibashi, Miyuki
2006   "Langue à cadre verbal ou langue à satellite ? Expressions de déplacement spontané en chinois mandarin et en japonais". *Trajectory Project Workshop*, 3 december 2006, Lyon.

Kopecka, Anetta — Bhuvana Narasimhan (edd.)
to appear   *Put and Take events: A crosslinguistic perspective*. Amsterdam: John Benjamins.

Kopecka, Anetta
2004   *Etude typologique de l'expression de l'espace : localisation et déplacement en français et en polonais*. [Doctoral dissertation, University of Lyon 2.]

Matsumoto, Yo
    2003   "Typologies of lexicalization patterns and event integration: Clarifications and reformulations", in: Shuji Chiba (ed.), 403-418.
Mitchell, Bruce
    1985   *Old English Syntax*. 2 vols. Oxford: Clarendon Press.
Ogura, Michiko
    2002   *Verbs of Motion in Medieval English*. Cambridge: D.S. Brewer.
Palek, Bohumil (ed.)
    1997   *Proceedings of LP'96*. Prague: Charles University Press.
Panther, Klaus-Uwe — Günter Radden (edd.)
    2004   *Motivation in Grammar*. Berlin: Mouton de Gruyter.
Shopen, Timothy (ed.)
    1985   *Language typology and syntactic description, vol. 3: Grammatical categories and the lexicon*. Cambridge: Cambridge University Press.
Sinha, Chris and Tania Kuteva
    1995   "Distributed spatial semantics". *Nordic Journal of Linguistics* 18:167-199
Stefanowitsch, Anatol — Ada Rohde
    2004   "The goal bias in the encoding of motion events", in: Klaus-Uwe Panther and Günter Radden (edd.), 249-268.
Talmy, Leonard
    1985   "Lexicalization patterns : semantic structure in lexical forms", in: Timothy Shopen (ed.), 57-77.
Talmy, Leonard
    2000   *Toward a cognitive semantics*. Bradford Books.

3 Distribution of OE *mid rihte* as an Adverbial of Propriety – with Special Reference to the Textual Variation

Kousuke Kaita, Chiba University, Graduate School

1. Introduction

The aim of this paper is to examine how an Old English (henceforth OE) adverbials *mid rihte* 'rightfully' and *rihtlice* 'rightly' vary and with which words they collocate as a sign denoting the notion of obligation or propriety.

English adverbs (or some phrases corresponding to it) can modify the verb or the whole sentence according to their sense.[1] As Nakao (2006: 64)[2] points out, sometimes an adverb can consist of a set phrase with an auxiliary in Modern English (henceforth MnE) (e.g. *I needs must rest me* in Shakes. *The Tempest* 3.3.4). Yamazaki (2001) points out the collocation of modal auxiliaries *could*, *might*, etc. with such adverbs of possibility as *possibly, conceivably, perhaps*, and *maybe*.[3] Collocation, literally defined in the present study as the co-occurrence of two or more words, is considered to be important in the historical linguistic study (e.g. grammaticalisation, see Akimoto 2002: 9).

In examining older languages it is necessary to consider style, genre, or even authors' preference for a text as we read the context. In OE as well as in MnE, such collocation of an (auxiliary) verb with an adverb is often found. When we give close attention to the texts, however, the distribution of the combinations are affected according to its style, genre, or collocation of words. It is not the intention of the present study to examine all the OE adverbials with their collocating verbs. Instead I intend to confine the consideration to the distribution of OE *mid rihte* and *rihtlice* with their collocating auxiliaries for obligation, to compare these two adverbials, and to conclude that *mid rihte* 'rightfully' can be functioning as an element compatible with such auxiliaries as *sculan* or *mōtan* and more remarkably *āgan to*, which has started from the use as a main verb at OE period, later showing the sense of auxiliary 'ought to'.

In the examples cited, italics, underlines, and translations are mine unless otherwise noted. The short titles of OE texts are based on *The Dictionary of Old English, Web Corpus* (henceforth *DOE Corpus*).

---

1 For the function of adverbs in detail, see Jackendoff (1972: Ch.3).
2 "Modals can be combined with such adverbial phrases as *nedes, of force*, and *by right* to reinforce their modal forces" (Nakao 2006: 64).
3 Lightfoot (1979: 92-97), citing Jackendoff's analysis of adverbs, made the semantic and syntactic analysis of adverbs parallel to that of modal auxiliaries.

2. OE '*āgan* + *to*-infinitive' construction with *mid rihte*

In Kaita (2006) I dealt with the formation of MnE auxiliary *ought to* in the usage of OE and Early ME *āgan* with *to*-infinitive by the help of examination of Ono (1989), who collected the Late OE examples[4] from *A Microfiche Concordance of Old English*. I list three examples in (1).

(1) a. *LkGl (Li)* 7.41
   an *ahte to geldanne* penningas fif fund (from Ono (1989: 75); italics his)
   'one had to pay five hundred pennies'
   b. *LawAfEl* 12.1
   Ðeah hwa gebycgge his dohtor on þeowenne, ne sie hio ealles swa ðeowu swa oðru mennenu: *nage* he hit ut on elðeodig folc to *bebycgganne*.   (from Ono (1989: 72); italics his)
   'Although one sells his daughter to foreigners, she is not entirely as the same slave as other male: he does not have her to sell onto foreign folk.'
   c. *LawDuns* 6
   Nah naðer *to farenne* ne Wilisc man Ænglisc land ne Ænglisc on Wylisc ðe ma, butan gesettan landmen,   (from Ono (1989: 73); italics his)
   'Foreign man ought not to go to the English land nor ought English (man) to go to the foreign (land) the more, except for settled native ones,'

According to *OED* (s.v. *ought* † 2.a.) (1a) is the first example of '*āgan* + *to*-infinitive'. In (1a) and (1b) the inflected infinitives are transitive verbs, while that of (1c) is an intransitive *faran*. In (1a) and (1b) of the '*āgan* + *to*-infinitive' constructions, if the transitive verbs are used with *āgan*, Ono points out the problem of ambiguity, asking whether the object should belong to *āgan* or to *to*-infinitive: "[a]*gan* + infinitive is ambiguous, when the verb combined with *agan* is transitive and has its own object, which can also be governed by *agan*" (Ono 1989: 77). On the other hand, as Ono points out, if the infinitive is intransitive the ambiguity does not occur: "there can be no ambiguity, when the verb combined with *agan* has a clause as object ... or when the verb is intransitive" (Ono 1989: 77).

In my examination what I found to be important for the history of *āgan to* is the collocation with *mid rihte*, together with the semantic-syntactic influence of *sculan* and *mōtan* as synonymous with *āgan* in the sense of obligation and alike in taking infinitival complement. For the collocation, if the ambiguous construction contains a sentence adverb *mid rihte* or *rihlice* meaning 'rightfully', the notion of obligation is interpreted and therefore such constructions of *āgan to* may be read as 'ought to'. The following examples (2) and (3) are ambiguous constructions with *mid rihte* and with *rihtlice* respectively, wherefore the ambiguity is avoided.

---

4   The examples of Ono (1989: 68-75) include what Callaway (1913: 80-81) has found.

(2) *HomU* 24 (Nap 25) 5
Forðam *nah* ænig man mid rihte *to fullianne* hæþenne man,
(from Ono (1989: 70); italics his)
'Therefore anyone ought not to baptise heathen man rightfully.'

(3) *Ch* 1084 (Harm 24) 9
þ he mote beon ælc þæra gerihta wurðe þæs þe he *ah* þær of rihtlice *to habbene* for minan lufan. (from Ono (1989: 73); italics his)
'that he is allowed to be worthy of each of the rights which he ought to have rightfully thereof for my affection.'

I owe the hint of this consideration to a New High German (henceforth NHG) adverbial phrase *mit Recht*, literally 'with right', as in (4).

(4) NHG adverbial phrase *mit Recht* 'rightfully, righteously'
Es wird *mit Recht* ein guter Braten gerechnet zu den guten Taten
(Wilhelm Buschs Sammlung, *Kritik des Herzens* (1874) cited from *Duden* (s.v. *Recht*))
'A good roast is rightfully counted as a good deed.'

From this observation of *mid rihte* and *rihtlice* I concluded that the ambiguous construction of '*āgan* + *to*-infinitive' could have a clear reading 'ought to' by the collocation of these adverbs, and such co-existence could play an important role for the formation of MnE *ought to* from the use of main verb into that of auxiliary, together with the change of the value of infinitival *to*.

Turning to OE *mid rihte*, *OED* also gives reference to the phrase, as in (5) and (6). For *rihtlice*, *OED* gives no exact reference for 'rightfully'.

(5) *OED* s.v. *right* 5. In prepositional phrases, *with*, *by*, or *of right*, = rightfully, properly, with reason or justice.[5]
† a. *with* (or *mid*) *right*. Obs.
The first example: 863 *Charter* in *O. E. Texts* 439
Sue ðer mid riahte[6] to ðem lande limpað.
'As it happens there to the land rightfully.'
The last example: *a*1400 (in *Relig. Pieces fr. Thornton MS.* 22)

(6) *OED* s.v. *right* 8. In prepositional phrases denoting justifiable title or claim to something:
a. *with right*. (In OE. *mid rihte*.)
The first example: *Beowulf* 2056[7]

---

5 Nakao (2006: 64) cites this signification in mentioning the phrase 'by right'.
6 The form *riahte* with *mid* in this text is the only example in *DOE Corpus*.
7 We will see the longer context in (9).

[He] þone maðþum byreð, þone þe ðu <u>mid rihte</u> rædan *sceoldest.*
'[He] bears the treasure, which you must have rightfully.'
The last example: 1599 (SHAKS. *Hen. V*, I. ii. 96)

OED does not give any account of the collocating words with *mid rihte* or *rihtlice*. The semantic distinction between these two significations, (5) and (6), seems unclear. The examples of *mid rihte* under either signification can be read as 'rightfully', i.e. 'it is proper (for someone to do something)'. The last example in (6) by Shakespeare (*May I with right and conscience make this claim?*) is translated into NHG by von Schlegel and Tieck (tr.) (1885) as *Kann ich nach Pflicht und Recht die Fordrung thun?* (spelling modernised) 'Can I make the claim according to obligation and right?', which does not seem to express the same thing if NHG translation had *mit Recht*. That is, *nach ... Recht* may modify the verb *thun* as an adverb of manner, whereas *mit Recht* may modify the whole sentence as a sentence adverb. However, *mid rihte* in *Beowulf* 2056 may well be assigned the reading 'rightfully', as supported from the similar reading of the line 424 in *Genesis B* which we will see in (10).

In subsequent sections I investigate how the distribution of *mid rihte* and *rihtlice* vary, and with which words they collocate as a sign of obligation or propriety. I will revisit the formation of *āgan to* at the end of this paper because I need to examine whether the sense of obligation of *āgan to* is really emphasised by the collocation.

3. The distribution and collocation of *mid rihte* / *rihtlice*
In the survey in *DOE Corpus* I adopted such spelling variants as *mid riht-*, *mid ryht-*, *mid reht-*, and *mid richt-* for *mid rihte*, and *rihtlice*, *ryhtlice*, and *rehtlice* for *rihtlice*. For convenience I describe the headwords of two adverbs as *mid rihte* and *rihtlice* respectively including each spelling variant in this paper. And the candidate words collocating with *mid rihte* or *rihtlice* taken into examination are *āgan to*, *bēon to*, *(ge)byrian*, *mōtan*, and *sculan* in the same clause. I selected these words because four of them are used as MnE auxiliaries of obligation, and also I took *(ge)byrian* for showing a considerable occurrence with the adverbs. The results in verse and gloss texts are shown in (7) and (8).

(7) Verse texts
    mid rihte: with *sculan* (3): And [0161 (520)], Beo [0570 (2053)], and ChristA,B,C [0102
        (378)]
        mōtan (2): GenA,B [0156 (421)] and Rid 40 [0008 (33)]
    rihtlice: Not found in the combination
(8) Glosses
    mid rihte: Not found in the combination
    rihtlice: with *bēon to* (1): LkHeadGl (Li) [0055 (54)]

The result in prose texts, which show the most occurrences among three texts, is displayed in the two Tables in the following page.[8]

In the Tables the prose texts are aligned almost chronologically according to the editions which the examples of *DOE Corpus* are based on, and I consulted for the alignment of texts Ker (1957: xiv-xix) and Clemoes (1959), but more specific identification of dates seems necessary.

For the results, in verse texts, *sculan* and *mōtan* with *mid rihte* are found in Early OE texts as in (9) and (10), while *rihtlice* was not found with any of the candidates. The commentary in Krapp and Dobbie (edd.) (1931-1953) does not refer to the *mid rihte* in these contexts.

(9) Beo [0570 (2053)]
    Nu her þara banena   byre nathwylces
    frætwum hremig   on flet gæð,
    morðres gylpeð,   ond þone maðþum byreð,
    þone þe ðu <u>mid rihte</u>   rædan *sceoldest*.
        (The text arranged according to Klaeber (ed.) 1950^3: 77)
'Now here some son of the murderers, exulting at decorated armour, goes to the hall, boasts of slaying, and bears the treasure, which you must have rightfully.'

(10) GenA,B [0156 (421)]
        Nu hie drihtne synt
    wurðran micle,   and *moton* him þone welan agan
    þe we on heofonrice   habban sceoldon,
    rice <u>mid rihte</u>;   is se ræd gescyred
    monna cynne.   (The text arranged according to Doane (ed.) 1991: 215)
'Now they are worthier for the Lord so much and are allowed to possess for themselves the happiness that we must have in heaven, the kingdom rightfully; the advantage is allotted in the mankind.'

---

8   The Tables include the data of negative contexts (described as "Neg."). Although not discussed as irrelevant to the present investigation, the consideration of such negative contexts seem to be important in that negation can play an important role in the entire meaning of a given sentence. In the data consulted in *DOE Corpus* such context with *mid unrihte* as the following can be found, although it does not show the combination with *sculan*, etc.;
    LawIAs [0012 (5)]
        Nelle ic, þæt ge me <u>mid unrihte</u> ahwar aht gestrynan; ...
    'I do not wish that you gain anything unrightfully in any way; ...'

Table 1: The result of *mid rihte* in prose texts (84 occurrences)

	CP	Bo	GD	HomS	HomU	WPol	WHom	HomM	WCan	Law	Comp	Ch	ChronF
āgan to (4)												4	
Neg. (8)				3		1			2	1			1
bēon to (1)			1										
(ge)byrian (32)				1	2	3				5	1	20	
mōtan (3)			2							1			
Neg. (1)					1								
sculan (35)	9	2	1	1	5	5	4	1		4	1	2	
Neg. (0)													
Total	9	2	1	4	10	7	8	1	2	11	2	26	1

Table 2: The result of *rihtlice* in prose texts (33 occurrences)

	CP	Mart	GD Pref	Æ CHom	Æ Abus Mor	HomS	ÆLS	ÆLet	WPol	ÆTemp
āgan to (2)										
Neg. (0)										
bēon to (4)		2	1							
(ge)byrian (6)										1
mōtan (2)										
Neg. (0)										
sculan (18)	1			2		1	1	1	1	4
Neg. (1)				1						
Total	1	2	1	3	1	1	1	1	4	1

	HomU	Law	WHom	Ch	Comp	Æ Abus Warn	ÆHom	LS	ChronE
āgan to	1			1					
Neg.									
bēon to			1						
(ge)byrian		1		3			1		
mōtan			2						
Neg.									
sculan	2			1	1	1	1		1
Neg.									
Total	3	1	3	5	1	1	1	1	1

Example (10), in which both *moton* and *mid rihte* are in the same clause, is the example of *mid rihte* with *mōtan*. The object *þone welan*, however, is followed by the relative clause containing *sceoldon*. Therefore we can say that *mid rihte* is syntactically not collocating with *sculan* in the same clause, but semantically associated to it.

In contrast to the data in verse texts, no data with *mid rihte* is found in glosses. Instead '*rihtlice* + *bēon to*' is found only once, where Latin *debere* is glossed to *rehtlice were* as in (11).

(11) LkHeadGl (Li) [0055 (54)]

OE:	fyr	innueard	hine cuoeð	ðærflicra	todælnise	woere gesended	&
Latin:	*Ignem*	*internam*	*se dicit*	*necessitudinum*	*diuissionem*	*missurum*	*et*
	onsione	heofnes	cunnande	<u>rehtlice</u> *were*	tíd	*to* oncnauanne	eawunga
	faciem	*caeli*	*probantes*	*debere*	*tempus*	*intellegere*	*manifestum*
	& æc	geðiodsumnise	to ðæm fionde	on	woeg	foresægeð	
	atque	*consentiendum*	*aduersario*	*in*	*uia*	*pronuntiat*	

(The text arranged according to Skeat (ed.) 1871-1887: 7-8)

'((The Gospel of) Luke) says (that) the internal fire should be put itself into the necessary division, and it would be a suitable time, knowing the sight of heaven, to understand plainly and also foretells the agreement to the fiend on the way.'

Here *rihtlice* may support the sense of *debere*, although I do not enter into this problem any further.

In the Tables there are four things to note. The first is the number of occurrences of 84 for *mid rihte* and 33 for *rihtlice*. The second thing is that through looking up the data of *rihtlice*, it seems that *rihtlice* can mean 'rightly'[9] as a manner adverb rather than 'rightfully' as a sentence adverb except for some example of *rihtlice* in *Chaters* which I mention in the subsequent section. The third thing is that the combination of '*sculan* + *mid rihte* or *rihtlice*' is found throughout from Early OE to Late OE. I give the examples for *mid rihte* and *rihtlice* from Early OE *Pastoral Care* as in (12) and (14), and Late OE *Institutes of Polity*[10] in (13) and (15). I have found ten examples in *Pastoral Care*.[11]

---

9   See *OED* s.v. *rightly* 1. "In accordance with equity or moral rectitude; justly, fairly, uprightly; in conformity with right conduct or procedure." (the first example: 805 *Charter* in *O.E. Texts* 442).

10 In the list of "Wulfstans Spracheigentümlichkeiten" (Jost (1950: 155-168)) the adverbials *mid rihte* and *rihtlice* are not referred to. For *Canons of Edgar*, another work of Wulfstan, however, Fowler (ed.) (1972: xxxi) includes *mid rihte* (and *mid unrihte*) in "[i]ntensifying adverbs and adverbial phrases" characteristic to Wulfstan's style.

11 There is no lexical variants for '*sculan* + *mid rihte* or *rihtlice*' between Cotton and Hatton MSS.

(12) CP [0089 (4.37.17)]
Forðan oft ðonne mon forlæt ðone ege & ða fæsðrædnesse ðe he mid ryhte on him innan habban *scolde*, hine spænð his mod to suiðe manegum unnyttum weorce.
'For often when one abandons the fear and the fortitude that he must have on himself inside rightfully, his mind misleads him to so many folly deeds.'

(13) WPol 2.1.1 (Jost) [0012 (10)]¹²
And ægðer he *sceal* beon mid rihte, ge milde ge repe, milde þam godum and styrne þam yfelum.
'And he must be both gentle and severe rightfully, gentle to the good and stern to the evil.'

(14) CP [0700 (20.149.24)]
Oððe eft ðæt he ryhtlice & stiðlice wrecan *sceolde*, ðæt he ðæt ne forielde, ðylæs se ryhtwislica anda acolige, ðæt he hit eft sua eaðe wrecan ne mæge, ðætte forðy to ungemetlice ne sie geliðod ðæm scyldgan, ðylæs him ðæs godan weorces lean losige ðe he mid ðære steore geearnian sceolde.
'Or again when he must persecute rightly and severely what he does not delay, lest the righteous zeal should grow cold, so that he cannot persecute it so easily again, so that the criminal is not softened too immeasurably lest he should lose the reward of good deed for himself which he must earn with the discipline.'

(15) WPol 2.1.1 (Jost) [0064 (59)]¹³
And hi *sceolan* leornian and rihtlice læran and ymb folces dæda geornlice smeagan.
'And they must learn and teach rightly and think about the deeds of people earnestly.'

The collocation with '*mōtan* / *bēon to* + *mid rihte* / *rihtlice*' was found rarely as in the examples from (16) to (19).

(16) HomS 2 (ScraggVerc 16) [0050 (139)]¹⁴
Broðor mine, us is þonne nu mycel neodþearf þæt we geleornian Godes geleafan swa us riht sie & we mid rihte cunnan & mid rihte ongitan magon & *moton*.
'My brothers, then it is now needed very much for us that we learn God's love as is right for us and we can and must know rightfully and understand rightfully.'

(17) WHom 18 [0048 (138)]
And an fulluht is eallum cristenum mannum gemæne, & þæt *mot* ure gehwylc rihtlice healdan gif we aht gefaran scylan; & se gehealt his fulluht rihtlice se þe gehealt Godes beboda.

---

12 Similar contexts are found in HomU40 (Nap50) [0008 (30)] and WPol 2.1.2 (Jost) [0005 (7)].
13 Similar context is found in WPol 2.1.2 (Jost) [0035 (42)].
14 In this example *mid rihte* occurs twice with single *mōtan*. In Table 1, however, this data is regarded as one pair of '*mid rihte* + *mōtan*'.

'And a baptism is common among all Christian people, and everyone of us must keep it rightly if we must undergo something; and he keeps his baptism rightly who keeps God's commands.'

(18) HomS 28 [0082 (200)]
Þam *is* þonne mid rihte *to* answarienne þæt us is se getriwesta gewita, seo soðfæstnys sylf, þæt is þonne ure drihten hælend crist se on helle astah and þanon eft lifiende com.
'Then it is rightful to answer for him that the most faithful sage, the faithfulness itself, is for us, that is then our Lord, Christ the Saviour, who descended to hell and came back from there alive.'

(19) Mart 5 (Kotzor) [0438 (My 4, A.14)][15]
Ða dagas *syndon* rihtlice *to* fæstenne, ond þara metta to brucenne ðe menn brucað on ðæt feowertiges nihta fæsten ær eastran.
'The days are to fasten rightly, and to partake of foods that men partake of on the fast of forty nights before Easter.'

The fourth thing to notify is that the occurrence of *āgan to* with both adverbials is distributed in Late OE texts, as in (2) and (3) as I have introduced. Some of the homilies for unspecified occasions are said to be ascribed to Wulfstan, although some scholars point out the authorship to other imitators of him. Even if these texts are not written by Wulfstan, the texts would date Late OE.

From these four points, what can be said about the collocation of '*sculan* + *mid rihte*' and '*āgan to* + *mid rihte*' is that *mid rihte* can well collocate with *sculan* meaning 'must', and this adverbial phrase may be compatible with such a context for obligation. If it is true, *mid rihte* may be a signal to denote that *āgan to* became an auxiliary for obligation from original *āgan to geldanne* construction as in (1a). That *mid rihte* can denote 'rightfully' rather than *rihtlice* does will support the reason why *mid rihte* can be found well with Late OE examples of *āgan to* collected by Ono (1989).

4. '(*Ge*)*byrian* + *mid rihte* / *rihtlice*' in *Charters*
The verb (*ge*)*byrian*, which can be used impersonally,[16] is not an auxiliary verb, but shows many occurrences in the collocation.

For the collocation with (*ge*)*byrian* in *Charters* in the previous Tables, twenty examples with *mid rihte* and three with *rihtlice* are found. *Charters* show some similar contexts as in the examples from (20) to (22), with other miscellaneous contexts in (23). Examples similar to these contexts are given at each of the footnote.

---

15 Similar context is found in Mart 4 (Sisam) [0020 (My 4, A.6)].
16 For the impersonal use, see Ogura (1986: 75-79, 85-90, 97).

(20) Ch 1047 (Rob 95) [0002 (4)][17]
& ic eom þæs mynstres mund & upheald & nelle geþafian þæt ænig mann geutige ænig þara landa þe mid rihte into þan halgan mynstre *gebyrige.*
'I am a guardian and supporter of the monastery and do not wish to endure that any man alienates any of the lands that rightfully belongs to the holy monastery.'

(21) Ch IWm (Galbraith 3) [0003 (7)][18] similar to (20)
And ic nelle gethafian thaet aenig man beo swa dorf thaet him fram hande drage heononforth aenig thera thinga thaes the he rihtlice age & into his <bisceoprice> *gebyrge* be minan fullan frieondscype & gif aenig man haefth aenige aehta ut of his landan gedon ic beode thaet hi bynnan thrym nythan ongean cuman & nan other ne sy be eallen than aehtan them age.
'And I do not wish to endure that any man is so needy that (he) withdraws from his hands henceforth any of the things that he rightfully has and that belongs to his bishopric by my full friendship and if any man has any of the property outdone from his land I command that he comes again within three nights and no other is the possession by all the properties for him.'

(22) Ch 988 (Harm 30) [0002 (2)][19]
& ic cyðe eow þæt ic hæbbe geunnan æþelnoðe arcebisceope ealre þare landare þe ælfmær hæfde & mid rihte into Cristes cyricean *gebyrað* binnan birig & butan on wuda & on felda swa full & swa forð swa ælfric arcebiscop hyre weold oþþe ænig his forgengena.
'And I show you that I have granted to Archbishop Æthelnoth all the land properties that Ælfmær had and that rightfully belong to Christian church inside town and except in wood and in field as fully and as far as the archbishop Ælfric or any of his predecessors controlled them.'

(23) Miscellaneous contexts in *Charters*
mid rihte with *āgan to* (2exs.): Ch 1503 (Whitelock 20) [0032 (71)] and Ch IWm (Dugdale 36) [0002 (2)]
(ge)byrian (3exs.): Ch 518 (Birch 1345) [0007 (4)], Ch 1478 (Rob 115) [0005 (9)], and Ch 1478 (Rob 115) [0008 (19)]
(ge)hīeran (1ex.): Ch 1240 (Harm 70) [0003 (5)]

---

17 Similar contexts are found in Ch 1067 (Harm7) [0003 (4)] and Ch 1118 (Harm 74) [0005 (9)]. Similar contexts but using *āgan to* instead of *(ge)byrian* are Ch 1096 (Harm 43) [0003 (6)] and Ch 1156 (Harm 115) [0003 (6)]. See the example (24).
18 Similar context is found in Ch IHen (BLAdd 29436) [0003 (12)].
19 Similar contexts are found in Ch 1054 (Kem890) [0001 (1)], Ch 1084 (Harm 24) [0003 (6)], Ch 1090 (Harm 35) [0002 (3)], Ch 1105 (Harm 55) [0002 (2)], Ch 1111 (Harm 64) [0002 (2)], Ch 1112 (Harm 65) [0002 (2)], Ch 1116 (Harm 69) [0003 (6)], Ch 1121 (Harm 77) [0002 (3)], Ch 1129 (Harm 85) [0002 (3)], Ch 1135 (Harm 91) [0002 (2)], Ch 1136 (Harm 92) [0002 (2)], Ch 1142 (Harm 98) [0002 (3)], and Ch 1146 (Harm102) [0002 (4)].
Similar contexts but using *(ge)hīeran* instead of *(ge)byrian* are Ch 1115 (Harm 68) [0002 (2)] and Ch 1241 (Harm 72) [0002 (2)].

sculan (2exs.): Ch Thomas (Liebermann) [0005 (4)] and Ch IWm (Douglas 7)
    [0005 (7)]
rihtlice with āgan to (1ex.): Ch 1084 (Harm 24) [0004 (9)][20]
(ge)byrian (1ex.): Ch I or IIWm (Salter) [0003 (6)]
sculan (1ex.): Ch 1454 (Rob 66) [0006 (11)]

In (22) (ge)hīeran 'to belong to' can sometimes be used.[21] Contexts such as (20), the contexts with *mid rihte*, mean that 'I will not endure that anything (right, land, etc.) that belongs to someone / some place is deprived of by others'. (21) is similar to (20) but *rihtlice* is used. The context in (22) denotes that 'I will show you that I have granted something that should belong to some place'. The important thing is that several examples of *Charters* contribute to the assessment of the function of *āgan to* as 'ought to'. The function of auxiliary of *āgan to* may become clear when we compare several contexts containing *gebyrian* in *Charters*.

(24) '*āgan to + mid rihte*' in *Charters*
    Ch 1096 (Harm 43) [0003 (6)][22]
    & ic nelle geþafian þæt him anig man fram hande teo anig þare gerihte þes þe he <u>mid richte</u> to habbene *ah* & ic him geunnen habbe.
    'And I do not wish to endure that any man deprives his hand of any of the right that he rightfully ought to have and I have granted to him.'

In examples (20) and (22) the verb *gebyrian* can mean 'to belong to', so that the contexts can be paraphrased as 'something belongs to someone / some place, etc. rightfully' denoting possession, while (almost) the same situation is expressed by '*āgan to + habban*' in (24), whose paraphrase can be 'someone ought to have some place, etc. rightfully'. It also seems obvious that *āgan to* in (24) functions as an auxiliary, because the notion of possession is retained in the verbal complement *to habbene*, not in *āgan* itself. In the contexts in *Charters* discussed in this section, *mid rihte* seems to be functioning for denoting legal obligation or righteousness.

Considering the context of *Charters* as legal documents, *mid rihte* in the contexts might possibly mean 'according to, with law' as a manner adverb. Even if *mid rihte* in *Charters* means it rather than 'rightfully', this phrase can be assessed to be compatible with such a context with *gebyrian* or *āgan to* or *sculan*. The texts of *Charters* examined in this paper date about Late OE period, and the date may give us the impression that these phrases show their original use of lit-

---

20 This context is what we have seen in (3).
21 Cf. NHG verbs *hören* 'to hear' vs. *gehören* 'to belong to'. For OE (*ge*)*hīeran*, see *OED* s.v. *hear* † 9. *intr.* "To be subject (*to*); to belong. *Obs.* [So MHG. *hœren*, beside *gehœren*.]" (the first example: c893 K. ÆLFRED *Oros.* I. i. § 22). The occurrence of (*ge*)*hīeran* is not included into the data of the Tables.
22 Also cited in Ono (1989: 73). A similar context is found in Ch 1156 (Harm 115) [0003 (6)].

eral 'with right' in *Charters* and may be functionally affecting other texts where *āgan to* appears as an adverb denoting propriety. Through looking at the data, however, the phrase '*sculan + mid rihte*' in *Pastoral Care* (see the examples (12) and (14)) or *Beowulf* (see the citation from *OED* in (6) and its longer context in (9)) will tell us that the function of denoting propriety may well be read and therefore the functional shift of *mid rihte* from its original sense of 'with right' to that of 'rightfully' would be hard to depict in the stage of Late OE period. Instead we should say that such (hypothetical) semantic shift had occurred rather early, and *mid rihte* exists as literal sense of 'with right' in *Charters*, and as another sense of 'rightfully' in *WPol* with *āgan to* in Late OE period. Therefore the adverb *mid rihte* in *Charters* can be semantically ambiguous, but at least shows the compatibility with the auxiliaries of obligation.

5. Conclusion

This study has started from the consideration of the history of '*āgan + to*-infinitive' construction as the ancestor of MnE *ought to* and proceeded to the distribution of *mid rihte* and *rihtlice* as well collocating adverbs in the construction. Through the present survey the following things can be pointed out.

In prose texts the distribution of *mid rihte* and *rihtlice* is different among texts and collocating words, though not definitely or complementarily. As in the Tables *mid rihte* collocates more with the auxiliaries of obligation than *rihtlice* does. For the semantics of these two adverbials it seems that *rihtlice* means 'rightly' as a manner adverb rather than 'rightfully' as a sentence adverb, although some similar contexts in *Charters* show the semantic ambiguity of these two. *Mid rihte* may qualify for a sentence adverb 'rightfully', and it may stylistically consist of a member of set phrases with other words, often found in homiletic or legal prose texts (e.g. *CP*, *HomU*, or *Charters*) in the use of some similar contexts. The collocation of *mid rihte* with words of obligation such as *sculan* (throughout OE texts), *mōtan*, or *bēon to* (though rare) would explain that this phrase is compatible with the context of obligation. '(*Ge*)*byrian + mid rihte*' as parallel to '*āgan to + mid rihte*' in *Charters* may suggest that the notion of obligation should be read in the legal contexts. Therefore it can be said that *mid rihte* supports a sense of obligation of *āgan to* – the sense it had possessed from the start but not exclusively– and *mid rihte* (rather than *rihtlice*) can function as the sign of obligation or propriety. From this point the formation of *āgan to* as an auxiliary may well be based (i) on the original sense of possession, (ii) on semantic and syntactic overlapping with *sculan* and *mōtan*, and (iii), as this present study has investigated, on the collocation with *mid rihte* in Late OE texts.[23]

---

[23] For another factor found in Kaita (2006) is the change of the function of infinitival *to*, which is not dealt with in this study. For the formation of the sense of MnE auxiliary *ought to*, see Kaita (2007).

I hope I have shown that, in order to understand what the text tells us, not only the analysis of the function of each part of speech but the role of collocation should be taken into consideration. This study states that the analysis of contexts needs the understanding of the function of each word in a given sentence. Collocation is considered to be an important factor in the field of linguistics such as grammaticalisation. I gave no remark to it, but I pointed out the importance of collocation from another angle of philological viewpoint.

As the problem for further research, (i) the collocation of *mid rihte* with other words in different clauses, (ii) what role the collocation with adverb plays for the formation of auxiliaries, and (iii) more specific examination of the distribution according to the deontic (root)/epistemic sense of modal auxiliaries can be listed for the study of auxiliary with adverbials.

References

Akimoto, Minoji
    2002   *Grammaticalization and Idiomatization*. Tokyo: Hitsuzi Shobo. [in Japanese]

Callaway, Morgan
    1913   *The Infinitive in Anglo-Saxon*. Washington, D. C.: Carnegie Institution.

Clemoes, Peter
    1959   "The Chronology of Ælfric's Works." *The Anglo-Saxons: Studies in Some Aspects of their History and Culture presented to Bruce Dickins*. London. rpt. in *Subsidia* 5: 1-37. SUNY-Binghamton: CEMERS, 1980.

Doane, A. N. (ed.)
    1991   *The Saxon Genesis: An Edition of the West Saxon Genesis B and the Old Saxon Vatican Genesis*. Wisconsin: University of Wisconsin Press.

Die Dudenredaktion
    2002   *Zitate und Aussprüche*. 2nd ed. (Der Duden Bd. 12). Mannheim: Dudenverlag.

Fowler, Roger (ed.)
    1972   *Wulfstan's Canons of Edgar*. EETS, o.s. 266. Oxford: Oxford University Press.

Harrison, G. B. (ed.)
    1968   *Shakespeare: the Complete Works*. New York: Harcourt Brace Jovanovich.

Jackendoff, Ray S.
- 1972 *Semantic Interpretation in Generative Grammar*. Cambridge, Mass.: MIT Press.

Jost, Karl
- 1950 *Wulfstanstudien*. Swiss Studies in English 23. Bern: Francke.

Kaita, Kousuke
- 2006 *The Semantic and Syntactic History of English Auxiliary* ought (to) - *with special Reference to the tendencies in Late Old and Early Middle English*. Unpublished MA thesis. Chiba University.
- 2007 "The Historical Formation of English Auxiliary *Ought to* – with special reference to Late OE and Early ME", *Studies on Humanities and Social Sciences of Chiba University* 15: 108-116.

Ker, N. R.
- 1957 *Catalogue of Manuscripts Containing Anglo-Saxon*. Oxford: Clarendon Press.

Klaeber, Frederick (ed.)
- 1950 *Beowulf and the Fight at Finnsburg*. 3rd ed. Boston: D. C. Heath and Company.

Krapp, G. P. – E. V. K. Dobbie (edd.)
- 1931-1953 *Anglo-Saxon Poetic Records*. I-VI. London: Routledge and Kegan Paul, New York: Columbia University Press.

Lightfoot, David
- 1979 *Principles of Diachronic Syntax*. Cambridge: Cambridge University Press.

Nakao, Yoshiyuki
- 2006 "The Interpretation of *Troirus and Criseyde* 3.587: '*syn I moste on you triste*'." In Michiko Ogura (ed.), *Textual and Contextual Studies in Medieval English: towards the Reunion of Linguistics and Philology*. Frankfurt am Main: Peter Lang. pp. 51-71.

Ogura, Michiko
- 1986 *Old English 'Impersonal' Verbs and Expressions*. Anglistica Vol. XXIV. Copenhagen: Rosenkilde and Bagger.

Ono, Shigeru
- 1989 *On Early English Syntax and Vocabulary*. Tokyo: Nan'un-do.

Simpson, J. A. – E. S. C. Weiner (edd.)
- 1989 *The Oxford English Dictionary*. 2nd ed. Oxford: Clarendon Press.

Skeat, Walter W. (ed.)
- 1871-1887 *The Gospel according to St. Matthew, St. Mark, St. Luke and St. John*. Cambridge: Cambridge University Press. rpt. Darmstadt: Wissenschaftliche Buchgesellschaft, 1970.

Sweet, Henry (ed.)
    1871   *King Alfred's West-Saxon Version of Gregory's Pastoral Care.* EETS, o.s. 45 and 50. rpt. Millwood, New York; Kraus Reprint, 1973.

University of Toronto
    n.d.   *The Dictionary of Old English, Web Corpus* [Internet]. Available from: <http://ets.umdl.umich.edu/o/oec/> [Accessed 30 August 2007]

Von Schlegel, W. A. – Ludwig Tieck (tr.)
    1885   *Shakespeares Sämtliche Dramatische Werke.* Zweiter Band. Berlin: A. Warschauer.

Yamazaki, Satoshi
    2001   "Bun-fukushi no Arawasu Kanousei no Doai to Chinjutsu-kanwateki-Houjodoushi tono Kyouki ni Tsuite." *Eigo Gohou Bunpou Kenkyu* 8: 181-184. [in Japanese]

4 The Prenominal Parefix *Ge-* in *Beowulf*
Yookang Kim, Hankuk University of Foreign Studies

1. Introduction
There have been a number of articles and monographs dealing with the subject of the English prefix *ge-* (Samuels 1949, Pilch 1951/2, Lindemann 1965, Kastovsky 1968, Koziol 1972, Niwa 1966, 1973, 1974, Stanley 1982, Lutz 1997, Dollinger 2001, among others). Many authorities agreed that the prefix was widely used in Germanic before nouns and verbs, and that it continued to appear in late Middle English (henceforth, ME) up to the end of the 15th century as well as in the Old English (henceforth, OE) period. In particular, the main function or the primary meaning of the prefix has been investigated. According to Mitchell and Robinson (1995: §138), the prefix combined with a verb has a perfective meaning while the nominal prefix *ge-* has the sense of collectivity (e.g., *ge-fera* 'companion'; *ge-winnan* 'get by fighting' vs. *winnan* 'to fight'). On the other hand, it has also been argued that the prefix did not have any transparent lexical meaning (Fijn van Draat 1902, Kastovsky 1968).

Most of the previous works have been concerned with the preverbal prefix, and research on the prenominal *ge-* has been comparatively smaller. As far as I know, Stanley (1982) is the only one that descriptively examines the prenominal prefix in OE and ME. This paper investigates the prenominal prefix *ge-* used in *Beowulf* with special attention to its semantic use. I argue that in the vast majority of *ge-*nouns used in the text, the prefix has a resultative meaning, consequently demonstrating that the traditional semantic account was incorrect or overgeneralised. The result of my case study reveals that in over 80% of *ge-*nouns the prefix has a transparent lexical meaning and the primary meaning is resultative rather than collective or associative.

2. Functions and Meanings of the Prefix *Ge-* in Early English
There have been many monographs and articles to deal with the subject of the subsequent development of OE *ge-* (especially the preverbal *ge-*) for the last two centuries. The general outline is clear. The prefix flourished in Germanic both when preverbal and when prenominal, and it died out in ME, lasting longest as a marker of past particles (ME *imātūrāte* 'matured', *iparepārāte* 'treated').[1] The development began in the Northern dialects in the tenth century, where it was practically completed by the 12th century, while in the Southern dialects itself in

---

[1] The OE *ge-* was used in reduced forms such as *y-* or *i-* in ME. According to Luick (1964: §325), the oldest form of the prefix in OE is *gi-* which occurred as *ge-* after AD 740. Pilch (1951/1952: 26) states that the sound for <g> in *ge-* was softened to /j/ in late OE and was then turned into [i] from around 1300 onwards (e.g., ME *ibrohte* 'brought').

later and was completed only in the 14th century (Lutz 1997: 278, Stanley 1982: 31, Pilch 1951/2: 24-6, Koziol 1972: §227). In Present-day English, the prefix survives as a prenominal only when it is no longer recognizable, e.g., in *alike* (OE *gelic* 'likewise'), *enough* (OE *genoh* 'enough'), *handiwork* (OE *handgeweorc* 'handiwork'). The prefix is found in OE as shown in (1).

(1) OE *Ge*-words

   a. verbs
   gehīeran 'to hear', geleornian 'depart', gegōdian 'to endow'

   b. nouns
   gesīþ 'companion', geset 'seat', geswing 'vibration'

   c. pronouns
   gehwer 'whoever', gehwilc 'whatever, whichever'

   d. adjectives
   gecynde 'natural', gefæg 'dear, pleasing', gelenge 'related'

   e. adverbs
   genoh 'enough', gelic 'likewise'

The function and the meaning of the prefix have been subject to research (Weick 1911, Pilch 1951/52, Niwa 1974, Lindemann 1970, Samuels 1949, Stanley 1982, Lutz 1997, Dollinger 2001, among others). Scholarly attention has over-emphasised research into verbal uses of the prefix whereas research on nominal *ge-* has been considerably smaller. Mitchell and Robinson (1995: §138) discriminate between *ge*-verbs and *ge*-nouns. According to them, the prefix has the sense of collectivity in some nouns (e.g., *ge-fera* 'companion, someone who travels with somebody') while in verbs, it has "a perfective sense", projecting the end or result of an action onto the verb (e.g., *ge-winnan* 'get by fighting', *winnan* 'to fight'). Namely, the prefix *ge-* is generally presented as a marker for collectivity in nouns and of perfective aspect in verbs. A number of previous studies draw a similar picture to the one in Mitchell and Robinson (1995). The following summary is an attempt to classify the approaches taken in the previous literature, yielding three groups of functions and meanings of *ge-*: (a) *ge-* as a meaningless morpheme; (b) *ge-* having transparent meanings; (c) *ge-* as a grammatical marker.

(a) *Ge-* as a meaningless morpheme
The idea that OE *ge-* has no meaning or function at all is not new. Fijn van Draat

(1902: 360) states that in the vast majority of cases OE *ge-* is a "meaningless appendage". More recently, a number of scholars have partially adopted this finding.

For deverbal nouns, Kastovsky (1968: 488) claims that in the majority cases *ge-* has no longer any meaning or function in OE and that its occurrences must be attributed to a "residual pattern probably no longer productive" (ibid.). Niwa (1974) also reveals that OE preverbal *ge-* has non-lexical meaning, only playing a grammatical or stylistic role.

(b) *Ge-* having transparent meanings
As Mitchell and Robinson (1995) observed, collectivity ('with, together') is the most widely attributed semantic meaning of *ge-*. This meaning of collectivity is applied to nouns and adjectives. Magoun (1930: 48e) iterates the collective use of the nominal prefix *ge-* and Voyles (1974: 123) also defines the function of the prefix as "collection" or "together, with". Kastovsky (1968: 488) also distinguishes between two types of collectivity: collectivity and associativity. According to him, collectivity implies a collectivity of persons or objects, such as in OE *gegeng* 'body of fellow travellers' while associativity indicates that the subject performs on overt or implied action in conjunction with somebody else, such as *gebedda* 'one who lies in bed with another one'.

It is also claimed that the prefix *ge-* marks repetition of an action in both verbs and nouns. The idea is found in Niwa (1966: 488) stating that *ge-* functions as an intensifier in OE verbs. Verbs are not the only part of speech to which this function is applied. Sprockel (1973: 38) detects it also in nouns, and calls it 'repeated action' as in OE *gebland* 'commotion' (from *blendan* 'to mix'), *geþring* 'tumult' (from *þringan* 'to press, throng, squeeze') or *gewinn* 'battle, repeated fighting' (from *winnan* 'to fight, strive').

Generalisation seems to be a function of *ge-* in pronouns. This meaning was first documented in pronouns by Weick (1911: 47) and also found in Magoun (1930). Generalisation is supposed to add a sense of 'indefiniteness, uncertainty' like in the following examples: *gehwer* 'whoever', *gehwilc* 'whatever, whichever'. This function is mostly found in pronouns.

(c) *Ge-* as a grammatical marker
It has been generally agreed that the preverbal *ge-* is a marker of perfective aspect (Pilch 1951/52: 130). As described above, a word like OE *faran* denotes 'to go, wander around aimlessly' whereas *gefaran* implies a goal, or OE *winnan* means 'to fight' but *gewinnan* 'to get by fighting, win' (Mitchell and Robinson 1995: §138).

Similarly, Pilch (1951/52: 198) reports that the preverbal *ge-* is a marker of the past participle (e.g., *gesette* 'to set, past participle' vs. *settan* 'to set, infinitive'). This idea is closely related to the hypothesis that *ge-* expresses perfective aspect.

Lastly, Lenz (1886) proposed that *ge-* transitivises intrasitive verbs, which is an idea supported by Pilch (1951/52: 135). For example, OE *gebiddan* means 'to worship somebody' while its simplex counterpart *biddan* denotes 'to ask, beg'.

I have briefly reviewed the previous works of the OE *ge-*, presenting an array of functions and meaning of the prefix. There are three points of view: (a) *ge-* had no significant meaning in OE; (b) *ge-* contributed to transparent semantic meaning; (c) *ge-* served as a grammatical marker. Functions (a) and (b) are applied to both nouns and verbs while function (c) only to verbs. Since this paper is concerned with *ge-*nouns, function (c) is excluded from consideration in this paper. My case study of *ge-*nouns in *Beowulf* reveals that the explanation (a) is not correct because there are many counter examples in which the prefix still has a transparent meaning. Furthermore, contrary to the previous view (b) that the nominal prefix *ge-* generally has a sense of collectivity (or associativity), I argue that the primary meaning of the prefix combined with nouns is resultative or causative rather than collective or associative.

3. Case Study: The Prenominal Prefix *Ge-* in *Beowulf*

As I described in section 2, it has been agreed that the prefix *ge-* was widely used in OE before nouns or verbs. This paper mainly deals with *ge-*nouns in *Beowulf* to investigate the function and the meaning of the OE prefix *ge-*. The date of *Beowulf* has been controversial, but considering linguistic, stylistic, historical, metrical and archaeological evidence, scholars suggested the date ranging from the eighth century to the eleventh century (Mitchell and Robinson 1998: 8). However, the poem is preserved in a single manuscript known as MS Cotton Vitellius A. xv in the British Library which was copied down in the late tenth century or perhaps the first decade of the eleventh (ibid.: 3). Therefore, it can be said that the present case study of *ge-*nouns in *Beowulf* provides an empirical evidence for the use of the prefix in late OE. The data used for this paper was drawn from Mitchell and Robinson's (1998) edition of *Beowulf,* and Toller's (1973) *An Anglo-Saxon Dictionary* is referred to in order to determine the lexical meanings of *ge-*tokens.

3.1. Data and Categories of Analyses

In *Beowulf*, I found 38 nouns and 3 pronouns combined with the prefix *ge-* in total.[2] The *ge-*nouns are listed below in (2).

(2) 41 *Ge-*nouns in Beowulf

    gebedda, gebrōþor, gebyrd, gedræg, gedryht, gefēa, gefeoht, geflit, gehwā, gehwæþer, gehwylc, gehygd, gehyld, gelād, gemēde, gemet, gemēting, gemynd, genip, gesacu, gescād,

---

[2] I will use the term *ge-*nouns for both pronouns and nouns combined with the prefix *ge-* throughout the paper.

gescæphwīle, gesceaft, gesceap, geselda, gesīð, geslyht, getrum, geþinge, geþōht, geþonc, geþræc, geþring, geþyld, gewæde, gewealc, geweald, geweorc, gewidre, gewif, gewrixle

The 41 *ge*-words were analyzed according to the following categories which are listed below in Table 1.

Table 1: Categories for the Analysis

ID	Form	Meaning	Frequency	Case	Number	Gender
1	gesacu	strife, hostility	1	n	s	f
Simplex Forms	Meaning	Related Ge-verbs	Meaning	Related Simplex Verbs	Meaning	
sacu	conflict, strife	gesacan	to strive, to oppose	sacan	to strive against, to contend	

(n = nominative, a = accusative, d = dative, g = genitive, i = instrumental, s = singular, p = plural, m = masculine, n = neuter, f = feminine)

The category 'Form' refers to the representative form of the relevant *ge*-tokens. Thus, all inflected forms (tokens) of the same word are not listed as separate words but counted as one word. For example, three different tokens of the word *geþinge* 'agreement' like *geþingo* 'agreement, a.p.', *geþinges* 'agreement, g.s.', *geþingea* 'agreement, g.p.' are classified as one word. Category 'Frequency' gives the total number of occurrences of tokens of the particular 'Form'. Category 'Simplex Form' provides information whether the noun without *ge-* is attested in *Beowulf* or in other texts. When a simplex form is found in Beowulf, the relative frequency of *ge*-types vs. simplex-types is given under the category 'Frequency': e.g., 2:1 (two occurrences of *ge*-types vs. one occurrence of simplex-types). The last two categories 'related *ge*-verbs' and 'related simplex verbs' give information of verbs related with *ge*-tokens. The relevant *ge*-verbs or simplex verbs are listed under the categories when they are attested either in *Beowulf* or in other OE texts.

3.2. Statistical Analysis of the Data
In this section, I provide a statistical analysis of *ge*-tokens based on the categories described in the previous section. Main questions for the analysis are as follows:

(a) What is the dominant case, gender, or number of *ge*-nouns?
(b) How frequently do *ge*-nouns occur?
(c) How many *ge*-nouns have their corresponding simplex nouns?
(d) How many *ge*-nouns have their corresponding *ge*-verbs or simplex verbs occurring without *ge-*?
(e) What is the main function or meaning of the nominal prefix *ge-*?

Let us begin with the case, gender, and number of *ge*-nouns.

3.2.1. Case, Gender, and Number of *Ge*-nouns

Among 41 *ge*-words found in *Beowulf*, three pronouns (*gehwā, gehwæþer, gehwylc*) are excluded because in many cases it is impossible to identify the gender of the pronouns without or even with contextual information. The total number of *ge*-tokens is 128 and their distributional feature is presented below in Table 2.

Table 2: Case, Gender, and Number of *Ge*-nouns

	Case	(128 tokens)				Gender	(38 nouns)		Number (128 tokens)	
	N	A	D	G	I	M	F	N	S	P
Total No.	19	54	31	21	3	7	8	23	106	22
%	14.8	42.1	24.2	16.4	2.3	18.4	21	60	82.8	17.1

As shown in Table 2, the figure for accusative forms is remarkable (42.1 %). In particular, dative and accusative forms account for 66.3 % of *ge*-tokens. It is not easy to figure out why the high proportions of *ge*-nouns occur as objective forms. I just speculate that this distribution may be related with the function or the meaning of *ge*-nouns. It may be possible to state that the perfective or resultative nouns might have been used in common as objectives of verbs or prepositions when they undergo an action or when an action is directed to them.

Table 2 also shows the high distribution of neuter nouns (60%) and singular forms (82.8%). It is also hard to provide a semantic interpretation of the high proportion of neuter nouns because OE gender is not natural but purely grammatical. However, the distribution of singular forms is understandable considering the fact that the prenominal use of *ge*- was common in the formation of abstracts (cf. Stanley 1982: 38). I reveal in section 3.2.4 that *ge*-nouns generally have an abstract meaning. That means that the semantic bleaching of the prefix *ge*- had already begun in late OE and that the prefix was being grammaticalised at that time. Since abstract nouns must be used as a singular form, it is natural to see the frequent use of singular forms of *ge*-nouns. Therefore, the high portion of singular forms support the idea that the prefix *ge*- is used to add an abstract meaning. The detailed discussion of this issue is provided in section 3.2.4 where I deal with the meaning of the prefix.

3.2.2. Frequency of *Ge*-Nouns

Table 3 presents how frequently *ge*-nouns occur in the text.

Table 3: Frequency of *Ge*-nouns in *Beowulf*

	Once	Twice	Three times	Four times	More than four times
Total No.	26	5	1	1	8
%	63.4	12.1	2.4	2.4	19.5

It is shown in Table 3 that 63.4 % of *ge*-nouns only occur once in *Beowulf*. It is premature to determine the reason for the rare use of individual *ge*-nouns from my relatively small body of evidence. However, the result suggested by Table 3 at least confirms Stanley's (1982: 37) speculation that *ge*-nouns are "readily formed but not habitually used."

3.2.3. *Ge*-forms vs. Simplex Forms

Let us return to the questions (c) and (d) regarding the alternation between *ge*-forms and their corresponding simplex forms without *ge*-. To provide a statistical analysis of the fluctuation, each of *ge*-nouns was morphologically traced back to their related forms derived from the same base: simplex nouns (e.g., *geslyht* 'battle' vs. *slyht* 'a stroke of lighting'), *ge*-verbs (e.g., *gemynd* 'memorial' vs. *gemyndigian* 'to remember') or simplex verbs (e.g., *gesceap* "shape' vs. *scippan* 'to create'). First, Table 4 offers the percentage of *ge*-nouns and their corresponding simplex nouns.

Table 4: *Ge*-nouns and Simplex Nouns

	No simplex nouns	Simplex nouns (*Beowulf*)	Simplex nouns (other texts)
Total No.	10	9	22
%	23.8	21.4	54.7

It can be seen in Table 4 that 23.8 % of the *ge*-nouns do not have their simplex counterparts while in 76.1 % their related simplex nouns are found (21.4 % in *Beowulf* and 54.7 % in other texts).[3] In the case of *ge*-nouns without having simplex forms, it may be speculated that OE native speakers cannot determine the meaning of the prefix without knowing the meaning of the base form which is used without the prefix. Therefore, considering the fact that about a quarter of *ge*-nouns in OE are used without having their *ge*-less variants, it may be stated that the prefix began to undergo semantic bleaching or grammaticalisation in the OE period. Nevertheless, as indicated in Table 4, there are still more than three quarters of *ge*-nouns occurring with their simplex nouns in OE texts and thus it can be speculated that the semantic bleaching or the grammmaticalisation of the prefix is

---

[3] I referred to Toller's (1973) *An Anglo-Saxon Dictionary* to find related simplex forms which are not used in *Beowulf*.

at its initial stage. I show in the following section that the prefix is not semantically blank but used as a meaningful unit.

In addition to their related simplex nouns, *ge*-nouns also have their verbal counterparts derived from the same base. The verbs appear either with or without the prefix *ge*-. Table 5 shows the percentage of the related (*ge*-) verbs.

Table 5: Related *Ge*-verbs or Simplex Verbs

	Only related *ge*-verbs	Only related simplex verbs	Both	Neither
Total No.	0	6	22	10
%	0	15.7	57.8	26.3

There is no *ge*-noun which only alternates with its related *ge*-verb without having any related simplex verbs while 15.5% of the nouns (e.g., *geslyht* 'battle' vs. *slihtan* 'to slay', **geslihtan*) appear only with their related simplex verbs. 57.8% of *ge*-nouns occur with both their related *ge*-verbs and simplex verbs (e.g., *geþinge* 'agreement' vs. *geþingan* 'to determine', *þingan* 'to invite') whereas there are 26.3% of the nouns without having their verbal counterparts (e.g., *geselda* 'companion' vs. **geseldan*, **seldan*).

3.2.4. The Meaning of *Ge*-nouns

In section 2, I provided a brief summary of the meanings or the functions of the prefix, reviewing relevant previous works. There have been two main claims on the nominal prefix *ge*-: (a) the prefix *ge*- is meaningless or (b) the nominal prefix *ge*- has a sense of collectivity while the verbal prefix *ge*- has a perfective meaning. My case study reveals that both of these findings are not correct. It is shown that the prefix *ge*- of most *ge*-nouns (80.5 %) found in *Beowulf* has a transparent meaning and that the dominant meaning of the prefix is resultative or causative rather than collective. Table 6 summarises the result.

Table 6: Meanings of the Nominal Prefix *Ge*- in *Beowulf*

	Collective/Associative	Meaningless	Generaliser	Others
Total No.	7	8	3	23
%	17.1	19.5	7.3	56.1

According to Table 6, only 8% of *ge*-nouns are used with a meaningless prefix *ge*- (e.g., *gewidre* 'storm, weather' vs. *weder* 'weather, storm') and in 17.1% of the nouns, the prefix has a sense of collectivity or associativity (e.g., *geþræc* 'pile, crowd' vs. *þræc* 'power, violence, force'). The meaning of generaliser is only applied to three pronouns (e.g., *gehwā* 'each, every' vs. *hwā* 'who'). More than half of *ge*-nouns (56.1%) are combined with *ge*- having other meanings. This result clearly shows that the traditional assumption that the nominal prefix *ge*- is meaningless or that the prefix has a sense of collectivity (associativity) is oversimplified or overgeneralised. (3) lists *ge*-nouns having another meaning and Table 7 manifests the percentage of the meanings of the nouns.

(3) *Ge*-nouns with non-collective *ge*-

(a) Resulatative (Causative)
gebyrd 'fate' (vs. byrd 'birth, native')
gefēa 'joy' (vs. feoh 'treasure, money')
gemet 'capacity, power' (vs. gemetan 'to measure')
genip 'mist, cloud' (vs. nīpan 'to darken, to become dark')
gesacu 'hostility' (vs. sacu 'conflict, strife')
gescad 'meaning, distance' (vs. scead 'reason, division')
gesceaft 'fate, world, decree' (vs. sceaft 'creation')
gesceap 'shape, nature, decree' (vs. gescippan 'to create')
geþinge 'result, outcome' (vs. þing 'thing, action, meeting')
geþoht 'determination' (vs. þoht 'thought, mind')
geþanc 'understanding' (vs. þanc 'kindly thought')
geþyld 'resignation' (vs. þyld 'patience')
gewealc 'attack, rolling' (vs. wealca 'roller, a garment that may be rolled round a person')
geweald 'protection, government' (vs. weald 'power')
geweorc 'a fort, a fortress' (vs. weorc 'work labour')
gewif 'web (of fate), an affection of the eye' (vs. wefan 'to weave')

(b) Repetitive
geflit 'competition' (vs. flit 'contention, strife')
gemind 'memorial, remembrance' (vs. gemyndigian 'to remember')
geslyht 'battle, fight' (vs. slyht 'a stroke of lighting, slaughter')

(c) Others
gehyld 'protector' (vs. hyld 'protection')
(Without attested corresponding forms)
gehygd 'thought, meditation'
gemēde 'consent, permission'
gescæphwīle 'destined hour'

Table 7: Percentage of non-collective meanings of *ge*-nouns

	Resultative (Causative)		Repetitive	Others
Total No.	Abstract	Non-abstract	3	4
	13	3		
%	80		15	5

As indicated in Table 7, in 3% of the nouns, the prefix has a repetitive meaning (e.g., *geslyht* 'battle, fight' vs. *sliht* 'a stoke of lightening, slaughter') and in 4% the meaning of the prefix cannot be determined due to the absence of their related forms. It is significant to note that 16 *ge*-nouns (80%) have a resultative (or causative) meaning (*geþinge* 'agreement, outcome' vs. *þing* 'meeting, condition'). Considering the fact that there are only 6 *ge*-nouns with the collective *ge-* (cf. Table 6), it can be stated that the primary meaning of the nominal prefix *ge-* used in *Beowulf* is resultative rather than collective. Furthermore, it should be noted that among the 16 *ge*-nouns with resultative prefix, 13 nouns have an abstract meaning (e.g., *geþoht* 'determination' vs. *geweorc* 'a fort, a fortress'). Namely, OE *ge-* is used as an abstract marker. This result accounts for why the majority of *ge*-nouns are used as singular forms (cf. Table 2). Abstract nouns must be singular. In addition, the large distribution of abstract *ge*-nouns indicates that grammaticalisation of the prefix is in progress in OE. However, as the prefix is still used as a meaningful morpheme, it may be stated that the grammaticalisation of the prefix is at an initial stage at the time of *Beowulf*.

3.3. Summarising and Interpreting the Results
The previous section has provided a statistical analysis of *ge*-nouns in *Beowulf*. Main findings are summarised below.

(a) Accusative and dative forms of *ge*-nouns show a high proportion and singular forms occur much more frequently than plural forms.
(b) Most *ge*-nouns appear only once in the text, which means that *ge*-nouns are not frequently used even though the affixation of *ge-* is not uncommon.
(c) A high portion of *ge*-nouns alternate with simplex nouns but there are also a quarter of *ge*-nouns without having their simplex counterparts.
(d) More than half of *ge*-nouns alternate either with their related *ge*-verbs or with their related simplex verbs whereas there is more than a quarter of the nouns without having their verbal counterparts. There is no *ge*-nouns which only alternate with their related *ge*-verbs without having their corresponding simplex verbs.
(e) Collective *ge*-nouns only account for 17.1 % and 19.5% of the nouns have the meaningless *ge-*. The majority of the *ge*-nouns, have the resulative (or causative) prefix resultative. Furthermore, most of the resultative *ge*-nouns have an abstract meaning.

In the light of the results summarised above, two issues concerning the nominal prefix *ge-* deserve to be discussed. The first one, which is the main focus of this study, is the meaning of the prefix *ge-*. Unlike the traditional account that the nominal prefix *ge-* is meaningless or collective, about 80% of *ge*-nouns examined in this paper have a transparent meaning and the primary meaning of the prefix is resultative while collective or associative meaning was secondary.

It is not easy to account for why the nominal prefix *ge-* comes to have a resultative meaning. I speculate that the resultative meaning of the nominal prefix is related with the perfective meaning of their verbal counterparts. Since the perfective aspect of *ge*-verbs denotes an action which is to be completed, their related *ge*-nouns are likely to denote something which results from or causes the action.

Second, even though the nominal prefix *ge-* is still used as a meaningful unit in most *ge*-nouns found in *Beowulf*, it cannot be denied that the prefix begins to undergo semantic bleaching and its grammaticalisation has already started. The result of this study supports this speculation. First, in many ge-nouns the prefix has an abstract meaning and thus most of the nouns are singular. It has been generally agreed that grammaticalisation involves patterns of conceptual transfer leading from concrete to less concrete domains of human experience (Heine 2004: 586). Furthermore, there are a quarter of *ge*-nouns without having their simplex nouns, in which cases the meaning of the prefix cannot be determined by OE native speakers so semantic bleaching is likely to occur to the OE prefix. However, as there are still a number of nouns combined with the meaningful *ge*-, it can be concluded that the grammaticalisation process of the OE *ge*- is at its intial stage.

4. Conclusion

In this paper, I have examined *ge*-nouns found in *Beowulf* with special attention to the meaning of the nominal prefix *ge*-. In contrast with the traditional semantic accounts that the nominal *ge*- was either meaningless or collective (or associative) if there was any transparent meaning of the prefix, the result of my case study revealed that most of *ge*-nouns had a transparent meaning and that the primary meaning of *ge*- was resultative (or causative) while collectivity was its secondary meaning. It was clearly manifested that the collective meaning of the nominal prefix was overgeneralised in the previous works.

This finding is significant because the resulative meaning has not been proposed as a possible meaning of the prefix in the previous literature. The previous works mainly focus on the verbal prefix *ge*-, providing comparatively little discussion of the nominal prefix *ge*-. If it is agreed that the OE nominal prefix *ge*- is resultative, it may be appropriate to investigate next how the prefix comes to acquire the resultative meaning. In this paper, without providing my own evidence I just speculated that the perfective meaning of the verbal prefix *ge*- had an impact on its nominal counterpart. I hope this speculation will be verified by following studies.

References

Dollinger, Stefan
    2001   "The Old English and Middle English Prefix *Ge-* as a Linguistic Replicator: A Morphological Case Study in a Neo Darwinian Framework", *VIEWS* 10(2): 3-29.

Fijn van Draat, P.
    1902   "The Loss of the Prefix Ge- in the Modern English Verbs and some of its Consequences", *Englische Studien* 31: 353-384.

Frančiška Trobevšek
1994 "The Old English Preverbal *Ge-* in the Light of the Theory of Language Change as Strengthening or Weakening", *Studia Anglica Posnaniensia* 28: 123-141.

Heine, Bernd
2004 *"Grammaticalization"*, in: Brian Joseph – Richard Janda (eds.), 575-601.

Joseph, Brian – Richard Janda
2004 *The Handbook of Historical Linguistics*. Oxford: Blackwell.

Kastovsky, Dieter
1968 *Old English Deverbal Substantives Derived by Means of a Zero Morpheme*. Esslingen: Langer.

Koziol, Herbert
1972 *Handbuch der Englischen Wortbildungslehre* 2, neu bearb. Aufl. Heidelberg: Winter.

Lenz, Philipp
1886 *Der Syntactische Gebrauch der Partikel Ge- in den Werken Alfred des Grossen*. Darmstadt: Otto.

Lindemann, J.W. Richard
1965 "Old English Preverbal *ge-*: A RE-examination of some Current Doctrine", *Journal of English and Germanic Philology* 64: 65-83.

Luick, Karl
1964 *Historiche Grammatik der Englischen Sprache*. ed. by F. Wild and Herbert Koziol. 2 vols. Oxford: Blackwell.

Lutz, Angelika
1997 "Sound Change, Word Formation and the Lexicon: The History of the English Prefix Verbs", *English Studies* 3: 258-290.

Magoun, Francis P. Jr.
1930 "Word Formation", in: M.H. Turk (ed.), 48c-h.

Mitchell, Bruce – Fred Robinson
1995 *A Guide to Old English*. 5th ed. Oxford: Blackwell..

Mitchell, Bruce – Fred Robinson
1998 *Beowulf: An Edition with Relevant Shorter Texts*. Oxford: Blackwell.

Niwa, Yoshinobu
1966 "The Preverb *Ge-* added to NIMAN in the OE Gloss to the Lindisfarne Gospels", *Studies in English Literature (Tokyo)* English Number: 65-79.
1973 *Old English Preverbal* Ge-. Tokyo: Shohakusha.
1974 "On the Collective Meaning of OE Preverb *GE-*", *Studies in English Literature (Tokyo)* English Number: 155-167.

Pilch, Herbert
1951/2 *Der Untergan des Präverbs je- im Englischen* [Doctoral dissertation. Kiel.]

Samuels, M.L.
1949 "The Ge-Prefix in the Old English Gloss to the Lindisfarne Gospels", *Transactions of the Philological Society* w/o volume number: 62-116.

Sprockel, C.
1973 *The Language of the Parker Chronicle. Vol.2 Word-Formation and Syntax.* The Hague: Nijhoff.

Stanley, E.G.
1982 "The Prenominal Prefix *Ge-* in Late Old English and Early Middle English", *Transactions of the Philological Society* w/o volume number: 25-66.

Turk, M.H.
1930 *An Anglo-Saxon Reader.* New York: Scribner.

Toller, Northcote
1973 *An Anglo-Saxon Dictionary: Based on the Manuscript Collections of Joseph Bosworth.* London: Oxford University Press.

Voyles, Joseph
1974 *West Germanic Inflection, Derivation and Compounding.* The Hague: Mouton.

Weick, Friedrich
1911 *Das Aussterben des Präfixes Ge- im Englishen.* Darmstadt: Wintersche Buchdruckerei.

5 Differences in Element Order between *Lindisfarne* and *Rushworth Two*
Tadashi Kotake, Keio University, Graduate School

1. Introduction

This paper discusses differences in element order between Aldred's gloss in the *Lindisfarne Gospels* (hereafter *Li*) and Owun's gloss in the *Rushworth Gospels*. The latter is generally called *Rushworth Two* (hereafter *Ru2*),[1] and believed to be copied from, or strongly affected by, Aldred's glosses.[2] This belief has averted researchers' attention from close comparison between the two, especially from syntactic viewpoints.[3] There are, however, a number of differences, and therefore, this study tries to analyse element order in these closely related texts in order to understand differences between the languages of the glossators. This study will also help us to understand more profoundly the relationship of the two interlinear glosses.

The syntax of an interlinear gloss is no doubt affected by that of its source language. Nevertheless, syntactic comparison between interlinear glosses to the same Latin text is often effective, if the two types of difference are clearly recognised and distinguished. In the present study, we call the two types Type A and Type B. Type A includes the instances where one of the two glossators deviates from the Latin element order and the other follows the Latin. Instances belonging to Type B are found when the glossators add elements not corresponding to anything in the Latin or when they expand Latin simple forms to Old English periphrastic forms. This distinction is important because differences in each type have different meanings: while instances from Type B are likely to reflect the languages of individual glossators because element order chosen by a glossator is not affected by Latin, Type A involves treatment of a certain Latin element order. This present study classifies differences in element order between *Li* and *Ru2* on the basis of these two types, which are dealt with in Sections 2 and 3 respectively. The following discussions are not exhaustive, but focusing on the repeatedly found instances, due to the limited space.

---

1 *Ru2* covers Mark, Luke and John, excluding the parts included in *Rushworth One*, i.e. from the beginning of Mark to 2:15 and John 18:1-3. The edition used for both *Li* and *Ru2* is Skeat (1871-1887).
2 For instance, Morrell (1965: 177) notes that "Owun [...] simply copied the Lindisfarne Gospels." Ker (1957: 352), though he also admits the possibility that Owun has copied *Li*, states that these two glosses share the same source.
3 Bibire and Ross (1981) list a variety of differences without detailed analyses of them. As to syntax, Ohkado (2007) deals with the differences between the two, and is referred to later in this paper (Section 3.3.).

2. Type A
2.1. Noun Phrase
Latin: N + Adj/Gen/Pron > OE: N + Adj/Gen/Pron or Adj/Gen/Pron + N[4]

As observed in the discussion by Ogura (2006: 105-108) of this order in the Old English Psalter glosses, there are two possible treatments of the normal Latin element order of noun phrases, N + Adj/Gen/Pron. A glossator may follow the order, giving word-for-word glosses. Some glossators, however, change the order so that the modifier precedes the noun.[5] Comparison between the two versions shows that Aldred deviates more frequently than Owun does. The following citation is very suggestive about this phenomenon.

(1) Jn 2.12[6]
Post hoc descendit capharnaum ipse et <u>mater eius</u> et fratres eius (Ru om.) et <u>discipuli eius</u>
Li: æfter ðis ðona astag ða burug he 7 <u>his moder</u> 7 his broðro 7 <u>his ðegnas</u>
Ru2: æfter ðisse ðona astag ða of burug he 7 <u>moder his</u> 7 his broðro 7 <u>ðegnas his</u>
WSCp: [Æ]fter þyson he 7 hys modor 7 his gebroðru 7 his leorning-cnihtas foron to capharnaum

Latin *mater eius* and *discipuli eius* are translated differently; whereas Owun follows the Latin element order, Aldred changes it. Although both of them have *his broðro* in the same order, this is presumably due to the Latin text of the Rushworth manuscript, which omits *eius* and has simply *fratres*. It is remarkable that Owun chooses the Old English order only when he inserts the modifier which does not have any corresponding Latin word in the manuscript he glosses. This presumably suggests that Owun feels at ease in using the Old English order, but he normally puts more importance on the Latin order. Table 1 summarises the difference.

---

4   Abbreviations used in this study: Adj = Adjective, C = Complement, Dat = Dative, Det = Determiner, Gen = Genitive, Inf = Infinitive, Mod = Modal, N = Noun, O = Object, Prep = Preposition, Pron = Pronoun, Rel = Relative, S = Subject, V = Verb.
5   For instance, Crowley (2000) deals with "Anglicized word order" in BL, Royal 2. A. XX. He also mentions the glossator of *Rushworth One* Farman, who tends to change this order. However, his comments on *Li* (Crowley 2000: 137-138), citing Nagucka (1997), that Aldred keeps the Latin element order "throughout that gloss to the four Gospels" is inaccurate as shown by the result of this study. Although Nagucka (1997: 181-182) indeed reports that the reverse order in Aldred's noun phrases is "infrequent and by no means a norm", she emphasises at the same time Aldred's inconsistency in giving the glosses, saying that he glosses "according to his own preferences at a given moment."
6   In all citations, emphases are mine. The Latin text is from the Lindisfarne MS with variant readings from the Rushworth MS in brackets. Comments in brackets refer to the preceding Latin word, unless the preceding set of words is in square brackets, which means that the comments refer to the whole words in the square brackets. Mere spelling variants are not reported.

Table 1: Treatment of Latin noun phrase N + Adj/Gen/Pron

	Mk	Lk	Jn	Total
Li N + Adj...: *Ru2* Adj...+ N	1	2	1	4
Li Adj... + N : *Ru2* N + Adj...	3	10	47	60

In addition to Aldred's freer way of glossing, change in his glossing practice can be pointed out from the table. In John, he employs the Old English element order much more frequently than in the other two gospels. In a few instances, Aldred uses both word orders in a double gloss, as *in gast halig ł in ðæm halge gaste* for *in spiritu sancto* (Jn 1.33), which is simply glossed with *in gaste halgum* in *Ru2*.

2.2. Prepositional phrases

2.2.1. Latin: Pron + *cum* > OE: Pron + *mið* or *mið* + Pron

Latin preposition *cum* can be used after a pronoun. Old English glossators may gloss by following the order of the Latin or change to the order *mið* (the predominant spelling of OE *mid* in *Li* and *Ru2*) + Pron. Owun prefers the former way while Aldred sometimes changes the order. As a result, the difference is observed in seven instances, of which five are found in John.[7] In the only instance (Lk 22.21) where Aldred glosses *mecum* with *mec mið*, following the order of Latin, Owun changes the order to *mið mec*.

2.2.2. Latin: Prep + Pron > OE: Prep + Pron or Pron + Prep

There are two instances of difference, when Latin prepositions are used before their objects, an order that is normally glossed word-for-word. One is found in Mk 4.41, where Latin reads *dicebant ad alterutrum*, glossed with *hia cuedon him bitwien* in *Li* and *cwedun bitwion him* in *Ru2*. The other instance is:

(2) Mk 8.33
uade retro me satana (Ru: satanas)
Li: geong on bæcc ł mec behianda ðu wiðerworda
Ru2: gong on bæclinc ł bihionda mec ðu wiðerworda
WSCp: Ga on-bæc satanas

Latin *retro me* is translated idiomatically in the first item of the double gloss in both versions, and the second one is the more literal translation, though the order differs. In these two instances, Aldred deviates from the Latin word order.

2.3. VC or CV

2.3.1. Latin CV > OE CV or VC

All the instances dealt with in this section involve the verb *esse* with its complements including participles. Four instances of this difference are found in John,

---

7 Mk 6.03, 14.7; Jn 13.33, 14.9, 14.16, 16.4, 17.24.

where Aldred deviates from Latin word order, choosing VC. The clause types are various; in the subordinate clause (Latin *quia*, Jn 10.13), in the question (Jn 12.38), and in the rhetorical questions (Latin *nonne*, Jn 10.34 and Latin *numquid* in Jn 18.35). On the other hand, Owun deviates from Latin word order in only one instance (Lk 13.12).

2.3.2. Latin VC > OE VC or CV
Although no clear instance of this difference is found, one instance should be noted, which involves a double gloss.

(3) Jn 12.33
hoc autem dicebat significans qua morte <u>esset moriturus</u>
Li: ðis uut*udl*ice he cuæð ł þ becnade ł of huælcu*m* deaðe <u>uere sueltende</u> ł gedeðet
Ru2: ðis wutudl*ice* cwæð ðæt becnade of hwelcu*m* deoðe <u>were deod ł sweltende wæs</u>
WSCp: Ðæt he sæde 7 tacnode hwylcum deaðe he wolde sweltan

Owun's double gloss is comparable with the first item in Aldred's double gloss. Owun's first gloss agrees with it in that the verb is in the subjunctive mood and the word order is VC. The second one has the same present participle in different order. In this case, Owun deviates from the Latin word order.

2.4. VO or OV
2.4.1. Latin VO > OE VO or OV
Although glossators normally follow Latin element order when Latin takes VO order, there are several instances where one of the two glossators deviates from the Latin. Aldred is the one who deviates in most cases, as follows:

(4) Jn 15.21
Quia nesciunt eum qui <u>misit me</u>
Li: foreðon nuu*t*ton hine ł ðone seðe <u>mec sende</u>
Ru2: forðon nutun hine seðe <u>sende mec</u>
WSCp: forþa*m* hi ne cunnon þæne þe me sende;

Aldred appears to prefer OV order in subordinate clauses; he glosses Latin Rel VO with OE Rel OV, in Jn 7.33, 8.18,[8] 12.48, as well as the citation above, and Latin *ut* (S)VO with *þte* (S)OV, in Jn 6.15, 11.53, and 17.1.The following is another instance of the change in the subordinate clause:

---

8   Latin text differs in this verse between the two texts, though both have *qui misit me* in the same order, which is glossed differently.

(5) Jn 9.35
   audiuit iesus quia eiecerunt eum foras
   Li: geherde se hælend forðon hine auorpon ut
   Ru2: giherde ðe hælend þte awurpon hine utt
   WSCp: Ða se hælend gehyrde þ hig hyne drifon ut.

Aldred's use of *forðon* in the citation is presumably due to the confusion of the two different uses of Latin *quia*, and it is frequently observed in his gloss. In this case, *quia* is used to introduce not an adverbial clause, but a noun object clause. In both cases, however, the clause should be considered as subordinate.[9] Even in a co-ordinate main clause, the same type of difference is found:

(6) Jn 8.20
   et nemo apprehendit *eum* quia necdum uenerat hora eius
   Li: 7 nænig *monn* hine gelahte forðon ne ðaget gecuom tid his
   Ru2: 7 nænig mon ne gilahte hine forðon ne ðagett comon tide his
   WSCp: 7 nan man hyne ne nam. forþam þe hys tid ne com þa gyt.

It should be noted that the negative particle *ne* precedes the verb only in *Ru2*, which is a natural reason for Owun to follow the VO order.[10] Yet it is striking that Aldred changes Latin VO order, even in the co-ordinate clause.

In two instances, Owun changes Latin VO to OE OV, while Aldred keeps the Latin order. In Jn 12.45, Aldred glosses Latin *qui misit me* with *seðe mec sende* by following the Latin order, whereas Owun changes it into OV order as *seðe mec sende*. The other instance also involves a relative clause, but it is necessary to give attention to the slight variation in Latin text:

(7) Jn 6.40
   haec est enim (Ru om.) uoluntas patris mei qui misit (Ru: messit) me
   Li: ðios is forðon uillo fador mines seðe sende mec
   Ru2: ðios is willa fædres mines seðe mec sende
   WSCp: Ðis is mines fæder willa þe me sende

The Latin text of the Rushworth manuscript has *messit* instead of *misit*, and the spelling *me-* might affect the placement of *mec* in his gloss.

Three points of significance are: (1) all these differences are found only in John, (2) the objects in all these instances are pronominal, and (3) it is likely that Aldred prefers the OV order to VO in subordinate clauses.[11]

---

9 The same kind of difference, though involving negative expression, is also found in Jn 8.55, where Latin *et si dixero quia non scio (Ru: nescio) eum ero similis uobis mendax* is glossesd with *7 gif ic cuoeðo þte ic hine nat ic beom gelic iuh leas* in *Li*, and *7 gif ic cweðo forðon ic ne wæt hine ic biom gilic iow leos* in *Ru2*.

10 Mitchell (1985: 661, §1599) mentions that "The OE verb is most commonly negated by the adverb *ne* immediately preceding it, no matter what the order of the other elements."

2.4.2. Latin OV > OE VO or OV

Two clear instances, with an ambiguous one, of this type are found. One is found in a main clause, where Aldred deviates by choosing VO order;

(8) Jn 15.20
si sermonem meum seruauerunt et uestrum seruabunt
Li: gif uord min gehealdon æc hia gehaldas iuer
Ru2: gif word min giheoldun 7 iower hia gihaldað
WSCp: Gif hi mine spræce heoldon hi healdað eac eowre;

The other clear instance is found in Jn 5.30, where the Latin relative clause *qui me misit* is glossed with *seðe mec asende* in *Li* and *seðe sendeð mec* in *Ru2*. In this case, Owun is the one who deviates, choosing VO order in the subordinate clause, and this agrees with the fact observed in the previous section that Owun mostly keeps VO order, when Aldred changes it to OV order. There is another instance which may be classified to this type, though it involves a difference in the Latin text:

(9) Jn 2.18
quod signum ostendis (Ru: ostendit) nobis quia (Ru: qui) haec facis (Ru: om.)
Li: huelc becon ðu ædeaues us forðon ðas ðu wyrces
Ru2: hwelc becun ðu æt-eowes us forðon wyrcas ðas
WSCp: hwylc tacn æt-ywst þu us forðam þe þu ðas ðing dest;

Aldred simply follows Latin element order, inserting the second person subject before the verb. The fact that the Latin text of the Rushworth manuscript lacks *facis* probably caused some trouble to the glossator. As is evident from that he correctly glosses *qui*, instead of *quia*, in his manuscript with *forðon*, Owun appears to try to give appropriate glosses to the defective Latin text. He feels the necessity to supply a verb, and he can do it without being affected by Latin word order. It is important that he chooses VO order in the subordinate clause, just as seen in the previous section. As we seen in citation (1) in the present study, Owun does not seem to hesitate to use the word order that is more natural to him when the Latin text lacks a corresponding word.

2.5. SV or VS
2.5.1. Latin SV > OE SV or VS

Four instances are found, all of which are in John. Aldred is the one who deviates in all of them. In Jn 9.4, the Latin temporal clause *donec dies est* is glossed with

---

11 It is likely that this means that Aldred tries to use Old English word order as in the case of noun phrases (Section 2.1.), because also *WSCp* uses OV order in all the instances dealt with in this section except for only one instance (Jn 17.1). On the other hand, Owun appears to give the Latin order higher priority.

ða huile *is dæge* in *Li* and ða hwyle *dæg is* in *Ru2*. Another instance is in Jn 12.31, where Aldred glosses Latin *nunc iudicium est mundi* with *nu is dom middangeordes*, while Owun keeps the Latin order, as *nu dom is middengeordes*. In Jn 6.42, the difference involves a rhetorical question staring with *nonne*.

(10) Jn 6.42
    et dicebant nonne hic est iesus (Ru om.) filius ioseph
    Li: 7 cuedon ahne is ðis se hælend sunu iosephes
    Ru2: 7 cwedun ahne ðis is suno iosepes
    WSCp: 7 hig cwædon; Hu nis þis se hælend iosepes sunu.

While all the three instances above involve *esse* and the BE-verb, the following is the only case where another verb is used.

(11) Jn 6.32
    amen amen dico uobis non moses dedit uobis panem [de caelo] (Ru om.)
    Li: soð is soð is þ ic cueðo iuh ne salde moisi iuh þ hlaf of heofnum
    Ru2: soðlice soð ic cweðo iow ne moyses salde iow hlaf
    WSCp: soð ic secge eow ne sealde moyses eow hlaf of heofnum.

Again, Aldred changes the order, and this may be due to the preceding negative particle *ne*.[12]

2.5.2. Latin VS > OE VS or SV
There are seven instances of this type, in five of which, all found in John, Aldred deviates from the Latin element order. In Jn 6.40, Latin *et resuscitabo ego eum* is glossed with *7 ic aueco hine* in *Li*, while the order is kept in *Ru2* as *7 aweco ic hine*. Another instance involves a negative expression:[13]

(12) Jn 8.44
    quia non est ueritas in eo
    Li: forðon soðfæstnise nis In him
    Ru2: forðon ne is soðfæstnis in him
    WSCp: forðam þe soðfæstnes nis on him;

---

12 One comparable instance is in Jn 16.22, where Latin *et gaudium uestrum nemo tollit (Ru: tollet) a uobis* is glossed by Aldred *7 gefea iuer / ne nimeð ænigmonn from iuh*, and by Owun *7 gifea iower nænigmon nimeð from iow*. In addition to the SV/VS difference, there is a difference in the use of negative particle. In *Li*, *ne* precedes the verb, while, in *Ru2*, *ne* is contracted with the subject and the order forms SV order.

13 Three other instances are in Jn 7.36, 12.26 and 14.3, where the Latin adverbial clause *ubi sum ego* is glossed differently. In all instances, Aldred chooses SV order, deviating from Latin. In 14.3, Aldred uses both word orders SV and VS as the double gloss *ðer ic beom / ðer am ic*, of which the second item with the order of Latin is followed by Owun.

In the other two instances, found in Mk 14.9 and Lk 22.60, however, Owun deviates. In the latter instance, the subject is not pronominal;

(13) Lk 22.60
et continuo athuc illo loquente <u>cantauit gallus</u>
Li: 7 sona forðor ða get hine sprecende <u>gesang se hona</u>
Ru2: 7 sona forðor ða-gett hine sprecende <u>ðe hona gisang</u>
WSCp: And þa hig þ spræcon samninga se hana crewo.

There seems a difference between John and the other two gospels: in John, this difference always involves Aldred's deviation, whereas Owun deviates from the Latin element order in Mark and Luke.

Summary of Type A

Differences belonging to this type can be summarised in Table 2 below. As a whole, it can be said that Aldred deviates from Latin element orders much more frequently than Owun does. It is also quite remarkable that these differences are found most frequently in John. This means that Aldred's way of glossing has changed in John's Gospel, whereas Owun maintains his practice unchanged.

Table 2: Summary of Type A

		Li deviates				*Ru2* deviates			
	Latin	Mk	Lk	Jn	Total	Mk	Lk	Jn	Total
2.1	N + Adj/Gen/Pron	3	10	47	60	1	2	1	4
2.2.1	Pron + *cum*	2	0	5	7	0	1	0	1
2.2.2	Prep + Pron	2	0	0	2	0	0	0	0
2.3.1	CV	0	0	4	4	0	1	0	1
2.4.1	VO	0	0	10	10	0	0	2	2
2.4.2	OV	0	0	1	1	0	0	1	1
2.5.1	SV	0	0	4	4	0	0	0	0
2.5.2	VS	0	0	5	5	1	1	0	2
	Total	7	10	76	93	2	5	4	11

3. Type B
3.1. Latin: N > OE: Det + N or N + Det

Since there is no article in Latin, Old English glossators may feel the necessity to add some article when translating a noun. As Ohkado (2006: 129) points out, there is no instance where a noun precedes a determiner in *Li*. In *Ru2*, however, we find such instances, for example:

(14) Jn 14.6
   ego sum uia et (Ru om.) ueritas et uita nemo uenit ad patrem nisi per me
   Li: ic am uoeg 7 soðfæstnise 7 lif nænig *monn* cuom to ðæm feder buta ðerh mec
   Ru2: ic am woeg soðfæstra 7 lif nænigmon com to feder ðæm buta ðerh mec
   WSCp: ic eom weg 7 soðfæstnys 7 lif. ne cym nan to fæder butan þurh me;

As a result, the difference is always the same way in the nine instances,[14] Aldred choosing the Det + N order and Owun the reverse. The following instance needs careful attention.

(15) Mk 7.26
   erat autem mulier gentilis [syrophoenissa genere] (Ru: sirophinis agere)
   Li: wæs uut*edlice* þ wif hæðen ðæs cynnes is nemned syro-phoenisa
   Ru2: 7 wæs wutud*lice* wif ðæt hæðen ðæs sirophinisca cynnes
   WSCp: Soðlice þ wif wæs hæðen. siorofenisces cynnes.

In this instance, *ðæt* appears to come just after the noun *wif* in *Ru2*, but in the manuscript *ðæt* is more likely to be connected with the adjective, *hæðen*. It can be inferred that Owun regards *ðæt hæðen* as a phrase in apposition with *wif*.

The instances where a single Latin noun is glossed with a noun phrase, with insertion of an adjective or a possessive pronoun, can be regarded as a variation of the difference dealt with above. For instance, in Mk 5.3, the Latin noun *domcilium* is glossed with *hus ł lytelo by* in *Li* and *hus ł byinge lytle* in *Ru2*. Two other instances are found: Mk 10.24, where *filioli* is glossed with *leafa suno* in *Li* and *sunu leofa* in *Ru2* and Jn 11.16, where *condiscipulos* with *his gefoerum* in *Li* and *gifoerum his* in *Ru2*.

3.2. Latin: Pron (Dat) > OE: Pron + Prep or Prep + Pron

Glossators may insert prepositions to express the sense denoted by the declension of a noun in Latin. In such instances, differences can be observed as to the placement of prepositions. This difference is confined to two types of verb, both with a dative pronoun; one is verbs of saying and the other verbs of motion. For instance, Latin *qui dixit mihi omnia* (Jn 4.29) is glossed with *seðe cueð me to alle* in *Li* and *seðe cwæð to me alle* in *Ru2*.[15] In Jn 4.51, Latin *serui occurrerunt ei* has different glosses, *esnæs gwurnun him togægnes* in *Li* and *esnas giurnon togægnes him* in *Ru2*. When these differences occur, the order is always consistent, Pron + Prep in *Li* and Prep + Pron in *Ru2*. In other words, postposed prepositions are avoided in Owun's gloss. It must be stressed here that seven instances of this difference are all found in John's Gospel.[16]

---

14 Mk 8.27, 13.20; Lk 11.47, 14.23, 20.1, 20.29, 20.32; Jn 11.8, 14.16.
15 For general and thorough survey of *cweðan* + *to*-phrase, see Ogura (1991).
16 Jn 4.29, 4.51, 6.30, 11.20, 11.23, 11.25, 20.29.

3.3. Verbal elements, Latin Single > OE Periphrastic

3.3.1. Latin: Passive (Single form) > OE: Periphrastic, BE + Part or Part + BE

When the Latin verb is a one-word passive form, Old English glossators have to expand it to a periphrastic forms. Ohkado (2007) deals with the difference in these element orders, pointing out that Owun prefers Part + BE order where Aldred uses BE + Part order as follows.

(16) Mk 14.41
ecce traditur filius hominis in manus peccatorum
Li: heono bið gesald sunu monnes in hond synnfullra
Ru2: heonu gisald bið sunu monnes in honda synn-fullum
WSCp: nu is mannes sunu gesealdon synfulra handa;

While this difference is repeatedly found[17], the next citation is the only instance where Aldred chooses Part + BE whereas Owun uses BE + Part order.

(17) Mk 4.21
numquid uenit lucerna ut sub modio ponatur aut sub lecto
Li: ahne l hueðer cuom leht-fæt l ðæccilla þte under mitta l fætt gesetted bið l under bed
Ru2: ahne l hwer cymeð lehtfæt l ðæcela þte under mitta l fæte bið giseted ðætte vnder bedde
WSCp: cwyst þu cymð þ leoht-fæt þ hit beo under bydene asette. oððe under bedde.

One thing that the present study can point out is that there are also differences in the similar construction with present participle as follows:[18]

(18) Mk 8.32
et palam uerbum loquebatur Et apprehendens eum petrus coepit increpare eum
Li: 7 eaunga word he wæs spræcend l he gespræcc 7 gelahte hine petrus ongann geðreadtaige hine
Ru2: 7 eowunga word sprecende wæs 7 to-gilahte hine petrus ongan giðreatiga hine
WSCp: 7 spræc þa openlice 7 þa nam petrus hine 7 ongan hine þreagean

Even when present participles are involved, the difference is consistently found in the four instances, Aldred choosing BE + Part and Owun Part + BE.[19] Furthermore, Aldred's preference for the order of BE + Part may be reinforced by its variations. When the BE verb is used with adjectives to expand Latin verbs or other constructions, the same difference can be observed. In Lk 1.14, for instance, the Latin verb

---

17 According to Ohkado (2007), 37 instances are found, and listed in Appendix 3. Note that this number includes the instances where Latin also takes *esse* + participle structure, i.e., those instances dealt with in 2.3.1. (two instances from the section involve participles, Jn 10.34 and 12.38). In his list, Lk 3.21 should be deleted because no relevant instance is found.
18 For the use of the periphrastic expression in translating Latin deponent verbs, see Kotake (2006: 46-47). Furthermore, Aldred uses the expression composed of BE verb + present/past participles in glossing Latin imperfect verbs (Kotake 2006: 38-40).
19 Mk 8.32, 10.32, 14.35 (bis).

gaudere is translated with the BE verb and an adjective, but the element order differs; BE + Adj (*biðon glæde*) in *Li* and the reverse (*glæde bioðun*) in *Ru2*. Similar instances are found in three instances (Mk 9.26, Lk 18.22,[20] Jn 18.14.), and the element order is always consistent.

3.3.2. Latin Verb > OE Modal + Inf or Inf + Modal

When Old English glossators feel the necessity to add a modal auxiliary verb to express the sense denoted by a certain morphological form in Latin,[21] the placement of such modals may differ. These instances are relatively frequent in Mark, with only one instance in Luke and no instance in John. The data almost agree with those provided by Ohkado (2007).

(19) Mk 4.13
  et quomodo omnes parabolas cognoscetis
  Li: 7 huu alle bispello gie ge-cunnas ł <u>gie cunna gie magon</u>
  Ru2: 7 hvv alle bispell gicunniga ł <u>magvun gicunniga</u>
  WSCp: 7 hu mage ge ealle bigspell witan;

In the instance above, the infinitive precedes the modal in *Li* and the reverse order is found in *Ru2*. Similar instances are in Mk 6.24[22] and 14.11. In the following instance, Aldred chooses Mod + Inf order, and Owun Inf + Mod.[23]

(20) Mk 14.1
  quomodo eum [dolo tenerent et occiderent] (Ru: tenerent et occiderent dolo)
  Li: huu hine mið facne gehealdon ł mæhton hia gehalda 7 ofslogon ł <u>hia mæhton of-slaa</u>
  Ru2: hu hiæ hine   giheoldun 7 oflsogun ł <u>of-sla mæhtun</u>
  WSCp: hu hi hine mid facne namon 7 of-slogon;

There is no clear tendency about element order in this type of difference. In this connection, it may be relevant that there are no instances in John, for it is in that gospel that clearly different tendencies between the two glosses, if there are any, are usually concentrated.

---

20 Latin *unum tibi <u>deest</u>* is glossed with *an ðe <u>is wona</u>* in *Li* and *an ðe <u>wona is</u>* in *Ru2*. The same Latin expression is translated with BE + Part in another instance (Mk 10.21), where the order also differs between the two glossators; Latin *unum tibi <u>deest</u>* is glossed with *an ðe <u>is forgeten</u>* in *Li* and *an ðe <u>forgeten is</u>* in *Ru2* (included in the 37 instances in Ohkado (2007)).

21 See Kotake (2006: 43-46) for the use. It also points out that Aldred tends to use modal auxiliary verbs in the second glosses. Such multiple glosses are also compared in the present study.

22 This instance also involves the placement of a subject. Latin *quid petam* is glossed with *hwæt <u>ic giuge wælle</u>* in *Li* and *hwæt <u>giowigo ih welle</u>* in *Ru2*.

23 Similar instances are in Mk 8.1 and Lk 19.23.

3.4. Latin V > OE SV or VS[24]

Since Latin verbal morphology is richer than that of Old English, glossators may have to add a subject which is expressed only by morphology in Latin. In such cases, the placement of a subject may differ between the two glossators. There are 19 instances of this type,[25] in 14 of which Owun chooses VS order and Aldred SV. Some of them involve questions.

(21) Mk 8.17
athuc caecatum habetis cor uestrum
Li: ðageon ł get ðiostrig ł blind is gie habbað hearta iuer
Ru2: ða geona ł   ðiostur ł blinde habbas ge heorta iowre
WSCp: gyt ge habbað eowre heortan geblende;

VS order may result in contraction as in Jn 16.5, where Latin *quo uadis* is glossed with *huidir ðu geongas* in *Li* and *hwider gongestu* in *Ru2*. In questions, Owun is more sensitive about the order, choosing VS order, than Aldred: similar instances are found in Mk 8.18, 11.29, Lk 3.10. Owun seems too sensitive in the following instance:

(22) Jn 14.4
et quo ego uado scitis et uiam scitis
Li: 7 ðidder ic geonga gie uutton 7 ðone uoeg gie uuton
Ru2: 7 ðider ic gongo wutas ge 7 ðo*ne* woeg giwutun
WSCp: 7 ge witon hyder ic fare 7 ge cunnon þæne weg.

Although *quo ego uado* is a noun object clause, it is not unlikely that Owun takes *quo* as interrogative, just as in the previous citation. Furthermore, *scitis*, which is usually taken as Jesus' assertive remark, could be read as question, since, just after this verse, Thomas says "domine nescimus quo uadis et quomodo possumus uiam scire." In questions, there is only one instance where Aldred chooses VS and Owun SV:

(23) Mk 15.34
quod est interpraetatum deus meus deus meus ut quid [dereliquisti me] (Ru: me diriliquisiti)
Li: þ is getrahted god min god min þte ł to huon forleortes ðu meh
Ru2: ðæt is gitrahtad god min god min þte ł to hwon mec ðu forl[e]te
WSCp: þ is on ure geðeode min god min god. hwi for-lete þu me;

Another possible tendency is that Owun prefers VS when the object precedes the verb. *Hoc faciam* in Jn 14.13 and 14.14 is glossed with *ðis dom ic ic (sic)* and *ðis*

---

24 In only one instance, the pattern "Latin S > OE SV or VS" is found. Latin *cui nomen gesemani* (Mk 14.33) is glossed with *ðæm is noma þ is on ebrisc* in *Li* and *ðæm noma is on ebrisc* in *Ru2*.
25 This number includes present participles and infinitives which are expanded to SV or VS.

dom ic, respectively in *Ru2*, while Aldred glosses ðis *ic uyrco ł ic doam* and ðis *ic doam ł ic uyrco*, respectively. Another instance is found in:

(24) Jn 15.15
quia omnia quaecumque audiui a patre meo nota feci uobis
Li: forðon alle ðaðe ł suæ huæd ic geherde from feder minum cuða ł cyðigo ic worhte iuh
Ru2: for-ðon alle ðaðe mið-ðy giherde ic from feder minum cyðe dyde iow
WSCp: forðam ic cyðde eow ealle þa þing þe ic gehyrde æt minum fæder.

It seems that the repeatedly found differences of SV and VS are mostly related to their grammatical environments. Owun is likely to prefer VS order in questions and when the object precedes the verb.

Summary of Type B

The differences of Type B are shown in Table 3 below. In some sections in Type B, the differences are consistent: in 3.1, Owun's choice of N + Det contrasts sharply with the absence of this word order in Aldred's gloss. Postposed prepositions are totally avoided in *Ru2*, whereas Aldred prefers them, especially in John, as shown in 3.2. In 3.3.1, the difference in expanding Latin verbs into periphrastic expressions is observed: Aldred prefers BE verb + participles/adjectives and Owun the reverse. 3.4 reveals Owun's fondness for VS order in some grammatical environments. In relation to Type A, 3.2 is the most interesting. The instances found in the section are completely confined to John, and they are due to the change in Aldred's way of glossing.

Table 3: Summary of Type B

	Latin	*Li*	*Ru2*	Mk	Lk	Jn	Total
3.1	N	Det + N	N + Det	2	5	2	9
		N + Det	Det + N	0	0	0	0
3.2	N (Dat)	Prep + N	N + Prep	0	0	0	0
		N + Prep	Prep + N	0	0	7	7
3.3.1	V	BE + Part (Pass)	Part (Pass) + BE	11	14	9	34
		Part (Pass) + BE	BE + Part (Pass)	1	0	0	1
	V	BE + Part (Pres)	Part (Pres) + BE	4	0	0	4
		Part (Pres) + BE	BE + Part (Pres)	0	0	0	0
3.3.2	V	Mod + Inf	Inf + Mod	2	1	0	3
		Inf + Mod	Mod + Inf	2	0	0	2
3.4	V	S + V	V + S	5	1	8	14
		V + S	S + V	2	1	2	5

4. Conclusion

The present study has pointed out that there is a considerable number of differences in element order between the two glosses, despite the fact that they are believed to be very closely related. By analysing such differences, it can be said that Aldred more frequently deviates from Latin element order than Owun does. This is presumably because of differences not in their language, but in their way of treating the Latin text. Even Owun chooses Old English orders where he needs to add words to defective Latin sentences. The largest difference lies in how much the glossators put priority on the Latin element order. Aldred is far more audacious in changing element order than Owun, who strictly follows the Latin. It is also significant that those instances classified under Type B, which are not affected by Latin element order, show some preferences of each glossator in element order, though further investigation is needed to explain the causes of such preference. Besides, the distribution of differences is highly likely to indicate the uniqueness of John's Gospel in the *Lindisfarne Gospels*.[26] The data clearly show that Owun does not simply copy from the *Lindisfarne Gospels*, but, if he uses it at all, he adjusts the exemplar, showing somewhat consistent intentions. The data may also be enough to question the unity of Aldred's gloss, because of the clear difference between John and the other two gospels, both in themselves and in their relation to Owun's gloss.

References

Bibire, Paul — Alan S.C. Ross
    1981   "The Differences between Lindisfarne and Rushworth Two", *Notes and Queries* 226 (2): 98-116.

Crowley, Joseph
    2000   "Anglicized Word Order in Old English Continuous Interlinear Glosses in British Library, Royal 2.A.XX", *Anglo-Saxon England* 29: 123-151.

Elliott, Constance O. — Alan S.C. Ross.
    1972   "Aldrediana XXIV: The Linguistic Peculiarities of the Gloss to St. John's Gospel", *English Philological Studies* 13: 49-72.

---

[26] This uniqueness has been pointed out by Elliott and Ross (1972). Their analysis clearly shows some linguistic features of Aldred's gloss confined to John's Gospel. Since their focus is on the form and the meaning of words, syntactic uniqueness is not mentioned in their article. They hypothesise, though they admit that it cannot be proved, Bedan influence on Aldred's gloss to John's Gospel. The syntactic uniqueness that the present study has pointed out may suggest the presence of a prose translation, because we have found many instances of deviation from Latin in terms of word order. This is, however, unlikely to be due to a hypothesised Bedan translation, if Ross (1969: 493) is right in suggesting that "what Bede was doing when he was translating was making a word-for-word gloss."

Kotake, Tadashi
2006 "Aldred's Multiple Glosses: Is the Order Significant?", in Michiko Ogura (ed.) 2006, 35-50.
Mitchell, Bruce
1985 *Old English Syntax*. 2 vols. Oxford: Clarendon Press.
Morrell, Minnie C.
1965 *A Manual of Old English Biblical Materials*. Knoxville: University of Tennessee Press.
Nagucka, Ruta
1997 "Glossal Translation in the *Lindisfarne Gospels according to St Matthew*", *Studia Anglica Posnaniensia* 31: 179-201.
Ogura, Michiko
1991 "*Cweðan + To* Dative of Person", *Neophilologus* 75: 270-278.
2006 "Element Order Varies: Samples from Old English Psalter Glosses", in Michiko Ogura (ed.) 2006, 105-126.
Ogura, Michiko (ed.)
2006 *Textual and Contextual Studies in Medieval English: Towards the Reunion of Linguistics and Philology*. Frankfurt am Main: Peter Lang.
Ohkado, Masayuki
2006 "On Word Order in Constructions with Two Predicates in Old English Interlinear Glosses", in Michiko Ogura (ed.) 2006, 127-145.
2007 "On Word Order in Old English Interlinear Gloss, with Special Reference to the *Lindisfarne* and *Rushworth Glosses*", in *Exploring the Universe of Language: A Festschrift for Dr. Hirozo Nakano on the Occasion of His Seventieth Birthday*. Edd. Amano Masachiyo. Nagoya: Department of English Linguistics, Nagoya University, 285-304.
Ross, Alan S.C.
1969 "A Connection Between Bede and the Anglo-Saxon Gloss to the Lindisfarne Gospels", *Journal of Theological Studies* 20(2): 482-494.
Skeat, Walter W. (ed.)
1871-1887 *The Holy Gospels in Anglo-Saxon, Northumbrian, and Old Mercian Versions, Synoptically Arranged, with Collations Exhibiting All the Readings of All the MSS.; together with the Early Latin Version as Contained in the Lindisfarne MS., Collated with the Latin Version in the Rushworth MS*. Cambridge: The University Press. [Mark (1871), Luke (1874), John (1878), Matthew (1887): reprint edition published in 1970, Darmstadt: Wissenschaftliche Buchgesellschaft]

6 An Aspect of OV Order in the *West Saxon Gospels* with Special Reference to the Collocation 'Verb + *God/Gode*'
Yoshitaka Kozuka, Aichi University of Education

1. Introduction

There have been a number of studies concerning the language of the *West Saxon Gospels* (hereafter *WSG*), but element order has rarely been discussed.[1] This is partly because this version is a free but relatively literal translation. Element orders in *WSG*, however, often show patterns which seem to be important for the study of Old English syntax. My aim in this paper is to discuss one such example, with focus on a particular type of verb-object phrase, verb+*god(e)*. In the following sections, I will first point out that this type of VO combination exhibits a noteworthy pattern of arrangement, and then argue that we can assume lexical as well as syntactic factors behind it.

2. Syntax in the combination 'V+*god(e)*'

It is necessary at the outset to make a clear definition of the phrases discussed in the present paper. By 'V+*god(e)*', I mean verb phrases where the noun *god* is a direct or indirect object, with or without modifiers, including not only monotransitive constructions (e.g. (1) and (2)), but also ditransitive constructions (e.g. (3)).[2]

(1) Lk 18:4
 þeah ic **god** ne **ondræde**. ne ic mán ne onþracige
(2) Jn 16:2
 Ac seo tid cymð þ ælc þe eow of-slyhð wenþ þ he **þenige gode**.
(3) Lk 21:4
 Soðes ealle þas **brohton gode** lác of hyra mycelan welan.

Combinations such as these occur 33 times in *WSG*.[3] Their syntactic patterns are shown in Table 1, where the examples are divided according to clause type and verb form, which have a significant influence on element order in Old English prose.

---

1 The most extensive study on element order in *WSG* is, to my knowledge, Kojima (1994-1996), who examines SV, SVC, and SVO in independent clauses. I have also dealt with several aspects of element order in this version (Kozuka 2006).
2 The quotations from *WSG* are all from the text in Cambridge, Corpus Christi College 140 in Skeat (1871-1887). In the present article, the Gospels according to St. Matthew, St. Mark, St. Luke and St. John are referred to as Mt, Mk, Lk and Jn, respectively.
3 Mt 5:8, 6:24, 9:8, 15:31; Mk 8:6, 14:23; Lk 2:13, 2:20, 2:22, 2:28, 5:25, 5:26, 7:16, 7:29, 13:13, 16:13, 17:15, 17:18, 18:2, 18:4, 18:43 (twice), 19:37, 21:4, 23:40, 23:47, 24:53; Jn 1:18, 8:27, 8:41, 9:24, 16:2, 21:19.

Table 1: Syntactic patterns of the combination 'V+*god(e)*' in *WSG*

	V=finite form				V=nonfinite form
	main clause			subordinate clause	
	coordinate		imperative	others		
	and	*ne*				
VO	2	0	1	3	2	0
OV	10	1	0	1	5	8

The figures above, roughly speaking, show standard syntactic patterns in Old English prose: objects tend to be put before the nonfinite verb, and often precede the finite verb in subordinate and coordinate clauses. However, one point is worthy of note in Table 1, namely, the high frequency of OV in main clauses beginning with *and* (hereafter *and*-clause): ten out of twelve, or about 83%. Examples (4)-(15) are all instances of 'V+*god(e)*' occurring in *and*-clauses:

VO (2 examples)
(4) Mt 9:8
    þa ondrédon hig hym 7 **wuldrodon god** þe sealde swylcne anweald mannum;
(5) Mt 15:31
    7 hig **mærsodon** israhela god;
OV (10 examples)
(6) Mk 8:6
    And [se hælend] nam þa seofon hlafas 7 **gode þancode**. 7 hi bræc
(7) Mk 14:23
    7 [se hælend] onfeng calice. 7 **gode þancas dyde** 7 sealde hi*m*.
(8) Lk 2:28
    he onfeng hine mid his handu*m*. 7 **god bletsode** 7 cwæð;
(9) Lk 5:25
    7 he sona be-foran him aras. ... 7 to his huse ferde 7 **god wuldrode**.
(10) Lk 5:26
    7 hig ealle wundredon 7 **god mærsodon** 7 wæron mid ege gefyllede. 7 cwædon.
(11) Lk 7:16
    Þa ofer-eode ege hig ealle. 7 hig **god mærsodon** 7 cwædon.
(12) Lk 7:29
    7 eall folc þis gehyrende sundor-halgan **god heredon** 7 gefullede on iohannes fulluhte;
(13) Lk 13:13
    þa wæs heo sona up arǽred. 7 heo **god wuldrode**;
(14) Lk 18:43
    7 eall folc **gode lof sealde** þa hig þ gesawon;
(15) Lk 19:37
    þa ongunnon ealle þa menego geblissian. 7 mid mycelre stefne **god heredon** be eallu*m* þa*m* mihtu*m* þe hig gesawun.

Comparing the two groups of instances above, VO and OV groups, we can clearly see a syntactic contrast between them: in both examples of VO, (4) and (5), the noun *god* is modified, as my underlining shows, while it is not modified in any of the examples of OV, (6)-(15). In other words, the object noun *god* with no modifier is regularly put before the finite verb in *and*-clauses.

Why does this regular preposing occur? What is readily supposed is that it would be due to two syntactic factors: the effect of the *and*-clause and the light weight of the object. In Old English prose, as mentioned above, objects are often placed before the finite verb in coordinate clauses, particularly in clauses introduced by *and* or *ne* "neither";[4] and 'light' objects are more likely to precede the finite verb. However, it should be emphasised here that these two factors do not always lead to OV, as is suggested in Tables 2 and 3. The former summarises the positions of nominal objects (i.e. VO/OV) appearing in the first three chapters in each Gospel; and the latter shows the relationship between the positions of nominal objects and their weight in *and*-clauses in the same parts of the Gospels.

Table 2: Positions of nominal objects in the first three chapters of each Gospel

	V=finite form					V=nonfinite form
	main clause				subordinate clause	
	coordinate		imperative	others		
	and	*ac*				
Mt	10/0		5/0	47/1	1/4	1/5
Mk	3/4	1/0	6/0	9/1	8/9	3/15
Lk	10/9		2/1	7/2	10/16	3/13
Jn	13/1		4/0	15/0	16/11	1/2
Total (VO/OV)	36/14	1/0	17/1	78/4	35/40	8/35

Note: For ease of comparison, examples of the following five structures are excluded from the statistics in Tables 2 and 3: interrogatives, double object constructions, topicalisations (e.g. OSV), inversions (e.g. VSO), and constructions with a complement (e.g. SVOC).

Table 3: Positions of nominal objects and their weight in *and*-clauses in the first three chapters of each Gospel

	weight (=number of words)			
	1	2	3	4 or more
Mt	3/0	6/0		1/0
Mk	0/1	2/2	0/1	1/0
Lk	2/7	4/2	3/0	1/0
Jn	4/1	8/0	1/0	
Total (VO/OV)	9/9	20/4	4/1	3/0

---

4 See Ohkado (2005: 196-282) for detailed data and discussion on the relationship between types of coordinate conjunction and element order.

These two tables indicate that *and*-clause and light weight are highly influential but not deciding factors for preverbal positioning. Examples (16) and (17) are good pairs of examples to illustrate the point, each demonstrating the positional variety of the same one-word noun object in *and*-clauses.

(16) a. Mt 1:23
    Soðlice seo fæmne hæfð on innoðe 7 heo <u>cenð</u> <u>sunu</u>;
                                            V O
    b. Lk 1:57
    Ða wæs gefylled elizabethe cenningtid. 7 heo <u>sunu</u> <u>cende</u>.
                                                    O   V
(17) a. Jn 1:32
    And Iohannes <u>cyþde</u> <u>gewitnesse</u> cweðende þ ic geseah ...
                          V   O
    b. Jn 1:34
    7 ic geseah 7 <u>gewitnesse</u> <u>cyðde</u> þ þes is godes sunu;
                           O   V

Given these figures and examples, the repeated and regular preposing of *god* in *and*-clauses seems to be somewhat exceptional. Although the significant involvement of syntactic factors is beyond doubt, we may presume the existence of additional factors which led the translator(s)[5] to the invariable arrangements.

3. Possible additional factor for the repetitive OV arrangements

A possible additional factor for the repeated OV arrangements mentioned above can be found in their lexical aspect. When looking at the verbs or verb phrases in the relevant OV instances (i.e. (6)-(15)), we can see that they are the same or similar in sense, denoting either "to thank" or "to praise", as summarised in Table 4.

Table 4: Verbs or verb phrases in '*god(e)* V' in *and*-clauses

"to thank"	"to praise"
þancian (Mk 8:6)	*bletsian* (Lk 2:28)
þancas don (Mk 14:23)	*herian* (Lk 7:29, Lk 19:37)
	mærsian (Lk 5:26, Lk 7:16)
	wuldrian (Lk 5:25, Lk 13:13)
	lof syllan (Lk 18:43)

This lexical feature is notable in relation to Old English poems, where OV phrases consisting of a noun denoting "God" and a verb denoting "to thank" or "to praise" occur frequently and formulaically. Using *A Microfiche Concordance to Old Eng-*

---

5   The authorship of *WSG* is uncertain, and several scholars have considered the problem, focusing on how many hands worked on the version, rather than who translated it. For a summary of previous studies on or related to this subject, see Kozuka (2006: 1-3).

lish and *the Dictionary of Old English Corpus in Electronic Form*,[6] I found nineteen instances of this type of phrase in eight poems, as listed in (18).

(18) Examples of 'GOD+verb of thanking or praising' in verse[7]
 Andreas (1011b **gode þancade**, 1267b **dryhten herede**, 1455b **dryhten herede**)
 Azarias (3b **dryhten herede**, 68b **þeoden heredon**, 155b **god bletsiað**)
 Beowulf (227b **gode þancedon**, 625b **gode þancode**, 1397b **gode þancode**, 1626b **gode þancodon**)
 Christ (1255b **gode þonciað**)
 Daniel (86b **gode þancode**, 281b **drihten herede**, 357b **ðeoden heredon**, 421b **god herigað**)
 Elene (961b **gode þancode**, 1138b **gode þancode**)
 Exodus (576b **drihten heredon**)
 Genesis (15b **þeoden heredon**)

All these instances appear in b-verses, and more importantly, all but one (*Daniel* 421b) constitute b-verses by themselves, as illustrated below, which means that this type of phrase is highly formulaic.

(19) *Andreas* 1011-13a
 Aras þa togenes, **gode þancade**[8]
 þæs ðe hie onsunde æfre moston
 geseon under sunnan.

(20) *Azarias* 155-57
 Nu we geonge þry **god bletsiað**,
 felameahtigne fæder in heofonum,
 þone soðan sunu ond þone sigefæstan gæst.

(21) *Daniel* 356b-60a
 Þær þa modhwatan
 þry on geðancum **ðeoden heredon**,
 bædon bletsian bearn Israela
 eall landgesceaft ecne drihten,
 ðeoda waldend.

Taken together, one possibility arises concerning the factors behind the repeated OV arrangements mentioned above: knowledge of this type of poetic formula

---

6 Using these two research tools, I examined instances containing *(ge)bletsian, (ge)herian, (ge)mærsian, (ge)þancian,* or *(ge)wuldrian.*

7 The quotations from poetic works are all based on *The Anglo-Saxon Poetic Records* (Krapp and Dobbie 1931-1953). For fuller citations, see Appendix.

8 The formula *gode þancode* is mentioned in Ogura (2003: 421) and Orchard (2003: 281). Ogura (2003: 414-27) offers a useful and exhaustive list of word pairs, formulas and formulaic systems with Old English words of emotion. Orchard (2003: 274-314) is also a good source of information, providing us with an extensive list of the repeated formulas in *Beowulf.*

might partly have contributed to the preference for OV in the identical or similar collocations. An instance notable from this perspective is found in Lk 23:47.

(22) Lk 23:47
Þa se hundred-man geseah þ þar geworden wæs. he **god wuldrode** 7 cwæð;

This example occurs in a main clause which does not begin with a coordinate conjunction, where a noun object rarely precedes the finite verb in Old English prose. In *WSG*, as was shown in Table 1, there appear four instances of 'V+*god*' in this type of clause (Lk 21:4, 23:47, Jn 1:18, 8:41), among which only the one cited above has a verb of praising/thanking (*wuldrian*) and shows OV order. In this instance, the collocation seems to be highly responsible for the choice of OV.

4. Comparison between OE and Latin versions
Lastly, let us turn to the Latin source of *WSG*.[9] Here, I would like to firstly examine whether or not the syntactic patterns described above are under a strong Latin influence, and subsequently take a close look at the translation method in two instances.

4.1. Latin texts for '*god(e)* V' in *and*-clauses
As I mentioned at the beginning, *WSG* is a more or less literal translation. We therefore need to see whether the patterns under consideration are Latinism or not. In (23), the syntactic structures in the Latin parts corresponding to the OV instances in question (i.e. (6)-(15)) are roughly summarised.

(23) Syntax of the Latin texts corresponding to the instances of '*god(e)* V' in *and*-clauses

OE	Latin
god(e) V (10 instances) →	V *deum/deo* (8 instances)
	deum/deo V (no instances)
	other structures (2 instances)

As shown in (23), the corresponding Latin parts never show OV (i.e. *deum/deo* V), but have the reverse order VO (i.e. V *deum/deo*) for the majority. Examples include:

---

9 The exact text of the Latin source of *WSG* is unknown. Several studies, such as Harris (1901) and Liuzza (2000: 1-49), demonstrate that the Latin original of *WSG* partly differs from the so-called Vulgate. However, based on the data provided in these studies, there seems to be no significant difference between the two Latin versions, as far as the present paper is concerned. Therefore, I used a modern Vulgate edition, Weber et al. (1994), for this study. The Latin texts cited here are all from this edition.

(24) Lk 13:13
    et confestim erecta est et **glorificabat Deum**
                                        V   O
    →þa wæs heo sona up aræred. 7 heo **god wuldrode**;
                                                           O   V

Thus, it can be said that the Latin source had no marked influence on the repeated choice of OV in question.

4.2. Noteworthy instances

I would like to discuss here the translation method in two instances, which will support the theory that the translator(s) had in mind OV phrases like *gode þancian* and *god herian* as set patterns. The first instance is in Mk 8:6.

(25) Mk 8:6
    And [se hælend] nam þa seofon hlafas 7 **gode þancode.** 7 hi bræc
    [et accipiens septem panes **gratias agens** fregit]
    'and he took the seven loaves, and after giving thanks he broke them'[10]

In this instance, the Old English version has *gode þancode* for Latin *gratias agens*, which literally means "doing thanks": the translator rendered the participial construction *gratias agens* into the past tense verb *þancode*, and put the object *gode* before the verb, despite the absence of an equivalent such as *deo* in the Latin version.[11] This preverbal addition of *gode* implies that *gode þancian* might have been a syntactically fixed collocation for the translator(s). A similar translation for *gratias agens* appears again in Mk, though it is more literal than the instance above.[12]

(26) Mk 14:23
    7 [se hælend] onfeng calice. 7 **gode þancas dyde** 7 sealde hi*m.*
    [Et accepto calice **gratias agens** dedit eis]
    'Then he took a cup, and after giving thanks he gave it to them'

The other instance to be noted is Lk 7:29.

(27) Lk 7:29
    7 eall folc þis gehyrende sundor-halgan **god heredon** 7 gefullede on iohannes fulluhte;

---

10   The Modern English translations given in this section are cited from the New Revised Standard Version.
11   Olsan (1973: 115-24) and Liuzza (2000: 51-61) illustrate and discuss the additions or expansions in *WSG* in detail, but neither mention these instances.
12   This type of addition, however, is not made elsewhere in *WSG*: there are at least five more instances of *gratias agere* that imply "to God" in the *Vulgate* (Mt 15:36, 26:27, Lk 22:17, 22:19, Jn 6:11), but *gode* is not added in these five instances.

[Et omnis populus audiens et publicani **iustificaverunt Deum** baptizati baptismo Iohannis]
'And all the people who heard this, including the tax collectors, acknowledged the justice of God, because they had been baptized with John's baptism.'

Remarkable in this instance is the use of *herian* "to praise" for the Latin verb *iustificare* "to justify". The Vulgate Gospels have seven instances of *iustificare* in total (Mt 11:19, 12:37, Lk 7:29, 7:35, 10:29, 16:15, 18:14), and in *WSG herian* is used for just one of them, Lk 7:29, while elsewhere, *gerihtwisian*, a word semantically closer to *iustificare*, is consistently employed, as seen in (28).

(28) Lk 16:15
ge synt þe eow sylfe beforan mannum **geriht-wisiaþ**.
[vos estis qui **iustificatis** vos coram hominibus]
'You are those who justify yourselves in the sight of others'

It is worth noting here that Lk 7:29 cited above is the sole instance where *iustificare* takes the object *deum*, which leads to the idea that the knowledge of the phrase *god herian* induced here the lexical choice *herian*, rather than the usual option *gerihtwisian*. This lexical variation sounds more interesting when we turn to the other Old English versions; the *Lindisfarne* and *Rushworth* Gospels (Skeat 1871-1887) invariably use *(ge)soðfæstian* "to justify" for *iustificare*. In addition, the Middle English version, the *Wycliffite Bible* (Forshall and Madden 1850), also employs only one word, *iustifien*, for translation. The comparison is summarised in Table 5.

Table 5: Translations of *iustificare* in the four versions of the Gospels

	WSG	*Lindisfarne*	*Rushworth*	*Wycliffite*(E/L)
Mt 11:19	gerihtwisian	(ge)soðfæstian	(ge)soðfæstian	iustifien
Mt 12:37	gerihtwisian	(ge)soðfæstian	(ge)soðfæstian	iustifien
Lk 7:29	herian	(ge)soðfæstian	MS lost	iustifien
Lk 7:35	gerihtwisian	(ge)soðfæstian	MS lost	iustifien
Lk 10:29	gerihtwisian	(ge)soðfæstian	MS lost	iustifien
Lk 16:15	gerihtwisian	(ge)soðfæstian	MS lost	iustifien
Lk 18:14	gerihtwisian	(ge)soðfæstian	(ge)soðfæstian	iustifien

Note: E/L=Earlier Version/Later Version

5. Conclusion

In the present paper, focusing on 'V+*god(e)*', I pointed out that the object noun *god* without any modifiers regularly precedes the finite verb in *and*-clauses, and considered the factors behind it. My supposition was that it could have been lexically as well as syntactically motivated; emphasis was put on the fact that the verbs or verb phrases in the instances are semantically identical or similar, denoting "to thank" or "to praise". Evidence suggested that the OV combinations consisting of *god(e)* and verbs of thanking or praising were set patterns for the translator(s), possibly under the influence of the verse tradition. Comparison between Latin and Old English versions told us that the repeated OV arrangements have no significant association with the syntax in the Latin original, and strengthened the view that the translator(s) regarded collocations such as *gode þancian* and *god herian* as set phrases. With these findings taken together, it was suggested that the idiomatic nature of this type of phrase was one factor contributing to the repeated preposing of *god(e)* in *and*-clauses.

References

The Dictionary of Old English Corpus
  1998 *The Dictionary of Old English Corpus in Electronic Form. TEI-P3 Conformant Version (for 3.5 inch floppies). 1998 Release.* Dictionary of Old English Project. Toronto: University of Toronto.
Forshall, J. — F. Madden (edd.)
  1850 *The Holy Bible, Containing the Old and New Testaments, with the Apocryphal Books, in the Earliest English Versions Made from the Latin Vulgate by John Wycliffe and his Followers.* Oxford: Oxford University Press. (reprint, 1982, New York: AMS Press)
Harris, L. M.
  1901 *Studies in the Anglo-Saxon Version of the Gospels. Part 1: The Form of the Latin Original, and Mistaken Renderings.* Baltimore: John Murphy Company.
Healey, A. diPaolo — R. L.Venezky (comp.)
  1980 *A Microfiche Concordance to Old English.* Toronto: University of Toronto.
Kojima, K.
  1994-1996 "Element Order Patterns in Independent Clauses in the West-Saxon Gospels: An Exhaustive Analysis (I-III)" *Gakujutsu Kenkyu (English Language and Literature)* 43 (1994): 63-74, 44 (1995): 19-29, 45 (1996): 1-14. School of Education, Waseda University.
Kozuka, Y.
  2006 *A Linguistic Study of the Authorship of the West Saxon Gospels.* Osaka: Osaka University Press.

Krapp, G. P. — E. van K. Dobbie (edd.)
    1931-1953 *The Anglo-Saxon Poetic Records. A Collective Edition.* New York: Columbia University Press; London: Routledge and Kegan Paul.

Liuzza, R. M.
    2000 *The Old English Version of the Gospels. Vol. II. Notes and Glossary.* EETS. O.S. 314.

The New Revised Standard Version
    1989 *The Holy Bible Containing the Old and New Testaments, New Revised Standard Version.* New York and Oxford: Oxford University Press.

Ogura, M.
    2003 "*Words of Emotion in Old and Middle English Psalms and Alliterative Poems.*" *Jimbun Kenkyu* (Chiba University) 32: 393-427.

Ohkado, M.
    2005 *Clause Structure in Old English.* Nagoya: Manahouse.

Olsan, L.T.
    1973 *The Style of the West Saxon Gospels.* Diss. Tulane University.

Orchard, A.
    2003 *A Critical Companion to Beowulf.* Cambridge: D. S. Brewer.

Skeat, W. W. (ed.)
    1871-1887 *The Gospels according to Saint Matthew, Saint Mark, Saint Luke, and Saint John in Anglo-Saxon, Northumbrian, and Old Mercian Versions, Synoptically Arranged, with Collations Exhibiting All the Readings of All the MSS.* Cambridge: Cambridge University Press.

Weber, R. et al. (edd.)
    1994 *Biblia Sacra iuxta Vulgatam Versionem* (Vierte, verbesserte Auflage). Stuttgart: Deutsche Bibelgesellschaft.

An Aspect of OV Order in the West Saxon Gospels 89

Appendix: Examples of 'GOD+verb of thanking/praising' in verse

Aras þa togenes,   **gode þancade**
þæs ðe hie onsunde   æfre moston
geseon under sunnan.   (*Andreas* 1011-13a)

                No on gewitte blon,
acol for þy egesan,   þæs þe he ær ongann,
þæt he a domlicost   **dryhten herede**,
weorðade wordum,   oððæt wuldres gim
heofontorht onhlad.   (*Andreas* 1265b-69a)

Swa se dædfruma   **dryhten herede**
halgan stefne   oððæt hador sægl
wuldortorht gewat   under waðu scriðan. (*Andreas* 1455-57)

Him þa Azarias   ingeþoncum
hleoþrede halig   þurh hatne lig,
dreag dædum georn,   **dryhten herede**,
wis in weorcum,   ond þas word acwæð:
"Meotud allwihta,   þu eart meahtum swið
niþas to nerganne.   (*Azarias* 1-6a)

              Wearð se hata lig
todrifen ond todwæsced,   þær þa dædhwatan
þry mid geþoncum   **þeoden heredon**,
bædon bletsian   bearn in worulde
ealle gesceafte   ecne dryhten,
þeoda waldend.   (*Azarias* 66b-71a)

Nu we geonge þry   **god bletsiað**,
felameahtigne   fæder in heofonum,
þone soðan sunu   ond þone sigefæstan gæst. (*Azarias* 155-57)

            Þanon up hraðe
Wedera leode   on wang stigon,
sæwudu sældon   (syrcan hrysedon,
guðgewædo),   **gode þancedon**
þæs þe him yþlade   eaðe wurdon.
            (*Beowulf* 224b-28)

Ymbeode þa   ides Helminga
duguþe ond geogoþe   dæl æghwylcne,
sincfato sealde,   oþþæt sæl alamp
þæt hio Beowulfe,   beaghroden cwen
mode geþungen,   medoful ætbær;
grette Geata leod,   **gode þancode**
wisfæst wordum   þæs ðe hire se willa gelamp
þæt heo on ænigne   eorl gelyfde
fyrena frofre.   (*Beowulf* 620-28a)

Ahleop ða se gomela,   **gode þancode**,
mihtigan drihtne,   þæs se man gespræc. (*Beowulf* 1397-98)

Eodon him þa togeanes,   **gode þancodon**,
ðryðlic þegna heap,   þeodnes gefegon,
þæs þe hi hyne gesundne   geseon moston. (*Beowulf* 1626-28)

Ðonne hi þy geornor   **gode þonciað**
blædes ond blissa   þe hy bu geseoð,
þæt he hy generede   from niðcwale
ond eac forgeaf   ece dreamas;
bið him hel bilocen,   heofonrice agiefen. (*Christ* 1255-59)

Wolde þæt þa cnihtas   cræft leornedon,
þæt him snytro on sefan   secgan mihte,
nales ðy þe he þæt moste   oððe gemunan wolde
þæt he þara gifena   **gode þancode**
þe him þær to duguðe   drihten scyrede. (*Daniel* 83-87)

Ða Azarias   ingeþancum
hleoðrade halig   þurh hatne lig,
dreag dæda georn,   **drihten herede**,
wer womma leas,   and þa word acwæð:
"Metod alwihta, hwæt!   (*Daniel* 279-83a)

Þær þa modhwatan
þry on geðancum   **ðeoden heredon**,
bædon bletsian   bearn Israela
eall landgesceaft   ecne drihten,
ðeoda waldend.   (*Daniel* 356b-60a)

An Aspect of OV Order in the West Saxon Gospels

    Hie **god herigað**,
anne ecne, and ealles him
be naman gehwam on neod sprecað,
þanciað þrymmes þristum wordum,
cweðað he sie ana ælmihtig god,
witig wuldorcyning, worlde and heofona. (*Daniel* 421b-26)

    Gode þancode,
wuldorcyninge, þæs hire se willa gelamp
þurh bearn godes bega gehwæðres,
ge æt þære gesyhðe þæs sigebeames,
ge ðæs geleafan þe hio swa leohte oncneow,
wuldorfæste gife in þæs weres breostum. (*Elene* 961b-66)

    Gode þancode,
sigora dryhtne, þæs þe hio soð gecneow
ondweardlice þæt wæs oft bodod
feor ær beforan fram fruman worulde,
folcum to frofre. (*Elene* 1138b-42a)

Hreðdon hildespelle, siððan hie þam herge wiðforon;
hofon hereþreatas hlude stefne,
for þam dædweorce **drihten heredon**,
weras wuldres sang; wif on oðrum,
folcsweota mæst, fyrdleoð golan
aclum stefnum, eallwundra fela.
    (*Exodus* 574-79)

Þegnas þrymfæste **þeoden heredon**,
sægdon lustum lof, heora liffrean
demdon, drihtenes dugeþum wæron
swiðe gesælige. (*Genesis* 15-18a)

7 Insubordination in Old English

Mitsuru Maeda, Yamaguchi University

1. Introduction

Old English (OE) is one of the languages that productively use the subjunctive mood. It occurred in various environments, including performative utterances such as (1).

(1) *feohte*   se   cempa on fyrdlicum truman
    fight:Subj:3sg Det warrior in warlike:D troop:D
    'Let the soldier fight in the warlike cohort.'   (*Lives of Saints* 31.1098)

This type of utterance is generally called "third-person imperative" or "jussive." Since the subjunctive in (1) is used in a main clause used performatively, I will call sentences like (1) "Performative Subjunctive Main Clauses" (abbreviated as PSMC's). Utterances like those in (2), which are rather formulaic and archaic in Present-day English (PE), are known to be their direct descendants:

(2) a. So *be* it.
    b. God *bless* you.

What is particular about PSMC's is that the subjunctive occurred in independent clauses. The subjunctive is widely known to be characterised as a "concomitant of subordination" (Bybee et al. (1994: 217)). In fact, as in other modern languages in Europe, the subjunctive in OE mostly occurred in various types of subordinate clause. Given this, one might regard PSMC's as an exceptional case, and ask why the subjunctive was used in a few very limited types of main clause. The purpose of the present paper is exactly to answer this question, and to demonstrate that PSMC's were derived from subjunctive noun clauses selected by performative main clauses[1] like *ic bidde* 'I command,' that is, they had originally been complement clauses, and later developed into main clauses. This kind of syntactic change is sometimes called "insubordination," i.e. a pattern of syntactic change that liberates a subordinate clause from dominance by the main clause (cf. Tabor and Traugott (1998)). Moreover, it will also be argued that this syntactic change was enabled by a type of semantic change I call "meaning possession."

---

[1] By "performative main clause" is meant those main clauses that are used to perform specific illocutionary acts, such as *I promise, I warn, I order*, etc. As Austin (1975) notes, they typically take the form of an active, simple form verb in the present tense with a first-person subject. When they do not have a first-person subject, as in the case of *It is necessary for you to attend the meeting* (uttered performatively), the speaker is understood as issuing a request.

The present paper is organised as follows. The next section is allotted to the presentation of some relevant facets of PSMC's. In section 3, I will turn to the syntactic development of PSMC's. There I will propose a scenario of how they developed from noun clauses. In section 4, I will introduce the concept of "meaning possession" as a pattern of semantic change, and argue that it enabled the syntactic development of PSMC's. Section 5 is a brief summary of this paper.

2. Performative Subjunctive Main Clauses in OE

In this section, I will first discuss some important properties of PSMC's as a preliminary step for the analysis in the following sections. Let us first consider the word order pattern of PSMC's. The most typical one is illustrated in (3):

(3) V_{Subj} S_{Nom} (... O_{Acc} XP ...)

In PSMC's, subjunctive verbs are most often located in the sentence-initial position and followed by overt nominative subjects (cf. (1)). On the other hand, sentences with the verbs in other positions, as in (4), are very rare:

(4) Ne heora nan   gerefscipe   oððe mangunge ne   *drife*
    Neg their none reeveship:A Conj mongering Neg undertake:Subj:3sg
    'Let none of them undertake any reeveship or mongering.'   (*ÆCHom*, ii, 94. 33)

Let us next turn to the four uses of PSMC's. Consider the examples in (5)-(8):

(5) a. *Beo*   þin   wif swylc swa uenus
       be:Subj:3sg your wife such   as Venus
       'Let your wife be like Venus.'   (*Lives of Saints* 8. 66)
    b. Ne *bepæce*   nan man hine   sylfne
       Neg deceive:Subj:3sg no   man him:A Ref:A
       'Let no man deceive himself.'   (*ÆCHom*, i, 52. 33)

(6) a. *wutum*   gongan to helpan   hild-fruman
       go:Subj:1pl go:Inf to help:Inf battle-chief:D
       'Let us go (to him) to help our war-leader.'   (*Beowulf* 2648)
    b. *fare*   we on ge-hende tunas
       go:Subj:1pl we in next:A   towns:A
       'Let us go into the next towns.'   (*Mark* 1. 38)

(7) *Gebide*   ge on berg
    wait:Subj:2sg you in barrow:D
    'Wait on the barrow.'   (*Beowulf* 2529)

(8) Alwalda þec   gode   *forgylde* ...
    almighty you:A good:D reward:Subj:3sg
    'May Almighty God reward you with good ...'   (*Beowulf* 955)

The examples in (5) are the instances of third-person imperatives, or *jussives*. On the other hand, those in (6) are *hortatives*, and they roughly correspond to sentences with *let's*. In this type of sentence, *uton*, which is the first-person plural, present subjunctive form of *witan* 'go,' was most often used as a kind of "hortative marker" (cf. (6a)).[2] Let us next turn to the example in (7). This kind of sentence is usually interpreted as a (polite) command, or *directive*. Sentences like (8) are so-called *optatives* (cf. *God save the Queen!*).

What seems to be syntactically deviant about PSMC's is this: although their main verbs are marked by the subjunctive, they are obviously main clauses. As noted above, the subjunctive is a mood whose occurrence is *mostly* restricted to subordinate contexts, to the extent that it can be regarded as a syntactic marker of subordination. Given this, one might speculate that PSMC's developed from a specific type of subordinate clause. In fact, I will argue that they actually did. This analysis gains support from their syntactic and functional properties.

3. Syntactic Development of PSMC's

In this section, I will consider how PSMC's were syntactically derived from the ordinary noun clause structure. Consider first the following list of OE predicates:

(9) *aliefan* 'allow, grant,' *bebeodan* 'command, require,' *beodan* 'command,' *biddan* 'ask, pray, command,' *forgiefan* 'grant, allow,' *neod* (*beon*) '(be) needful,' *willan* 'desire,' etc.

These are the most typical predicates which often took subjunctive noun clauses (SNC's). Like their PE counterparts, these predicates functioned as performative main clauses (PMC's; see fn. 1):

(10) a. ic ðe bebeode ... þæt þu þæt nænegum men *cyðe* ...
I you:D require:1sg Comp you it no one:D tell:Subj.3sg
'I require you not to tell it to anybody.' (*Bede* 266. 28)
b. Ic bidde þe ... þæt þu me gelæde to minum earde
I pray:1sg you:D Comp you me:A lead:Subj:2sg to my:D country:D
'I pray that you will bring me to my country.' (*Lives of Saints* 30. 343)

These typical performative utterances are so functionally parallel to PSMC's that one cannot ignore the affinity between them.

It is my contention that the starting point of the development of PSMC's was the ellipsis of PMC's like *ic bidde* 'I command' in (10b). This hypothesis would

---

2   When the subject of a PSMC was in the first person plural, *uton* was most often used as a kind of introductory particle, as *let's* in PE is. Mitchell (1985: 374) notes that Ælfric tended to prefer using *uton*; in fact, the number of hortative PSMC's with *uton* is overwhelming in *ÆCHom* and *Lives of Saints*. It is often analyzed as an interjection, while Mitchell argues that it was a verb. In my opinion, it was on the process of being grammaticalised as a hortative particle. Incidentally, when *uton* is used, PSMC's often lack an overt nominative subject.

gain support from the functional similarity between sentences like (10) and PSMC's. However, to establish it firmly, we must find some syntactic evidence that clearly points to their subordinate origin. The best way to do this is to find PSMC's with the complementiser *þæt*, a hallmark of noun clauses. Although all of the examples I have collected do not have *þæt*, Visser (1966: 806) cites examples like (11) and notes that they are occasionally found in OE texts like Ælfred's *Cura Pastoralis*:

(11) a. *þætte* unlærede ne dyrren underfon lareowdom
    Comp unlearned Neg dare:Subj:3pl receive:Inf teaching:A
    'Don't let the unlearned dare to take up teaching.'   (*Cura Pastoralis* 24. 14)
  b. *þætte se* reccere his godan weorc for gielpe anum ne do ...
    Comp Det teacher his good:A work:Acc for arrogance:D strong:D Neg do:Subj:3sg
    'Don't let the teacher do his virtuous work for strong arrogance.' (*Cura Pastoralis* 140. 14)

The existence of examples like (11) cogently argues for the claim that PSMC's derived from SNC's.

Let us next consider how the typical surface order of PSMC's, which is illustrated in (12a) below, was syntactically derived:

(12) a. [V_{subj} S_{Nom}. ... (... O_{Acc} XP ...)]   (surface order)
  b. [$_{CP}$ 0 [$_{IP}$ S_{Nom}. ... (... O_{Acc} XP ...) V_{subj}]]   (base structure)

As noted above, PSMC's typically had the subjunctive verb in the sentence-initial position. First, OE was a typical SOV language (cf. Fischer et al. (2000)), so the base-generated position of a verb can be assumed to be somewhere toward the right periphery of VP (often the sentence-final position). If this is correct, the underlying structure of (12a) should be something like (12b). Why, then, was the verb located in the clause-initial position (the head of CP)? Given that subject-verb inversion was widely used in OE, it can be assumed that the surface order in (12a) resulted from verb-fronting, as in (13):

(13) [$_{CP}$ [$_C$ V_{subj1}] [$_{IP}$ S_{Nom}. ... (... O_{Acc} XP ...) t$_1$]
   ↑_____|
      Verb-fronting

There have been a plenty of proposals as to why a finite verb in main clauses should be fronted to C^0 in Germanic languages (cf. Ohkado (2001: 26-28)). According to these proposals, verb-fronting is triggered to fill the empty C^0 position. If this is correct, the verb-fronting in (13) could have been related to the ellipsis of *þæt*.

In fact, there are a number of instances of verb-fronting which seem to be triggered by the ellipsis of a C^0 element. For example, in PE, the ellipsis of the

conditional *if*, an instance of C⁰, obligatorily triggers Subject-Aux Inversion, as in (14):
(14) a. If I *were* in your place, ... ⇒ *Were* I in your place, ...
  b. If it *should* be true, ... ⇒ *Should* it be true, ...

Note, however, that in the case of PSMC's, verb-fronting was not obligatory, given the existence of examples like (4) above (though they are only rarely found). In OE, the surface order in (12a) was at best the strongly preferred one.[3]

Another, more direct support for the present analysis comes from the situation in French. French also has the equivalents of PSMC's, and they are still productively used:

(15) a. *Que*   Dieu vous   bénisse!
      Comp God you:A bless:Subj:3sg
      'May God bless you.'   (Jones (1996: 181))
    b. *Qu'*il   vienne   me   voir   demain!
      Comp+he come:Subj:3sg me:A see:Inf tomorrow
      'Let him come to see me tomorrow.'   (Ibid.)

They usually have the complementiser *que* 'that,' which points to the subordinate origin of French PSMC's. However, when they are used as optatives, as in (15a), *que* is sometimes omitted, as in (16):

(16) *Vive*   la   France!
    live:Subj:3sg Det France
    'Long live France!'   (Kurata (1995: 116))

As this example shows, when *que* is omitted, verbs are *preferably* (not obligatorily) fronted to the clause-initial position, as if they did so to fill the empty C⁰ position. According to Kurata (1995), the ellipsis of PMC's like *Je souhaite* 'I wish' is the first step in the derivation of French PSMC's. He also assumes that the subsequent ellipsis of *que* is closely related to verb-fronting. Then, the example in (16) is derived as in (17):

(17) *Je souhaite*   que   la France *vive*.
    I wish:1sg Comp Det France live:Subj:3sg
    'I hope France will live.'

  STAGE 1: Ellipsis of the PMC (= *Je souhaite* 'I wish')
         ⇒ ~~Je souhaite~~ [CP [C que] [IP la France [VP vive]]]

---

3   From a functional point of view, it can be assumed that the verb-fronting was an attempt to indicate grammatically the non-declarative nature of PSNC's.

STAGE 2: Ellipsis of *que*:
  ⇒ [$_{CP}$ [$_C$ ~~Que~~] [$_{IP}$ la France [$_{VP}$ vive]]]

STAGE 3: Fronting of the verb to the empty C^0 slot:
  ⇒ [$_{CP}$ [$_C$ Vive$_1$] [$_{IP}$ la France [$_{VP}$ t$_1$]]]
      ↑_____|
      Verb-fronting

Since French PSMC's are still productively used, the intuition behind this analysis would be very suggestive for the present purpose. In fact, the analysis is in a sense so suggestive that it already foreshadows the direction of the present analysis of PSMC's: in the spirit of the analysis in (17), one can propose the course of the development of PSMC's in (18):

(18) The syntactic development of PSMC's:
  Ic bidde þæt he do ... 'I command that he do ...'
  PMC [$_{CP}$ [$_C$ *þæt*][$_{IP}$ S$_{Nom}$ V$_{subj}$ ... (... O$_{Acc}$ XP ...)]]

STAGE 1: Ellipsis of the PMC:
  ⇒ ~~Ic bidde~~ [$_{CP}$ [$_C$ þæt][$_{IP}$ S$_{Nom}$... (... O$_{Acc}$ XP ...) V$_{subj}$]]

STAGE 2: Ellipsis of *þæt*:
  ⇒ [$_{CP}$ [$_C$ ~~þæt~~][$_{IP}$ S$_{Nom}$ ... (... O$_{Acc}$ XP ...) V$_{subj}$]]

STAGE 3: Fronting of the verb to the empty C^0 slot:
  ⇒ [$_{CP}$ [$_C$ V$_{subj1}$][$_{IP}$ S$_{Nom}$ ... (... O$_{Acc}$ XP ...) t$_1$]]
      ↑_____|
      Verb-fronting

This analysis is fully compatible with the above discussion about PSMC's. First, the assumption of the ellipsis of a PMC accounts for the functional similarity between performative sentences with PMC's and PSMC's and occasional inclusion of *þæt* in PSMC's (cf. (11)). More than that, one can treat both OE and French PSMC's in parallel fashion, which seems to be a very natural orientation.

4. Meaning Possession
Syntactically, the above analysis of PSMC's might be sufficient for accounting for the surface order of PSMC's. However, from a functional point of view, there is a serious difficulty yet to be solved. Consider (17)-(18) again. Both analyses assume the ellipsis of a PMC as a first step of the derivation. The very assumption seems to be theoretically impossible. This is because the ellipsis of a meaningful element such as a PMC must observe *Recoverability Condition on Deletion* (RCD), which requires that an element can be deleted only in the context of another element which it is identical to (cf. Sag (1980: 16)). Given this, for the ellip-

sis of a PMC to be possible, there must be some preceding utterance that enables the hearer to recover its semantic content. Consider the following dialog:

(19) A: I'm in the mood for strawberry shortcake. How about it? You make the best.
B: Sorry. It's too late.
A: *To make shortcake?* C'mon, what's so time-consuming about that?

In PE, an infinitive complement can be left alone by the ellipsis of the main clause only when there is some preceding utterance which points to the semantic content of the latter. In (19), no problem with the RCD would occur, since there is indeed an element that guarantees the recoverability of the missing main clause. Specifically, *it's too late* in B's utterance provides the key to interpret *To make shortcake?* as "Is it too late to make shortcake?"

However, the ellipsis of a PMC out of the blue is quite different. This type of ellipsis does not make sense and always results in ungrammaticality. Consider the following examples (supposing they are uttered out of the blue):

(20) a. *(I promise) never to leave you alone.
b. *(I require) that this be done right away.

Since the unrecoverable ellipsis of a PMC is not allowed in PE, we should not assume that it was possible in OE, too. Then how about the ellipsis of a PMC assumed in the derivation of PSMC's? First, PSMC's are very unlikely to be uttered in response to the interlocutor's previous utterance. This is because illocutionary acts like issuing a command or making a request are often done out of the blue. In fact, I cannot imagine a command being issued as a response to some previous utterance. Given this, why, then, did the ellipsis of a PMC not violate the RCD?

The key to answer this question, I believe, lies in the fact that there are plenty of cases in languages of the world where the meaning of an element changed as a result of being collocated with another. In such cases, the two elements involved were originally not related either syntactically or semantically. They first happened to be collocated for some discourse purpose, such as emphasis or reinforcement of a certain function, but later the collocation got conventionalised and eventually developed into a *quasi-idiomatic* relationship.

Let us take as an example the adverbial usage of *but* in (21). The meaning of *but* here can approximately be paraphrased as 'only':

(21) He is *but* a child.

This usage of *but* dates back to the combination of *ne* + *butan* in OE:

(22) þær   næran   *butan* twegen dælas
    there Neg+be:Pst:3pl except two   portions
    'There were only two portions.'   (*Orosius* I. i.)

According to *OED*, "[b]y the omission of the negative accompanying the preceding verb ..., *but* passes into the adverbial sense of: *Nought but, no more than, only, merely*" (see also Stern (1931: 264)) In short, *He is but a child* derived from something like *He is not but a child* by the ellipsis of *not*. Note that in (22), *ne* (here amalgamated with *wæran* 'were' by cliticisation (cf. Ohkado (1996)) and *butan* were simply collocated to periphrastically express the concept of 'only.' The relevant meaning of *butan* here was approximately 'except,' so if it was combined with the negation *ne* 'not,' it would yield a reading like 'not except ...' (> 'not other than ...'), which naturally leads to the concept of 'only.'

At first *ne* and *butan* were obviously both syntactically and semantically unrelated, but they were combined with each other by a strong *functional relationship*, i.e. a relationship motivated by some discourse purpose. As noted above, the practice of combining *butan* with *ne* must have started as a strategic and innovative way of expressing the concept of 'only.' Interestingly enough, after this relationship was strengthened enough to be called a quasi-idiomatic one, the negative *ne* got omitted by ellipsis. Since *ne* is a meaningful element, this ellipsis is expected to have had a potent influence on the interpretation of a sentence, but actually the remaining half of the pair, *butan*, took over the meaning of *ne*, so that no notable change in meaning occurred. It seems that the negative meaning of *ne* was somehow absorbed into *butan*.

Moreover, there are also a number of cases where the illocutionary force of an utterance type seems to be of external origin, i.e. it seems to have been "imported" from outside through collocation with another element. For example, let us examine how greeting formulas like *good morning* developed. They are very simple in form, but they take on the illocutionary force of greeting. Since *good morning* is an ordinary noun phrase, it is assumed not to have an illocutionary force by itself. Where, then, did the illocutionary force come from? The answer is quite obvious from a diachronic point of view: these greeting formulas trace back to performative utterances of the form <*I wish you* + NP>, as in (23):

(23) a. Good morning.   <   *I wish you* a good morning.
    b. A merry Christmas.   <   *I wish you* a merry Christmas.

I wish you originally signaled the illocutionary force of greeting, but today it is totally missing. This is a diachronic result of a type of ellipsis sometimes called "clipping" (cf. Stern (1931)), and it is indeed a very pervasive phenomenon (cf. *Thank you* < *I thank you*). Although the ellipsis of *I wish you* was once simply a choice to make the utterance short, now it has already disappeared from the syntactic structure altogether. Nevertheless, the illocutionary force of *I wish you* is present as if it were still overtly expressed. As in the case of *ne* + *butan*, it seems as if the meaning of *I wish you* was absorbed into the following NP.

In both of the above examples, there is seemingly a missing part in the syntactic structure, but not in the semantic structure. For example, in the case of *but* in (21), the meaning of the missing negative is somehow still alive in *but*. Such a lingering meaning of a disappeared part is just like a spirit without a body. Like a spirit, a meaning separated from its phonological form can be transferred to another element. In this way, the process of meaning transference is somewhat like the possession of the body by a spirit, so I have (somewhat jokingly) chosen to call it "meaning possession." It can be defined as a "pattern of semantic change thereby an element E_1 receives a certain component of meaning from another element E_2, which is syntactically located in the outside of E_1 and has a certain functional relationship with it."

This process is schematically illustrated in Figure 2. Suppose there are two elements, E_1 and E_2, and they have a certain *functional relationship* (FR), a relationship motivated by some discourse purpose. This is indicated by the dotted line between E_1 and E_2. In the first stage of development, the sequence of $<E_1 (...) E_2>$ is simply a preferred collocation, and the two elements are still regarded as syntactically and semantically unrelated. However, if the functional relationship is later strengthened in a local context by being frequently collocated, it may develop into a *quasi-idiomatic relationship* (QIR, indicated by the solid line):

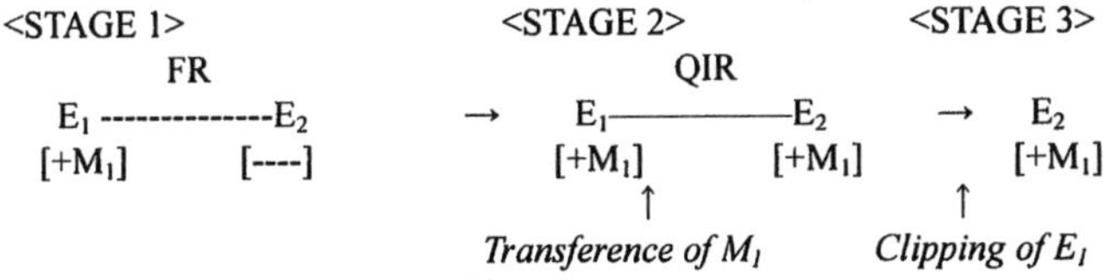

<STAGE 1>   <STAGE 2>   <STAGE 3>
     FR   QIR
E_1 -------- E_2 → E_1 ———— E_2 → E_2
$[+M_1]$ $[----]$ $[+M_1]$ $[+M_1]$ $[+M_1]$
                            ↑   ↑
                      Transference of M_1   *Clipping of E_1*
Figure 2

This is the second stage. I assume that this is the very point that transference of M_1 to E_2 takes place. As a result, both E_1 and E_2 mean M_1. Since they share exactly the same meaning component, one of them is no longer necessary, and is in fact redundant. In such a situation, one of the two elements would very likely be omitted, since language in general does not prefer more than one element in a sentence to express the same meaning. Since E_2 is semantically more informative than E_1 (the former now means M_1 in addition to its original meaning), it is natural that the latter should eventually be omitted by clipping (the third stage).

Consider again the development of *but* in (21) whose putative course of development is illustrated below (NEG stands for the negative meaning of *ne*):

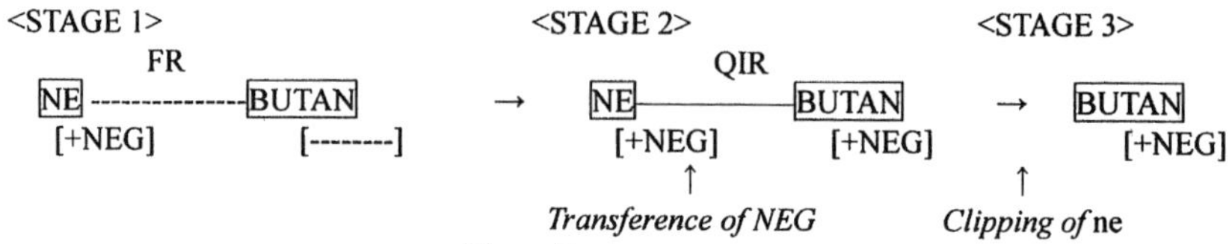

```
<STAGE 1>                      <STAGE 2>                    <STAGE 3>
      FR                           QIR
 |NE|----------|BUTAN|    →   |NE|------|BUTAN|     →    |BUTAN|
 [+NEG]        [--------]      [+NEG]    [+NEG]          [+NEG]
                                  ↑                          ↑
                          Transference of NEG        Clipping of ne
                                Figure 3
```

In the first stage, *ne* and *butan* were merely a preferred collocation. The transference of NEG to *butan* is assumed to have taken place at the time when the FR between them was strengthened into a QIR. This enabled the ellipsis of *ne* in the third stage. Let us now consider why we must postulate the transference of NEG to *butan*. If *ne* had been omitted as it stood, it would have violated the RCD. This is because it is a meaningful element, and usually the ellipsis of a negation drastically changes the reading of an utterance. In short, the RCD compels us to postulate a semantic change that had an effect of transferring NEG from *ne* to *butan*.

Let us next consider the development of the greeting formulas in (23) above. It seems that it can also be explained by use of meaning possession. If so, the course of development can be described as in Figure 4 (IL$_G$ stands for the illocutionary force of greeting):

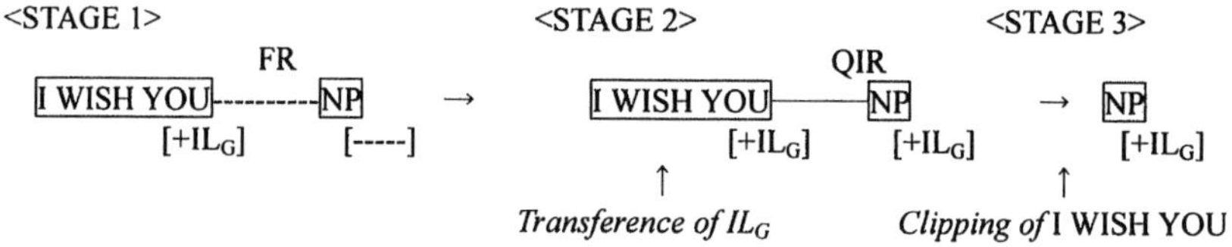

```
<STAGE 1>                          <STAGE 2>                       <STAGE 3>
         FR                            QIR
 |I WISH YOU|--------|NP|    →   |I WISH YOU|------|NP|    →       |NP|
  [+IL_G]            [-----]      [+IL_G]          [+IL_G]         [+IL_G]
                                      ↑                                ↑
                             Transference of IL_G         Clipping of I WISH YOU
                                   Figure 4
```

In fact, this type of explanation is in any case required, since otherwise the ellipsis of *I wish you* in Figure 4 must have violated the RCD (a greeting can be done out of the blue). However, this case is a bit more complicated than that of *but*. One might ask what kind of FR held between *I wish you* and the following NP. I take it to be created by what Morgan (1978) calls a "convention of usage." It is the process of pairing an utterance pattern (sentence form) with a specific discourse purpose. This pairing may be strengthened enough to become a convention.

For example, Morgan speaks of the development of *good-bye*. This formula is a shortened form of *May God be with you*, a formula of prayer. The reason that the latter became a formula of greeting is that the speakers of that time happened to prefer to say it as a valediction. So it might have been pure chance that the way of greeting later caught on among speakers. In this process, greeting by saying *May God be with you* came to become a convention of usage. In the case of greeting formulas in (23), using <*I wish you* + NP> for greeting must at first have been a newly innovated way of greeting. But this practice somehow caught on in the society, and the utterance pattern was strongly paired with the act of greeting, strongly enough to be called a convention of usage. At this stage, the sequence <*I wish you* + NP> was regarded as a specialised pattern of greeting. That is, the sequence became a functional unit motivated by a specific discourse purpose (i.e. greeting). As a result of this, then, a quasi-idiomatic relation was created between *I wish you* and the following NP. This, I believe, set the stage for transference of IL$_G$ from *I wish you* to the following NP.

Let us now return to the development of PSMC's. The above analysis of greeting formulas in (23) serves as a good starting point. Recall that the major problem with the analysis in (18) was that the ellipsis of PMC's assumed in the first stage of development must have violated the RCD. But we now have a strong device to solve the problem: meaning transference. Therefore, my answer to the question above is simple: the relevant meaning component of PMC's was transferred to the SNC's before they got omitted by clipping, as illustrated in Figure 5.

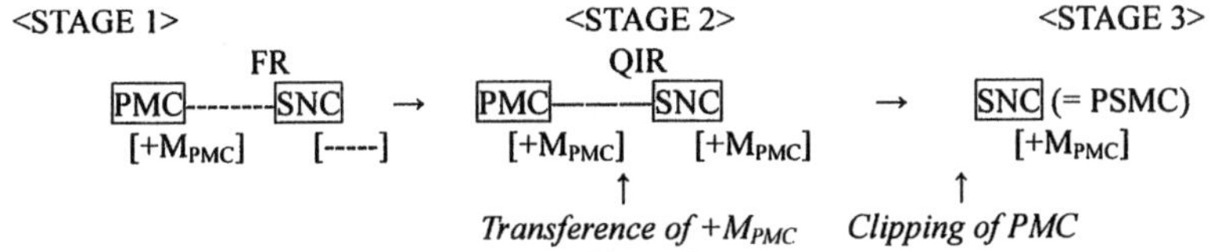

<STAGE 1>   <STAGE 2>   <STAGE 3>

$$\begin{array}{ccc}
\text{FR} & \text{QIR} & \\
\boxed{\text{PMC}}\text{------}\boxed{\text{SNC}} \rightarrow & \boxed{\text{PMC}}\text{------}\boxed{\text{SNC}} \rightarrow & \boxed{\text{SNC}}\,(=\text{PSMC}) \\
[+M_{PMC}]\quad [\text{-----}] & [+M_{PMC}]\quad\quad [+M_{PMC}] & [+M_{PMC}] \\
& \uparrow \quad\quad\quad\quad\quad\uparrow & \\
& \textit{Transference of} +M_{PMC}\quad \textit{Clipping of PMC} &
\end{array}$$

Figure 5

The combination of a PMC and an SNC was originally merely one of the two possible patterns of complementation. In fact, an infinitival clause was also used instead of an SNC without any notable change in meaning. However, this utterance pattern <PMC + SNC> somehow came to be increasingly recognised as a conventional way of performing certain illocutionary acts, which eventually yielded a convention of usage; in other words, the sequence <PMC + SNC> is strongly paired with performance of these acts (the first stage). This created an FR between the two, which eventually developed into a QIR (the second stage). This was in my opinion, the very moment when meaning transference occurred: the relevant meaning component of the PMC's (M_{PMC} in Figure 5) was transferred to the SNC's, which made a PMC unnecessary to perform the illocutionary acts. The RCD no longer prevented the ellipsis of PMC's, since the recoverability of their meaning was "internally" satisfied. Later this ellipsis somehow became canonical, and before long PMC's disappeared from the syntactic structure altogether as a result of reanalysis. This is the last stage of the development.

There is yet another point to be addressed. In the case of *ne-butan*, the relationship which eventually led to meaning transference was *one-to-one*. As for *I wish you*-NP, it was *one-to-many*, i.e. *I wish you* was related to a number of NP's. In the case of PSMC's, it was *many-to-one*: SNC's were related to various performative predicates. Therefore, we must assume that the form of meaning transference with PSMC's was rather different from those with the former two cases. It seems that in the case of the latter, the transferred meaning is extracted from those elements which together constitute the *source* of meaning transference (cf. Maeda (2006)). I have called this process "abstraction." What is abstracted is a common meaning component shared by all the source elements involved.

Consider now the meanings of performative predicates in (9) again. All of them could be used to perform illocutionary acts by which a speaker sought to realise his or her desire, such as issuing an order, making a request, asking for permission, etc. Therefore, at least when they were used as PMC's and collocated with SNC's, all of them implied, or were at least compatible with, "I want X to happen" (here "I" is added because PMC's are always understood as having a first-person subject; cf. fn. 1). Consider again the examples in (10). In these examples, the speaker is making a request, so he or she surely wants the event described in the SNC's to take place (if he or she is sincere). Given this, the meaning component abstracted and transferred from a number of PMC's to SNC's can be described as "I want X to happen." To summarise, the process of meaning possession in Figure 5 should be elaborated as Figure 6:

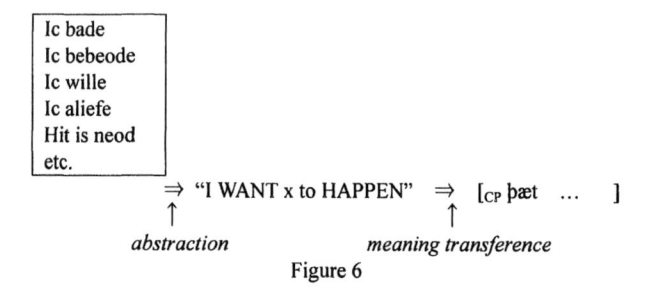

```
Ic bade
Ic bebeode
Ic wille
Ic aliefe
Hit is neod
etc.
         ⇒  "I WANT x to HAPPEN"  ⇒  [CP þæt  ...  ]
         ↑                            ↑
      abstraction              meaning transference
                    Figure 6
```

The common meaning component "I want X to happen" is first extracted from a number of PMC's (abstraction), which is then transferred to SNC's (meaning transference).

If this analysis is correct, we can explain how the range of readings of PSMC's in (5)-(7) were yielded. Consider first the reading of (5b), repeated here:

(5) b. Ne *bepæce*   nan man hine   sylfne
       Neg deceive:Subj:3sg no   man him:A Ref:A
       'Let no man deceive himself.'

The reading of (5b), roughly speaking, consists of the constructional template "I want X to happen" and the propositional content of SNC's (which substitutes for the variable X). Therefore, the reading of (5b) is something like "I want <no man deceiving himself> to happen," which would have actually been interpreted as "I pray any man not to deceive himself." Let us next turn to (6b), repeated here:

(6) b. *fare* we on ge-hende tunas
   go:Subj:1pl we in next:A   towns:A
   'Let us go into the next towns.'

Examples like (6) with a first-person, plural subject are construed as hortatives. Under the present analysis, (6b) means something like "I want <us going into the next towns> to happen," or "I want us to go into the next towns," which would have implied "Let's go into the next towns." As for (7), it means something like "I want <you waiting on the barrow> to happen," or "I want you to wait on the barrow," which could have been construed as a command.

(7) *Gebide*   ge on berg
   wait:Subj:2sg you in barrow:D
   'Wait on the barrow.'

Note that the difference in reading among (5b), (6b) and (7) is obviously due to the person of the subject of PSMC's. In other words, it derives from the combination of "I want X to happen" and clauses with subjects in different persons.

Finally, the optative interpretation of PSMCs like that in (8) is somewhat problematic, since the person of the subject of PSMC's does not seem to be relevant to the interpretation, i.e. the subject of optative PSMC's could in principle be in any person (cf. *May you be very happy*; *May I be happy forever*). In this connection, I argued in Maeda (2006) that optatives are jussives directed to some supernatural being (typically God). In fact, when a jussive is directed to God, it can only be interpreted as an optative. Consider the example in (25):

(25) Please God, let her telephone me.   (*Collins Cobuild Advanced English Dictionary*)

Since this jussive is directed to God, not anyone around, it cannot be interpreted as issuing a command or making a request. Therefore, it is necessarily interpreted as a wish. If this analysis is correct, the optative readings of PSMC's are merely a special case of jussive readings.

This way, if we assume that the meaning component approximately described as "I want X to happen" was transferred from PMC's to SNC's, we can easily explains the four readings of PSMC's observed in OE texts. Furthermore, it also enables us to account for the reason why the ellipsis of PMC's postulated in (18) did not violate the RCD: as a result of meaning transference, PSMC's came to embrace the meaning of PMC's and be able to satisfy the RCD "internally."

5. Conclusion

In this paper, I mainly made two points. First, I argued that PSMC's were derived from SNC's selected by PMC's like *ic bidde* 'I command.' The most telling evidence for this hypothesis is the existence of PSMC's with *þæt* (cf. (11)). The beginning of this development is assumed to be the ellipsis of the PMC and its conventionalisation. The surface order of PSMC's in (12a) is derived by the ellipsis of *þæt* and associated fronting of the subjunctive verb. The putative course of development is summarised in (18). However, this scenario would be very problematic, since the ellipsis of a PMC assumed in (18) seems to violate the RCD: since PMC's like *ic bidde* are meaningful, they cannot be omitted unless they are uttered as a response to the interlocutor's previous utterance. However, it seems very unlikely that the putative ellipsis of PMC's was done in this way. My second claim is that a type of semantic change which I called "meaning possession" occurred in the utterance pattern <PMC + SNC> before the ellipsis of the PMC was done. This change had the effect of transferring a meaning component extracted from various of PMC's to SNC's, and as a result of this, isolated SNC's (= PSMC's) could satisfy the RCD "internally." I argued furthermore that the component transferred can be approximately described as "I want X to happen," and the four readings of PSMC's can be assumed to occur by combining this component with clauses with subjects in different persons.

References

Austin, James L.
    1975   *How to Do Things with Words*. (2nd ed.) Cambridge, Massachusetts: Harvard University Press.

Bybee, Joan, Revere Perkins, and William Pagliuca
    1994   *The Evolution of Grammar: Tense, Aspect, and Modality in the language of the world*: Chicago: The University of Chicago Press.

Fischer, Olga, Ans van Kemenade, Willem Koopman and Wim van der Wurff
    2000   *The Syntax of Early English*. Cambridge: Cambridge University Press.

Jones, Michael A.
    1996   *Foundations of French Syntax*. Cambridge: Cambridge University Press.

Kurata, Kiyoshi
    1995   *Du Français en Japonais*. Tokyo: Taishukan Publish Company.

Maeda, Mitsuru
    2006   "Insubordination and Semantic Change", *English and English-American literature* 41: 47-85

Mitchell, Bruce
    1985   *Old English Syntax*, Vol. 1. Oxford: Clarendon Press.

Morgan, J. L.
    1978   "Two Types of Convention in Indirect Speech Acts", in Cole, Peter. (ed.), *Syntax and Semantics* 9: *Pragmatics*. New York: Academic Press, 261-280.
Ohkado, Masayuki
    1996   "NEG1 Constructions in Old English," *English Linguistics* 13: 277-298.
    2001   *Old English Constructions with Multiple Predicates*. Tokyo: Hituzi Shobo.
Sag, Ivan
    1980   *Deletion and Logical Form*. New York and London: Garland Publishing, Inc.
Stern, Gustaf
    1931   *Meaning and Change of Meaning*. (Reprint). Westport, Connecticut: Greenwood Press, Publishers.
Tabor, Whitney and Elizabeth C. Traugott
    1998   "Structural Scope Expansion and Grammaticalization", in Ramat, Anna G. and Paul J. Hopper (eds.), *The Limits of Grammaticalization*. Amsterdam: John Benjamin, 229-272.
Visser, Frederikus Th.
    1966   *An Historical Syntax of the English Language*, vol. 2. Leiden: E. J. Brill.

8 Variant Readings in the Two Manuscripts of the West Saxon Gospels: MSS CCCC 140 and CUL Ii.2.11

Michiko Ogura, Chiba University

1. Introduction

The original manuscript of the West Saxon Gospels is said to have been lost before the extant four manuscripts of the 10th and 11th century: Corpus Christi College, Cambridge 140 (MS. Cp), Bodley 441 (MS. B), Cotton Otho C. 1 (Vol. I) (MS. C) and University Library, Cambridge Ii.2.11 (MS. A). The relation between these manuscripts and later ones is presented by Skeat (1878: x):[1]

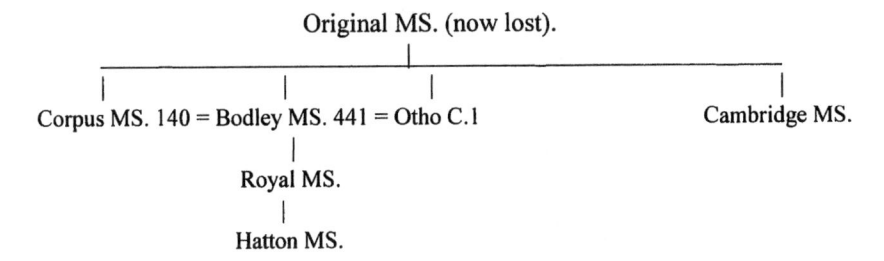

```
                    Original MS. (now lost).
        _____|_____
        |         |          |                    |
Corpus MS. 140 = Bodley MS. 441 = Otho C.1    Cambridge MS.
                    |
                Royal MS.
                    |
                Hatton MS.
```

The resemblance between the three manuscripts (Cp, B and C) is notable, while the peculiarity of MS. A is quite independent.[2] From the explanation of Liuzza (1994), the innovative attitude of A's scribe is obvious in the way of paraphrasing, making paragraphs with additional instructions,[3] and not correcting but changing the original readings.[4]

---

1 W. W. Skeat (ed.), *The Gospel according to Saint Luke* (1878; rpt. 1970), p. x.
2 Liuzza (1994), pp. lv-lvi: "A avoids the errors of CpBC, while containing a number of mechanical errors not found in other MSS ... . Its text therefore represents neither a descendant nor an ancestor of CpBC."
3 *Ibid.*, p. lvii: "It is also by far the most elaborate copy: paraphrasing is much fuller, and most paragraphs are preceded by a textual apparatus consisting of OE rubrics (indicating the mass at which the Gospel passage is to be read) and Latin incipits (containing the first words of the periscope). These features of A's design suggests that it is a later version of the unadorned translation found in CpBC; a sophisticated design and lectionary system are more likely to have been added than omitted in the dissemination of a text." Additional texts in Old English are tantamount to 75 in Mt, 27 in Mk, 45 in Lk (comparatively infrequent) and 60 in Jn. There are a few parts of verses omitted in each Gospel and many words and parts of words added by a later hand.
4 *Ibid.*, p. lvii: "CpBC may preserve an original reading, even a mistaken one, which A has altered."

The aim of this paper is to classify the differences between MS. Cp and MS. A, to exemplify major differences, and to show which can be the most significant differences as free translation of virtually the same Latin original.[5]

2. Lexical differences

MS. Cp is dated 995 or XI[1] (originated in Bath) and MS. A 1050 or XI[3rd quarter] (originated in Exeter).[6] The lexical choice, therefore, does not show a dialectal difference but a difference in choice among the synonyms. Typical instances are (Cp) *befrinan* vs. (A) *acsian* (Mt 2.7), (Cp) *gebolgen* vs. (A) *gedrefed* (Mt 2.16), (Cp) *mid* vs. (A) *wið* (Mt 6.1), (Cp) *bearn* vs. (A) *sunu* (Mt 20.20, 26.64), (Cp) *gefylstan* vs. (A) *gemyltsian* (Mt 15.25), (Cp) *wircan* vs. (A) *don* (Mt 1.24), (Cp) *faran* vs. (A) *feran* (Mk 5.17), (Cp) *gram* vs. (A) *yrre* (Mk 14.6), (Cp) *secgan* vs. (A) *cweðan* (Mk 14.57), (Cp) *hrægl* vs. (A) *clap* (Lk 2.12), (Cp) *gehæftan* vs. (A) *geswencan* (Lk 8.37), (Cp) *oferwinnan* vs. (A) *oferswiðan* (Lk 11.22), (Cp) *folc* vs. (A) *mænigeo* (Jn 6.2), and (Cp) *gan* vs. (A) *gangan* (Jn 7.33). I find 44 instances of different choice in Mt, 27 in Mk, 45 in Lk and 27 in Jn. The lexical choice is not so complete as found in the Psalter glosses[7] that MS. A is not systematic in choosing renderings for particular Latin words.

3. Prepositions

Prepositions are not indispensable in renderings as long as the case endings are reliable in understanding the context. Compare, for instance, Mt 5.22 [*quia autem dixerit fratri suo*] (Cp) *Soþlice se þe segð hys breðer* vs. (A) *Soðlice se þe segð to his breðer* with Lk 20.42 [*Dixit Dominum Domino meo*] (Cp) *drihten sæde to minum drihtne* vs. (A) *dryhten sæde minum dryhtne*. Prepositions often differ as in the following example (underline mine):

(1) Jn 17.15 [Non rogo ut tollas eos de mundo, sed ut serues eos ex malo.]
 Cp: Ne bidde ic þ þu hi nyme of middanearde. ac þ þu hi gehealde of yfele;
 A: Ne bydde ic þ ðu hig nyme of myddanearde. ac þ ðu hig gehealde fram yfele.
 'I do not pray that thou shouldest take them out of the world, but that thou shouldest keep them from evil.'

The statistic result can be summarised as in Table 1.[8]

---

5 It is a composite version of the non-Vulgate versions. Here I use Wordsworth-White (1973) as one of the closest editions.
6 See Liuzza (1994) and Ker (1957).
7 For the "Winchester" words, see Hofstetter (1988).
8 Differences are: *on* vs. Ø, *mid* vs. Ø, Ø vs. *to*, Ø vs. *on*, Ø vs. *myd*, *to* vs. *on*, *mid* vs. *wið*, *of* vs. *on* in Mt; *on* vs. Ø, *in* vs. *into* in Mk; *to* vs. Ø (twice), *æt* vs. Ø, Ø vs. *to* (three times), *of* vs. *on*, *æt* vs. *on*, *on* vs. *of* in Lk; *fram* vs. Ø, *on* vs. Ø, Ø vs. *of*, Ø vs. *on*, *of* vs. *on* (twice), *æt* vs. fram, of vs. fram, of vs. myd, of vs. oð, on vs. on 'ł of' in Jn.

Table 1: Different choice of prepositions

	Mt	Mk	Lk	Jn	Total
Cp / Ø	2	1	3	2	8
Ø / A	3	0	3	2	8
Cp / A	3	1	3	7	14

N.B. Cp / Ø = a preposition found in Cp does not appear in A
Ø / A = a preposition found in A does not appear in Cp
p / A = prepositions differ in Cp and A

4. Prefixes

Prefixes are also likely to change, appear, or disappear, as long as they are semantically insignificant. For instance, Lk 7.5 [*et synagogam ipse aedificauit nobis*] (Cp) ⁊ *he us ure samnunge getimbrode* vs. (A) ⁊ *he us ure gesamnunge tymbrode* 'and he built us our synagogue', Jn 6.13 [*Collegerunt ergo, et impleuerunt duodecim cophinos fragmentorum*] (Cp) *hi gegaderedon* ⁊ *fyldon twelf wyligeon fulle þæra brytsena* vs. (A) *hig gaderodon* ⁊ *gefyldon twelf wylian fulle þæra gebrytsena* 'they gathered (them) and filled twelve baskets with full of the fragments', and the *a-/on-* correspondence particularly found in Mk, e.g. Mk11.18 [*timebant enim eum*] (Cp) *þeh hi him adredon hine* vs. (A) *þeh hig hyne hym ondredon* 'yet they were afraid of him'. Sometimes he different choice of prefixes become significant lexically and stylistically, though not semantically. E.g.

(2) Mt 10.41 [Qui recipit prophetam in nomine prophetae, mercedem prophetae accipiet: et qui recipit iustem in nomine iusti, mercedem iusti accipiet.]
Cp: Se þe underfehð witegan on witegan naman he onfehþ witygan mede. And se þe <u>underfehþ</u> rihtwisne on rihtwises naman he onfehþ rihtwies mede.
A: Se ðe underfehð witegan on wytegan naman he onfehð witegan mede. ⁊ se ðe <u>onfehð</u> ryhtwisne on ryhtwises naman. he onfehð ryhtwises mede.
'He who receives a prophet in the name of a prophet shall receive a prophet's reward; and he who receives a righteous man in the name of a righteous man shall receive a righteous man's reward.'

The statistic result is summarised in Table 2. The use and non-use of a prefix in the same context is much the same in the number of occurrences, and the alteration of prefixes is often found in Mk and Lk.

Table 2: Different choice of prefixes

	Mt	Mk	Lk	Jn	Total
Cp / Ø	21	7	12	5	45
Ø / A	12	9	18	7	46
Cp / A	6	23	39	1	69

5. Pronouns and particles

Function words, especially demonstrative pronouns, personal pronouns and particle *þe*, are often added or subtracted.[9] It is typical of West Saxon manuscripts to insert a nominative personal pronoun which does not appear in Latin: e.g. Mt 8.25 [*et suscitauerunt eum*] (Cp) ⁊ *hy awehton hyne* vs. (A) ⁊ *awehton hyne*. Particularly in Mt a demonstrative pronoun in a phrase in MS. Cp appears in possessive in MS. A: e.g. Mt 21.8 [*in uia*] (Cp) *on þone weg* vs. (A) *on hys weg*. Sometimes a demonstrative pronoun used as a relative can be expressed by a personal pronoun as a variant, or vice versa, e.g.

(3) Lk 9.24 [Qui enim uoluerit animam suam saluam facere, perdet illam: nam qui perdiderit animam suam propter me, saluam faciet illam.]
    Cp: Se þe wyle hys sawle hale gedon; se hig forspilþ; witodlice se ðe his sawle for me forspilð he hi gehælð;
    A: Se þe wyle hys sawle hale gedon se hig forspylð. Witodlice se ðe his sawle for me forspylð. se hig gehælð.
    'He who wishes to make his soul whole (he) will destroy it. Truly he who destroy his soul for the sake of me (he) will make it whole.'

Table 3 summarises the result. (The pronouns are classified into nominative, genitive, dative and accusative so that we may find which case is involved most in variant readings.

Table 3: Different choice of pronouns

Cp / A	Mt	Mk	Lk	Jn	Total
Nom	8 / 8	4 / 4	4 / 10*	4 / 11**	20 / 33
Gen	1 / 5	1 / 0	2 / 0	0 / 2***	4 / 7
Dat	4 / 1	1 / 2	2 / 3	2 / 7	9 / 13
Acc	4 / 1	0 / 1	1 / 0	1 / 2	6 / 4

N. B.   * 4 instances in a later hand
       ** 2 instances in a later hand
       *** 1 instance in a later hand

---

9   For other function words, and (⁊) is added or subtracted in the manuscripts, regardless of the original Latin. The choice of additional and (together with *and cwæð*) can be summarised as follows.

Cp / A	Mt	Mk	Lk	Jn	Total
And−	1 / 0	3 / 2		0 / 1*	4 / 3
L$_1$ and L$_2$	3 / 2	2 / 1	0 / 2*	1 / 0	6 / 5
Cl$_1$ and Cl$_2$	3 / 1	2 / 5	3 / 4	1 / 4	9 / 14
and cwæð	0 / 1	0 / 1			0 / 2

N. B.   And   − = And used initially; L = lexeme; Cl = clause
          * one instance of the occurrences in a later hand
Another structure is '*ne* V (S) *na*'; *na* is added twice in Mt and once in Jn in MS. A, and once in Mk and once in Lk in MS. Cp.

þæge is a form exclusively found in MS. Cp in the four earlier manuscripts, denoting 'they, them, those' (Mt 20.9, Jn 4.40, 10.16, 12.20, 14.12), which corresponds to *þa* or *þe* in MS. A.[10]

(4) Jn 14.12 [et maiora horum faciet, quia ego ad Patrem uado.]
    Cp: ⁊ he wyrcð maran þon*ne* <u>bæge</u> synt forþam þe ic fare to fæder.
    A: ⁊ he wyrcð maran þonn*e* <u>þa</u> synd. forþa*m* ðe ic fare to fæder.
    'and he does (the works) more than these are, because I go to my father'

6. Verb forms
6.1. 'V *ge/we*'
Verb forms often disagree in the two manuscripts. The feature that looks most characteristic of MS. A is the use of 'V-*on* (or V-*að*) *ge/we*' in contrast with 'V-*e ge/we*' in MS. Cp.[11] According to the Old English grammar, the first and second person plural verb endings can be reduced to -*e* in VS order,[12] but it is not a strict rule. Two types of constructions are notable in rendering Latin, as seen in (5) and (6).[13]

(5) Mt 23.9 [Et patrem nolite uocare uobis super terram]
    Cp: ⁊ <u>ne nemne ge</u> eow fædyr ofer eorþan.
    A: ⁊ <u>ne nemnon ge</u> eow fæder ofer eorðan.
    'and do not call you yourselves father upon the earth'

(6) Jn 7.31 [Christus cum uenerit, numquid plura signa faciet quam quae hic facit?]
    Cp: <u>Cweþe ge</u> wyrcð crist ma tacna þon*ne* he cymð þon*ne* þes deð.
    A: <u>Cweðað ge</u> wyrcð cryst ma tacna. Þonn*e* he cymð þonne ðes deð.
    'Do you say that Christ will work, when he comes, more miracles than this (man) does?'

6.2. Infinitives and participles
Verb forms ending in *–an*, (*to*) *–anne/-enne* and *–ende* can be variants, together with present and preterit forms. This is partly because of the free translation, i.e.

---

10 See Ogura (2001).
11 Mt 6.34 [nolite ... esse] (Cp) Ne beo ge vs. (A) Ne beon ge; Mt 23.9 [nolite uocare] (Cp) ne nemne ge vs. (A) ne nemnon ge; Mt 25.38 [uidimus] (Cp) gesawe we vs. (A) gesawon we; Mt 25.45 [nec ... fecistis] (Cp) ne dyde ge vs. (A) ne dydon ge; Mk 4.13 [cognoscetis] (Cp) mage ge ... witan vs. (A) magon ge ... witan; Lk 7.24 [existis] (Cp) ferde ge vs. (A) ferdon we (sic); Lk 12.4 [Ne terreamini] (Cp) ne beo ge bregyde vs. (A) ne beoð ge bregyde; Jn 7.31 [Numquid] (Cp) Cweþe ge vs. (A) Cweðað ge; Jn 9.41 [non haberetis] (Cp) næfde ge vs. (A) næfdon ge; Jn 14.5 [possumus ... scire] (Cp) mage we ... cunnan vs. (A) magon we ... cunnan.
12 See Campbell (1959), § 730.
13 For the structural devises in translating Latin rhetorical questions and the reason why cweðan is used therein, see Ogura (1984).

the scribe can either follow the original which is close to Latin or use his West Saxon phrasings. I choose three examples for illustration.[14]

(7) Mt 13.17 [Amen quippe dico uobis: quia multi prophetae et iusti cupierunt uidere quae uidetis, et non uiderunt: et audire quae auditis, et non audierunt.]
Cp: Soþlice on eornust ic eow secge þ manega witegan ⁊ rihtwise gewilnudon þa þing to geseonne þe ge geseoþ ⁊ hig ne gesawon; ⁊ <u>gehyran</u> þa þing þe ge gehyrað. ⁊ hig ne gehyrdon;
A: Soðlice on eornost ic eow secge þ manega witegan ⁊ ryhtwise gewylnedon þa þing to geseonne þe ge geseoð. ⁊ hig ne gesawon. ⁊ <u>to gehyranne</u> þa ðing þe ge gehyrað. ⁊ hig ne gehyrdon.
'Truly in earnest I say to you that many prophets and righteous men wished to see those things which ye see, and did not see them; and to hear those things which ye hear, and did not hear them.'

(8) Lk 12.45 [et coeperit percutere pueros et ancillas, et edere, et bibere, et inebriari]
Cp: ⁊ agynð beatan þa cnihtas ⁊ þa þinena. ⁊ <u>etan</u> ⁊ <u>drincan</u> ⁊ <u>beon</u> oferdruncen.
A: ⁊ agynð beatan þa cnyhtas ⁊ þa þynena. ⁊ <u>etað</u> ⁊ <u>dryncað</u> ⁊ <u>beoð</u> oferdruncene.
'(the servant) shall begin to beat the men-servants and maid-ervants and to eat and drink and be drunken'

(9) Jn 7.25 [Nonne hic est quem quaerunt interficere?]
Cp: hu nis ðis se ðe hi seceað <u>to ofsleande</u>:
A: hu nys þys se. þe hig secað <u>to ofsleanne</u>
'Isn't this he whom they seek to kill?'

The use of the infinitive in Cp in (7) can be caused by the distance from the main verb *gewilnudon*. In (8) Cp, as Latin reads, uses infinitives which agree with *beatan*, while A uses present forms which agree with *agynð*. In (9) (and some other examples in footnote 14) it looks as if the *–ende/-enne* interchange, which probably originated from assimilation and became obvious after early Middle English, has already started in late Old English.

6.3. Negative contraction

The negative contraction is said to be a West Saxon feature,[15] and so the interchangeability between the contracted and the non-contracted forms in the two manuscripts is not so frequent. Thus *neom* in Cp corresponds to *ne eom* in A four

---

14 Other examples are: Mt 2.22 [*ire*] (Cp) *farende* vs. (A) *faranne*; Mk 6.6 [*docens*] (Cp) *lærde* vs. (A) *lærende*; Lk 1.21 [*mirabantur*] (Cp) *wundrodon* vs. (A) *wundrigende*; Lk 4.28 [*audientes*] (Cp) *gehyrende* vs. (A) *gehyrde*; Lk 5.13 [*extendens*] (Cp) *apenede* vs. (A) *apenigende*; Lk 5.17 [*ad sanandum*] (Cp) *to gehælende* vs. (A) *to gehælenne*; Lk 9.2 [*praedicare*] (Cp) *to bodianne* vs. (A) *bodigende*; Lk 9.31 [*completurus erat*] (Cp) *to gefyllende* vs. (A) *to gefyllene*; Lk 24..21 [*esset redempturus*] (Cp) *to alysenne* vs. (A) *alysende*.
15 See Levin (1958).

times (Mt 3.11, Lk 15.19, 18.11, Jn 3.28). Here I quote one example, together with he only instance of *ne dyde/nydde*.

(10) Lk 15.19 [et iam non sum dignus uocari filius tuus:]
  Cp: nu ic <u>neom</u> wyrðe þ ic beo þin sunu nemned
  A: nu ic <u>ne</u> <u>eom</u> wyrðe þ ic beo þyn sunu genemned
  'now I am not worthy to be called thy son'

Cf. 15.21 (*Cp* = *A*) nu ic <u>ne</u> <u>eom</u> wyrþe þ ic þin sunu beo genemned

(11) Mk 5.10 [Et deprecabatur eum multum. Ne se expelleret extra regionem.]
  Cp: ⁊ he hine swyðe bæd þ he hine of þam rice <u>ne</u> <u>dyde</u>.
  A: ⁊ he hyne swyðe bæd. þ he hyne of þam rice <u>ne</u> <u>nydde</u>.
  'and he prayed him so much that he should not make him go out of the country'

7. Element order

Word order or element order varies in many more ways than is necessary. Table 4 is given to show how often the two manuscripts differ in element order, which is closer to Latin, and how ambiguous the renderings can be.

Table 4: Where and how the element order differs in Cp and A

	Mt	Mk	Lk	Jn	Total
Cp ≠ A	33	23	23	19	98
(Cp = Latin)	(20)	(7)	(8)	(3)	(38)
(A = Latin)	(5)	(13)	(6)	(5)	(29)
(OE ≠ Latin)	(8)	(3)	(9)	(11)	(31)

Thus the different order of the renderings of *amen dico uobis/tibi* can be regarded as stylistic variants, e.g.

(12)   Cp   A
      [Amen (amen) dico uobis]
Mt 18.18   Soþlice ic secge eow   Soþlice ic eow secge
Mt 23.36   Soþlice ic eow secge   Soþ ic secge eow
Jn 6.26   Soþ ic eow secge   Soþ ic secge eow
       [Amen dico tibi]
Mt 5.26   Soþes ic secge þe   Soþes ic þ secge

The element order may vary and, as a result, one follows Latin order and the other does not, as in

(13)   *Cp* follows Latin order   *A* follows Latin order
     Mt 1.18 [in utero habens]   Mt 3.14 [tu uenis]
     Cp: on innoðe hæbbende   *Cp*: cymst ðu
     A: hæbbende on innoðe   *A*:   þu cymst

Mk 16.16 [baptizatus fuerit]
Cp: gefullod bið
A: bið gefullod
Lk 10.34 [oleum et uinum]
Cp: ele ⁊ win
A: win ⁊ ele
Jn 2.4 [mihi et tibi]
Cp: me ⁊ þe
A: þe ⁊ me

Mk 7.32 [adducunt ei]
Cp: hine bædon
A: bædon hyne
Lk 19.43 [uenient ... in te]
Cp: to ðe cumað
A: cumað to ðe
Jn 9.2 [interrogauerunt eum]
Cp: hine axodon
A: acsedon hyne

But when we find (more than) two elements for (virtually) one Latin lexeme, and moreover, when it is outside the regulation of Old English grammar,[16] we cannot tell which should be appropriate for a particular context: e.g. Mt 2.4 [*nasceretur*] (Cp) *accenned wære* vs. (A) *wære accenned*; Mk 2.26 [*non licet*] (Cp) *ne alyfede næron* vs. (A) *næron alyfede*; Lk 8.39 [*fecit*] (Cp) *gedon hæfð* vs. (A) *hæfð gedon*; Jn 13.26 [*dedit*] (Cp) *he sealde hyne* vs. (A) *he hyne sealde*. The general tendency of the Synoptic Gospels tells us that VO, SV and V Prep-ph (prepositional phrase) are frequently found in A, where OV, VS and Prep-ph V are chosen in Cp, but the element order varies so widely that the order seems subsidiary to the case distinction and/or stylistic collocation of late West Saxon variety.

8. Other differences

Now let us see some more examples that illustrate those differences which lead to different interpretations. Example (14) illustrates A's peculiar reading that differs from Cp and Latin, which might be caused by a spelling mistake of *nyme* for *mine* and results in the subsequent addition of ⁊ before the original main verb *wyrce*.

(14) Lk 22.11 [Dicit tibi magister: Ubi est diuersorium, ubi Pascha cum discipulis meis manducem?]
   Cp: Ure lareow þe segð hwar ys cumena hus. þar ic <u>mine eastron wyrce</u> mid minon leorningcnihtum;
   A: Ure lareow þe segð hwar ys cumena hus. þar ic <u>nyme eastron</u>. ⁊ <u>wyrce</u> myd mynum leorningcnyhtum.
   'Our Lord says to thee, Where is the guest-chamber, where I keep (eat) my Easter with my disciples?'

Example (15) shows a lexical difference, which can be a mistake of MS.A and leads to a slightly different interpretation.

(15) Lk 3.14 [Neminem concuitatis, neque calumniam faciatis: et content; estote stipendiis uestris]
   Cp: Ne <u>tále</u> ne doð. ⁊ beoð eð-hylde on eowrum andlyfenum;
   A: Ne <u>stale</u> ne doð. ⁊ beoð eð-hylde on eowrum ⁊lyfenum.
   'Do no false accusation (Do no theft) and be satisfied with your living'

---

16 Like the so-called "emphatic order"; see Andrew (1940).

Example (16) is another lexical difference, where Cp chooses a verb different from Latin.

(16) Jn 7.17 [Si quis uoluerit uoluntatem eius facere, cognoscet de doctrina, utrum ex Deo sit, an ego a me ipso loquar.]
　　Cp: gyf hwa wyle his willan don he <u>gecwemð</u> be þære lare hwæþer heo si of gode hwæþer þe ic be me sylfum sprece;
　　A: gif hwa wyle hys wyllan don. He <u>gecnæwð</u> be þære lare hwæðer heo sig of gode. hwæþer þe ic be me sylfum spece.
　　'if any man wishes to do his will, he knows of the teaching, whether it be from God or whether I speak about myself'

There are at least five examples in which *hi(g) ne* and *hine* are involved. In (17)[17], (18)[18] and (19) the readings of Cp are correct, no matter which form it chooses.

(17) Mt 17.16 [et optuli eum discipulis tuis, et non potuerunt curare eum.]
　　Cp: ⁊ ic brohte hyne to þinum leorningcnihtum: ⁊ <u>hig ne</u> mihton hyne gehælan;
　　A: ⁊ ic brohte hyne to þynum leorning-cnihtum. ⁊ <u>hyne</u> myhton hyne gehælan.
　　'and I brought him to thy disciples, and they could not cure him'

(18) Mk 16.14 [quia his qui uiderant eum resurrexisse, non crediderant.]
　　Cp: forðam þe hi ne gelyfdon þam ðe <u>hine</u> gesawon of deaþe arisan.
　　A: forþamðe hig ne gelyfdon þam ðe <u>hig ne</u> gesawon. of deaðe arysan.
　　'because they did not believe them who saw him risen from death'

(19) Jn 8.27 [Et non cognouerunt quia Patrem eis dicebat.]
　　Cp: ⁊ <u>hig ne</u> undergeton þ he tæalde him god to fæder;
　　A: ⁊ <u>hig hyne</u> undergeaton. þ he tealde hym god to fæder.
　　'and they did not understand that he told them God as father'

In (20) the reading of A is correct as a rendering of Latin *none*.[19]

(20) Jn 4.35 [Nonne uos dicitis, quod ad huc quattuor menses sunt, et messis uenit?]
　　Cp: <u>Hyne</u> secge ge þ nu gyt synt feowur monðas ær man ripan mæge
　　A: <u>hu ne</u> secge ge. þ nu git synd feower monþas ær man rypan mæge
　　'Do ye not say that there are yet four months before one could reap?'

In (21) A is right in using *ne* once, as is Latin; it is not necessary to repeat *ne* in the second clause in co-ordination.

17　Mt 17.15 in Riuzza (1994).
18　The main verb is *gelyfan* and it is negated, and so the occurrence of pleonastic *ne* is not totally implausible, but the chance of the verb to be used in such a construction is far less than the case of *tweogan* or *wenan*. See Ogura (1986) and (2007).
19　Cf. (6) and (9), and see Ogura (1984).

(21) Jn 12.40 [Excaecauit oculos eorum, et indurauit eorum cor: ut non uideant oculis, et intellegant corde]
    Cp: he ablende hyra eagan. ⁊ ahyrde hyra heortan þ hi <u>ne</u> geseon mid hyra æagon ⁊ mid hyra heortan <u>ne</u> ongyton.
    A: he ablende heora eagan. ⁊ ahyrde heora heortan þ hig <u>ne</u> geseon myd heora eagon. ⁊ myd heora heortan ongitan.
    'he blinded their eyes and hardened their heart so that they should not see with their eyes (n)or understand with their heart'

In (22) *ne* appears mistakenly in Cp, and in (23) Cp should translate *non* either in the form *ne wæs* or *næs*.

(22) Lk 7.8 [Nam et ego homo sum sub potestate constitutus,]
    Cp: Ic <u>ne</u> eom an man under anwealde gesett;
    A: Ic eom an man under anwealde gesett.
    'I am a man set under authority'

(23) Mt 22.11 [et uidit ibi hominem non uestitum ueste nuptiali]
    Cp: þa geseah he þær ænne mann þe <u>wæs</u> mid gyftlicum reafe gescryd.
    A: þa geseah he þær ænne man þe <u>næs</u> myd gyftlicon reafe gescryd.
    'then he saw there a man, who was not clad with a wedding garment'

I give two examples of verb-adverb combination, which present different element orders. This possibility of the change of order is one of the characteristic features of free translation and probably the illustration of changing phases of English constructions.

(24) Mt 27.60 [et aduoluit saxum magnum ad ostium monumenti, et abiit.]
    Cp: ⁊ he <u>to awylte</u> mycelne stan to hlide þære byrgene. ⁊ ferde syþþan;
    A: ⁊ he <u>wylede to</u> mycelne stan to hlide þære byrgenne. ⁊ ferde syððan.
    'and he rolled a great stone to the opening of the sepulchre and then departed'

(25) Jn 11.41 [Iesus autem eleuatis sursum oculis, dixit: Pater, gratias ago tibi quoniam audisti me.]
    Cp: Se hælend <u>ahof upp</u> his eagan ⁊ cwæð. fæder, ic do þe þancas forþam þu gehyrdest;
    A: Se hælend <u>ahof</u> his eagan <u>up</u> ⁊ *cwæð.* fæder ic do þancas þe forþam þu gehyrdest me.
    'The Lord lifted up his eye and said, Father, I thank thee, because thou heardest (me).'

In (24) 'Adv + prefix-V' in Cp corresponds to '(non prefix) V + Adv' in A. The order in Cp can be either an older one[20] or a literal one influenced by *ad-* in *aduoluit*. In (25) the oldest variety can be *upp ahof, but there is no obvious reason why one reading should be *ahof upp his eagan* and the other *ahof his eagan up*, except that *up(p)* and *ut* are adverbs most likely to be postposed.

---

20 See Hiltunen (1984).

9. Summary

MS. A is probably later than MS. Cp, but it is a mixture of preservation and innovation. I cannot find any basic or drastic reform of rendering the Gospels in MS. A, except that the manifold division of paragraphs and interpreting additions may indicate a practical use of the manuscript. Most variants are semantically insignificant, but some of those which I have discussed here in this paper are stylistic varieties often originated from he repetitive, contrasting, or rhetorical expressions of Latin constructions. Similar sentences with slight differences or modifications in a few lexemes can be effective to hear or read but require great care in translating or copying so as not to be misspelled. A mere slip of the pen might haven given birth to a new reading or understanding of an old context. Variant readings of the two manuscripts represent the West Saxon features of rendering and naturalising the foreign forms and structures while the scribes are handing down the content of the Gospels as faithfully as possible.

References

Editions

Liuzza, R. M. (ed.)
    1994   *The Old English Version of the Gospels. Vol. I Text and Introduction*. Oxford: Oxford University Press.
    2000   *The Old English Version of the Gospels. Vol. II Notes and Glossary*. Oxford: Oxford University Press.

Skeat, W. W. (ed.)
    1871-87   *The Gospel according to St. Matthew, St. Mark, St. Luke and St. John*. Cambridge; rpt. Darmstadt: Wissenschaftliche Buchgesellschaft, 1970.

Wordsworth, J. — H. I. White (eds.)
    1973   *Nouum Testamentum Latine*. London: The British and Foreign Bible Society.

Studies

Andrew, S. O.
    1940   *Syntax and Style in Old English*. Cambridge: Cambridge University Press.

Campbell, Alistair
    1959   *Old English Grammar*. Oxford: Clarendon Press.

Hiltunen, Risto
　1983　　　*The Decline of the Prefixes and the Beginnings of the English Phrasal Verb*. Turku: Turun Yliopisto.

Hofstetter, Walter
　1988　　　"Winchester and the standardization of Old English vocabulary", *Anglo-Saxon England* 17: 139-161.

Ker, N. R.
　1957　　　*Catalogue of Manuscripts containing Anglo-Saxon*. Oxford: Clarendon Press.

Levin, Samuel R.
　1958　　　"Negative Contraction: An Old English and Middle English Dialect Criterion", *JEGP* 57: 492-501.

Ogura, Michiko
　1984　　　"*Cwyst þu* as an OE Interrogative Equivalent", in: S. Ono, *et al* (eds.), *Studies in English Philology and Linguistics in Honour of Dr. Tamtsu Matsunami*. Tokyo: Shubun International, 14-33.
　1986　　　"OE Verbs of Thinking", *Neuphilologische Mitteilungen* 87: 325-341.
　2001　　　"Late West Saxon Forms of the Demonstrative Pronouns as Native Prototypes of *they*", *Notes & Queries* 246.1: 5-6.
　2007　　　"ME *douten* and *dreden*", in: G. D. Caie (ed.), *The Power of Words: Essays in Lexicography, Lexicology and Semantics in honour of Christian Kay*. Amsterdam: Rodopi, 117-130.

9 Stylistic Fronting in Old English Prose
Masayuki Ohkado, Chubu University

1. Introduction
Ohkado (2006) examines word order phenomena in two types of constructions involving two predicates in the *Lindisfarne Gloss*, which is written in the Northern dialect of Old English. It is demonstrated that in Participle Constructions, constructions involving the combination of BE and past participle, the absence of subjects leads to the increase in frequency of the head-final 'participe-BE' patterns, whereas in Modal Constructions, constructions involving the combination of modal verb and infinitive, the presence or absence of subjects does not seem to affect the choice between head-initial and head-final patterns.

This paper extends the database to Old English prose and examines whether the observations made in the *Lidisfarne Gloss* can also be seen in prose texts.

2. Modal and Participle Constructions in the *Lindisfarne Gloss*
Modal Constructions and Participle Constructions are illustrated in (1) and (2), respectively.

(1) Constructions with Modal Verbs + Infinitives (Modal Constructions)
  a. Modal Constructions
    MV (Modal-Verb) Order
    OE: seðe uutedlice *wælla suoeriga* in gold   temples
    Latin: qui autem   *iurauerit*   in aurum templi
    'if anyone swears by the gold of the temple' (Matthew 23.16)
  b. VM (Verb-Modal) Order
    OE: huæt *gespræcca scilo*
    Latin: quid *loquamini*
    'what to say' (Matthew 10.19)
(2) Participle Constructions (BE = beon, wesan, weorþan) + Past Participle)
  a. BV (BE-Verb) Order
    OE: and *weron gefulwad* in Iordanen from him
    Latin: et *baptizabantur* in iordane ab eo
    'they were baptized by him' (Matthew 3.6)
  b. VB (Verb-BE) Order
    OE: huer crist   *accenned were*
    Latin: ubi christus *nasceretur*
    'where the Christ was to be born' (Matthew 2.6)

As shown in these examples, Modal and Participle Constructions can be head-initial or head-final: The (a) examples are head-initial and the (b) examples are head-final.

In these constructions, pronominal subjects which are not present in the Latin original are sometimes added as illustrated in (3) and (4).

(3) Modal Constructions with Subject
   a. OE: *ic* cearro vel *ic* willo cerre in hus min ðonaic cuom
      Latin: reuertar in domum mean undeexiui
      'I will return to the house I left.' (Matthew 12.44)
   b. OE: huæt *ge* gebrucca scile
      Latin: quid manducetis
      'what you will eat or drink' (Matthew 6.25)

(4) Participle Constructions with Subject
   a. OE: þæt *he* were gefulwad from him
      Latin: ut baptizaretur ab eo
      'to be baptized by John' (Matthew 3.13)
   b. OE: þæt *hia* gesene sie from monnum
      Latin: ut uideantur ab hominibus
      'to be seen by men' (Matthew 6.5)

There is an important difference between Modal and Participle Constructions with respect to the relation between the presence or absence of subjects and the choice between head-initial and head-final order. This is illustrated in table 1 and table 2.

Table 1: MV/VM Order and the Presence/Absence of Subjects
(Modal Constructions)

	With Subject	Without Subject	total
MV Order	34 (61.8%)	21 (38.2%)	55
VM Order	16 (48.5%)	17 (51.5%)	33

Degrees of freedom: 1
Chi-square = 1.49445614035088
For significance at the .05 level, chi-square should be greater than or equal to 3.84.
The distribution is not significant.
p is less than or equal to 1.

Table 2: BV/VB Order and the Presence/Absence of Subjects
(Participle Constructions)

	With Subject	Without Subject	total
BV Order	62 (22.5%)	214 (77.5%)	276
VB Order	8 (2.6%)	300 (97.4%)	308

Degrees of freedom: 1
Chi-square = 54.4563250784388
p is less than or equal to 0.001.
The distribution is significant.

In Participle Constructions the choice between the two word order patterns is affected by the presence or absence of a subject: Examples with subjects tend to show head-initial BV order while those without subjects prefer head-final VB order. In contrast, in Modal Constructions such tendencies are not observed.

Ohkado (2006) proposes that these differences between Modal and Participle Constructions are accounted for in terms of stylistic fronting, which is observed in Modern Icelandic and older stages of the Scandinavian languages including Old Norse, as shown in (5).

(5) ... at *heriat* var í ríki hans.
    that harried was in kingdom his
    '... that was harried in his kingdom.' (Trips (2002: 276))

Stylistic fronting fronts participles or adjectives if there is a subject gap as schematically illustrated in (6).

(6) [subject gap] BE Participle/Adjective =>

 [Participle/Adjective] BE _____

Ohkado (2006) suggests that the existence of stylistic fronting in the *Lindisfarne Gloss* is attributed to Scandinavian influences starting from the Viking invasions of England. For possible influences of the Viking invasions in Old English in different constructions, see Kroch and Taylor (1997). For arguments for the existence of stylistic fronting in Middle English, see Trips (2002).

3. Other Interlinear Glosses

If the differences between Modal and Participle Constructions are due to the Scandinavian influences, it is expected that Modal and Participle Constructions in interlinear glosses written in dialects other than northern do not show the behavior observed in the *Lindisfarne Gloss*.

This expectation is indeed borne out: Ohkado (2007) shows that the behavior of Modal and Participle Constructions in the *Rushworth Gloss* is as expected. In the *Vespersian Pslater Gloss*, which is written in the Mercian dialect, and in the *Regius Psalter Gloss*, which is written in the West Saxon dialect, the absence of subjects does not lead to higher frequencies of head-final patterns in Participle Constructions as illustrated in table 3 and table 4.

Table 3: BV/VB Order and the Presence/Absence of Subjects in the *Vespasian Psalter* Gloss

	With Subject	Without Subject
BV Order	38 (100.0%)	188 (100.0%)
VB Order	0 (0.0%)	0 (0.0%)
Total	38	188

Table 4: BV/VB Order and the Presence/Absence of Subjects
in the *Reguius Psalter* Gloss

	With Subject	Without Subject
BV Order	51 (83.6%)	140 (94.0%)
VB Order	10 (16.4%)	9 (6.0%)
Total	61	149

The figures given in tables 3 and 4 are in conformity with Ogura's (2004: 33) remarks that "A [-type glosses, represented by the *Vespasian Psalter Gloss*] tends to use a fixed gloss but D [-type glosses, represented by the *Regius Psalter Gloss*] tries several ways of translation." In the *Vespasian Psalter Gloss* all the instances exhibit head-initial BV order. In contrast, in the *Regius Psalter Gloss*, head-final VB order as well as head-initial BV order is observed. It is to be noted that in the *Regius Psalter Gloss*, where both patterns are seen, examples with subjects prefer head-final VB order and those without subjects tend to show head-initial BV order, an opposite tendency to what is seen in the *Lindisfarne Gloss* (cf. also Ogura (2003, 2006)). Although more detailed studies should be done here, we can at least say that the tendency for Participle Constructions without subjects to prefer head-final VB order is not observed in two representative glosses written in dialects other than the Northumbrian.

Since there is little examples of Modal Constructions, no comparison between Modal and Participle Constructions can be made, but at least the behavior of Participle Constructions in these two glosses is as expected, or at least not incompatible with our expectation.

4. Old English prose texts
Let us now examine whether Old English prose texts behave in similar fashion with interlinear glosses.

4.1. Data
The data used here have been extracted from the *York-Toronto-Helsinki Parsed Corpus of Old English Prose* (Taylor et al. (2003)), henceforth the YCOE. The texts analyzed are restricted to those containing more than 10,000 words, which are given in Table 5, since smaller texts only include a limited number of relevant examples.

Table 5: The List of the Texts Analyzed

Text name	File name	Ms. Date	Dialect*	Latin Translation	Word Count
Ælfric's Catholic Homilies I	cocathom1.o3	2	WS	No	106,173
Ælfric's Lives of Saints	coaelive.o3	2	WS	No	100,193

Text name	File name	Ms. Date	Dialect*	Latin Translation	Word Count
Ælfric's Catholic Homilies II	cocathom2.o3	2	WS	No	98,583
Gregory's Dialogues (C)	cogregdC.o24	2	WS/A/M	Yes	91,553
Bede's History of the English Church	cobede.02	2	W/A	Yes	80,767
West-Saxon Gospels	cowsgosp.o3	2	WS	Yes	71,104
Cura Pastoralis	cocura.o2	1	WS	Yes	68,556
Ælfric's Homilies Supplement	coaelhom.o3	various	WS	No	62,669
Heptateuch	cootest.o3	2	WS	Yes	59,524
Orosius	coorosiu.o2	1	WS	Yes	51,020
Boethius, Consolation of Philosophy	coboeth.o3	1	WS	Proem: No, Body: Yes	48,443
Vercelli Homilies	coverhom	1		?	45,674
Blickling Homilies	coblick.o23	2	WS/A	No	42,506
Anglo-Saxon Chronicle E	cochronE.o34	3	WS/X	?	40,641
Bald's Leechbook	colaece.o2	1	WS/A	Yes	34,727
The Homilies of Wulfstan	cowulf.o34	various	WS	No	28,768
Anglo-Saxon Chronicle D	cochronD	2		?	26,691
Martyrology	comart3.o23	2	WS/A	No	25,781
Gregory's Dialogues (H)	cogregdH.o23	2	WS	Yes	25,593
Anglo-Saxon Chronicle C	cochronC	2		?	22,463
Herbarium	coherbar	2	WS/A	Yes	22,213
Benedictine Rule	cobenrul.o3	2	WS	Yes	20,104
Chrodegang of Metz	cochdrul	2	?	Yes	18,386
St Augustine's Soliloquies	cosolilo	3	WS	Yes	15,856
Anglo-Saxon Chronicle A	cochronA.o23	1	WS	No	14,583
Ælfric's Letter to Sigeweard (Z)	colsigewZ	3		No	10,420
Byrhtferth's Manual	cobyrhtf.o3	2	WS	Yes	10,243

* Abbreviations in Dialect: WS = West Saxon, M = Mercian, A = Anglian.

Since stylistic fronting is a phenomenon typically observed in subordinate clauses, the data considered in the following are limited to subordinate clauses.

When we consider the potential effect of the absence of subjects, we have to take into account the fact observed in Ohkado (2001a). In Ohkado (2001a) it is shown that in Modal and Participle Constructions the presence or absence of extra elements, notably full NP objects and prepositional phrases, is relevant to the choice between head-initial and head-final patterns: In examples with no extra elements, head-final patterns are preferred while in examples with extra elements, head-initial patterns tend to be observed as schematically illustrated in (7) and (8).

(7) Modal Constructions
    a. Without Extra Elements
       (Subject) **Verb Modal**
    b. With Extra Elements
       (Subject) Object/PP, etc. **Verb Modal**=>
       (Subject) **Modal** Object/PP, etc. **Verb** or (Subject) **Modal Verb** Object/PP, etc.

(8) Participle Constructions
    a. Without Extra Elements
       (Subject) **Verb BE**
    b. With Extra Elements
       (Subject) PP, etc **Verb BE**=>
       (Subject) **BE** PP, etc. **Verb** or (Subject) **BE Verb** PP, etc.

In Ohkado (2001a) this tendency is accounted for by assuming that in clauses with extra elements verb phrases headed by infinitives are heavy. So in accordance with the generally observed tendency in Old English that heavy elements tend to undergo rightward movment, the verb phrases are moved to the right as shown in (9).

(9) (Subject) [$_{VP}$ **Verb**] $_{[light]}$ **Modal or BE**
    (Subject) [$_{VP}$ Extra Element **Verb**] $_{[heavy]}$ **Modal or BE**

It should be noted that the negating particle *ne* and personal pronoun objects are not counted as extra elements since they are clitics and do not make the relevant verb phrases heavy.

(10) a. þeahþe sume mensingan **ne** cunnon
      although some mensing not can
      'although some men cannot sing' (ÆCHom I, 9.150.30)
   b. hwi heora God **him** andwyrdan **ne** mihte
      why their God them answer not could
      'why their God could not answer them' (ÆCHom I, 31.456.2)

In order to exclude the potential effect of extra elements, we will concentrate on examples with no extra elements. The constructions examined in the present investigation are summarised in (11).

(11) Examples Examined
    a. Modal Constructions with No Extra Elements
      (i) genuine example
      (ii) with the negating particle *ne*
      (iii) with an accusative personal pronoun object
      (iv) with a dative personal pronoun object

b. Participle Constructions with No Extra Elements
   (i) genuine example
   (ii) with the negating particle *ne*
   (iii) with a dative personal pronoun object

4.2. Search method

The search was conducted by using CorpusSearch 2, which is a program written by Beth Randall for analyzing syntactically annotated corpora. In line with the proposal made in Ohkado (2001b) that in studies based on corpora the search methods should be made explicit so that the interested readers can verify the results by conducting their own search, the basic content of the command files used for the present search is given in (12). The line numbers are only for explanatory purposes and are not present in the original command files.

(12) The Basic Content of the Command Files
```
1: node: IP-SUB*
2: query: (IP-SUB* iDomsTotal 3)
3: AND (IP-SUB* iDominates NP-NOM*)
4: AND (NP-NOM* iDominates N^N|NR^N)
5: AND (IP-SUB* iDominates *MD*)
6: AND (IP-SUB* iDominates *VB*)
7: AND (*MD* Precedes *VB*)
8: AND (NP-NOM* Precedes *MD*)
9: AND (*MD* iDominates ![1]¥**)
10: AND (*VB* iDominates ![2]¥**)
```

The first line specifies that the searched node is labeled as subordinate clause. The second line states that the node immediately dominates just three elements. These elements are specified in the third, fifth, and sixth lines: The nominative subject in line 3, modal verbs in line 5, and infinitives in line 6. The fourth line specifies that the subject is a common or proper noun. The last part in the fourth line is replaced by (13a) when examples with personal pronoun subjects are searched for, and by (13b) when examples with empty subjects are searched for.

(13) a. Personal Pronoun Subject
      N^PRO
   b. Empty Subject
      ¥*con¥*|¥*exp¥*|¥*pro¥*|¥*T¥**

The seventh and eighth lines specify the order of the three elements. The seventh line states that the modal verb precedes the nonfinite verb and the eighth line states that the subject precedes the modal verb. These specifications search for strings with the head-initial pattern illustrated in (14a).

(14) a. Head-Initial Pattern
       subject modal verb (infinitive)
     b. Head-Final Pattern
       subject verb (infinitive) modal

For examples with head-final patterns, these two lines are replaced by (15).

(15) For Head-Final Patterns
```
AND (NP-NOM* Precedes *VB*)
AND (*VB* Precedes *MD*)
```
The ninth and tenth lines exclude cases where modal and nonfinite verbs are empty. Thus, the command file with the specifications in (12) searches for the structure given in (16).

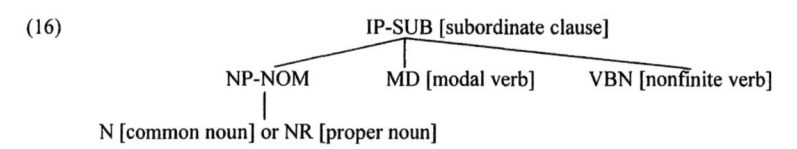

(16)
```
                    IP-SUB [subordinate clause]
           ┌─────────────────┼─────────────────┐
        NP-NOM         MD [modal verb]    VBN [nonfinite verb]
           │
   N [common noun] or NR [proper noun]
```

(17) is an example found by this search.

```
(17) (CP-ADV (C +t+at)
     (IP-SUB (NP-NOM (D^N +t+at) (ADJ^N halige) (N^N husl))
             (MDPS sceole)
             (VB fynegian)))
     (. ,))
     (ID colwsigeXa,+ALet_1_[Wulfsige_Xa]:134.177))
```

Since the negating particle *ne* is treated as a separate item in the corpus, examples with it should be searched for separately by using the command given in (18).

(18) For Examples with the Negating Particle
```
 1. node: IP-SUB*
 2. query: (IP-SUB* iDomsTotal 4)
 3. AND (IP-SUB* iDominates NP-NOM*)
 4. AND (IP-SUB* iDominates NEG)
 5. AND (NEG iDominates ne)
 6. AND (NP-NOM* iDominates N^N|NR^N)
 7. AND (IP-SUB* iDominates *MD*)
 8. AND (IP-SUB* iDominates *VB*)
 9. AND (*MD* Precedes *VB*)
10. AND (NP-NOM* Precedes *MD*)
11. AND (*MD* iDominates ![1]¥**)
12. AND (*VB* iDominates ![2]¥**)
```

Two lines dealing with the negating particle, the fourth and fifth lines in (18) are added, and accordingly, the number of elements dominated by the IP-SUB node is changed from 3 to 4 as stated in the second line.

For examples with a personal pronoun object, the content of the command file is as illustrated in (19).

(19) For Examples with a Personal Pronoun Object
```
1.  node: *IP-SUB*
2.  query: (IP-SUB* iDomsTotal 4)
3.  AND (IP-SUB* iDominates NP-NOM*)
4.  AND (IP-SUB* iDominates NP-ACC)
5.  AND (NP-ACC iDominates PRO^A)
6.  AND (NP-NOM* iDominates N^N|NR^N)
7.  AND (IP-SUB* iDominates *MD*)
8.  AND (IP-SUB* iDominates *VB*)
9.  AND (*MD* Precedes *VB*)
10. AND (NP-NOM* Precedes *MD*)
11. AND (*MD* iDominates ![1]¥**)
12. AND (*VB* iDominates ![2]¥**)
13. AND (NP-ACC iDominates ![3]¥**)
```

The fourth and fifth lines deal with personal pronoun objects. The specifications in (19) are for examples with an accusative object. For examples with a dative object, these lines are replaced by (20).

(20) For Examples with a Dative Object
```
AND (IP-SUB* iDominates NP-DAT)
AND (NP-DAT iDominates PRO^D)
```

For Participle Constructions, the specifications for two verbal elements are as illustrated in (21).

(21) For Participle Constructions
   a. BE = *BED*|*BEP*
   b. Participle = *VBN*

Thus, the relevant part of (18) and (19) are replaced by the specifications in (21).

Note that since pronoun objects found in Participle Constructions are usually dative, and not accusative, examples with accusative objects are not searched for.

4.3. Results
The results of the investigation are given in table 6 and table 7

Table 6: Word Order in Modal Constructions

	NP Subject		Pronoun Subject		Empty Subject	
	MV	VM	MV	VM	MV	VM
Genuine	7	8	57	77	8	31
With Negative *Ne*	1	7	4	19	1	9
With Accusative PRO (without *Ne*)	5	10	38	73	11	58
With Accusative PRO (with *Ne*)	1	6	7	20	2	2
with Dative PRO (without *Ne*)	0	3	6	15	0	16
With Dative PRO (with *Ne*)	2	4	1	3	1	1
Total	16 (29.6%)	38 (70.4%)	113 (35.3%)	207 (64.7%)	23 (16.4%)	117 (83.6%)

Table 7: Word Order in Participle Constructions

	NP Subject		Pronoun Subject		Empty Subject	
	BV	VB	BV	VB	BV	VB
Absolutely 3	145	217	117	217	34	70
With Negative *Ne*	8	3	8	3	13	0
With Dative PRO (without *Ne*)	4	6	1	5	4	82
with Dative PRO (with *Ne*)	0	0	0	0	1	0
Total	157 (41.0%)	226 (59.0%)	126 (35.9%)	225 (64.1%)	52 (25.5%)	152 (74.5%)

It appears that the frequencies of head-final patterns in clauses with an empty subject are slightly higher in Modal Constructions but it is not the case in Participle Constructions. In reality, however, there are significant differences among texts and we should not claim that these observations apply to Old English texts in general. Therefore, examining individual texts is necessary.

However, the texts containing enough examples are limited as listed in (22) and (23).

(22) Texts Having 10 or More Examples of Modal Constructions with PRO and ZERO Subjects
aelive (Ælfric's *Lives of Saints*), cathom2 (Ælfric's *Catholic Homilies II*), cura (*Cura Pastoralis*), wsgosp (*West-Saxon Gospels*)

(23) Texts Having 10 or More Examples of Participle Constructions with NP, PRO and ZERO Subjects
aelive (Ælfric's *Lives of Saints*), bede (Bede's *History of the English Church*), cathom1 (Ælfric's *Catholic Homilies I*), cura (*Cura Pastoralis*), gregdC (Gregory's *Dialogues* (C)), wsgosp (*West-Saxon Gospels*)

Only three of these texts, that is, *aelive, cura* and *wsgosp* are listed in both cases and they are the first candidates to be examined in detail. However, since *cathom1*, and *cathtom2* are written by the same author (Ælfric) as *aelive*, the figures concerning these texts are also considered. Below, the figures concerning these three texts are put together and treated as representing the language of Ælfric.

The figures concerning these three texts are given in tables 8, 9, and 10.

Table 8: Word Order in *aelive, cathom1*, and *cathom2*

| | NP Subject || PRO Subject || ZERO Subject ||
	MV/BV	VM/VB	MV/BV	VM/VB	MV/BV	VM/VB
Modal	3 (18.8%)	13 (81.3%)	30 (32.6%)	62 (67.4%)	9 (21.4%)	33 (78.6%)
Participle	29 (61.7%)	18 (38.3%)	56 (37.6%)	93 (62.4%)	21 (33.3%)	42 (66.7%)

Table 9: Word Order in *cura*

| | NP Subject || PRO Subject || ZERO Subject ||
	MV/BV	VM/VB	MV/BV	VM/VB	MV/BV	VM/VB
Modal	(1)	(0)	11 (35.5%)	20 (64.5%)	1 (8.3%)	11 (91.7%)
Participle	11 (91.7%)	1 (8.3%)	8 (40.0%)	12 (60.0%)	2 (9.5%)	19 (90.5%)

Table 10: Word Order in *wsgosp*

| | NP Subject || PRO Subject || ZERO Subject ||
	MV/BV	VM/VB	MV/BV	VM/VB	MV/BV	VM/VB
Modal	(1)	(1)	12 (85.7%)	2 (14.3%)	7 (70.0%)	3 (30.0%)
Participle	28 (70.0%)	12 (30.0%)	17 (65.4%)	9 (34.6%)	16 (47.1%)	18 (52.9%)

The figures concerning Participle Constructions in tables 8-10 are unexpected. In all the texts clauses with an empty subject exhibit higher frequencies of head-final patterns than clauses with a full NP or pronoun subject. Moreover, Clauses with a pronoun subject shows higher frequencies of head-final patterns than clauses with a full NP subject. Thus, there seems to be a hierarchy illustrated in (24).

(24) The Frequencies of Head-Final Patterns in Participle Constructions (VB)
clauses with an   >   clauses with a   >   clauses with a
empty subject   personal pronoun subject   full NP subject

It seems that the differences between clauses with an empty subject and those with an overt subject is best accounted for by assuming that the language of these texts does have stylistic fronting. Therefore, contrary to our observations in interlinear glosses, we have to assume that the West-Saxon dialect of Old English has stylistic fronting.

The differences between clauses with a personal pronoun subject and those with a full NP subject can be accounted for by the assumption that personal pronoun subjects in the West-Saxon dialect are clitics so that the subject position is virtually empty, to which participles can be fronted as schematically illustrated in (25).

(25) C-subject$_{[clitic]}$ [   ]   BE   Vparticiple

The figures concerning the *Lindisfarne Gloss* seem to suggest that this option is not available in the gloss. This analysis might be independently supported by the fact pointed out by Kroch and Taylor (1997) that personal pronoun subjects in the *Lindisfarne Gloss* can undergo subject-verb-inversion in parallel fashion with full NP subjects, which is not the case in the West-Saxon dialect.

The figures concerning Modal Constructions with a full NP subject are limited and we cannot draw a definite conclusion about these clauses. However, there are differences between clauses with an empty subject and those with a personal pronoun subject. Again, clauses with an empty subject show higher frequencies of head-final patterns than those with a personal pronoun subject. The natural conclusion to be drawn here seems to be that in the West-Saxon dialect infinitives in Modal Constructions as well as participles can undergo stylistic fronting.

In the original formulation of Maling (1990), which is a reprint of Maling (1980), infinitives are not listed among elements that can undergo stylistic fronting, and Willson (2001: 134) explicitly states that, "[f]ronting of infinitives in MnICe [Modern Icelandic] is marginal outside of fixed expressions such as *vera má* 'it may be' (in MCs [main clauses]) and *hvað sem koma skal* 'whatever happens' ...." Willson also points out that in older stages infinitives could undergo stylistic fronting as illustrated in (26).

(26) Ertu   Gísli sá   er   finna vildir   Gretti Ásmundarson?
     are-you Gísli that who   find wanted Grettir Ásmundarson
     'Are you the Gísli who was looking for Grettir Ásmundarson?' (Willson (2001: 134))

The existence of such examples as (26) suggests that Old Norse had a version of stylistic fronting that could apply to infinitives.

Since stylistic fronting seems to be observed in the West-Saxon dialect, we are forced to reconsider our assumption that stylistic fronting in Old English, which seems to be observed in the *Lindisfarne Gloss*, is due to the Scandinavian invaders. It seems more likely that the operation is a common property of North and West Germanic languages.

5. Conclusion

This paper examines whether or not the tendency observed in the *Lindisfarne Gloss* is seen in Old English prose in general. It has been shown that:

(A) Stylistic fronting is observed in Old English prose texts written in the West-Saxon dialect.
(B) Stylistic fronting in Old English prose texts written in the West-Saxon dialect can apply to infinitives as well as participles, which is not the case in the *Lindisfarne Gloss*, where the operation does not apply to infinitives.
(C) In clauses with a personal pronoun subject elements undergoing stylistic fronting can move to the empty slot. This option is available in Old English prose written in the West-Saxon dialect, but not available in the *Lindisfarne Gloss*.
(D) The difference between the availability of the subject slot between Old English prose written in the West-Saxon dialect and the *Lindisfarne Gloss* is attributed to the different nature of subject personal pronouns (cf. Kroch and Taylor (1997)).
(E) The lack of stylistic fronting in the *Regius Psalter Gloss* written in the West-Saxon dialect is left unaccounted for.
(F) Stylistic fronting is a common property of North and West Germanic languages and its presence in the *Lindisfarne Gloss* cannot be solely attributed to the Scandinavian invaders.

References

Kroch, Anthony — Ann Taylor
    1997   "Verb Movement in Old and Middle English: Dialect Variation and Language Contact," in Ans van Kemenade and Nigel Vincent (edd.), *Parameters of Morphosyntactic Change*. Cambridge: CambridgeUniversity Press, 297-325.

Maling, Joan
    1980   "Inversion in Embedded Clauses in Modern Icelandic," *Íslenski málog almenn málfræði* 2, 175-193.

1990 "Inversion in Embedded Clauses in Modern Icelandic," in Joan Maling and Annie Zaenen (eds.), *Modern Icelandic Syntax (Syntax and Semantics 24)*. New York: Academic Press, 71-91.

Ogura, Michiko
2003 "The Variety and Conformity of Old English Psalter Glosses," *English Studies* 84, 1-8.
2004 "Lexical Comparison between the Glosses of the *Vespasian Psalter* and the *Regius Psalter*," *Poetica* 62, 17-36.
2006 "Element Order Varies: Samples from Old English Psalter Glosses" in Michiko Ogura (ed.) *Textual and Contextual Studies in Medieval English: Towards the Reunion of Linguistics and Philology*. Frankfurt: Peter Lang, 105-126.

Ohkado, Masayuki
2001a *Old English Constructions with Multiple Predicates*. Tokyo: Hituzi Syobo.
2001b "Database and Historical Studies," *The History of English* (the Korean Society for the History of the English Language) 11, 125-147.
2006 "On Word Order in Constructions with Two Predicates in Old English Interlinear Glosses," in Michiko Ogura (ed.) *Textual and Contextual Studies in Medieval English: Towards the Reunion of Linguistic and Philology*. Frankfurt: Peter Lang, 127-145.
2007 "On Word Order in Old English Interlinear Glosses, with Special Reference to the *Lindisfarne* and *Rushworth Glosses*," in Masachiyo Amano, Kozo Kato, Makiyo Niwa, Ko-ichiro Hamasaki, Tomoyuki Tanaka, Yusaku Oteki, Kay Nakago, and Eiko Mizuno (edd.) *Exploring the Universe of Language: A Festschrift for Dr. Hirozo Nakano on the Occasion of His Seventieth Birthday*. Nagoya: Nagoya University, 285-304.

Taylor, Ann — Anthony Warner — Susan Pintzuk — Frank Beths
2003 *The York-Toronto-Helsinki Parsed Corpus of Old English*. York: Department of Language and Linguistic Science, University of York.

Trips, Carola
2002 *From OV to VO in Early Middle English*. Amsterdam: John Benjamins.

Willson, Kendra
2001 "Old Icelandic Topicalization and the Emergence of Stylistic Fronting," in Arthur Holmer, Jan-Olof Svantesson and Åke Viberg (eds.) *Proceedings of the 18th Scandinavian Conference of Linguistics, Vol. 2*. Lund: Lund University, 127-137.

10 The Old English Adjective *sĭht*

Aurelijus Vijūnas, National Kaohsiung Normal University

1. Introduction

In Old English *Corpus Diplomaticus Aevi Saxonici* (henceforth: "CD") there is attested a hapax word-form *sihtre*. This form occurs in a description of land boundaries, and the context is provided below:

> ...of þā treowe on þone elebeam styb þonon on ceolbaldes wylle of þā wylle on cytasihtes ford of þā forda to wulfrices gemǣre þonon to hordhlince ufeweardum of þā hlince on <u>sihtre</u> mǣde norþeweardre swa forþ on cenelmes stān... '...from that tree till the olive-tree stump, from there till Ceolbald's well, from that well till Kite-stream's (?) ford,[1] from that ford till Wulfric's boundary, from there till the upper part of Hoard-linch, from that linch till the <u>s.</u> meadow in the north, and then forward till Cenelm's (?) stone...' (CD III.430)[2]

The word-form *sihtre* appears to modify the feminine noun *mǣde* 'meadow' (dat.sg.), and its ending *-re* looks like an adjectival feminine dative singular ending, cf. OE *gōd* 'good' (nom.sg. masc./fem./neutr.) vs. *gōd-re* (dat.sg. fem.), *hwīt* 'white' vs. *hwīt-re*, etc. The nominative singular form of this adjective can therefore be reconstructed as *siht*. The length of the root vowel is not entirely clear, since length is not marked accurately in this manuscript. As one can see from the passage above, vowel length is correctly indicated in the noun *stān* 'stone' (< Proto-Germanic **staina-*), but in the rest of the words containing long vowels or the broken Old English diphthongs length is not indicated, cf. *treowe* for *trēowe*, *gemǣre* for *gemǣre* (< PGmc. **-mairija-*), *mǣde* for *mǣde* 'meadow' (← PGmc. **mǣđwōi*), etc. The superscript mark over the vowel in the pronoun *þā* (4x) denotes not length but rather indicates that the word is to be read with a final nasal, viz. *þām* 'that' (by-form of *þǣm*; dat.sg. masc./neutr.; < pre-OE **þaim-*).

The adjective *siht* (or *sĭht*) was not included in J. Bosworth's *Anglo-Saxon Dictionary* (1st edition 1838), but appears in Toller's *Anglo-Saxon Dictionary Supplement* and is glossed 'drained' (BTS: 703).

In more recent times, the adjective *siht* was treated by F. Heidermanns in his *Etymologisches Wörterbuch der germanischen Primäradjektive* (1993). Unlike BTS, Heidermanns interpreted the root vowel of this adjective as long,

---

1 The place-name *Cytasiht* is probably a compound of *cȳta* 'kite' (or 'buzzard') and *siht* 'stream, flowing' (for the discussion of semantics, see section 4 below).
2 Translation mine.

reconstructing the nominative singular form as *sīht*. Also the semantic analysis was different in the new treatment: Heidermanns glossed this adjective as 'wet'.³

In this article I would like to return to this Old English adjective once again, re-examining its synchronic meaning and structure, as well as derivation.

2. Heidermanns' analysis of the adjective *sĭht*

In his *Etymologisches Wörterbuch*, Heidermanns interpreted the adjective *sīht* as a thematised reflex of an earlier Proto-Germanic athematic adjective **senχ-t-* which, in turn, would have reflected a Proto-Indo-European *t*-stem adjective **senk-t-* built to the Indo-European verbal root **sek-* 'seep away, dwindle' (G. 'versickern, versiegen').⁴ The consonant *n* appearing in the nominal derivative **senk-t-* was explained by Heidermanns as the familiar Indo-European *n*-infix which relatively frequently occurs in present tense verbal formations. According to the analysis presented, the adjective *sīht* also possesses cognates in other West Germanic languages, viz. Middle High German *sīhte* 'shallow' (> Modern German *seicht* 'id.') and Swiss German *sīht* 'very wet'.⁵

Heidermanns' interpretation of the history of the Old English adjective *sĭht* poses various problems. The semantic parallel between OE *sīht* and the German forms would only be true in such a case if the meaning of the Old English adjective indeed were 'wet'. However, Heidermanns' provided no argumentation in favour of such a semantic interpretation, and, as was said above in section 1, the meaning of this adjective has also been glossed as 'drained' (cf. BTS). As will be shown below in section 3, such a semantic interpretation is equally plausible.

A different semantic problem arises between the meaning of the reconstructed Indo-European verbal root **sek-* vs. the two German adjectives: whereas the meaning of the root **sek-* suggests drying up, the adjectives *sīht* and *sīht(e)*⁶ suggest wetness. The Swiss German adjective *sīht* and MHG *sīht(e)* most likely derive not from the root **sek-*, but rather from another Indo-European verbal root, viz. **seng̑ʰ-* 'sink, fall down',⁷ and reflect an ancient *to*-participle **seng̑ʰ-to-* (← **sn̥g̑ʰ-tó-* 'lowered, sunken') which underwent a relatively complex

---

3 Heidermanns (1993: 70).
4 Heidermanns (1993: 479).
5 Heidermanns (1993: 479).
6 The spelling *sīht(e)* is preferable, because *e*-less forms occur in Middle High German as well (see M. Lexer 1876: 920).
7 Contra Heidermanns, who claimed that "zu den starken Verben **seiga-/*seihʷa-* [< IE **seik̑ʰ-*; A.V.] 'sinken, tropfen, seihen' [...] oder **senkʷa-* 'sinken' besteht angesichts von Stamm- bildung, Bedeutung und außergerm. Etymologie keine direkte Verbindung" (Heidermanns 1993: 479).

morphological and semantic development, first being nominalised by the process of vṛddhiisation, and eventually adjectivised.[8]

Another problem is the reconstruction of the Indo-European *t*-stem adjective **senk-t-* itself. Although the existence of *t*-stem adjectives in Proto-Indo-European has also been suggested by E. Seebold who reconstructed a Proto-Indo-European *t*-stem adjective **lengʷh-ot-* 'light' (→ PGmc. **lenχta-* > E. *light*, German *leicht* etc.),[9] more recent studies of Indo-European primary *t*-stems have revealed that all substantival Indo-European primary *t*-stems were nouns.[10] Instead of the reconstruction proposed by Seebold, the development of the Proto-Germanic adjective **lenχta-* can be more plausibly explained in a way similar to that of the Swiss adjective *sīht* and the Middle High German adjective *sīht(e)*. According to this alternative interpretation, PGmc. **lenχta-* reflects an ancient *to*-participle **h₁lṇgʷh-tó-* 'easily moved' (~ √**h₁lengʷh-* 'move easily, lightly').[11]

One could slightly modify Heidermanns' theory by reconstructing the Indo-European *t*-stem **senk-t-* as a noun instead of an adjective. This, however, would create structural problems. First, no other Indo-European *t*-stem noun is built to an infixed verbal root, although several early primary *t*-stems were built to roots that are known to have formed *n*-presents, cf. the Indo-European *t*-stems **gʷo/erH-t-* 'praising' (→ Latin *grātēs* 'gratitude', Oscan *brateis* 'favour')[12] and **h₃ro/eiH-t-* 'flowing' (→ Vedic *rít-* 'stream' [hapax; RV vi.57.4a]). These two nouns were built to the Indo-European roots **gʷerH-* 'praise' resp. **h₃reiH-* 'flow', and there are attested several infixed verbal stems formed from these roots, cf. Ved. *gṛṇā́ti* 'praise' (< **gʷṛ-ne-H-*), Younger Avestan *-gərəṇte* 'id.' (< **gʷr-n-H-*),[13] Ved. *riṇā́ti* 'flow' (< **h₃ri-ne-H-*), Greek ὀρίνω (Lesbian) and ὀρῑ́νω (Attic) 'id.' (< **h₃ri-n-H-*), etc. Second, even if the putative noun **senk-t-* were an exception, the *e*-grade would appear in the wrong place in the root, as in infixed formations it normally appears after the nasal, cf. IE **gʷṛ-ne-H-* and **h₃ri-ne-H-* shown above. Therefore, the expected shape of the *n*-infixed *t*-stem **senk-t-* should have been **snek-t-*.

---

8 The process of vṛddhiisation of several Indo-European participles as well as the development of Swiss German *sīht* and Middle High German *sīht(e)* are discussed in more detailed in A. Vijūnas (2006: 124f.).
9 Seebold (1981: 295f.).
10 See E. Rieken (1999: 83-100), B. S. Irslinger (2002: 37-46), A. J. Nussbaum (2004), Vijūnas (2006).
11 For a more detailed analysis see A. Bammesberger (1990: 256) and Vijūnas (2006: 123f.).
12 See H. Rix (2000).
13 Cf. LIV.210.

3. Problems in the historical analysis of *sĭht*

Before venturing into alternative historical analyses of OE *sĭht*, it may be useful to consider the synchronic meaning of this adjective. As was said in section 1 above, two rather different interpretations have been suggested: 'drained' (BTS) resp. 'wet' (Heidermanns).

Theoretically, both meanings are plausible. As the words *wylle* 'well', *hlinc* 'linch, link (a ridge or hills nearby a body of water)', and *siht* 'stream' imply, ground water and various water bodies were present in the area. Therefore, one could argue that the meadow could have been subject to seasonal floodings (e.g., in spring), or, alternatively, was permanently wet or swampy. This would support Heidermanns' semantic interpretation. However, the older semantic analysis as presented in BTS is equally plausible: the presence of water in the vicinity of this meadow could also support the idea that it was a drained old swamp or wetland.

The exact meaning of the adjective *sĭht* is of crucial importance both for the determination of the length of the root vowel as well as the historical interpretation of the word itself. In the case the adjective *sĭht* should have a long *ī*, it would be tempting to connect it etymologically with the two German adjectives mentioned in section 2 above (as per Heidermanns [*mutatis mutandis*]). A weak point of this interpretation is that one would have to reconstruct a long vowel in the root of *sihtre*. It is certainly possible to argue that absence of the length mark over a phonologically long vowel would not be a very unusual mistake, since vowel length is frequently marked very arbitrarily in medieval manuscripts; however, in the case of *sihtre*, an entirely different – and much simpler – historical and semantic interpretation is possible if one takes the length of the vowel at face value, viz., interpreting it as a short vowel /ĭ/.

If the vowel *i* is short, derivation from the vṛddhiied participle **seng^u-to-* becomes impossible on phonological grounds, and, as a consequence, *siht* would have to be disconnected from Middle High German *sīht(e)* and Swiss German *sīht*.

The adjective *siht* with a short *ĭ* could be successfully derived from another Indo-European verbal root, viz. **seik^u-* 'spill out'. In the pre-Germanic dialectal area, the meaning of this root was further transformed into 'strain' and 'sink, be lowered, fall', as is suggested by multiple Germanic derivatives, cf. OHG *sīhan*, OE *sēon*, Old Frisian *sīa* 'strain' (< PGmc. **sīχwan-*), Old Icelandic *sía* (< PGmc. **sīχwōn-*), OHG *sīha*, OE *seohhe*, OIc. *sía* 'strainer, sieve' (< **sīχwōn-*), OHG/ OE *sīgan*, OIc. *síga* 'fall, be lowered, sink' (< PGmc. **sīgwan-*), etc. The ancestor of the Old English adjective *siht* could have been built from this root, too, and originally it would have been a *to*-adjective **sik^u-tó-* 'strained' or 'lowered'.

The derivation of OE *siht* from the Indo-European participle **sik^u-tó-* is free of problems both phonologically and semantically. The Indo-European **sik^u-tó-*

would have regularly developed into Proto-Germanic *siχta-,[14] and thence to Old English sĭht. The adjectivisation of ancient to-participles in Germanic is normal, and similar examples can be adduced, cf. PGmc. *đau-þ/đa- 'dead' (< virtual *dhou-to-), *kal-đa- 'cold' (< virtual *g/ĝol-tó-), etc. The secondary development of the meaning 'strained, lowered' to 'drained' is fairly easy to imagine: as drainage canals are dug, the water from the drained area sinks down, seeping through the soil like through a strainer.

Such a historical interpretation of the adjective sihtre can be quite attractive for various reasons: first, in such a case, one does not need to assume a long vowel where it is not written. Second, when the development is presented in this way, it looks simpler than the newer alternative analysis, and one can avoid two typologically rather rare phenomena: the vr̥ddhiisation of an ancient participle and the subsequent adjectivisation of the resulting vr̥ddhi noun.[15]

4. Excursus: Old English *Cýta-siht*

In the same passage occurs a compound noun *Cýta-siht* (spelled <cytasihtes> [gen.sg.]). It is apparently a name of some stream, as is implied by the immediately following word *ford* 'ford'. The first member of this compound most likely means 'kite (bird of prey)', cf. OE *cýta* 'id.', whereas the second member is curiously similar to the adjective *sĭht*.

The second member *-siht* most likely is a noun 'stream'. Such a semantic interpretation is supported by the Old English nouns *blōd-sihte* 'bloodstream' and *ūt-siht(e)* 'diarrhea, dysentery' (lit. 'out-flowing'), in both of which *siht(e)* means 'stream' or 'flowing'.[16]

The history of the noun *siht* is fairly straightforward. This noun derives from the Indo-European verbal root *seikʷ- discussed in section 4 above, and originally it must have been formed as a *ti*-stem verbal abstract *sikʷ-ti-. The original meaning of such a formation would have been 'spilling; straining', but in the course of time it developed into 'trickling' and eventually 'small stream' or just 'stream'.

The root vowel of the noun *siht* is most likely historically short, as *ti*-stems built to *CeRC* roots normally exhibit the zero grade of the root.[17] If the root vowel is short also in the adjective *sĭht*, the two words would be genetically

---

14 Labialisation regularly disappeared in clusters, cf. IE */nókʷ-t-/ 'night' > PGmc. *naχt-, IE */h₁lengʷh-to-/ 'light' > PGmc. *linχta-, etc.
15 Adjectivisation of nouns is a much rarer phenomenon than the reverse, although a certain number of examples can be adduced, e.g. OE *cēap* 'bargain' (noun) → ME *chēpe* 'cheap' (adj.), OIc. *hljóð* 'sound; silence' (old vr̥ddhi noun) → *hljóðr* 'silent', also late OE *standard* 'distinctive ensign' (noun; first attested in XII c.; ← Old French) → *standard* 'serving as a standard of measurement' (adj.; first attested in XVII c., cf. OED), etc.
16 The forms ending in *-e* imply a late transfer of *sĭht* to the *n*-stem inflectional class.
17 For a more detailed discussion of the ablaut of Indo-European *ti*-stems see B. Vine (2004).

related. However, if the root vowel in the adjective is long, the noun *sīht* and the adjective *sīht* would be genetically unrelated.

References

Bammesberger, A.
1990 *Die Morphologie des urgermanischen Nomens.* Heidelberg: Carl Winter Universitätsverlag.
Bosworth, J.; T. N. Toller.
1838 *An Anglo-Saxon Dictionary.* Based on the manuscript collections of the late Joseph Bosworth. Edited and enlarged by T. Northcote Toller. Oxford University Press. Second impression, printed photographically from sheets of the first edition of 1898 in Great Britain.
BTS *Supplement to An Anglo-Saxon Dictionary.* Based on the manuscript collections of Joseph Bosworth. By T. Northcote Toller (with revised and enlarged addenda by Alistair Campbell). Oxford University Press, 1921.
CD *Codex Diplomaticus Aevi Saxonici.* Opera Johannis M. Kemble. Tomus III. Londini: Sumptibus Societatis, 1845 (Kraus Reprint Ltd. Vaduz, 1964).
Heidermanns, F.
1993 *Etymologisches Wörterbuch der germanischen Primäradjektive.* Berlin – New York: Walter de Gruyter.
Irslinger, B. S.
2002 *Abstrakta mit Dentalsuffixen im Altirischen.* Heidelberg: Carl Winter Universitätsverlag. g.
Lexer, M.
1876 *Mittelhochdeutsches Wörterbuch.* Zweiter Band. N – U. Leipzig: Verlag von S. Hirzel.
LIV *Lexikon der indogermanischen Verben.* Zweite, erweiterte und verbesserte Auflage bearbeitet von Martin Kümmel und Helmut Rix. Wiesbaden: Dr. Ludwig Reichert Verlag, 2001.
Nussbaum, A. J.
2004 "A -t- Party". Presentation handout, the 16th UCLA Annual Indo-European Conference, 2004.
OED *Oxford English Dictionary* (www.oed.com).

Rieken, E.
1999 *Untersuchungen zur nominalen Stammbildung des Hethitischen.* StBoT 44. Wiesbaden.

Rix, H.
2000 "Oskisch *brateis bratom*, lateinisch *grates*." In *Anusantatyai: Festschrift für Johanna Narten* (herausgegeben von Almut Hintze und Eva Tichy), 207-29. *MSS Beiheft* 19.

Seebold, E.
1981 *Etymologie. Eine Einführung am Beispiel der deutschen Sprache.* München: Verlag C. H. Beck.

Vijūnas, A.
2006 *The Indo-Primary* t-*Stems*. Dissertation. University of California, Los Angeles.

Vine, B.
2004 "On PIE Full Grades in Some Zero-Grade Contexts: *-tí-, *-tó-." In *Indo-European Formation: Proceedings of the Conference Held at the University of Copenhagen. October 20th-22nd, 2000* (edited by James Clackson and Birgit Anette Olsen), 357-79. Copenhagen: Museum Tusculanum Press.

11 The Ambiguous or Polysemous Compounds in *Beowulf* Revisited: *æscholt* and *garholt*[1]

Hideki Watanabe, Osaka University

One salient stylistic feature of Old English poems is the frequent use of compounds and a certain type is particularly interesting.[2] That is 'double-form compounds,' made of two synonymous words. Walter A. Berendsohn (1935) called them *Doppelformen*. Among them the form *holtwudu* arrests our attention as it denotes a forest at line 1369, but it refers to a shield at line 2340 in the epic.[3]

(1) þær mæg nihta gehwæm   nið-wundor seon,
    fyr on flode;   no þæs frod leofað
    gumena bearna   þæt þone grund wite.
    ðeah þe hæð-stapa   hundum geswenced,
    heorot hornum trum   *holt-wudu* sece,
    feorran geflymed,   ær he feorh seleð,
    aldor on ofre,   ær he in wille,
    hafelan hydan.   Nis þæt heoru stow;   (*Beowulf* 1365-72)[4]

(2) Heht him þa gewyrcean   wigendra hleo
    eall-irenne,   eorla dryhten,
    wig-bord wrætlic;   wisse he gearwe,

---

1   This paper is written on the basis of my previous consideration of the polysemous compounds in *Beowulf*, which appeared in Chapter IX of *Metaphorical and Formulaic Expressions in Old English Reconsidered* (Tokyo: Eihosha, 2005). The conclusion was read at the 19th conference of The Japan Society for Medieval English Studies at Tokyo University of Foreign Languages (December, 2004).
2   As for the number of compounds in *Beowulf*, Charles Leslie Wrenn in the introduction of his edition of *Beowulf* says he collects 903 nominal compounds in the 3,182 lines, of which 518 are peculiar to this epic. Arthur Gilchrist Brodeur gives the same number for "distinct substantive adjectives" (*The Art of Beowulf* (1959), p. 7). Thomas Gardner presents the figure of 1070 ("The Old English Kenning: A Characteristic Feature of Germanic Diction" *Modern Philology* (1969) No. 67 p. 109-17), while Professor Tsunenori Karibe counts about 700 substantive compounds, 250 genitive combinations, and 400 compound adjectives (*The Narrative World of Beowulf* (2006) p. 173).
3   All the quotations are from the edition of Wrenn and Bolton (1973).
4   Roy Micheal Liuzza's translation: "every night one can see there an awesome wonder,/ fire on the water. There lives none so wise/ or bold that he can fathom its abyss./ Though the heath-stepper beset by hounds,/ the strong-horned hart, might seek the forest,/ pursued from afar, he will sooner lose/ his life on the shore than save his head/ and go in the lake—it is no good place!"

þæt him *holt-wudu*   helpan ne meahte,
lind wið lige.   (*Beowulf* 2337-41a)[5]

In Example (1) the dismal and dreary forest near Grendel's den is depicted, into which a hart, a male deer, driven by hounds seeks shelter. In Example (2) Beowulf ordered an iron shield to be made, who thought a wooden shield is useless against the dragon's fire. This is the case of metonymy. In this way one and the same compound has two different referents: a large group of trees and a manufactured wooden article.

I have already discussed the *Beowulf*-poet's intentional use of the same compounds with different meanings and referents (in Watanabe 2006), showing the cases of *wælfyr* (1119 cremation; 2582 dragon's fire), *hildeleoma* (1143 a sword; 2583 dragon's fire), and *guðwine* (1810 a sword Hrunting; 2735 a warrior), so *holtwudu* is not unique with double readings in the same form, but it is very remarkable because it is made of two synonymous nouns, *holt* and *wudu*. Both nouns, *holt* and *wudu*, are polysemous and ambiguous even as a simplex: the former can be a single tree or a group of trees, that is a forest, and the latter can refer to a tree, a timber, a rood, a spear-shaft, or a ship. When they are combined, they are still more ambiguous in the relationships between the elements.[6]

In *Beowulf* there are many compounds denoting weapons, where other cases of Doppelformen are found. Among them I would like to take up the cases of *æscholt* at line 330 and *garholt* at 1834, of which the base noun is also *holt*, an intrinsically ambiguous word:

(3)   þa hie to sele furðum
in hyra gryre-geatwum   gangan cwomon,
setton sæ-meþe   side scyldas,
rondas regn-hearde,   wið þæs recedes weal;
bugon þa to bence,   byrnan hringdon,
guð-searo gumena.   *Garas stodon,*
sæ-manna searo,   *samod ætgædere,*
æsc-holt ufan græg;   wæs se iren-þreat
wæpnum gewurþad.   (*Beowulf* 323b-31a)[7]

---

5   Roy Micheal Liuzza's translation: "Then the lord of men bade them make,/ protector of warriors, a wondrous war-shield,/ all covered with iron; he understood well/ that wood from the forest would not help him,/ linden against flames."

6   While the main factor in choosing the first element of a compound is the alliterative scheme of the line, a talented poet might well try to be explicit and choose the right element, when resorting to compounding, to produce *sundwudu* at line 208 (ship), *mægenwudu* at line 236 (spear), *gomenwudu* at line 1065 (harp or lyre [laiər]), or *bælwudu* at 3112 (funeral pyre).

7   Roy Micheal Liuzza's translation: "when right to the hall/ they went trooping in their terrible armor./ Sea-weary, they set their broad shields,/ wondrously-hard boards, against the building's wall;/ they sat on a bench—their byrnies rang out,/ their soldiers' war-gear; their spears stood,/ the gear of the seamen all together,/ a gray forest of ash."

(4) Gif ic þæt gefricge   ofer floda begang,
þæt þec ymb-sittend   egesan þywað,
swa þec hetende   hwilum dydon,
ic ðe *þusenda þegna* bringe,
hæleþa to helpe. Ic on Higelac wat,
Geata dryhten,   þeah ðe he geong sy,
folces hyrde,   þæt he mec fremman wile
wordum ond weorcum,   þæt ic þe wel herige
ond þe to geoce   *gar-holt* bere,[8]
mægenes fultum,   þær ðe bið manna þearf. (*Beowulf* 1826-35)[9]

The passage presented as Example (3) depicts the arrival of Beowulf and his fourteen followers in Denmark. They set their spears against the wall of Heorot before entering the Danish royal hall. Note the words in italics. At lines 328-9 the poet clearly states that *garas stodon/ .../ samod ætgædere* (spears stood all together). The following phrase with the compound in question, *æsc-holt ufan græg*, is a variation to *garas* and here "a forest of spears with grey tops" is, I believe, a fine instance of metonymy-based metaphor, for spears are long wooden objects.

Contrastively in Example (4) Beowulf is making a farewell speech and promising to come back to the Danes with an armed force when neighboring tribes threaten to invade the land as he has done this time to come with his retainers and exterminate the two monsters. Is the hero saying that he will come back with a single spear in hand? Or is he resorting to a metaphor which likens a military troop to a forest of spears?

Interpretations of the two words have wavered between their literal and figurative senses as well as singularity and plurality. That they are tautological and refer to a single spear is the belief prevalent among the *Beowulf* scholars. Almost all editors from Wyatt onward and all the dictionaries of Old English and their revised editions which register *æsc-holt* and *gar-holt* as headwords take them as tautological compounds. *A Thesaurus of Old English* by Kay and Roberts uniquely registers them under the heading "a group of spear" as against its source dictionaries, *Bosworth and Toller* and *Clark Hall*.[10] It was Fred C. Robinson and Caroline Brady who almost simultaneously but independently in 1979 reached the figurative interpretation of the compound as 'forest of spears.' See "Two Aspects of Variation in Old English Poetry" and "Weapons in *Beowulf*: An Analysis of the Nominal Compounds and Evaluation of the Poet's Use of Them." Robinson

---

8   The compound *garholt* is peculiar to *Beowulf* but *æscholt* also appears in *The Battle of Maldon* (Offa gemalde æscholt asceoc (230))with the literal sense of "spear-wood."
9   Roy Micheal Liuzza's translation: "If ever I hear over the sea's expanse/ that your neighbors threaten you with terror/ as your enemies used to do,/ I will bring you a thousand thanes,/ heroes to help you. I have faith in Hygelac—/ the Lord of the Geats, though he be young,/ shepherd of his people, will support me/ with words and deeds, that I might honor you well/ and bring to your side a forest of spears,/ the support of my might, whenever you need men."
10 Volume I, p. 605.

acknowledges Brady's suggestion that Arthur Gilchrist Brodeur in his *Art of Beowulf* (1959) has already proposed the figurative reading of *garholt*. Brodeur, however, gives no reasons for his interpretation at all. Twenty years after Brodeur, Robinson strengthened the case for the metaphorical interpretation by mentioning Latin writings which use the same figure, the later Icelandic tradition with a system of kennings based on warriors as trees, and, most significantly, the case of the similar figure in the Old English epic *Exodus*.[11] Brady compares various appellations for a heap of spears carried by Beowulf's retainers in the same passage and concludes that the sense of *æsc-holt* is substantiated by *heresceafta heap* "heap of war-shafts" at line 335 and *wælsceaftas* "slaughter-shafts" at 398.[12] But neither of them relates *garholt* with *æsc-holt* in any significant way. It is Fred C. Robinson's and Caroline Brady's arguments that my paper intends to follow and complement, presenting further supporting evidence from the stylistic and thematic point of view.

In the most extensive treatment of the nominal compounds for "weapon" in the epic, Caroline Brady re-examines, and discards, the traditional renditions of those compounds given by most authoritative editors. Brady asserts, "Only analysis *in context*, the immediate context in which it stands and any additional context in which it or a closely related appellation stands *within the same poem*, can determine whether or not any appellation in *Beowulf* is truly a figure of speech of any kind." So I would like to reconsider the immediate contexts of the passages in which the two compounds appear.

Let us look at Example (4) once again. In Example (4) *þusenda þegna* and its variation, *hæleþa*, is an object of the verb *bringan* while the compound *gar-holt* is an object of the verb *beran*. If we look at the passage from a wider perspective of thematic resonance, a parallel structure will emerge, as is shown in Figures One and Two:

---

11 Robinson refers to *ferrea silva* "a forest of iron" at line 47 of the Latin version of *Waldere*, an illustrative instance of influence from *Aeneid* and other Latin writings. He also gives Old Norse *hildmeiðr, vighlynr, geira viðr*. But his reference to *oferhalt wegan* in *Exodus* (157b) seems decisive in supporting the metaphorical interpretation of *garholt*. See "Two Aspects of Variation in OE Poetry," pp. 135-6.

12 Caroline Brady, "Weapons in *Beowulf*: An Analysis of the Nominal Compounds and Evaluation of the Poet's Use of Them," *Anglo-Saxon England* 8 (1979) pp. 130-1.

Figure I. Thematic and Verbal Repetitions in the Epic (Ring Composition)[13]
(A (B (C (D (...) D) C) B) A) : Motifs at the Beginning and the End of the Poem
(adapted from Niles (1979)

A:	Eulogy for Scyld
B:	Scyld's Funeral
C:	History of Danes before Hroðgar
D:	Hroðgar's Order to Build Heorot

D:	Beowulf's Order to Build his Barrow
C:	History of Geats after Beowulf
B:	Beowulf's Funeral
A:	Eulogy for Beowulf

Figure II. The Parallel and Chiastic Structure in the Two Sentences
(a (b (c (d (...) d) c) b) a) : Wordings in the Passage

A:
þæt þec ymb-sittend egesan þywað,
swa þec hetende hwilum dydon,(a)
ic ðe þusenda þegna(b) **bringe**,(c)
hæleþa(b) to helpe.(d) (*Beowulf* 1827-30a)

'(if I hear) that neighboring tribes fright thee,
as your enemies used to do to you,
I will **bring** thousands of thanes
of warriors to your aid.'

B:
ond þe to geoce(d) gar-holt(b) **bere**, (c)
mægenes fultum, (b) þær ðe bið manna þearf. (a)
(*Beowulf* 1834-35)

'(I will) **bring** a forest of spears to your aid
with the armed force, when you are in need of men.'

---

[13] "This [the theory of Ring Composition] had been introduced to *Beowulf* studies," Thomas Shippey summarises, "some years before H. Ward Tonsfeldt (1977). Tonsfeldt follows recent trends in Homeric scholarship, in which it has been pointed out how often Homer organizes motifs in a chiastic rather than a parallel structure: not A, B, C, A^1, B^1, C^1, but A, B, C, C^1, B^1, A^1. Tonsfeldt finds a number of such "ring structures" in *Beowulf* and states that "the repetitious arrangement of narrative agents within a nearly static structure is the essence of the poet's technique" (452). Ward Parks's article of 1988 gives further examples and notes that a major function of a ring structure is to integrate digressions with main narrative by linking the two or by framing a "core episode"; ring systems provide both bridges and interfaces, and create an effect not of disclosing narrative so much as unfolding it from within. Like Niles, parks and Tonsfeldt deal with old criticisms of the structure of *Beowulf* not by denying them but by seeing them as features of a different, nonclassical rhetoric exemplified also in the recently acquired records of oral epic." *A Beowulf Handbook* (1997: 171-2). Tonsfeldt analyzes the structures of 11. 129b-49a, 237-70, 1017-168, 1885b-924, 2355-72 and 2426-512a. Ward Parks reassesses the ring structure at "catalyz[ing] a movement into or out of digressions or between plot segments."

What is intriguing in analysing this passage, then, is to see the choice and arrangement of words which would correspond to the overall structure called Ring Composition. John D. Niles explains the structure as "certain ways in which the poem shows patterning in its larger structure as well as on the level of the formulaic word or phrase."[14] He aptly defines the patterning elsewhere as "a chiastic design in which the last element in a series in some way echoes the first, the next to the last the second, and so on.[15] If we follow the line, we can instantly perceive a formal coincidence between its macro- and microstructures. The epic begins and ends with a eulogy for the legendary king Scyld and the old king Beowulf, which are followed and preceded, respectively, by the scenes of their funerals. After and before these funerals come the histories of Danes before Hroðgar and of Geats after Beowulf.

In the same way the passage in question begins and ends with causal clauses tagged (a) and each element and its counterpart occurs in the reversed order: (a) (b) (c) (d) and (d) (c) (b) (a). Within the passage the hero's promise to help King Hroðgar is repeated with different wordings and in the two statements, (A) and (B), each element appears in the reversed order. Put together there emerges a chiasmatic or mirrored structure in the two sentences, which would be missed when seen separately. This kind of repetition of elements, scattered throughout the poem, is too clear to be fortuitous.[16] Thus the reading of *gar-holt* as denoting "a forest of spears" will be supported by its counterpart in the preceding sentence, *þusenda þegna*, "thousands of thanes."[17]

---

14 John D. Niles, 1983. *Beowulf: The Poem and Its Tradition.* p. 152.
15 John D. Niles, 1979. "Ring Composition and the Structure of *Beowulf*," *PMLA* 94, p. 924. Niles here analyzes the scenes of the three great fights and the overall structure of the epic.
16 Well before the theory of Ring Composition, Adeline Courtney Bartlett in her *The Larger Rhetorical Patterns in Anglo-Saxon Poetry* (1935) proposed "envelope patter" in order to unify the "group of verses bound together by the repetition at the end of (1) words or (2) ideas or (3) words and ideas which are employed at the beginning. In the course of her discussion she explained that the pattern originates in "the chiastic arrangement" of the elements (pp. 9-11).
17 Here it may be interesting to know that William Morris, a translator of *Beowulf*, in his rendering of *The Story of Sigurd the Volsung and the Fall of the Niblungs* coined a compound *spear-wood* to describe Gothic soldiers moving toward their enemy: "up the steep came the Goth-folk, and the spear-wood drew anigh." (William Morris, 1911. *The Story of Sigurd the Volsung and the Fall of the Niblungs* p. 15)William Morris, 1910-11. The Collected Works of William Morris: With Introductions by His Daughter May Morris. 24 Vols. London: Longmans Green and Company. Volume XII. *The Story of Sigurd the Volsung and the Fall of the Niblungs.* That the compound *garsecg* "spear-warrior" denotes a sea might be comparable to the case of *garholt*, where a forest is the vehicle of the metaphor for "a troop of soldiers." In Shakespearean tragedy we have another instance of a forest of troops: "Macbeth shall never vanquish'd be, until/ Great Birnam wood to high Dunsinane hill/ Shall come against him." (*Macbeth* IV, i, 92-4). Vainly convinced, the regicidal hero was shocked by the messenger's ill-fated report to tell: "As I did stand my watch upon the hill,/ I look'd toward Birnam, and anon, methought,/ The wood began to move." (*Macbeth* V, v, 32-4). In *Macbeth* the troops of

Then the question arises: Does the poet use the verb *beran* to describe a war commander leading his army elsewhere in the epic? The verb *beran* as a simplex occurs 34 times in *Beowulf*. It appears with various words for objects, where the nouns for defensive and offensive weapons make up a prominent group. Among those sentences with the verb *beran*, I would like to call the reader's special attention to the following two instances. In Examples (5) and (6) the subject of the verb *beran* is Beowulf himself:

(5) Ic þæt þonne forhicge, swa me Higelac sie,
 min mon-drihten, mōdes bliðe,
 þæt ic *sweord* bere oþðe *sidne scyld*,
 geolo-rand to guþe; ac ic mid grape sceal
 fon wið feonde ond ymb feorh sacan,
 lað wið laþum; (*Beowulf* 435-40a)[18]

(6) "Nolde ic *sweord* beran,
 wæpen to wyrme, gif ic wiste hu
 wið ðam aglæcean elles meahte
 gylpe wiðgripan, swa ic gio wið Grendle dyde;
 ac ic ðær heaðu-fyres hates wene,
 oreðes ond attres; forðon ic me on hafu
 bord ond byrnan. (*Beowulf* 2518b-24a)[19]

In these speeches by *Beowulf*, where the hero declares his battle-readiness, it is manifestly shown that his main offensive weapon is a sword, not a spear. As a nephew to King Higelac, Beowulf was bestowed with King Hreðel's corslet on his departure from the Geatland, which was to guard the hero against the fearful attack of Grendel's mother. Before diving into the haunted mere of the monsters, he was entrusted with a renowned sword, Hrunting, by Unferð. The vanquishing hero was given a set of Danish royal armor, including King Healfdene's sword, a corslet, helmet, and the golden banner; but no spear is mentioned in the treasure-giving scene. Accordingly in the passage quoted as Example (4), it is *sweord*, not *garholt*, that would be the object of the verb *beran*, if Beowulf would declare that he would return and wield a weapon and fight in person to help Hroðgar.

 Malcolm and Macduff carry a bough, not a spear, in order to camouflage their movement but resemblance in the two scenes is conspicuous: soldiers with a wood in their hands. They are metonymically and metaphorically a group of trees, a forest.

18 Roy Micheal Liuzza's translation: "so too I will scorn—so that Hygelac,/ my lieage-lord, may be glad of me—/ to bear a sword or a broad shield,/ a yellow battle-board, but with my grip/ I shall grapple with the fiend and fight for life,/ foe against foe."

19 Roy Micheal Liuzza's translation: "I would not bear a sword/ or weapon to this serpent, if I knew any other way/ I could grapple with this great beast/ after my boast, as I once did with Grendel;/ but I expect the heat of battle-flames there,/ steam and venom; therefore shield and byrnie/ will I have on me."

On their arrival at Heorot, Beowulf and his followers set their spears against the wall of the hall and the poet presents the bunch of spears as "a forest grey on top". In the farewell speech given to Hroðgar, Beowulf repeatedly promises the Danish king an aid in his need. Is it a far-fetched idea if we think that in the farewell speech the poet elaborately recalls the image of a forest of spears, the first awe-inspiring impression of the foreign troop to the Danes, who have long been in need of a hero to destroy the monster Grendel? If we follow the theory of Ring Composition, we will get still another instance of the repeated theme or element in an envelope structure: At the arrival and the departure of Beowulf's party at Heorot, the image of a forest of spears appears, enclosing the narrative parts of Beowulf's two great fights in Denmark. Now the case for taking both compounds to be metaphorical and resounding to each other seems inescapable.[20]

Caroline Brady argues that "Brodeur alone thus far in print has taken it correctly as 'forest of spears.'" (p. 130)' But this comment of hers is rather misleading. As they are silent about the early editors and translators, I would like to add something else. Well before the important discussions by Brodeur, Brady and Robinson, Moriz Heyne (5th edition revised by Socin, 1888) presented this compound as a kenning for "a forest of javelins" in his glossary: "Wald aus Speeren, d. i. Speermenge." Following the fourth edition by Heine (1879) Harrison and Sharp in the United States gave the modern rendering "forest of spears, i.e. crowd of spears" in their Glossary and went on to say that the compound would "more properly means *spear-shaft*; (as a Doppelformen) referring to *asc-holt* at line 330 in their Notes. And as early as in 1892 Professor John Earle translated the compound as "a forest of spears." Very interestingly but bewilderingly Heyne's second reviser Levin Schücking discarded the figurative sense and registered its literal interpretation in the glossary: 'Speerholz, Speerschaft.'

Since the beginning of the second half of the last century we saw sporadic emergence of the figurative reading of the compounds. Edwin Morgan and Burton Raffel brought the two instances together in the plural before Michael Alexander gave "a grove of grey-tipped spears" in 1973. It was Michael Swanton who, for the first time in translation, presented the two instances as figurative in his unified renderings: 'a forest of ash-grey shafts' (330) and 'a forest of spears' (1834). And finally Roy Michael Liuzza (2000) decisively noted this figurative sense of the two compounds in concert.

---

20 There are two instances of compound outside *Beowulf*, which are perhaps illuminating in assessing the artistry of the *Beowulf*-poet. First, The compound *asc-holt* also appears with the literal sense of "spear-wood" in *The Battle of Maldon*(230): Offa gemalde æscholt asceoc. Then we should note the unique interpretation of *garbeam* (Exodus 246) for a warrior by Brodeur, who explains that "a warrior is a 'spear-tree,' presumably, because he stands armed unshakable in battle, as a tree stands in the forest." in *The Larger Rhetorical Patterns in Anglo-Saxon Poetry* (p. 12). She later in the book puts forward the affinitive metaphorical interpretation of *asc-holt* and *gar-holt* in concert.

Recent editors like Jack and Mitchell & Robinson seem to follow this revival of figurative interpretation, and will in turn exert an influence on the latest translations after Liuzza.[21] Thus the general scholarly consensus on *garholt*, and *æscholt*, too, swung from the figurative interpretation at the end of the nineteenth century to the literal one in the first half of the twentieth century, and, once again, swung back to its original interpretation at the turn of the century.[22]

I presented here a few pieces of supporting evidence for the unified readings of the two compounds, *æsc-holt* and *gar-holt*. This metaphorical interpretation of the two compounds would not just contribute to understanding the thematic resonances or verbal coincidences in the epic. But in a wider sense this would also show that the cases of prescience by early editors and translators of Old English poems, especially those who were active at the turn of the last century, might perhaps be greater than has been realised.[23]

Table 1. Modern English Equivalents for *æscholt* and *garholt* in *Beowulf*

Editors and Commentators	*æscholt* in 330	*garholt* in 1834
Heyne (5th., 1888) rev. by Adolf Socin	Eschenholz, Eschenschaft	Wald aus Speeren, d.i. Speermenge* (pl.)
Harrison & Sharp (1883; 4th. 1991) (Following Heyne (4th. 1879))	------	Forest of spears, i. e. crowd of spears (Glossary); more properly means spear-shaft; cf. *asc-holt*. (Notes)
Wyatt (1894)	ash wood, spear	spear-shaft, spear
Sedgfield (2nd., 1913)	spear	shaft of javelin
Heyne (12th., 1918) rev. by Levin Schücking	Eschenholz, Eschenschaft	Speerholz, Speerschaft
Wyatt rev. by Chambers (1920)	[ASH-wood] spear	Spear-HOLT, spear-shaft, spear
Hoops (1932)	das von oben (gesegen) graue Eschenholz**	und dir zur Hilfe das Speerholz trage***
Klaeber (1950)	ash wood, i.e. spear	spear-shaft, i.e. spear
Wrenn (rev., 1958)	ash-wood, *hence* spear	spear-shaft
Heyne (17th, 1961) rev. by Else von Schaubert	Eschenholz, Eschenschaft	Speerholz, Speerschaft
Nickel (1982) (Strauss Glossar)	Speer (aus Eschenholz)	Speerholz, Speerschaft
Jack (1994)	ash-wood	**forest** of spears (pl.)
Mitchell & Robinson (1998)	ash **forest**, stack of ash spears (pl.)	**forest** of spears (pl.)

---

21 Puhvel clearly states that his translation "is based primarily on Fr. Klaeber's edition." He is "also indebted to the editions of C. L. Wrenn and W. F. Bolton and Bruce Mitchell and Fred C. Robinson, especially in connection with disputed textual element, some of which also come in for attention in Notes and Comments." (p. vii)

22 Heaney well captures and powerfully describes the figure in his rendering of the passage with the compound: 'I raise a hedge of spears around you.'

23 My paper might be regarded as an attempt to supplement Liuzza's renderings and Mitchell and Robinson's glossarial explanation which are silently given.

Translators	*æscholt* in 330	*garholt* in 1834
B. Thorpe (3rd., 1889) Half-line edition with translation	the ash-wood grey above (665)	the javelin-shaft (3673)
J. Earle (1892) Prose	ash-timber with tip of grey	a **forest** of spears
W. Morris (1895) Verse	the ash-holt grey-headed	the spear-holt
C. G. Child (1904) Prose	the shafts of ash-wood gray above (pl.)	the spear's shaft
W. Huyshe (1907) Prose	the ashen wood, grey at the point	the shafted spear
W. E. Leonard (1923) Verse	their ash-wood, gray-tipped spears (pl.)	ashen spear
F. Gummer (1910) Verse	Gray-tipped ash	(ielding) the war-wood
P. K. Gordon (1926)	the spears...of ash wood grey at the tip (pl.)	a spear
C. W. Kennedy (1940) Verse	their stout spears...shaped of ash (pl.)	stout ash-spear
Clark Hall (1940) Verse Revised by Wrenn and Tolkien	the ash-spear, grey at the tip	my shafted spear
E. Morgan (1952) Verse	the spears, ash-cut, grey-tipped (pl.)	war-spears (pl.)
B. Raffel (1963) Verse	Their ash-wood spears Gray-tipped and straight (pl.)	our battle-sharp spears (pl.)
D. H. Crawford (1966) Verse	the grey-tipt ashwood	my shafted spear
K. Crossley-Holland (1968) Verse	a grey-tipped **forest** of ash spears (pl.)	spear shafts(pl.)
M. Alexander (1973) Verse	an ash-wood grey-tipped	a **grove** of grey-tipped spears (pl.)
E. T. Donaldson (1975) Prose	ash steel-gray at the top	Spears (pl.)
H. D. Chickering, Jr. (1977)	Straight ash, gray points. (pl. ?)	By help pf spear-wood
M. Swanton (1978) Prose	a **forest** of ash-grey shafts (pl.)	a **forest** of spears (pl.)
S. A. J. Bradley (1982) Prose	shafts of ashwood grey at their tips (pl.)	spear
S. B. Greenfield (1982) Verse	an ash-**forest** tipped with gray (pl.)	a **forest** of spears (pl.)
C. B. Hieatt, rev. (1983) Prose	the ashwood gleaming gray at the tip	a spear
J. Porter (1984) Verse	ash-wood tipped with grey	the power of spear-shafts (pl.)
B. F. Huppé (1987) Verse	gray-tipped spears of trusty ash (pl.)	Spears (pl.)
R. P. M. Lehmann (1988) Verse	ashenshafts, gray-tipped (pl.)	my shafted spear
J. Porter (1991) Verse	ash-wood tipped with grey	spear-shafts bear (pl.)
F. Rebsamen (1991)	gray-tipped treelimbs (pl.)	a **forest** of spears (pl.)
S. Heaney (1999,2000, 2002) Verse	a stand of greyish tapering ash	(I raise) a hedge of spears (around you) (pl.)
Roy M. Liuzza (2000)	a gray **forest** of ash (pl.)	a **forest** of spears (pl.)
A. Sullivan & T. Murphy (2004)	their sturdy spears in a row, gray from the ash grove (pl.)	a **thicket** of spears (pl.)
M. Puhvel (2006)	Grey-tipped ash spears (pl.)	a **forest** of spears (metaphor for "a large army" (note p. 108))
D. Kaufman (2006)	their ashen spears, gray-tipped(pl.)	bring spear shafts to you(pl.)
E. L. Risden (2006)	an ash-holt with gray tops (pl.)	bear spear-shafts (pl.)

(pl.) refers to the modern renderings indicating plurality and words printed in bold are for the metaphorical interpretation.

References

Bartlett, Adeline Courtney
    1935   *The Larger Rhetorical Patterns in Anglo-Saxon Poetry*. New York: Columbia University Press.

Berendsohn, Walter A.
    1935   *Zur Vorgeschihte des Beowulf*. Copenhagen: Levin and Munksgaard.

Bjork, Robert E. and Niles, John D. (eds.)
    1997   *A Beowulf Handbook*. Lincoln: University of Nebraska Press.

Brady, Caroline
    1979   "Weapons in *Beowulf*: An Analysis of the Nominal Compounds and Evaluation of the Poet's Use of Them," *Anglo-Saxon England* 8: 79-141.
    1983   "Warriors in *Beowulf*: An Analysis of the Nominal Compounds and Evaluation of the Poet's Use of Them," *Anglo-Saxon England* 11: 199-246.

Brodeur, Arthur Gilchrist
    1959   *The Art of Beowulf*. Berkeley: University of California Press.

Cronan, Dennis
    2003   "Poetic Meanings in the Old English Poetic Vocabulary," *English Studies* 84: 397-425.

Gallasch, Linda
    1979   *The Use of Compounds and Archaic Diction in the Works of William Morris*. Berne: Peter Lang & Co. Ltd.

Isaacs, Niel D.
    1962   "Six *Beowulf* Cruces" *Journal of English and Germanic Philology* 61: 119-28.
    1967   "The Convention of Personification in *Beowulf*" *Old English Poetry* ed. by R. P. Creed (Brown University Press) 215-48.

Lee, Alvin A.
    1998   *Gold-Hall and Earth-Dragon: Beowulf as Metaphor*. Toronto: University of Toronto Press.

Marquardt, Hertha
    1933   "Fürsten- und Kriegerkenning im *Beowulf*" *Anglia* 55: 390-5.
    1938   *Die Altenglischen Kennigar: Ein Beitrag zur Stilkunde altenglischer Dichtung*. Halle.

Miki, Yasuhiro
    2006   "Compounds in *Beowulf*: Hordweard and a Theme of the Poem" *Studies in Medieval English Language and Literature*. 21: 83-95.

Niles, John D.
> 1979 "Ring Composition and the Structure of *Beowulf*," *PMLA* 94: 924-35.
> 1981 "Compound Diction and the Style of *Beowulf*," *English Studies* 62: 489-503.
> 1983 *Beowulf: The Poem and Its Tradition*. Cambridge, Massachusetts: Harvard University Press.

Orchard, Andy
> 2003 *A Critical Companion to Beowulf*. Cambridge: D. S. Brewer.

Owen-Crocker, Gale R.
> 2000 *The Four Funerals in Beowulf*. Manchester: Manchester University Press.

Parks, Ward
> 1988 "Ring Structure and Narrative Embedding in Homer and *Beowulf*," *Neuphilologische Mitteilungen* 89: 237-51.

Roberts, Jane, Kay, Christian, and Grundy, Lynne (eds.)
> 1995 *A Thesaurus of Old English*. King's College London.

Robinson, Fred C.
> 1979 "Two Aspects of Variation in Old English Poetry," *Old English Poetry: Essays on Style*. Los Angeles: University of California Press. 127-45.
> 1985 *Beowulf and the Appositive Style*. Knoxville: The University of Tennessee Press.

Taylor, Paul Beekman
> 1986 "The Traditional Language of Treasure in *Beowulf*" *Journal of English and Germanic Philology* 85: 191-205.

Tonsfeldt, H. Ward
> 1977 "Ring Structure in *Beowulf*," *Neophilologus* 61: 443-52.

Watanabe, Hideki
> 1988 "Monsters Creep?: the Meaning of the Verb *scriðan* in *Beowulf*," *Studies in Language and Culture*. Osaka University. 14: 107-20.
> 1993 "Some Neglected Aspects of Meaning of the Old English Noun-Verb Combination *egesa stod*," *Studies in Medieval English Language and Literature*. Tokyo: The Japan Society for Medieval English Studies. 8: 25-37.
> 1998 Review of *A Thesaurus of Old English*. *Studies in English Literature*. English Number. Tokyo: The English Literary Society of Japan. 132-8.
> 2000a "Final Words on *Beowulf* 1020b: *brand Healfdenes*," *Neuphilologische Mitteilungen* 100: 51-7.

2000b	"Quotations from *Beowulf* and Other Old English Poems in *the Oxford English Dictionary*," *Lexicographica* Series Maior. Tübingen: Max Niemeyer. 103: 263-9.
2001	"Notes to Clark Hall's Treatment of the Hapax Legomena and Hard Words in *Beowulf*," *Studies in Language and Culture*. Osaka University. 27: 211-32.
2002a	"*A Thesaurus of Old English* Revisited," *Lexicographica* Series Maior. Tübingen: Max Niemeyer. 109: 313-24.
2002b	Review: *Beowulf: A New Verse Translation* by Seamus Heaney. Bilingual Edition. Farrar, Straus and Giroux; New York, 2000. *Studies in English Literature,* English Number. Tokyo: The English Literary Society of Japan. 43: 55-62.
2004	"The Textual Significance of the Sentences in the Form of *þæt wæs god cyning* in Old English Poems," *Approaches to Style and Discourse*. Osaka: Osaka University Press. 135-64.
2005	*Metaphorical and Formulaic Expressions in Old English Reconsidered*. Tokyo: Eihosha.
2006a	"Sword, Fire and Dragon: Polysemous Compounds in *Beowulf* Reconsidered with Special Reference to *nacod nið draca* (2273) and *þæt wæs modig secg* (1812)," *Textual and Contextual Studies in Medieval English: Towards the Reunion of Linguistics and Philology*. Bern: Peter Lang. 193-204.
2006b	"Beowulfiana in Japan: A Brief Survey of the Past 75 Years with Special Focus on the Japanese Translations and Interpretive Studies," *Studies in Medieval English Language and Literature*. 21: 45-54.

12 A Reconsideration of the Reliability of Alliterative Evidence for the Sound System of Old English: Does Old English Poetry Work Aurally or Visually?

Tomonori Yamamoto, Keio University, Graduate School

1. Introduction

There have been two views in Old English scholarship when considering the sound system of Old English on the basis of the alliterative evidence in the poetic corpus. Some scholars like Penzl (1947: 34) think that alliteration may have been visually-based in OE:

(1) All words with initial *c* alliterate with one another in Old English poetry. This fact is not conclusive evidence against a phonemic split, because it may have been due to a poetic tradition of the kind that is responsible for Modern English 'eye-rhymes'.

His line of argument is that alliteration provides no evidence for the sound system of OE if one letter alliterates with itself. However, other scholars like Minkova (2003: 78-87) think that alliteration is phonologically-governed and aurally-based, and the alliterative evidence found in the OE poetic corpus is reliable for the reconstruction of the sound system.

A key question underlying these two interpretations of alliterative evidence is whether this poetic practise works aurally or visually in the OE poetic MSS, and some orthographic and paleographic aspects of the manuscripts will also lead us to a more general question: does Old English poetry work aurally or visually? In other words, the reliability of alliterative evidence for the sound system of Old English has a close connexion with the problem of whether apparently graphic devices found in the poetic MSS have been set up to work aurally for audiences or visually for readers.

In the next section, the paper discusses briefly whether "eye-rhyme", mentioned by Penzl (1947: 34), is appropriate or not when we consider alliteration in Old English. In Section 3 and Section 4, the paper reconsiders apparently graphic devices in OE poetic MSS, which can provide orthographic and paleographic evidence that OE poetry works aurally in principle. In Section 5 the paper argues that vocalic alliteration or apparently abnormal alliteration can provide evidence that the alliterative system of Old English is set up not on a visual, but aural basis. In the conclusion, it will be confirmed that alliteration is phonemically-based in Old English and reliable for the reconstruction of the sound system.

2. "Eye-alliteration" in Anglo-Saxon England?

The comment of Penzl (1947: 34) clearly means that alliteration may have been visually-based in Old English. Still, it seems to be worth checking what the definition of "eye-rhyme" is in English literature. Schipper (1910: 278) defines eye-rhyme as follows:

(2) ... a class of imperfect rhymes came into existence in consequence of the change in the pronunciation of certain vowels, from which it resulted that many pairs of words that originally rhymed together, more or less perfectly, ceased to be rhymes at all to the ear, although, as the spelling remained unaltered, they retained in their written form a delusive appearance of correspondence.

Kaluza (1911: 174) states that "... especially since the eighteenth century, departures have been made from the strict rule that rime must be correct for the ear." Below are cited examples from Kaluza (1911: 174) for eye-rhyme:

(3) *love: prove – love: grove – come: home – one: alone – blood: stood – done: gone – burn: mourn – profound: wound – forth: worth – sword: word – are: faire*

Given the definition and examples of "eye-rhyme", the probability of such a phenomenon in the OE period needs to be reconsidered. Could we suppose that scribes or authors in the OE period would have composed alliterative poems or poetic MSS not for reading them aloud, but only for reading them visually or silently with literary consciousness of "delusive appearance of correspondence in their written form" like writers or readers "especially since the eighteenth century"? The following comment of Harris (1954: 53-54) answers this question:

(4) It would seem unlikely that any such sophisticated literary device as "eye-alliteration" would have been used, or at least so consistently, by the early scribes.

Alliterative evidence in the present paper supports this comment, and this point will be mentioned later.

3. Cynewulf's runic signature in *Elene*

One of the strongest pieces of evidence that OE poetic MSS work visually may be Cynewulf's runic signature; however, Kenneth Sisam (1953) argues that the signature works aurally for an audience in principle as well as visually in the manuscripts. Cynewulf's runic signature occurs in *Fates of the Apostles*, *Elene*, *Christ*, and *Juliana*, but for considerations of space the one occurring in *Elene* is here selected as an example. Below are cited from *ASPR* lines 1256b-1270a of the poem, in which the runic signature appears:[1]

---

1   As for the facsimile of the passage cited in (5), see folio 133r reproduced in Celia Sisam (1976). Kenneth Sisam (1953: 27) gives his translation of this passage.

(5)   A wæs secg oð ðæt
cnyssed cearwelmum,   ᚳ drusende,
þeah he in medohealle   maðmas þege,
æplede gold.   ᚣ gnornode
ᚾ gefera,   nearusorge dreah,
enge rune,   þær him ᛗ fore
milpaðas mæt,   modig þrægde
wirum gewlenced.   ᛚ is geswiðrad,
gomen æfter gearum,   geogoð is gecyrred,
ald onmedla.   ᚣ wæs geara
geogoðhades glæm.   Nu synt geardagas
æfter fyrstmearce   forð gewitene,
lifwynne geliden,   swa ᛚ toglideð,
flodas gefysde.   ᚠ æghwam bið
læne under lyfte;

Sisam (1953: 23) points out that Cynewulf expresses clearly the reason why he signed his poems, twice in *Fates of the Apostles* and again in *Juliana*: 'I beg every man who repeats this poem to remember me *by name* in my need', in which he asks for prayers. Sisam (1953: 25) also discusses why Cynewulf used not the usual Latin acrostic but runes when signing his poems:

(6) But this method [the usual Latin acrostic] would not serve Cynewulf. It depended on each verse beginning a new line, and Old English verse was written continuously, like prose. More important still, it was intended for the eye of a reader, whereas a vernacular poet addressed himself primarily to the ear of a listener. It is doubtful whether any listener could follow the Latin method. Cynewulf used runes because, while they were obvious to a reader, they made possible the communication of his name to an audience in a way at once memorable and sure. An Anglo-Saxon hearing *cēn*, *ȳr*, would know at once that he was dealing with runes; his attention would be directed at once to the task of solution because runes sometimes played a part in Old English riddles; and he would listen closely for the succession.

In addition, Sisam (1953: 25-27) thinks that it would be less probable for Cynewulf to use *cēne* and *yfel* as standing for *cēn* and *ȳr* runes, which are the substitutions suggested by modern critics, because *cēne* and *yfel* are the more common adjectives, while *cēn* and *ȳr* had no currency as words in Old English, so that no audience, when they heard *cēne* and *yfel* in their common meanings, could be expected to guess that these common words stood for *cēn* and *ȳr* runes. His conclusion is that Cynewulf used *cēn* and *ȳr* runes as simple letter-names that would serve as warnings to an audience that less obvious letter-names would follow.

Here can be mentioned two more points arguing that the runes work aurally as well: as Sisam (1953: 25-26) points out, *ūr* did not occur as a word in Old English, but to a listener it is identical with the personal pronoun meaning 'our.' The other point is that the runes used in the poem clearly participate in alliteration, while they are not visually identical with the letters involved in alliteration of the lines. This can be evidence that alliteration is set up not on a visual, but aural basis.

4. Visual aspects of poetic MSS in Anglo-Saxon England

Visual aspects of poetic MSS in Anglo-Saxon England, such as layout, lineation, and punctuation, are cues closely related with reading of poetic discourse. A full detailed account of this theme would require careful studies of visual conventions in the manuscripts, and also include the orality/literacy problem, which is too complicated to be discussed in this paper; here are discussed only statements which summarise characteristics of poetic MSS in Anglo-Saxon England, but could be enough to argue against the idea of "visual alliteration" for OE poetry.

O'Keeffe (1990: 21-22) suggests that the use of visual cues for reading of poetic discourse was not as consistent or systematic in OE poetic MSS as in that in Latin:

(7) ... the physical evidence of the writing of these poetic works – their irregular spacing of free morphemes, highly individual and sporadic capitalization and punctuation, and copying of verse without regard to length of line – argue that the visual conventions which provided necessary information for the reading of contemporary verse in Latin ... were unnecessary for Old English. Verse in Old English was read in a different way from verse in Latin.

Huisman (1998: 100) mentions how a text in an OE poetic MS would be recognised as poetry without consistent visual conventions that could "distinguish a text of poetic discourse from other categories of discourse":

(8) The signification of a text as poetry could be heard when the text was read aloud, in the phonic patterns of rhythm and alliterative links.

Given these characteristics of the visual cues used in OE poetic MSS, it is doubtful that "visual alliteration" alone could have been used or accepted in a consistent or systematic way by the early scribes or readers, considering the inconsistency and low salience of visual conventions in OE poetic MSS; rather, it seems to be a more likely supposition that the vernacular manuscript culture in Anglo-Saxon England is orally/aurally-based, which would be one of reasons for the inconsistent use of visual conventions in OE poetic MSS.

5. Alliterative evidence

When we turn to the alliterative evidence, we find plentiful exceptions to the visual consistency that "visual alliteration" would seem to require. Vocalic and other types of visually inconsistent alliteration seem to argue against such visual alliteration. This suggests that alliteration is set up not on a visual, but oral/aural basis. Before the paper gives some of evidence below, the following points should be noted: the editions used in the present study are the *Anglo-Saxon Poetic Records*

(*ASPR* hereafter) and Rosier (1964-1966) for "Instructions for Christians"; this study follows the accepted readings and the extensively reconstructed passages (lines 96-122 of *Fates of the Apostles*, for example) in *ASPR* and Rosier (1964-1966), unless the MS readings are specifically mentioned below; from the present study are excluded lines that are too defective (short of a half-line, for example) for us to observe alliterative patterns; the abbreviated titles of poems are based on Mitchell, Ball, and Cameron (1975-1979); the numbers are those of the lines in *ASPR* or Rosier (1964-1966); the alliterating elements in question are highlighted in boldface; in the footnotes are given full lists of lines where apparently abnormal alliteration occurs.

In the poetic corpus, 342 relevant instances of apparently abnormal alliteration are found.[2] It seems unnecessary to count the total frequency of vocalic alliteration, because it is widely attested in Old English poetry, and has been well discussed in the previous studies. Only some examples are cited in (9):[3]

(9) Beo 392   aldor Eastdena,   þæt he eower æþelu can,
    Beo 3138   ad on eorðan   unwaclicne,
    Ex 509   ealles ungrundes   ænig to lafe,
    El 229   Ða wæs orcnæwe   idese siðfæt,
    PPs 143,13,3 þæt hi unrihtes awa tiligean.
    Met 29,50 on uprodor   ælbeorhta leg,
    Brun 31   eorlas Anlafes,   unrim heriges,
    Exhort 60 eard and eþel.   Uncuð bið þe þænne

Ogura (2004: 25) reports that the double alliteration of the same vowel is exceptional. Kaluza (1911: 121) suggests "glottal stop" (which, of course, is not represented orthographically) as the real alliterating element in this type of alliteration.[4]

---

2   Ogura (2004: 24-26) notices the same types of alliteration as those illustrated in (9) to (19) in the present paper, and cites some examples, with consideration of alliterative patterns in the Old Saxon *Heliand*. However, she relates these types neither to the problem of whether OE poetry works aurally or visually nor to the reliability of the evidence for the reconstruction of the sound system of OE; what she intends is to cite exceptional patterns of alliteration in OE alliterative verses so as to sketch and detect the diachronic changes in alliterating elements from OE to ME, that is, from structurally essential to artfully ornamental alliteration in some way in medieval English poetry. In addition, she does not give statistics and lists of the alliterative evidence of these types in OE. Accordingly, it seems reasonable to survey them again here with some illustrative examples and lists of the alliterative evidence for each type.

3   Noteworthy are the compounds whose first element *and-* (or *ond-*) is abbreviated with ꝥ in OE poetic MSS. Compounds of this type sometimes participate in vocalic alliteration, and GuthA 210, where *ondsacan* occurs, is a case in point. This type of alliteration can be compared to those cited in (22) and (23) below. Lines of this type are excluded from this study, because the abbreviation ꝥ is always spelt out in *ASPR*.

4   Minkova (2003) examines this "glottal stop" for the "vowel alliteration riddle" in Chapter 4.

In the poetic corpus, biblical proper names sometimes show word-initial *h* + a vowel, which may alliterate with a vowel. It should be noted that this *h* can be either historic or inorganic. There are 19 instances for this type of alliteration, some of which are cited in (10):[5]

(10) Dan 1   Gefrægn ic **H**ebreos   **ea**dge lifgean
     And 779   beodan **H**abrahame   mid his **ea**forum twæm
     Fates 36   fore **H**erode   **ea**ldre gedælan,
     Jul 673   **H**eliseus   **eh**stream sohte,
     Jud 180   **H**olofernus   **u**nlyfigendes,
     PPs 132,3,2 swa **æ**þele deaw   on **H**ermone,

Unferð, a proper name of Germanic origin, occurs in the Beowulf manuscript with an inorganic *h* word-initially, which is usually emended. It participates in vocalic alliteration three times out of all the four occurrences.[6] Below is cited one of its examples, which could be compared to the examples of biblical proper names cited in (10) above:

(11) Beo 499   **U**nferð maþelode,   **E**cglafes bearn,
                 [MS H**V**N ferð]

There are instances similar to this. Biblical proper names, such as *Hierusalem*, *Hieryhco*, and *Hieremie*, having *h* + *i* word-initially, may alliterate with [j] or [g], spelt *i* or *g*. There are 26 instances for this type of alliteration, some of which are cited in (12):[7]

(12) Dan 2   in **H**ierusalem,   **g**oldhord dælan,
     El 273   **g**uðrofe hæleþ   to **H**ierusalem
     ChristC 1134 in **H**ierusalem   **g**odwebba cyst
     Hell 128   ond fore **H**ierusalem   in **I**udeum,
     PPs 146,2,1 Eft **H**ierusalem   **g**eorne drihten
     MSol 201   **H**ieryhco, **G**alilea,   **H**ierusalem
     KtPs 134   **H**ierusolimę,   **g**od lifiende.
     Instr 155   Spræc **G**od **g**eara   to **H**ieremie,

---

5 Gen A 224 / Dan 1 / And 756, 779, 793, 1324 / Fates 36 / Jul 25, 160, 293, 673 / Jud 7, 21, 46, 180, 250, 336 / PPs 132,3,2 / Seasons 120.
6 Beo 499, 1165, 1488.
7 Dan 2 / El 273 / ChristB 533 / ChristC 1134 / GuthA 813 / Hell 99, 128 / PPs 64,1,3; 67,26,4; 78,3,2; 101,19,3; 115,8,5; 121,2,3; 121,3,1; 121,6,2; 127,6,3; 134,22,5; 136,5,1; 136,6,2; 136,7,3; 146,2,1; 147,1,1 / MSol 201, 235 / KtPs 134 / Instr 155.

Proper names of exotic origin sometimes have *ph* word-initially, and they may alliterate with [f]. There are four instances for this type, two out of which are cited in (13):[8]

(13) PPs 134,9,3 and þa Pharaones folce gecyðde
   Men 81   Philippus and Iacob, feorh agefan,

The word *psalterio* with *ps* word-initially may alliterate with [s] on all the four occurrences in PPs only, one out of which is cited in (14):[9]

(14) PPs 107,2,2 on psalterio þe singan mote,

In four instances found in the poetic corpus, *th* may alliterate with [θ], spelt *þ* or *ð*.[10] The alliterating words seem to be *Thomas* and *thronum*. In (15) is cited one example for each word:

(15) Fates 50 Swylce Thomas eac þriste geneðde
   Summons 2 ðeoda þrymcyningc thronum sedentem

In three instances, proper names of exotic origin with *z* word-initially may alliterate with [s], as is shown in (16).[11]

(16) Rid 40,68 nis zefferus, se swifta wind,
   PPs 82,9,2 Zeb and Zebee and Salmanaa,
   Men 136 Zebedes afera. And þæs symle scriþ

In 123 instances, words with *g* word-initially seem to alliterate with [j], spelt *i*.[12] Most of the instances contain biblical proper names, but some have an adverb *iu* or a compound whose first element is *iu-* (or *io-*). The example from *Instr* has *iugoð* as an alliterating word. Some examples are cited in (17):

---

8 Fates 37 / PPs 134,9,3; 135,15,1 / Men 81.
9 PPs 91,3,2; 107,2,2; 143,10,3; 149,3,3.
10 Fates 50 / Men 223 / Summons 2, 25.
11 Rid 40,68 / PPs 82,9,2 / Men 136.
12 Gen A 1078, 1174, 1552, 1604, 1921, 1932, 1967 / Ex 312, 330, 588 / Dan 314, 707 / Sat 185, 573 / And 12, 166, 489, 560, 754, 794, 966, 1408, 1516 / Soul I 60 / Dream 28 / El 209, 216, 268, 278, 328, 418, 586, 600, 609, 627, 655, 667, 682, 806, 836, 859, 874, 921, 923, 934, 976, 1032, 1202 / ChristB 633, 637 / ChristC 1476 / GuthA 40 / Az 31 / Phoen 549 / Jul 28, 96, 106, 131, 148, 167, 316, 531, 540, 628, 703 / Sea 83, 92 / Vain 57 / OrW 11 / Pan 21 / Hell 50 / Beo 2459, 2931, 3052 / Jud 13, 40, 123, 132, 144, 168, 256, 333, 341 / PPs 52,8,1; 74,8,6; 75,1,1; 75,5,2; 77,6,2; 77,23,3; 77,67,1; 78,7,1; 79,1,3; 83,7,3; 84,1,3; 86,1,3; 93,7,3; 98,4,3; 104,6,3; 104,9,3; 104,15,4; 104,19,2; 104,36,3; 113,1,3; 113,3,2; 113,5,2; 113,7,3; 118,9,1; 131,2,3; 131,5,3; 134,4,1; 145,4,2; 147,8,2 / Met 1,1; 1,42; 26,35; 26,47 / WaldB 7 / DEdg 8 / Men 10, 109 / Creed 29 / Seasons 62 / Instr 237.

(17) Dan 707	gold in Gerusalem,	ða hie Iudea
Sat 185	goda bedæled,	iudædum fah,
Soul I 60	ne nan þara goda	þe ðu iu ahtest,
Az 31	ond Iacobe,	gæsta scyppend.
Sea 92	gomelfeax gnornað,	wat his iuwine,
Beo 2931	gomela iomeowlan	golde berofene,
PPs 113,3,2	for him Iordanen	gengde on hinder.
WaldB 7	golde gegirwan	(iulean genam),
DEdg 8	Iulius monoð,	þær se geonga gewat
Instr 237	Gode oððe monnum	on iugoð þeowa,

In 14 instances, [k] or [tʃ], spelt *c*, alliterates with *k*.[13] Three instances are shown in (18):

(18) Beo 665	cwen to gebeddan.	Hæfde kyningwuldor
PPs 62,10,1	Kynincg sceal on drihtne	clæne blisse
Men 31	his cyme kalend	ceorlum and eorlum

In the following two instances from *Met*, cited in (19), the word for 'the Greeks' with *g* word-initially may alliterate with *c* and *k*, if this *g*, as Krapp (1932b: 227) notes, arises because Junius was merely unsettled in the spelling of this word, spelt with initial *c* in the other Metra:[14]

(19) Met 1,56	kyningas cyðdon.	Wæs on Greacas hold,
Met 1,66	comen on þa ceastre,	lete Greca witan

In the instance cited in (20), *f* seems to alliterate with [f], spelt *u*:[15]

(20) MCharm 12,6 Under fot wolues, under ueþer earnes,

The line cited in (21) may be evidence that the Latin word *rex*, if taken for *cyning*, can participate in alliteration:[16]

(21) El 610 oncyrran rex genioðlan; he wæs on þære cwene gewealdum):

Roman numerals may participate in alliteration if expanded into Old English numerals, which seems to suggest that alliteration could make them work orally/aurally, because they are not visually identical with the letters involved in

---

13 Beo 665, 3171 / PPs 62,10,1; 104,10,2; 144,4,1 / DEdw 5, 18, 23 / Men 7, 31, 52 / Pr 42 / CPEp 26 / Instr 250.
14 Met 1,56; 1,66.
15 MCharm 12,6.
16 El 610.

alliteration of the lines. There are 62 instances for this type of alliteration, some of which are cited in (22):[17]

(22) Gen A 1192   V and syxtig,   þa he forð gewat,
El 829   under turfhagan,   þæt he on XX
Rid 22,1   Ætsomne cwom   LX monna
Beo 2401   Gewat þa XIIa sum   torne gebolgen
DEdw 6   XXIIII,   freolic wealdend,
MSol 263   Se fugel hafað   IIII heafdu
Creed 35   and he XL daga   folgeras sine

The same comment seems to be applicable to runes used in poetry as to roman numerals. There are 74 instances with runes apparently alliterating. As mentioned in the discussion of Cynewulf's runic signature, runes could work aurally as well as visually. Some examples are cited in (23):[18]

(23) Husb 49   Gecyre ic ætsomne   ·ᚻ·ᚱ· geador
Rid 64,1   Ic seah ·ᛈ· ond ·ᛁ·   ofer wong faran,
Beo 913   ᛉ Scyldinga.   He þær eallum wearð,
WaldA 31   ealdne ᛉ   oðða her ær swefan,
MRune 1   ᚠ (feoh) byþ frofur   fira gehwylcum.

In *MSol*, two instances at least cited in (24) may be evidence that the separate letters of which the text of Pater Noster is composed could alliterate with a vowel in the second half-line.[19] Dobbie (1942: 163) notes that the alliteration of line 108a falls on both *N* and *O*, since *N* was pronounced "en", while in line 123 *L* can be alliterating because of its pronunciation "el". If this is right, it might be possi-

---

17 Gen A 1120, 1126, 1141, 1154, 1192, 1215, 1217, 1232, 1238, 1417, 2041, 2042, 2301, 2304, 2346 / Ex 232 / Fates 86 / Soul I 36 / El 3, 285, 326, 379, 634, 694, 743, 829, 832, 1227 / Az 171, 174 / Jul 678 / Rid 13,1; 13,2; 22,1; 22,3; 22,4; 86,4 / Beo 147, 207, 379, 2401 / CEdg 20 / DEdw 6, 20 / MSol 14, 47, 215, 232, 248, 263, 272 / Men 30, 38 / Creed 35 / MCharm 2,4; 2,30; 2,32; 2,33; 2,39; 2,42; 2,45; 2,46.
18 Fates 98, 100, 101, 102, 103, 104 / El 788 (MS), 1089 (MS), 1257, 1259, 1260, 1261, 1263, 1265, 1268, 1269 / ChristB 797, 800, 804, 805, 806, 807 / Jul 704, 706, 708 / Rid 19,1; 19,2; 19,5; 19,6; 19,8; 24,7 (MS); 24,8; 24,9 / Husb 49, 50 / Ruin 23 / Rid 64,1; 64,2; 64,3; 64,4; 64,5; 64,6 / Beo 913, 1702 / WaldA 31 / MRune 1, 4, 7, 10, 13, 16, 19, 22, 25, 27, 29, 32, 35, 38, 41, 45, 48, 51, 55, 59, 63, 67, 71, 74, 77, 81, 84, 87, 90. As regards the word *wyn* occurring in El 788 and 1089, see Krapp (1932a: 144): the runic symbol in the MS is expanded in the edition. As regards the letter *X* in Rid 24,7 see Krapp and Dobbie (1936: 334): they note that it was undoubtedly intended for a rune, and in the edition they print it as a majuscule, while it is a minuscule in the MS.
19 MSol 108, 123.

ble that in these two instances pronunciation of the separate letters could make alliteration in an oral/aural way.[20]

(24) MSol 108 ·N· and O s[..]od, æghwæðer brengeð
    MSol 123 Đonne hine I and ·Ť·L· and se yrra ·ʞ·C·

5. Conclusion

The present paper discusses whether alliteration works aurally or visually. The view of Sisam (1953) on Cynewulf's runic signature is that Cynewulf, considering his audience as well as readers, incorporated his signature into his poems so that it could work aurally as well as visually. This suggests that such a visual convention set up in a highly literate way does not necessarily preclude that Old English poetry works in an oral/aural way; rather, it could work aurally as well as visually. The visual aspects of the poetic MSS in Anglo-Saxon England suggest that the use of "visual alliteration" in Old English is unlikely, because it would be improbable for such a visually sophisticated literary device to be established in OE poetic MSS whose physical evidence does not show systematic consistency in the use of visual cues relevant to reading of poetic discourse. It seems that "eye-rhyme" in modern poetry should be based on well-established visual conventions, including orthography. Alliterative evidence in the present study, since it shows basically visual inconsistency and phonetic/phonological consistency of alliteration, suggests that alliteration is not set up on a visual, but aural basis, and reliable for the reconstruction of sound system of OE. This said, OE consonantal alliteration in the same graph in most cases seems to suggest that alliteration is phonemically-based, provided that the graphetic system reflects the phonological system in principle.

References

Dobbie, Elliott Van Kirk (ed.)
    1942   *The Anglo-Saxon Minor Poems*. The Anglo-Saxon Poetic Records VI. New York: Columbia University Press, London: Routledge and Kegan Paul.
    1953   *Beowulf and Judith*. The Anglo-Saxon Poetic Records IV. New York: Columbia University Press.

---

20 Judging from the pronunciations of letters mentioned in Ælfric's *Grammar* (see Zupitza 1880: 5-6), here may be added MSol 89, 93, 94, 96, 98, 111, 118, 127, 134, though Dobbie (1942: 162-163) does not mention these instances from the viewpoint of alliteration. Provisionally the present study does not count these nine lines in the total frequency of apparently abnormal alliteration.

Harris, David Payne
　1954　　　*The Phonemic Patterning of the Initial and Final Consonant Clusters of English from Late Old English to the Present: A Structural Approach to their Historical Development*. Ph. D. Dissertation, University of Michigan.

Huisman, Rosemary
　1998　　　*The Written Poem: Semiotic Conventions from Old to Modern English*. London and New York: Cassell.

Kaluza, Max
　1911　　　*A Short History of English Versification, from the Earliest Times to the Present Day*. tr. by A. C. Dunstan. London: George Allen.

Krapp, George Philip (ed.)
　1931　　　*The Junius Manuscript*. The Anglo-Saxon Poetic Records I. New York: Columbia University Press, London: Routledge and Kegan Paul.
　1932a　　*The Vercelli Book*. The Anglo-Saxon Poetic Records II. New York: Columbia University Press.
　1932b　　*The Paris Psalter and the Meters of Boethius*. The Anglo-Saxon Poetic Records V. New York: Columbia University Press, London: Routledge and Kegan Paul.

Krapp, George Philip – Elliott Van Kirk Dobbie (edd.)
　1936　　　*The Exeter Book*. The Anglo-Saxon Poetic Records III. New York: Columbia University Press, London: Routledge and Kegan Paul.

Minkova, Donka
　2003　　　*Alliteration and Sound Change in Early English*. Cambridge: Cambridge University Press.

Mitchell, Bruce – Christopher Ball – Angus Cameron
　1975　　　"Short Titles of Old English Texts". *Anglo-Saxon England* 4: 207-221.
　1979　　　"Short Titles of Old English Texts: Addenda and Corrigenda". *Anglo-Saxon England* 8: 331-333.

Ogura, Michiko
　2004　　　"Variations and Diachronic Changes of Alliterative Patterns and Alliterating Elements". *Anglo-Saxon, Norse, and Celtic Studies: Report on the Research Projects* 80, ed. by Michiko Ogura, 23-49. Chiba: Graduate School of Social Sciences and Humanities, Chiba University.

O'Keeffe, Katherine O'Brien
　1990　　　*Visible Song: Transitional Literacy in Old English Verse*. Cambridge: Cambridge University Press.

Penzl, Herbert
   1947   "The Phonemic Split of Germanic *k* in Old English". *Language* 23: 34-42.

Rosier, James L. (ed.)
   1964   "'Instructions for Christians': A Poem in Old English". *Anglia* 82: 4-22.
   1966   "Addenda to 'Instructions for Christians'". *Anglia* 84: 74.

Schipper, Jakob
   1910   *A History of English Versification*. Oxford: Clarendon Press; rpt. Honolulu, Hawaii: University Press of the Pacific, 2000.

Sisam, Celia (ed.)
   1976   *The Vercelli Book: A Late Tenth-Century Manuscript Containing Prose and Verse, Vercelli Biblioteca Capitolare CXVII*. Early English Manuscripts in Facsimile 19. Copenhagen: Rosenkilde and Bagger.

Sisam, Kenneth
   1953   "Cynewulf and his Poetry". *Studies in the History of Old English Literature* by Kenneth Sisam, 1-28. Oxford: Clarendon Press.

Zupitza, Julius (ed.)
   1880   *Ælfrics Grammatik und Glossar*. Erste Abteilung: Text und Varianten. Berlin: Weidmann.

13 Object Movement in Old English Subordinate Clauses[1]

Tomohiro Yanagi, Chubu University

1. Introduction

Within generative grammar, one of the main concerns of Old English (OE) syntax is to examine whether the underlying structure is head-initial or head-final, and numbers of attempts have been made (Kemenade (1987), Koopman (1990), and Pintzuk (1999), among others). This paper is concerned with the object-verb pattern (i.e. the head-final pattern) in subordinate clauses, and argues that there are two types of object-verb pattern in OE.

In OE subordinate clauses objects can either precede or follow adverbs. This is illustrated in (1) and (2), where the objects and adverbs are in boldface and italics, respectively.

(1) a. Ða ofðuhte pharao þæt he **þæt folc** *swa freolice* forlet.
      then repented Pharaoh that he the people so freely let
      'Then Pharaoh repented that he had so freely let the people depart'
      (ÆCHom II 12.112.86)
   b. Saul to cyninge ongean godes willan. þeah ðe he **hit** *geðyldelice* forbære.
      Saul to king against god's will though he it patiently endured
      'Saul for king, against the will of God, though he patiently endured it'
      (ÆCHom II 4.35.180)

(2) a. nis þeahhwæðere be him geræd þæt *he handlinga* **ænigne mann**
      not-is however about him read that he by-hand any man
      acwealde;
      killed
      'it is not, however, read of him that he killed any man with his own hands.'
      (ÆCHom I 27.400.12)
   b. He swor þæt he on æfnunge æt his heafde *witodlice* **hi** gesawe;
      he swore that he in evening at his head certainly them saw
      'He swore that he certainly saw them at his head in the evening.'
      (ÆCHom I 30.437.240)

It is generally assumed that both of the patterns in (1) and (2) are treated as the 'object-verb' order, but they may have different structures. In this paper we assume that while in sentences (2) the objects may occupy the base-generated position, the sentences in (1) may be derived by moving the objects leftward.

---

[1] I would like to express my gratitude to Masachiyo Amano, Masayuki Ohkado, Tomoyuki Tanaka, Michio Hosaka, Hideki Watanabe, Yasuaki Ishizaki, Mitsuru Uchida, and Manfred Marcus for their valuable comments and suggestions. All remaining errors, of course, are my own.

Under this assumption, the present paper further explores what causes objects to move out of VP in OE subordinate clauses, on the basis of the data retrieved from the parsed corpus of Old English, and argues that there is a landing site above the VP available for both nominal and pronominal objects.

2. Preliminaries
2.1. Database

The database used for the present study is *The York-Toronto-Helsinki Parsed Corpus of Old English Prose* (hereinafter, YCOE; Taylor et al. 2003).[2] The syntactic and part-of-speech annotations of the YCOE were used to collect data from the corpus by utilizing the Java-based searching program, *CorpusSearch 2*, created by Beth Randall.[3] This program is powerful to search for lexically and syntactically annotated configurations of any complexity, by combining simple commands. As a sample, one of the command sets used for the present study is given below.

command set
query: (IP-SUB* iDominates NP-NOM)
AND (IP-SUB* iDominates NP-ACC)
AND (NP-ACC iDominates N^A|NR^A)
AND (IP-SUB* iDominates ADV*)
AND (ADV* iDominates !¥**)
AND (IP-SUB* iDominates *VBD*|*VBP*)
AND (NP-ACC iPrecedes ADV*)
AND (ADV* iPrecedes *VBD*|*VBP*)

This command set is to extract sentences with the 'accusative noun and adverb' order in subordinate clauses.[4]

The data to be examined are restricted to simple sentences in subordinate clauses. Simple sentences are the ones that consist of a finite verb, object, adverb, and prepositional phrases, but without a modal or auxiliary (*beon* 'be' and *habban* 'have'). There are two reasons for this restriction. One is to exclude sentences derived through complex operations, such as Verb (Projection) Raising and Extraposition. The other reason is that if verb movement takes place in subordinate clauses, the underlying 'object-verb' order is preserved; in main clauses a finite verb moves up to C through T, resulting in the derived

---

2 The overall description of the YCOE tagset can be seen at
   http://www-users.york.ac.uk/~lang22/YCOE/YcoeHome.htm.
3 *CorpusSearch 2* can be freely downloaded at http://corpussearch.sourceforge.net/.
4 The commands 'iDominates' and 'iPrecedes' mean 'immediately dominates' and 'immediately precedes', respectively. For the exhaustive list of commands see at the URL in note 3.

'verb-object' order (see Section 2.2 for verb movement and the specific structures).

2.2. Theoretical Assumptions

Here I will make some theoretical assumptions. This paper assumes the 'traditional' clause structure of OE syntax in (3), where VP and TP are head-final, while CP is head-initial.

(3) OE clause structure

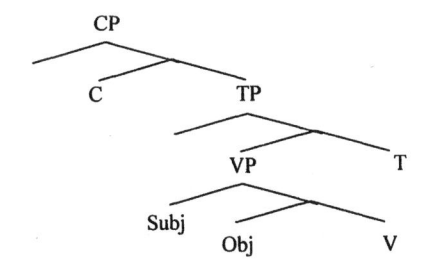

```
        CP
       /  \
      C    TP
          /  \
         VP   T
        /  \
      Subj
           \
           Obj   V
```

In main clauses the finite verb raises to the head of TP and further moves up to C, and a topic element (e.g. an object or adverb) occupies the specifier of CP, as illustrated in (4). This yields the so-called Verb-Second sentences.

(4) verb movement in main clause

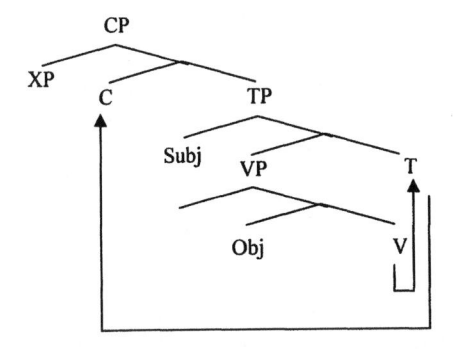

```
          CP
         /  \
        XP   \
            C   TP
               /  \
             Subj  \
                   VP   T
                  /  \
                Obj   V
```

In subordinate clauses, the head of CP, where a finite verb is located in main clauses, is occupied by a complementiser, such as *þæt* 'that' and *gif* 'if.' This prevents the finite verb from moving up to the head of CP and the finite verb stays at the head of TP, resulting in the verb-final structure, as illustrated in (5).

(5) verb movement in subordinate clause

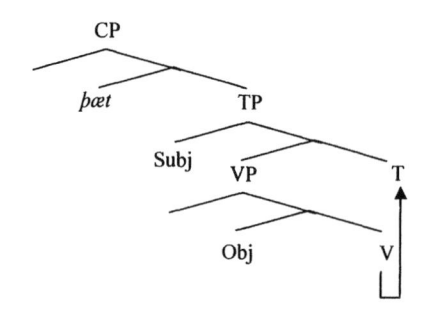

```
              CP
             /  \
           þæt   TP
                /  \
              Subj  \
                    VP      T
                   /  \     ↑
                 Obj   V────┘
```

The next section provides examples concerning the 'adverb-object' order and the 'object-adverb' order.

3. Word Order of Adverb and Object
3.1. Word Order of Adverb and Noun

Let us begin with examples of the 'adverb-noun' order. The number of these examples found in the YCOE is 266. Two examples are given in (6). In what follows the relevant object nouns and pronouns are in boldface, and the adverbs are in italics.

(6) the 'adverb-noun' order (266 exx.)
    a. Þa axode hine. seo eadige fæmne. hwi he *swa hrædlice*. **his gereord** forlete.
        the asked him the blessed female why he so   quickly his meal   left
        'The blessed female then asked him why he so quickly left his meal?'
                                                                   (ÆCHom II 10.89.294)
    b. Wæs þy feorðan geare Osredes rices þæt Cenred, se   Myrcna rice
        was the fourth year Osred   reign that Cenred   who Mercia realm
        æþelice sume tide forewæs, 7 *micle æþelicor*   **þæt anweald**
        nobly some time for was and much more nobly   the authority
        þæs rices   forlet.
        the kingdom   let
        'In the fourth year of the reign of Osred, Cenred, who for some time nobly ruled over the realm of Mercia, much more nobly resigned the authority over his kingdom.'
                                                                      (Bede 5.17.448.21)

Next we take examples of the 'noun-adverb' order. There were 287 examples found in the corpus. Two of them are given in (7).

(7) the 'noun-adverb' order (287 exx.)
    a. and wæron for ði   þa gebytlu   on ðam   dæge *swiðost* geworhte.
        and were therefore the building on the   day   chiefly made
        ðe he **ða ælmessan** *gewunelice* dælde;
        that he the alms   usually   distributed

'and therefore was the building chiefly made on the day on which he usually distributed alms.' (ÆCHom II 23.203.123)
b. Wæs his gewuna þæt he ða **stowe** *gelomlice* sohte for intingan
   was his habit that he the place frequently visit for matter
   stilnesse 7 his deagolra gebeda,
   stillness and his secret prayer
   'He was wont often to visit the place for the sake of retirement and prayer in secret'
   (Bede 3.14.202.11)

3.2. Word Order of Adverb and Pronoun

Let us turn to word order variation of an adverb and a pronoun. In contrast to the 266 occurrences of the 'adverb-noun' pattern, the 'adverb-pronoun' pattern is much less frequent: only 37 examples were found in the corpus. See examples (8).

(8) the 'adverb-pronoun' order (37 exx.)
    a. and filigde Criste. for ðan ðe he mid ungesewenlicere onbryrdnysse
       and followed Christ because he with invisible stimulation
       his mod lærde. swa swa he mid his worde. *wiðutan* **hine** clypode;
       his mind instructed as he with his word without him called
       'and followed Christ, because with invisible stimulation he instructed his mind, as he with his word called him from without.' (ÆCHom II 37.273.30)
    b. 7 þa ongunnan ærest wið heora fynd feohtan, þa þe monige gear
       and then began first against their enemies fought who many years
       ær **hi** onhergedon 7 hleoðedon.
       before them wasted and spoiled
       'Then for the first time they began to resist their enemies, who now for many years had wasted and spoiled them.' (Bede 1.11.48.22)

Object pronouns occur much more frequently before adverbs, rather than after adverbs. We found 385 examples, of which two examples are given in (9).

(9) the 'pronoun-adverb' order (385 exx.)
    a. Þa arn se ceorl geond ealle ða stræt. dæges and nihtes. dreorig
       then ran the churl through all the street day and night dismally
       hrymende. oð þæt ða heafod men **hine** *hetelice* swungon. æne. and
       crying until the chief men him severely scourged one and
       oðre siðe. oð þæt ða ban scinon.
       other time until the bones appeared
       'Then the churl ran through all the street, day and night, dismally crying, until the chief men severely scourged him, once and a second time, until the bones appeared;'
       (ÆCHom II 18.173.118)
    b. We asetton, swa swa usser Drihten Hælende Crist in menniscum
       we set as our Lord Saviour Christ in human
       lichoman sealde his discipulum, ða ðe **hine** *ondweardlice* gesegon
       body delivered his disciples who him present saw
       7 gehyrdon his word.
       and heard his words

'We set down, as our Lord and Saviour Christ, being in a human body, delivered to his disciples, who there saw him face to face, and heard his words.' (Bede 4.19.310.25)

3.3. Summary

The frequencies of the 'adverb-object' and the 'object-adverb' orders are summarised in Table 1.[5]

Table 1. Frequencies of the 'Adverb-Object' and 'Object-Adverb' Orders

	adverb-object	object-adverb	total
noun	**266** (48.1%)	**287** (51.9%)	**553** (100%)
pronoun	**37** (8.8%)	**385** (91.2%)	**422** (100%)
total	**303** (31.1%)	**672** (68.9%)	**975** (100%)

($\chi^2 = 172.884$; d.f. = 1; $p < 0.001$)

As we can see in this table, (i) in the case that the object is a noun, the frequency of the 'object-adverb' order is a little higher than that of the 'adverb-object' order (51.9% vs. 48.1%); (ii) when the object is a pronoun, by contrast, the 'object-adverb' order is much more frequent than the 'adverb-object' order (91.2% vs. 8.8%); and (iii) the distribution of the object and the adverb is statistically significant ($p < 0.001$).

The following section discusses the results obtained from the corpus search.

4. Discussion
4.1. What Derives Object Movement?

In order to examine what factor causes object movement in OE subordinate clauses, we classify the examples in terms of their clause types, the 'heaviness' of objects and the 'definiteness' of objects. Note that the discussion in this section is limited to nominal objects, since pronominal objects are 'light' and 'definite' by nature.

Clause Type

The first classification was made based on the clause type in which the relevant word orders are contained. In the YCOE, subordinate clauses are further divided into several clause types, such as adverbial clause, relative clause, indirect question, *þæt*-clause, and so on. Each of the subordinate clauses is labelled with one of the tags listed in (10).

---

[5] Throughout this paper the chi-square values were obtained by using the following Web-based calculators: Web-based Fisher's Exact Test Calculator designed by Shigenobu Aoki (http://aoki2.si.gunma-u.ac.jp/exact/fisher/getpar.html) and JavaScript-STAR version 4.4.0 created by Hiroyuki Nakata (http://www.kisnet.or.jp/nappa/software/star/).

(10) subordinate clause types
- CP-ADV   adverbial clause
- CP-CAR   clause-adjoined relative
- CP-CLF   *it*-cleft
- CP-CMP   comparative
- CP-DEG   degree complement
- CP-EOP   empty-operator CP
- CP-FRL   free relative
- CP-QUE   indirect question
- CP-REL   relative clause
- CP-THT   *þæt* complement

Of the clause types in (10), the three most frequent clause types are adverbial clauses, relative clauses, and *þæt* clauses. The numbers of these types are more than 80 in total each; each of the other clause types have less than 20 relevant examples of both 'adverb-object' and 'object-adverb' orders. The frequencies concerning the three clauses are given in Table 2.

Table 2. Classification according to Clause Type

	adverb-object	object-adverb	total	χ^2 (1)	*p*
adverbial clause	68 (52.3%)	62 (47.7%)	130 (100%)	0.276	n.s
relative clause	35 (41.2%)	50 (58.8%)	85 (100%)	2.647	n.s
þæt clause	37 (44.6%)	46 (55.4%)	83 (100%)	3.522	n.s

As can be seen in Table 2, the 'adverb-object' order appears to be slightly preferred in adverbial clauses while in relative and *þæt* clauses the 'object-adverb' order appears to be slightly preferred. These distributions based on the clause type, however, are not statistically significant, as indicated in the rightmost column (headed by italicised *p*). It could therefore be concluded that the clause type has no (or little) effect on object movement in OE subordinate clauses.

'Heaviness' of Object

Next, the examples were classified according to the 'heaviness' of their objects. Here the notion 'heaviness' is defined simply as 'the number of words which constitutes the object.' Two criteria were used to classify the examples: more than three words and more than two words. Table 3 and Table 4 show the results, respectively.

Table 3. Classification according to 'Heaviness' of Object (Three Words)

	adverb-object	object-adverb	total
> 3 words	10 (25.0%)	30 (75.0%)	40 (100%)
≤ 3 words	256 (49.9%)	257 (50.1%)	513 (100%)
total	266 (44.6%)	287 (55.4%)	553 (100%)

($\chi^2 = 9.218$; d.f. = 1; $p < 0.01$)

Table 4. Classification according to 'Heaviness' of Object (Two Words)

	adverb-object	object-adverb	total
> 2 words	43 (31.4%)	94 (68.6%)	137 (100%)
≤ 2 words	223 (53.6%)	193 (46.4%)	416 (100%)
total	266 (44.6%)	287 (55.4%)	553 (100%)

($\chi^2 = 20.381$; d.f. = 1; $p < 0.001$)

If an object consists of more than three words, it tends to precede an adverb; if an object consists of three or less than three words, there is no big difference in frequency between the 'adverb-object' and 'object-adverb' orders (49.9% vs. 50.1%). This contrast is almost true of the distribution of the other case, as shown in Table 4. Objects of more than two words tend to precede adverbs (68.6%), and no clear difference in frequency between the two word orders was found when an object contains two or less than two words (53.6% vs. 46.4%).

The examples in (11) and (12) involve the three-word objects. In (11) the object precedes the adverb, and in (12) the object follows the adverb.

(11) and   mid   micclum   hreame   his   sið   bemænde,   swa   þæt   ða   gebroðru
    and   with   much   cry   his   lot   bewailed   so   that   the   brothers
    ða   deofellican   stemne *swutellice*   gehyrdon;
    the   devilish   voice   plainly   heard
    'and with a great cry bewailed his lot, so that the brothers plainly heard the devilish voice'
    (ÆCHom II 11.97.181)

(12) Gif   hi   *soðlice*   **þone halgan fæder**   oncneowon.   ðonne   underfengon   hi
    gif   they   truly   the   holy   father   known   then   received   them
    mid   geleafan   his   ancennedan   sunu.   þe   he   asende   to   middanearde;
    with   belief   his   only-begotten   son   that   he   sent   to   world
    'For if they had known the Holy Father, then would they with belief have received his only-begotten Son, whom he sent to the world' (ÆCHom II 13.133.177)

It should be noted in Tables 3 and 4 that the *p*-value for the classification based on more than two words is less than that for the classification based on more than three words, and that an object which consists of more than two or three words, tend to precede an adverb.

'Definiteness' of Object

Finally, in addition to the two classifications presented so far, one more classification was made according to the definiteness of objects occurring before or after adverbs.

'Definiteness' can be defined syntactically or semantically. This paper employs the syntactic definition of 'definiteness': nouns with 'determiners', nouns with possessives, and proper nouns are definite. Here, determiners are *se* 'the, that' and *þes* 'this', and their inflected forms. Pronouns are also definite, but they are excluded from the calculation for the reason mentioned above. Indefinite nouns are the ones without determiners or possessives. The result is summarised in Table 5.

Table 5. Classification according to 'Definiteness' of Object

	adverb-object	object-adverb	total
definite	**100** (42.4%)	**136** (57.6%)	**236** (100%)
indefinite	**166** (52.4%)	**151** (47.6%)	**317** (100%)
total	**266** (48.1%)	**287** (51.9%)	**553** (100%)

($\chi^2 = 5.412$; d.f. = 1; $p < 0.05$)

When an object is definite, the 'object-adverb' order is more frequent than the opposite order. The distribution in Table 5 is statistically significant at the 0.05 significance level. It could be concluded that when an object is definite, the 'object-adverb' order is slightly preferred. Though, it seems that the definiteness of the object cannot be a decisive factor for object movement. The examples of definite and indefinite objects are given in (13) and (14), respectively.

(13) definite object
    a. Se þe ðas ðing *gecneordlice* begæð. he gegrypð untwylice
        he who these things sedulously performs he seized undoubtedly
        þæt behatene rice mid gode 7 eallum his halgum;
        the promised kingdom with God and all his saints
        'He who sedulously performs these things, seizes undoubtedly the promised kingdom with God and all his saints.' (ÆCHom I 25.385.181)

    b. 7 cwæð. Eala ðu cniht. þe ðurh þines flæsces luste
        and said O thou youth who through thy flesh's lust
        hrædlice þine sawle forlure;
        early thy soul lost
        'and said "O thou youth, who through thy flesh's lust hast early lost thy soul;"' (ÆCHom I 4.211.138)

(14) indefinite object
    a. Se færð to his tune 7 forsihð godes gearcunge. se þe *ungemetlice*
        he goes to his farm and neglects God's preparation who immoderately

eorðlice teolunge begæð to þan swiþe þæt he his godes dæl
earthly pursuits attends to the strong that he his God's portion
forgymeleasað;
neglects

'He goes to his farm and neglects God's preparation, who immoderately attends to earthly pursuits to that degree that he neglects God's portion.' (ÆCHom I 35.478.84)

b. þonne fylge we Drihtnes swæþe, þæt is gif we **oþre men** *teala*
then follow we Lord's footsteps that is if we other men well
læraþ, & hie be urum larum rihtlice for Gode libbaþ,
teach and they about our lore rightly for God live

'then follow we the Lord's footsteps, that is, if we teach other men well, and they rightly after our lore live to God;' (HomS 21 [BlHom 6] 75.160)

Here a brief comparison is made with Object Shift in Icelandic. In Icelandic, only definite objects can be shifted. In (15) and (16) italics and boldfaces are mine.

(15) a. Hún keypti *ekki* **kaffi**.
she bought not coffee
b. *Hún keypti **kaffi**ᵢ *ekki* tᵢ
'She didn't buy coffee.' (Thráinsson (2001: 151))
(16) a. Nemandinn las *ekki* **bókina**.
student-the read not book-the
b. Nemandinn las **bókina**ᵢ *ekki* tᵢ
'The student didn't read the book.' (Thráinsson (2001: 148))

In (15) *kaffi* 'coffee' is an indefinite object, and it cannot precede the negative adverb *ekki* 'not'. In contrast, *bókina* 'the book' in (16) is definite, and it can precede the negative *ekki* 'not' as well as follow it.[6] This contrasts with the distribution of objects in OE shown in Table 5. In OE indefinite objects as well as definite ones can precede adverbs. In this respect, object movement observed in OE subordinate clauses has a different property from Object Shift observed in Icelandic.

This section can be summarised as follows:

Summary
(i) The clause type has no (or little) effect on the position of objects in relation to adverbs.
(ii) 'Heavy' objects, which consist of more than two words, precede adverbs more frequently than they follow them.
(iii) The 'definiteness' of objects may have an effect on the word order of object and adverb.

---

6 For discussion of Object Shift in Icelandic and other Scandinavian languages, see also Holmberg (1986), Holmberg and Platzack (1995), and Vikner (2006).

4.2. Landing Site for Moved Object

This section discusses the syntactic position where the object can move up to. The basic clause structure for OE subordinate clauses is given in (17).

(17) OE subordinate clause

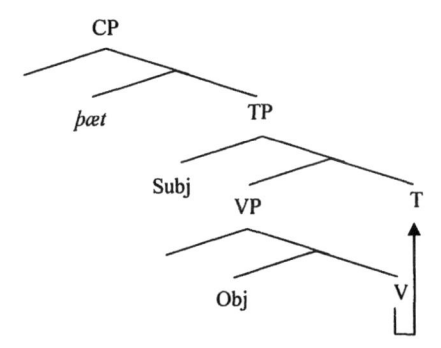

```
          CP
         /  \
       þæt   TP
            /  \
          Subj  \
               VP      T
              /  \     ↑
            Obj   V____|
```

Sentences like (6) and (8), where the object follows the adverb, indicate that an adverb occurs above the VP, given that adjunction to the bar-level category is not allowed (cf. Chomsky 1995). Then, let us assume that an adverb is adjoined to VP, as illustrated in (18).

(18) subordinate clause with adverb

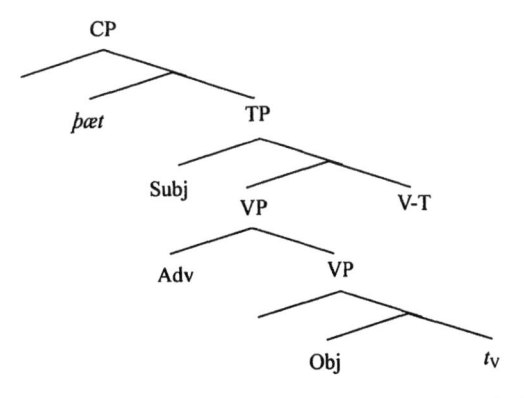

```
          CP
         /  \
       þæt   TP
            /  \
          Subj  \
               VP         V-T
              /  \
            Adv   VP
                 /  \
               Obj   t_v
```

Given (18), the subordinate clause headed by *hwi* 'why' in (6a), repeated here as (19a), would have the structure in (19b). In this, no object movement takes place.

(19) a. hwi he *swa hrædlice*. **his gereord** forlete.
       why he so quickly his meal left
    b. [CP hwi [TP he [VP *swa hrædlice* [VP [Obj **his gereord**] t_V] forlete]

By contrast, sentences like (7), where the object precedes the adverb, are derived by moving the object across the adverb adjoined to VP. In (18), however, there is no landing site for the moved object between the subject and the VP. As seen from the sentences in (7), the moved object cannot go across the subject. Then, we assume a functional projection, called FP, above the VP, as in (20).[7]

(20) movement of nominal object in subordinate clause

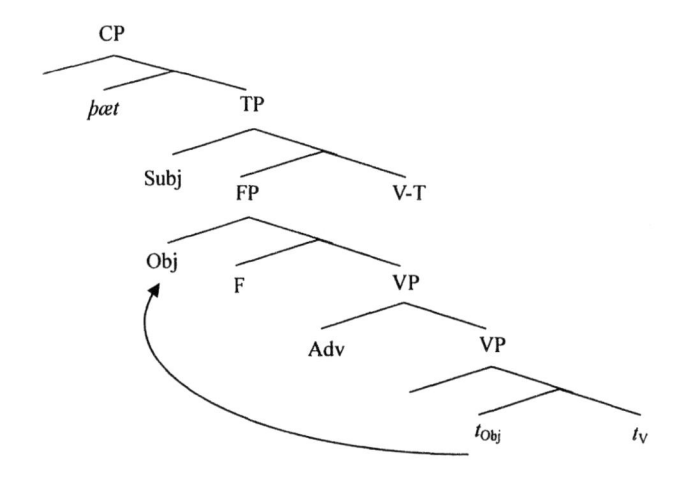

```
            CP
           /  \
         þæt   TP
              /  \
           Subj   \
                 /  \
                FP   V-T
               /  \
             Obj   \
                  /  \
                 F    VP
                     /  \
                   Adv   VP
                        /  \
                      t_Obj  t_V
```

The subordinate clause in sentence (7a), repeated here as (21a), is derived by moving the object to the specifier of FP. This is illustrated in (21b) and (21c).

(21) a. ðe he ða ælmessan *gewunelice* dælde;
       that he the alms   usually   distributed
  b. [_CP ðe [_TP he [_FP [_VP *gewunelice* [_VP [_Obj ða ælmessan] t_V]]] dælde]]
  c. [_CP ðe [_TP he [_FP [_Obj ða ælmessan] [_VP *gewunelice* [_VP t_Obj t_V]]] dælde]]

One might argue that there is an alternative operation: adjunction of an object to VP. This operation, however, may not be motivated theoretically, if pronominal objects are taken into account. Pronominal objects can also precede adverbs, but they are not a maximal projection and cannot be adjoined to VP, a maximal projection. Head elements like pronouns are adjoined to another head if motivated. It can thus be assumed that pronominal objects are adjoined to the head of FP. This is called *cliticisation* in the literature. (cf. Kemenade (1987), Koopman

---

7   The functional projection FP might be related to 'definiteness' or 'heaviness' of objects, as suggested in Section 4.1., but the determination of its nature is left open for future research.

(1990), and Pintzuk (1996), among others). This is schematically illustrated in (22).

(22) movement of pronominal object in subordinate clause

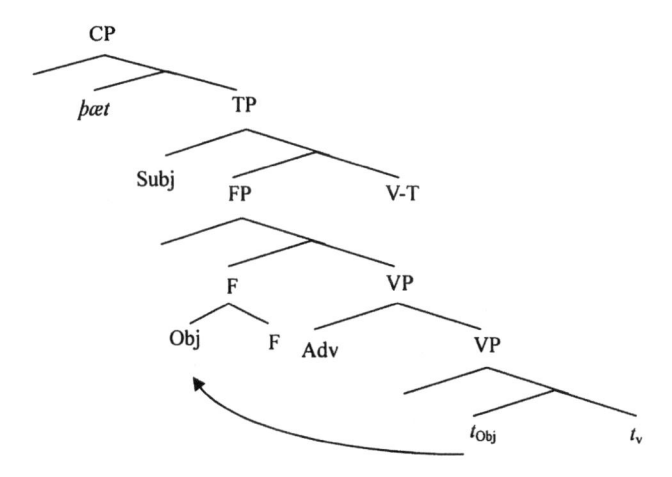

```
              CP
             /  \
           þæt   TP
                /  \
             Subj   \
                    FP        V-T
                   /  \
                  F    VP
                 / \
               Obj  F   Adv    VP
                                / \
                             t_Obj  t_v
```

The sentence of (9a), repeated here as (23a), is derived by cliticising the pronoun to the head of FP. This is illustrated in (23b) and (23c).

(23) a. oð þæt ða heafod men **hine** *hetelice* swungon.
    until the chief men him severely scourged
  b. [_CP_ oð þæt [_TP_ ða heafod men [_FP_ [_VP_ *hetelice* [_VP_ [_Obj_ **hine**] t_V]]] swungon]]
  c. [_CP_ oð þæt [_TP_ ða heafod men [_FP_ **hine**-F [_VP_ *hetelice* [_VP_ t_{Obj} t_V]]] swungon]]

To summarise, when an object precedes an adverb, a nominal object moves to the specifier of FP while a pronominal object is adjoined to the head of FP. Their final landing sites are different, but both are within the same functional category.

5. Concluding Remarks

It has been shown in this paper, based on the data retrieved from the YCOE, that (i) the 'object-adverb' order is much more prominent when the object is pronominal than when it is nominal; (ii) the 'heaviness' of the object may be related to the determination of word order of an adverb and object; and (iii) when an object is definite, the 'object-adverb' order is preferred. However, it is still unclear which is the decisive factor to distinguish between the 'object-adverb' and 'adverb-object' orders. This paper also argued that the functional projection FP is projected above VP and that nominal objects move to the specifier of FP and pronominal objects are adjoined to the head of FP.

References

Chomsky, Noam
    1995   *The Minimalist Program.* Cambridge, MA: MIT Press.
Clemoes, Peter (ed.)
    1997   *Ælfric's Catholic Homilies: The First Series.* EETS SS 17.
Godden, Malcolm (ed.)
    1979   *Ælfric's Catholic Homilies: The Second Series.* EETS SS 5.
Holmberg, Anders
    1986   *Word Order and Syntactic Features in Scandinavian Languages and English.* PhD Dissertation, University of Stockholm.
Holmberg, Anders – Christer Platzack
    1995   *The Role of Inflection in Scandinavian Syntax.* New York: Oxford University Press.
Kemenade, Ans van
    1987   *Syntactic Case and Morphological Case in the History of English.* Dordrecht: Foris.
Koopman, Willem
    1990   *Word Order in Old English: With Special Reference to the Verb Phrase.* Ph.D. Dissertation, Amsterdam University.
Miller, Thomas (ed.)
    1890-1898   *The Old English Version of "Bede's Ecclesiastical History of the English People".* EETS 95, 96, 110 and 111. [reprinted in 1959–1953]
Morris, Richard (ed.)
    1874-1880   *The Blickling Homilies.* EETS 58, 63 and 73
Pintzuk, Susan
    1996   "Cliticization in Old English", in *Approaching Second: Second Position Clitics and Related Phenomena* Edd. Aaron L. Halpern and Arnold M. Zwicky. Stanford: CSLI Publications, 375–409.
    1999   *Phrase Structures in Competition: Variation and Change in Old English Word Order.* New York: Garland.
Taylor, Ann – Anthony Warner – Susan Pintzuk – Frank Beths
    2003   *The York-Toronto-Helsinki Parsed Corpus of Old English Prose.* University of York.

Thorpe, Benjamin (ed.)
 1844–46   *The Homilies of the Anglo-Saxon Church*. 2 vols. London: Ælfric Society.

Thráinsson, Höskuldur
 2001   "Object Shift and Scrambling", in *The Handbook of Contemporary Syntactic Theory*. Edd. Mark Baltin and Chris Collins, Malden, MA: Blackwell, 148–202.

Vikner, Sten
 2006   "Object Shift", in *The Blackwell Companion to Syntax, Vol. III*. Edd. Martin Everaert and Henk van Riemsdijk, Malden, MA: Blackwell, 392–436.

Part II
Middle English

14 New Impersonal Verbs in Some Late Fourteenth-Century English Texts[1]
Ayumi Miura, University of Tokyo, Graduate School

1. Introduction and Review of Gaaf (1904)

In the history of English, the late fourteenth century is generally considered to mark the middle of a transition from impersonal constructions to personal constructions. According to Gaaf (1904), the process of transition started from the first half of the fourteenth century, and for most of the verbs the old construction survived until about 1500. On the other hand, not a few verbs made their first appearances in impersonal constructions during the fourteenth and fifteenth centuries. Gaaf refers to these two centuries as "a period of confusion" (§171) because older (i.e. impersonal) constructions and new (i.e. personal) constructions coexisted as synonyms.

The main subject of this paper derives from the following passage from Gaaf (ibid.):

(1) It is not surprising that during the two centuries the struggle was going on between A and D constructions [= impersonal and personal constructions respectively], mistakes were occasionally made, i.e. A constructions were sometimes employed where they were entirely out of place, e.g.:
Piers Plowm. C XIV 153, þer-of *me wondrede;* Destr. of Troy 9821, *wonders vs* noght;*) Prov. of Hendyng 156, Sore *may him drede;* Chaucer, Canterb. T. B 3918, Cyrus sore *him dradde;* Secr. Secret. 3rd. transl. 153/2, *hym mervelid* of Suche an Shape; similar inst. in Towneley Pl. 90/156 and 93/257.
Such mistakes could, of course, only be made when A constructions were still in general use.

Here Gaaf employs the term "mistakes", by which he means personal verbs that developed an impersonal construction. All the three verbs raised in the above quotation, *wondren, dreden* and *merveillen,* were originally personal verbs, but in Gaaf's argument, they were incorporated as impersonal verbs in Late Middle English. Such phenomena run counter to the shift from impersonal to personal constructions that is said to have been in progress in the period. However, the impersonal use of the three verbs should not simply be dismissed as the result of mistakes. In the above quotation Gaaf cites only two instances of impersonal constructions with *wondren,* both from the late fourteenth century, without any further explanations. This might lead us to erroneously believe that the use of *wondren* in impersonal constructions is sporadic enough to be regarded as a mistake. On the contrary, *MED* gives several other examples from various works (s.v. *wondren* 1. (c), 2. (c), 3. (c)), and the earliest instance is from the oldest manuscript of the

---
1 I am very grateful to Dr. Jun Terasawa for his useful comments and suggestions on the first draft of this paper. Thanks are also due to Dr. Hywel Evans for stylistic improvement.

South English Legendary, which is generally dated the end of the thirteenth century (see D'Evelyn and Mill 1957, Vol. III: 2). Since the impersonal use of *wondren* originated before the fourteenth century, it is inappropriate to cite it as an example of mistakes arising from syntactic confusion during the period of transition.

The two examples of the impersonal *dreden* in the quotation (1) do not exactly qualify as evidence that *dreden* was used in impersonal constructions because both of these instances are in fact ambiguous between an impersonal construction and a reflexive construction. The citations below provide a larger context in which these examples occur:

(2) Mon þat is luef don ylle,
     When þe world goþ after is wille,
     Sore may him drede;   (*The Proverbs of Hendyng* 154-6)[2]
(3) This riche Cresus, whilom kyng of Lyde,
     Of which Cresus Cirus soore hym dradde,
     Yet was he caught amyddes al his pryde,
     And to be brent men to the fyr hym ladde.   (Chaucer MkT(7) 2727-30)[3]

Gaaf seems to think that *drede* in the citation (2) lacks a nominative subject and that the preverbal *him* is an objective resumptive pronoun referring to *Mon þat is luef don ylle*. This is a possible interpretation, but it is also straightforwardly possible to take the first line as the nominative subject of *drede* and *him* as the reflexive pronoun. The *OED* dates the use of *dreden* in reflexive constructions from the early thirteenth century to the middle of the nineteenth century (s.v. *dread* †4) and *MED* also from the early thirteenth century onwards (s.v. *drēden* 1. (b)), so the reflexive interpretation is historically justified here. This also holds true with the citation (3). We cannot entirely deny the possibility that *dradde* in the second line is used impersonally, with the preverbal *hym* functioning as a resumptive objective pronoun referring to *Cirus* in the same line. However, it would be much more natural to take *hym* as a reflexive pronoun and *Cirus* as the nominative subject of *dradde*.[4]

Although the two examples cited by Gaaf are not perfect examples of impersonal constructions with *dreden*, it does not mean that *dreden* was never used as an impersonal verb in the history of English. Neither the *OED* nor *MED* enter the impersonal use of *dreden*, but the following quotations confirm that *dreden* was used in impersonal constructions not only in Late Middle English but also in Early Middle English:

---

2 The text consulted here as well as in Gaaf (1904) is Böddeker (1878).
3 All citations from Chaucer in this paper are from Benson (1988). References and short titles are in general those used in Benson (1993).
4 Incidentally, *MED* quotes the citation (3) as an example of the reflexive use (s.v. *drēden* 1. (b)).

(4) The dayes moore and lenger every nyght
    Than they ben wont to be, hym thoughte tho,
    And that the sonne went his cours unright
    By lenger weye than it was wont to do;
    And seyde, "Ywis, me dredeth evere mo
    The sonnes sone, Pheton, be on lyve,
    And that his fader carte amys he dryve." (Chaucer Tr 5.659-65; hereafter emphasis mine)
(5) "For þe ȝwyle þe chartre is i-hol: ȝeot euere-more me dredeth;
    Are heo beo to douste i-brent: siker lijf ne mai ich lede."
    (*South English Legendary*. St. Theophilus (MS. Laud 108) 175-6)[5]

We may also note that *ofdreden*, a verb derived from *dreden*, is attested as an impersonal verb in Early Middle English. *MED* provides the following two instances (s.v. *ofdrēden* (c)):

(6) Wel sore hyre of dradde
    Þat horn child ded were
    For þe ryng was þere (*King Horn* (MS. Laud Misc. 108) 1205-7)
(7) Þarfore me of-dredeþ sore
    Þe kniȝt him haue take.' (*Reinbrun* 75. 4-5)

It is interesting to note that the verb in (6) is replaced with *dreden* in another manuscript of about 1260, Cambridge MS. Gg.4.27.2: *Sore hure dradde*. The ultimate origin of the impersonal use of *dreden* can thus be traced back to a time before the fourteenth century, so we cannot support Gaaf's apparent claim that the impersonal *dreden* is an instance of mistakes made in the period of transition.

The impersonal use of *merveillen* should also not be understood as the result of the syntactic confusion in the period of transition because the usage had already existed in Old French before the verb was borrowed into English in the late fourteenth century (see *AND* s.v. *merveiller*). There are several verbs whose impersonal usage is ascribable to the loan translation from Old French. The English language most probably borrowed not only the verb *merveillen* itself but also its usage in Old French at the same time.[6]

---

5   We have to admit that the imperfect rhyme casts doubt on the authenticity of this reading, which appears in the oldest (dated 1280-90 in Horstmann (1987: x)) of all the existing manuscripts of the *South English Legendary*. It is interesting to observe that the later manuscript, Cambridge Corpus Christi College 145 in the early fourteenth century, has a personal construction in the corresponding line with a perfect rhyme:
    For þe wile þe chartre is ihol · euere mo ich drede
    Ar he[o] be[o] to doust ibarnd · siker lif nemay ich lede (181-2)
6   The *OED* quotes the earliest instance of the impersonal use of *merveillen* from the early fourteenth century (s.v. *marvel* †3. †b.), but the usage was apparently still not firmly established in late fourteenth-century English. This can be seen from the following citations from Chaucer's *Boece*, which draws largely on Jean de Meun's Old French translation of the Latin

Although published more than a century ago, Gaaf (1904) remains the most authoritative study. However, since his argument contains inaccuracies, as we have seen, the verbs that began to be used as impersonal verbs in the period of transition need to be reconsidered. As a preliminary survey, I shall compare the verbs used in impersonal constructions in the works of Chaucer, Gower, the *Gawain*-poet and Langland and attempt to show that factors other than the syntactic struggle between impersonal and personal constructions can be raised for the impersonal use of what were originally personal verbs in the works of the four poets.[7]

2. Data

An alphabetical list of all the verbs employed in *methinks*-type impersonal constructions in the English works of the four poets appears in the appendix.[8] The number of verbs is the largest for Chaucer (36), followed by Gower (30), the *Gawain*-poet (26) and Langland (21). The majority of these verbs have already been found in impersonal constructions since Old English or Early Middle English, whereas there are a number of verbs whose impersonal use is first attested in the period contemporary with the four poets. These verbs imply that the practice of creating new impersonal verbs was still alive even during the period of transition.

---

original. Chaucer uses the verb several times in his works, but never as an impersonal verb (the text of Jean de Meun is based on Machan and Minnis (2005)):

(a) JM: Mais forment me merveil pour quoi tu es malades puis que tu es mis en si salvable sentence. (Book 1 p6. 15-6)

   Ch: But owgh! I wondre gretly, certes, whi that thou art sik, syn that thow art put in so holsome a sentence. (22-4)

(b) JM: Lors dis je: "Trop me merveil et sui tous eshabiz de ce que tu me proméz si grans choses. (Book 4 p.2 1-2)

   Ch: Thanne seide I thus: "Owh! I wondre me that thow byhetist me so grete thinges. (1-2)

Here Chaucer avoids a direct translation of the Old French impersonal construction and instead adopts a semantically similar but syntactically distinct construction. Chaucer may have known that the impersonal use of *merveillen* already existed in the English of his day, but he probably thought that it would still sound exceptional to his contemporaries. This attitude is contrary to that of Gower and Langland, who, although only once (*CA* V 4481) and twice (*PPl.B* XI 350, 359) respectively, employ *merveillen* in impersonal constructions.

7 Editions consulted for the works of Gower, the *Gawain*-poet and Langland are as follows: Macaulay (1969) for *Confessio Amantis*; Anderson (1969) for *Patience*; Anderson (1977) for *Cleanness*; Gordon (1953) for *Pearl*; Tolkien and Gordon (1967) for *Sir Gawain and the Green Knight*; and *Piers Plowman* for Schmidt (1995).

8 By *methinks*-type impersonal constructions, I mean impersonal constructions where a verb occurs with an objective personal pronoun but without a formal subject *it*, just like *methinks*. Examples of *ben* plus an adjective or a past participle type such as *me is bettre* and *me was taught*, which are called "phrasal impersonals" and "impersonal passives" respectively in Denison (1990: 125), are outside the scope of the present study because, strictly speaking, they are different in character from our *methinks*-type impersonal constructions.

I shall concentrate on these newly employed impersonal verbs and point out the most significant factor that enabled each poet to use them.

3. Analysis

There is common agreement that a choice of impersonal constructions is dependent on the context or their typical meaning such as "unvolitionally/unself-controllably involved in the situation" suggested by McCawley (1976: 194). I do not intend to challenge this, but context should not be regarded as the ultimate determinant. It seems very unlikely that a poet alters an originally personal verb into an impersonal verb simply because the meaning he wants to express coincides with that of an impersonal construction. Context matters only on condition that the verb has both personal and impersonal uses, while the verbs to be discussed in this paper have been attested only as personal verbs until the late fourteenth century. For this reason, I shall exclude considerations of context from the following argument. I shall first discuss new impersonal verbs shared by more than one poet and then those found in only one of the four poets.

3.1. New Verbs Shared by More than One Poet

Two verbs fall into this category: *happen* (shared by Chaucer and Gower) and *wrethen* (shared by the *Gawain*-poet and Langland). Gaaf (1904: §24) notes that *happen* is not found in impersonal constructions until about 1340, but he does not argue how this usage developed. We may assume that synonyms like *bitiden* and *fallen*, which had been used as impersonal verbs since the Early Middle English period, played a part.

The impersonal use of *wrethen* appears to have been quite rare: the *OED* cites just one instance from the *Wars of Alexander* (s.v. †*wrethe* v.[1] 1. c.), while *MED* quotes only one example each from the *Gawain*-poet and Langland, in addition to the one cited in the *OED* (s.v. *wratthen* 1. (f) and *wrēthen* 1. (e)). The verb itself had been in use since Old English, and it is hard to explain the reason for the sudden introduction of the impersonal use in Late Middle English. Again we may point out the role of semantic analogy with verbs expressing displeasure (such as *lothen* and *misliken*), but perhaps another more significant factor is the clause in which the verb occurs. Both instances in Langland and the *Gawain*-poet are found in conditional clauses beginning with *if* and *and* respectively. Such subordinate clauses are named "stereotyped impersonal clauses" in Masui (1964: 180-90) because impersonal constructions are very frequently found there. This implies that not only semantic factors but also syntactic factors were relevant in the rise of new impersonal verbs during the period of transition:

(8) And if hym list for to laike, thanne loke we mowen
 And peeren in his presence the while hym pleye liketh,
 And <u>if hym wratheth</u>, be war and his wey shonye.' (*Piers Plowman B*. Prol. 172-4)
(9) 'I woled wyt at yow, wyȝe,' þat worþy þer sayde,

'<u>And yow wrathed</u> not þerwyth, what were þe skylle
Þat so ʒong and so ʒepe as ʒe at þis tyme,
So cortayse, so knyʒtyly, as ʒe ar knowen oute— (*Sir Gawain* 1508-11)

3.2. New Verbs Found in Chaucer Alone

Other than *dreden* mentioned above, there are three verbs which are found in Chaucer alone and whose earliest occurrence in impersonal constructions belongs to the period contemporary with him: *availen*, *remembren* and *suffisen*:

(10) So hath your beautee fro your herte chaced
   Pitee, that <u>me</u> ne <u>availeth</u> not to pleyne, (MercB 14-5)
(11) "<u>Me remembreth</u> it wel," quod I; "and I confesse wel that I ne wyste it nat. (Bo3 pr12.17-8)
(12) "<u>Suffyseth me</u> to love you, Rosemounde,
   Thogh ye to me ne do no daliaunce." (Rosem 15-6)

For all of these three verbs, *MED* quotes the earliest instance of the impersonal use from Chaucer's works (s.v. *availen* 1a. (c), *remembren* 1d., *suffisen* 1c. (c)). It is important to note that all of these are loanwords from Old French and that they had already been used as impersonal verbs before they were borrowed into English (see *AND* s.v. *valer*², *suffire*; *OED* s.v. *remember* 6. a.). The impersonal usage in Old French is very likely to have encouraged Chaucer to employ these verbs in impersonal constructions in English as well. This can be seen most clearly in his use of *remembren*. Miura (2007) pointed out that more than half of the examples of impersonal constructions with *remembren* in Chaucer occur in *Boece*, which is very faithful to Jean de Meun's Old French prose translation. In addition, most of the instances in *Boece* are literal or nearly literal translations of Old French impersonal constructions with *remembrer* or its synonyms such as *membrer* or *souvenir*. Most importantly, the texts that are generally assigned earlier dates than *Boece* lack instances of impersonal constructions with *remembren*. We may hypothesise that Chaucer adopted the impersonal use of this verb into his works during his translation of Boethius. Existing constructions in Old French provided a pattern for introducing new impersonal verbs in English.

3.3. Verbs Found in Gower Alone

Two verbs whose date of first appearance belongs to the late fourteenth century are exclusive to Gower, i.e. *bilongen* and *supposen*, neither of which is taken up in Gaaf's study. The following examples are both quoted in *MED*:

(13) Bot er the time that he spede,
   Ther is no sleihte at thilke nede,
   Which eny loves faitour mai,
   That he ne put it in assai,
   As <u>him belongeth</u> forto done. (I 687-91)

(14) Bot al to lytel him supposeth,
    Thogh he mihte al the world pourchace; (V 22-3)[9]

As far as I am aware, *bilongen* is the only verb whose first instance of the impersonal use is ascribed to Gower (see *MED* s.v. *bilōngen* 3.), while *supposen* as an impersonal verb is first attested in Trevisa's *Polychronicon* (see *MED* s.v. *suppōsen* 1. (c)), which was composed in the same period as *Confessio Amantis*. The use of *supposen* in impersonal constructions was therefore not peculiar to Gower in late fourteenth-century English, and *AND* does not recognise the impersonal use of the Old French counterpart *supposer*. It is difficult to explain why the impersonal usage of these two verbs developed after all, but the influence of synonymous impersonal verbs, i.e. *deinen* for *bilongen* and *thinken* and *semen* for *supposen*, must have been at work at least to some extent. However, it should also be noted that Gower employs impersonal constructions with *bilongen* exclusively in the *as*-clause. The following are the other two instances of impersonal constructions with *bilongen* in *Confessio Amantis*:

(15) And afterward, as him belongeth, (V 4268)
(16) Bot this I seie natheles,
    As me belongeth forto seie. (V 7370-1)

These are further examples of "stereotyped impersonal clauses" mentioned above. We may argue that the common structural pattern for impersonal constructions facilitated the impersonal use of *bilongen*, in addition to the semantic analogy.

3.4. New Verbs Found in the *Gawain*-poet Alone

Of the verbs whose first use as an impersonal verb was in the late fourteenth century, *displesen* is the only verb found in the *Gawain*-poet alone among the four poets.[10] Neither the *OED* nor *MED* has a section on the impersonal use under the entry for this verb,[11] nor is it mentioned in Gaaf (1904). However, there are two possible instances in *Sir Gawain and the Green Knight*. The use of *displesen* in *methinks*-type impersonal constructions does not seem to be attested elsewhere, so the following examples may be regarded as the *Gawain*-poet's unique usage, although the latter is inflectionally more likely to be a reflexive construction:[12]

---

9   The *OED* quotes this instance as the intransitive use with an inverted construction (s.v. *suppose* †1.†d.).
10 Although not in *methinks*-type impersonal constructions, Chaucer uses *displesen* in impersonal constructions involving the formal subject *it* three times in his works (WBPro(3) 293, RomB 3661, RomC 7495).
11 The *OED* integrates the impersonal use under the transitive use, although the term "impersonal" is not used (s.v. *displease* 2.).
12 Ogura (1991: 75) summarises the interpretative problems with these examples as follows:

(17) 'And þerfore, I pray yow, <u>displese yow</u> noȝt,
And lettez be your bisinesse, for I bayþe hit yow neuer
to graunte;   (1839-41)
(18) Bot on I wolde yow pray, <u>displeses yow</u> neuer: (2439)

Like several other verbs mentioned above, the impersonal use of *displesen* is supported by that of *desplere* in Old French (see *AND* s.v. *desplere*). When we consider the fact that *Sir Gawain and the Green Knight* abounds in words and phrases of Old French origin (see Tolkien and Gordon 1967: 140), it is quite possible that the impersonal use in Old French encouraged the *Gawain*-poet to think that he could extend the usage to English.

3.5. New Verbs Found in Langland Alone

The number of verbs used in *methinks*-type impersonal constructions in Langland is the smallest of all the four poets, and almost all the verbs are shared by at least one of the other poets. This may give the impression that Langland is comparatively conservative in his choice of impersonal verbs, but there are two noteworthy verbs that indicate his readiness to employ new impersonal verbs: *cheven* and *loven*. Neither of these verbs is treated in Gaaf (1904).

Both the *OED* (s.v. †*cheve* 4. b.) and *MED* (s.v. *chēven* 4. (b)) register the following instance in the B-Text of *Piers Plowman* as the earliest impersonal use of *cheven*:

"Norman Davis takes the verb from [*sic*] in (1) [= our (17)] as the impersonal subjunctive; then *displese yow noȝt* may mean 'let it not displease you'. He takes the verb form in (2) [=our (18)] as the reflexive imperative plural; then *displeses yow neuer* may mean 'never displease yourself', that is, 'never take offence'. But *MED* quotes (1) [= our (17)] as an example of the reflexive use.
One of the causes of the disagreement in interpretation lies in the form of the verb. A verb in the 'impersonal' use takes the third person singular, but *–s* drops when it is used in the subjunctive. The imperative plural may take *–eþ* or *–eth*, developed from *–aþ*, but *–es* can appear as a variant."
Ogura's summary is not sufficient to explain the "disagreement in interpretation" of (17). According to Tolkien and Gordon (1967: 147), the imperative plural has three endings in *Sir Gawain and the Green Knight*: *-(e)s*, *-ez* and *-e*, the last of which is crucial when we interpret the form of the verb in (17). Note also that the verb in (18) can be taken as the indicative present third person singular form, in view of the fact that an indicative form is occasionally found where a subjunctive form is expected to occur (see Tolkien and Gordon 1967: 146). In short, examples (17) and (18) are both subject to two readings: (17) is possible both as the impersonal subjunctive and as the reflexive imperative plural, whereas (18) can be understood both as the impersonal indicative and as the reflexive imperative plural. However, it is better to take (17) as an impersonal construction and (18) as a reflexive construction, since *–e* is infrequent as the imperative plural ending and the use of an indicative form instead of a subjunctive is rather uncommon.

(19) For if thei bothe pleyne, the poore is but feble,
And if he chide or chatre, hym cheveth the worse. (XIV 226-7)

Judging from the fact that *AND* does not mention the impersonal usage for the Old French counterpart, the use of *cheven* in impersonal constructions may be peculiar to English. One possible factor behind the development of this usage is again a semantic analogy with verbs such as *bitiden*, *fallen* and *happen*, all of which mean some happening or occurrence. However, the impersonal use in (19) is better understood as a kind of a common formula rather than an idiosyncratic usage of Langland's. The identical expression appears in the *Destruction of Troy*, another alliterative work of the late fourteenth century:

(20) The Troiens full tyte were tyrnit to ground:
Thurghe Achilles chiualry, hom cheuyt the worse. (5984-5)

Contrary to *cheven*, *loven* is not recognised as an impersonal verb either in the *OED* or in *MED*, so the following two instances of impersonal constructions can be considered as Langland's unique inventions:

(21) Patriarkes and prophetes and apostles were the children,
And Crist and Cristendom and alle Cristene Holy Chirche
In menynge that man moste on o God bileve,
And there hym likede and lovede, in thre [leodes] hym shewede. (XVI 198-201)
(22) 'The Fader was first as a fust with o fynger folden,
Til hym lovede and liste to unlosen his fynger
And profrede it forth as with a pawme to what place it sholde. (XVII 139-41)

In both of these instances *loven* is coordinated with a synonymous impersonal verb. We have to admit that the citation (21) prevents us from concluding with certainty that *loven* was actually used as an impersonal verb: we sometimes encounter cases where a verb that was never used as an impersonal verb in the history of English is coordinated with an impersonal construction, without being preceded by a nominative subject (see Nakao 1972: 299). In (22), on the other hand, *loven* is unquestionably used as an impersonal verb since it is immediately preceded by an objective pronoun. As far as I know, the impersonal use of *loven* does not seem to occur elsewhere, but Langland would not have employed *loven* in impersonal constructions if it had sounded very unnatural to his contemporaries.[13] The following quotations (23) and (24) may provide a clue to understanding the elsewhere unattested impersonal use of *loven*:

---

13 It may be worth noting that *biloven*, which was derived from *loven*, was attested as an impersonal verb in the early thirteenth century (see *OED* s.v. *belove* †1. and *MED* s.v. *bilōven* 1.), although the usage does not seem to have existed in the fourteenth century.

(23) It is *licitum* for lewed men to segge the sothe
If <u>hem liketh and lest</u> — ech a lawe it graunteth;   (XI 96-7)
(24) 'Right so,' quod the renk, 'reson it sheweth,
That he that knoweth clergie kan sonner arise
Out of synne and be saaf, though he synne ofte,
If <u>hym liketh and lest</u>, than any lewed, leelly.   (XII 170-3)

Since both *listen* and *liken* are among the most frequent impersonal verbs in *Piers Plowman*, these instances can be regarded as the prototype of (21) and (22): in (21) *loven* is substituted for *listen* whereas in (22) it replaces *liken*. Langland could certainly have used the prototypical form in (21) and (22) as well, but he may have found *loven* contextually more suitable than *listen* or *liken*. We may surmise that synonymity with *listen* and *liken* has encouraged Langland towards the nonce invention of the impersonal *loven*.

4. Concluding Remarks

As far as the four poets are concerned, the development of new impersonal verbs is generally attributed to at least one of the following three factors: semantic analogy with existing impersonal verbs, occurrence in stereotyped clauses for impersonal constructions such as *if*-clauses, and existing Old French impersonal constructions. The last factor is particularly relevant in the works of the four poets. Nearly half of the verbs mentioned in this paper are used as impersonal verbs in Old French. It is easy to imagine that a calque from established patterns in Old French was a quick way to increase the number of impersonal verbs in English. Although the number of verbs is only a handful, each of the four poets representing the late fourteenth century did allow a countertrend towards the transition from impersonal to personal constructions.

References

Primary Sources

Anderson, J. J. (ed.)
    1969   *Patience*. Manchester: Manchester University Press.
    1977   *Cleanness*. Manchester: Manchester University Press.
Benson, Larry D. (ed.)
    1988   *The Riverside Chaucer*. 3rd ed. Oxford: Oxford University Press.

Böddeker, K. (ed.)
1878   *Altenglische Dichtungen des MS. Harl. 2253.* Berlin: Weidmannsche Buchhandlung.
D'Evelyn, Charlotte — Anna J. Mill (edd.)
1956-59   *The South English Legendary: Edited from Corpus Christi College Cambridge MS. 145 and British Museum MS. Harley 2277 with Variants from Bodley MS. Ashmole 43 and British Museum MS. Cotton Julius D. IX.* EETS o.s. 235, 236, 244. London: Oxford University Press.
Gordon, E. V. (ed.)
1953   *Pearl.* Oxford: Clarendon Press.
Hall, Joseph (ed.)
1901   *King Horn: A Middle-English Romance.* Oxford: Clarendon Press.
Horstmann, Carl (ed.)
1987   *The Early South-English Legendary or Lives of Saints: I. MS. Laud, 108, in the Bodleian Library.* EETS o.s. 87. Millwood: Kraus Reprint.
Macaulay, G. C. (ed.)
1969   *The English Works of John Gower.* 2 vols. EETS e.s. 81-82. Rpt. London: Oxford University Press.
Machan, Tim William — A. J. Minnis (edd.)
2005   *Sources of the Boece.* Athens: University of Georgia Press.
Panton, G. A. — D. Donaldson (edd.)
1968   *The "Gest Hystoriale" of the Destruction of Troy: An Alliterative Romance Translated from Guido de Colonna's 'Hystoria Troiana': Edited from the Unique Manuscript in the Hunterian Museum, University of Glasgow* EETS o.s. 39, 56. Rpt. as one volume. London: Oxford University Press.
Schmidt, A. V. C. (ed.)
1995   *The Vision of Piers Plowman: A Critical Edition of the B-Text Based on Trinity College Cambridge MS B.15.17.* 2nd ed. London: J. M. Dent.
Tolkien, J. R. R. — E. V. Gordon (edd.), Norman Davis (rev.)
1967   *Sir Gawain and the Green Knight.* 2nd ed. Oxford: Clarendon Press.
Zupitza, Julius (ed.)
1966   *The Romance of Guy of Warwick: Edited from the Auchinleck MS. in the Advocates' Library, Edinburgh and from MS. 107 in Caius College, Cambridge.* EETS e.s. 42, 49, 59. Rpt. as one volume. London: Oxford University Press.

Secondary Sources

Benson, Larry D. (ed.)
   1993   *A Glossarial Concordance to the Riverside Chaucer*. 2 vols. New York: Garland.

Denison, David
   1990   "The Old English Impersonals Revived", in *Papers from the 5th International Conference on English Historical Linguistics: Cambridge, 6-9 April 1987*. Edd. Sylvia Adamson et al. Amsterdam: John Benjamins, 111-40.

Gaaf, Willem van der
   1904   *The Transition from the Impersonal to the Personal Construction in Middle English*. Heidelberg: Carl Winter.

Kurath, Hans— S. M. Kuhn — R. E. Lewis (edd.)
   1952-2001   *Middle English Dictionary*. Ann Arbor: University of Michigan Press. [cited as *MED*]

Masui, Michio
   1964   *The Structure of Chaucer's Rime Words: An Exploration into the Poetic Language of Chaucer*. Tokyo: Kenkyusha.

McCawley, Noriko A.
   1976   "From OE/ME 'Impersonal' to 'Personal' Constructions: What is a 'subject-less' S?", in *Papers from the Parasession on Diachronic Syntax, April 22, 1976*. Edd. Sanford B. Steever, Carol A. Walker, and Salikoko S. Mufwene. Chicago: Chicago Linguistic Society, 192-204.

Miura, Ayumi
   2007   "The Impersonal Verb *remembren* in Chaucer Revisited", *Language and Information Sciences* 5: 213-28.

Nakao, Toshio
   1972   *History of English II*. Vol. 9 of *Outline of English Linguistics*. Tokyo: Taishukan. [in Japanese]

Ogura, Michiko
   1991   "*Displese yow* and *displeses yow*: OE and ME Verbs Used Both 'Impersonally' and Reflexively", *POETICA* 34: 75-87.

Simpson, J. A. — E. S. C. Weiner (edd.)
   1989   *The Oxford English Dictionary*. 2nd ed. 20 vols. Oxford: Clarendon Press. [cited as *OED*]

Stone, Louise W. — William Rothwell (edd.)
   1977-92   *Anglo-Norman Dictionary*. London: Modern Humanities Research Association. [cited as *AND*]

New Impersonal Verbs in Some Late Fourteenth-Century English Texts 199

Appendix: Data

Figures under the column "Earliest Date" are the dates of the earliest quotation of the verb in *methinks*-type impersonal constructions. Blank spaces mean that the impersonal use of the verb is not explicitly mentioned in the dictionary. Blank spaces under the column "Number of Examples" mean that the verb is not attested as an impersonal verb in the poet.

Table 1: Alphabetical list of verbs used in *methinks*-type impersonal constructions

Verb	Earliest Date		Number of Examples			
	OED	MED	Chaucer	Gower	*Gawain*-poet	Langland
athinken	1250	c1300	2	—	—	—
availen	—	c1385	5	—	—	—
bifallen	c1175	c1300	1	2	—	2
bihoven	c950	1131	11	1	20	1
bilongen	1413	c1375	—	3	—	—
bisemen	a1225	c1225	—	1	—	—
bitiden	c1175	a1225	—	1	1	1
cheven	1377	c1378	—	—	—	1
deinen	1297	c1325	7	2	—	—
displesen	—	—	—	—	2	—
dreden	—	—	1	—	—	—
dremen	c1250	c1300	2	—	—	1
eilen	1086	—	—	1	—	—
failen	a1300	c1300	—	3	—	3
fallen	1297	c1200	6	1	1	1
forthinken	a1300	a1393	—	2	1	—
gamen	c1205	c1275	1	—	—	—
geinen	c1200	c1225	3	—	1	—
gremen	a1310	c1225	—	—	1	—
greven	c1230	c1390	3	6	—	—
happen	c1375	c1380	3	1	—	—
hungren	950	c1175	—	1	—	1
lakken	a1175	a1225	17	26	1	5
liken	c1200	c1150	56	42	24	26
limpen	c888	c1175	—	—	2	—
listen	971	c1150	303	91	12	13
longen	c893	c1200	2	5	1	—
lothen	a1225	c1230	—	—	—	1
loven	—	—	—	—	—	2
merveillen	c1325	c1380	—	1	—	2
meten	c1000	c1300	16	—	—	3

Verb	Earliest Date		Number of Examples			
	OED	*MED*	Chaucer	Gower	*Gawain*-poet	Langland
minnen	a1300	c1200	—	—	1	—
misbifallen	a1225	a1250	—	1	—	—
misfallen	1340	1340	1	—	—	—
mishappen	c1330	c1385	1	—	—	—
misliken	c1250	c1300	1	—	1	—
mosten	a1300	a1300	4	—	—	—
neden	c1125	c1230	31	15	1	9
oughten	a1300	a1250	41	15	2	—
paien	—	c1300	—	—	1	—
quemen	—	c1300	—	2	—	—
recchen	a1225	c1230	12	8	—	—
remembren	c1374	c1390	8	—	—	—
repenten	13..	a1400	4	1	1	1
reuen	a1000	c1200	2	1	1	—
semen	c1300	c1300	34	12	3	—
shamen	c897	a1150	1	—	—	—
smerten	c1200	a1225	11	—	—	—
suffisen	c1385	c1375	7	—	—	—
supposen	—	a1387	—	1	—	—
thinken	c888	a1126	171	120	31	37
thirsten	c897	a1150	1	2	—	1
thurven	c1200	c1175	13	2	—	—
tiden	c1000	c1300	3	—	—	—
wanten	a1225	c1225	2	—	2	1
wlaten	c1000	c1230	—	—	1	—
wondren	c1300	c1300	—	—	1	—
worthen	a1330	a1225	—	—	2	—
wrethen	a1400	c1378	—	—	1	1

15 The Rise of *because* in Middle English
Rafał Molencki, University of Silesia, Poland

1. Introduction
In this article I discuss the sudden emergence and the subsequent very rapid growth of usage of the adverbial subordinator *because* in late Middle English. I will try to find the explanation why this word came to replace the original English causal connective *forthi* so quickly and became the chief subordinating conjunction of cause in the 15th century. I will present a detailed survey of how *because* became the most important causal subordinator in a very short time by means of several cycles of grammaticalisation. I will also show that contrary to what we find in dictionaries, the phrase is not a direct French loanword and appeared in English much later than *OED* suggests. Finally, I will present strong evidence that the origins of *because* are to be found in England rather than in continental French.

The language material for the study comes from several electronic corpora (*DOE* corpus, *OED, MED*, the Helsinki corpus, the Helsinki corpus of older Scots), from Visser (1963-1973), several Middle English anthologies and some Early English Text Society editions of Middle English texts. The short titles of the texts follow the standard conventions for Old English (*DOE* and Mitchell 1985) and Middle English (*MED*). The quotations from the the Helsinki corpora are marked according to the textfile codes used by the compilers (cf. Kytö 1993). The Anglo-French data mostly come from *Foedera*.

2. Old English
Old English made use of a complex conjunction made up from the preposition *for* + followed by the dative or instrumental of the neuter demonstrative pronoun, usually univerbated to *forþon, forþam, forþæm* (depending on the period and the dialect – northern texts prefer *forþon*), *forþy*, often followed by the subordinating particle *þe* (later *þæt, þat*) We find analogous formations in Slavonic (cf. Polish *dlatego że*, Czech *pro to že*) and Romance (French *parce-que*, Spanish *porque*, Italian *perché*) – cf. Kortmann (1997: 199). According to Rissanen (1998: 394) the presence of the subordinating element *þe/þæt* is the evidence of the growing need for marking the subordination. Indeed, his study of the clause markers in the three subsequent Old English periods of the Helsinki corpus shows a steady growth: 850-950 23% of *þe*, 950-1050 – 30 %, 1050-1150 – 52 %. The *þe/þæt* forms are very rare in OE poetry, which is the evidence of its archaic character. The phrase *forþon* could mark both the clause of reason and the clause of consequence:

strictly causal sense:

(1) *Bo* 42 Ða cwæð ic: Hwy? Ða cwæð he: **For ðon þe** we witon swiðe lytel ðæs þe ær us wæs buton be gemynde 7 be geascunge.

explanatory sense:

(2) *Chr.* 891 Sume men cweþaþ on Englisc þæt hit sie feaxede steorra. **forþæm** þær stent lang leoma of.

Other causal conjunctions are discussed in detail by Mitchell (1985), who in §3037 draws our attention to the fact that *OED* notes no examples of *for* [alone] as a causal conjunction before c1150. But van Dam (1957) finds earlier examples, e.g. *ChronE* 251.31 (1123) and a singular example from *Gregory's Dialogues* with variant manuscript forms. However, Mitchell believes that "*for* has only a shaky claim to being a causal conjunction in OE". Witness:

(3) *ChronF* 995.45: ac ða hi to Rome coman, þa nolde se papa naht don, **far** hi ne brahtan nan gewrit.

3. Early Middle English

In early Middle English we find the same markers of cause as in Old English, but one can observe the gradual elimination of *forþon* by the early 14th century. Last *forþan þe* is attested in *The Bodleian Homilies* (c1175,?OE) and *The Trinity Homilies* (a1225,?a1200), thus texts which are known to have been versions of Old English texts:

(4) a1225(?a1200) *Trin.Hom.* 107 Leomene fader we clepeð ure drihten, **for þan þe** he sunne atend.

Last instances of *forþan þæt* are found in (southern) *Ayenbite of Inwit*:

(5) c1340 *Ayenb.* Þet wes betokned ine samson þe stronge þet, **uorþan þet** he let him ouercome be ane wyfmanne, he uorleas his her of his heauede.

Forthi continues longer and as a conjunction is always followed by subordinating *þe/þat* according to *MED*:

(6) 1137 *Peterb.Chron.* Ðis gære for þe king Stephne ofer sæ to Normandi; & ther wes underfangen, **forði ðat** hi uuenden ðat he sculde ben alsuic alse the eom wes, & **for** he hadde get his tresor; ac he todeld it & scatered sotlice.

(7) ?c1200 *Orm.* 115 Icc hafe itt don **forrþi þatt** all Crisstene follkess berrhless Iss lang uppo þatt.

(8) c1230(a1220) *Ancr.* 41b (*Corp.Chr.*) freinið hwet itidde of ezechie þe gode king **for þi þ** he schawde þe celles of his aromaz.

(9) a1425(a1382) *WBible* 2 Kings 3.30   Therfor Joab and Abisay...slewen Abner, **forthi that** he hadde slayn Asahel.
(10) c1475(?c1400) *Wycl.Apol.* 69   He schal bere þe wickidnes wiþ te synnar, **for þi þat** he is cause.

The simple *for* in this function is quite well attested in early Middle English:

(11) 1123 *Peterb.Chron.* Ac hit naht ne beheld **for** se biscop of Aæres byrig wæs strang.
(12) ?c1200 *Orm.* 15 E33whær þær þu shallt findenn hemm..**Forr** whase mot to læwedd follc Larspell..tellen, He mot wel ekenn mani3 word.
(13) a1250 *Cristes milde moder* 39   Þer ne mei non ualuwen, **uor** þer is eche sumer.

And in the earliest ME texts *that* was appended to *for*, especially in North-East Midlands (*Ormulum, Trinity Homilies*)

(14) ?c1200 *Orm.* 3826 þa wakemenn to frofrenn **Forr þatt** hi wisste wel þatt te33 Off himm fordrædde wærenn.
(15) c1250 *Owl&N.* 365   An seist, **forþat** ich fleo bi ni3te þat ich ne mai iso bi li3te.

Nevertheless the instances of *for that* are relatively infrequent in Middle English and according to Rissanen (1998) they become really common in the 16th century, when most of other complex adverbial subordinators ending in *that* became obsolete (*if that, when that*, etc).

Additionally in the early 14th century we can witness the appearance of *for-why* (especially in the North, with the spelling *forqui*), cf. Lenker (2007). Witness the conjunctions in the following *Cursor mundi* manuscripts (line 3500):

(16) þe fader luued esau for fode, **For-qui þat** he was archer gode   *Cotton*
    þe fader loued esau for fode. **for-quy þat** he was archer gode   *Fairfax*
    þe faþer loued Esau for fode, **For-þi þat** he was an archer gode   *Göttingen*
    þe fadir loued esau for fode, **For** he was an archer gode   *Trinity*

MED lists some other examples of *forwhy* between 1330 and 1500, e.g. Chaucer's:

(17) a1425(c1385) Chaucer *TC* 1.714 Certeinly namore harde grace May sitte on me, **forwhy** ther is no space.
(18) a1425(?a1400) Chaucer *RRose* 1741 But certes, the arowe that in me stod Of me ne drew no drope of blod, **For-why** I found my wounde all dreie.

Forthy was used both as an adverb, as in (19) below, and as a subordinating conjunction:

(19) a1300 *Jacob&J.* 144 Of Egiptene speche couþe he no þing; **For þi** he wepte sore.

Then the adverbial *forthy* came to be replaced with *therefore* – in this respect we can see a systematic difference between northern vs. southern MSs of *Cursor mundi*. In the first 4500 lines of the poem the southern Trinity MS does not have *forthy* at all – it is systematically replaced with *therefore*, e.g.

(20) **For-þi** he left þat cursed lede and went vnto his auen dede. *Cotton* 1745
 for-þi he left þat cursed lede and wro3t forþ his awen dede *Fairfax*
 For-þi he sone he left þat cursid lede, And went him to his aun dede. *Göttingen*
 Þerfore he lefte þat cursede lede And went & dud his owen dede *Trinity*

On the other hand, the conjunction *forthy* is more and more often reduced to simple *for* (see 11-13 and especially 16 above):

(21) Mi leif sun, i will þe warn, **For-qui** þou ert mi derest barn. *Cotton* 3626
 Mi leue son I wol þe warn **For** þou art my derrest barn. *Trinity*

In the early 14th century we can observe the semantic extensions of other adverbial subordinators to the function of causal subordinators: *since, als/as*, especially introducing the given information at the beginning of the complex sentence (cf. Molencki 2003, 2007). *For* seems to specialise then as an exponent of explanation, giving new information, and is rare at the beginning of the sentence. It is predominantly found as a coordinating marker, while *forthy* tends to introduce the strict cause.

4. The rise of *because*
4.1. Etymology
In the late 14th century a new device for expressing causal relationship appears in English. These are phrases with the noun CAUSE, most notably the prepositional phrase *by (the) cause*, the parent of *because*. Obviously, the noun is derived from Latin *causa*, whose regular phonetic development in Central Old French and Norman was *chose*. But in later medieval times, as is well known, *moyen français* underwent the process of re-Latinisation, and according to etymological French dictionaries the first instances of the noun *cause* in French are recorded in 1180. More or less at the same time we find the earliest English instance of *cause*, in the sense of 'reason or ground for action, motive', first attested in *Ancrene Wisse*:

(22) c1230(?a1200) *Ancr.* 87a **Cause** is hwi þu nit dudest, oðer hulpe oþre þerto, oðer þurh hwet hit bigon.

However, these seem to be rather isolated uses – I do not find any whatsoever in the Helsinki Corpus. Only one example is attested in Kentish *Ayenbite* 1340. *MED* quotes some other instances of *cause* in *South English Legendary* (c1300) in the sense of 'a matter of legal controversy', but it is not until the mid-14th century that *cause* is found in English in its present (and now prototypical) sense of 'source, origin, root':

(23) c1350(a1333) Shoreham *Poems* 115.13 **Cause** of alle þyse dignyte.. Was godes owene grace.

But the examples do not become plentiful until Chaucer when *cause* readily cooccurs with the prepositon *by*, thus bringing about the rise of a new English conjunction. It is based on the French strategy for forming complex conjunctions, e.g. *par cause que*. Bonnard – Régnier (1997: 220) also mention "locutions composées" *por o que* – from *pro hoc quod* and *por ço (ce) que* – from Vulgar Latin *pro eo quod*, as in

(24) c1200 *Aucassin et Nicolette* XX.10 si fist faire une mot rice feste, **por çou qu**'il cuida Aucassin son fil conforter.
(25) 1279 *Foedera* Et, **pur ce ke** nus vodrum ke cele chose se preyt, vos priums ke vous voylleyt acorder; **kar** nus entenduns ke ce est vestre prou & vestre honur.

4.2. Causal connection in medieval French

The coordinating conjunction of explanation in French (and other Romance languages) was *car* derived through grammaticalisation from the Vulgar Latin phrase *qua re* (*by what thing/by what cause*), ablative of *res* acquiring the sense of *cause*, just like Old English *þing*. The grammaticalisation of the phrase was accompanied by the phonetic attrition, hence in Old French we find *quar, quer, qar, kar, car* (cf. de Dardel 2002 and 25 above):

(26) c1090 *Roland* 2454 Charle, chevalche, **car** tei ne falt clartet!
(27) c1140 *Le charroi de Nîmes* 474 Demi mon regne, se prendre le volez, Vos doin ge. sire, volantiers et de grez; **Quar** de grant foi vos ai toz jorz trové Et par vos sui roi de France clamé.

The word *cause* is not attested in *La chanson de Roland* yet. Some early instances in Anglo-Norman appear in the early entries of *Foedera*, which is a collection of legal documents and historical chronicles written in French and Latin in England between 1256 and 1383, e.g.:

(28) 1282 *Foedera* E ei troue que, **por ceste cause** avant que je fusse ore derierement vostre seneschaus, e apres, aucunes procurations ont este cassees, en la cort de France.
(29) 1301 *Foedera* Et toutes foiz veut & promet le diz Rois de France, que les dites terres, chatiax, seignories, forteresces, & toutes les choses, qui seront mises en sa main **pour ceste cause**.

In French etymological dictionaries (also in Guiraud 1963: 112-114) the first quotations of the complex conjunction/preposition *à cause que/par cause que; à cause de/par cause de* are attested in the classical French period, i.e. the 16th century:

(30) Corneille *D.San.* 50 Sa naissance inconnuee est peut-être sans tache: vous la présumez basse **à cause qu'**il la cache.
(31) Mme de La Fayette: Je couche chez nos voisins, **à cause qu'**on bâtit devant mes fenêtres.

In Modern French the conjunctions *à cause que, par cause que* are used in argot (nonstandard varieties) and in Canadian French – but such usage is strongly criticised by prescriptive grammarians. Here are some instances googled out from Belgian and Canadian websites:

(32) Je ne bois pas de café, **à cause que** ça me tue l'estomac.
    (http://monavissurtout.blogspot.com)
(33) Lorsque ce crétin annoncera sa retraite **par cause que** le hockey n'est plus un travail rentable!
    (http://www.rds.ca/hockey/talkbacks/182342/64601.html; common in sports columns)

There do not seem to be any attested examples of the conjunction in medieval continental French. But – interestingly – one can find numerous instances in the Anglo-French dialect that developed in England after the Norman Conquest. The first Anglo-Norman examples are only about one generation earlier than the Middle English instances of *by cause (that)*. The following three examples illustrate the grammaticalisation path whereby the noun *cause* (still preceded by the definite article *la* in 34) became a part of the phrase *par cause de*, which had the force of a preposition:

(34) 1312 *Foedera*   que seneschal & garde de terre poet & deit faire, **par la cause de** son office.
(35) 1315 *Foedera*   faites solempnement contre nos diz enemiz, si les faites publier par voz teres, si que vous ne s'en puist excuser **par cause de** ignorance.
(36) 1345 *Foedera*   si que vous ne s'en puist excuser **par cause de** ignorance.

Further on, the complex conjunction *par cause que/a cause que* appeared:

(37) 1344 *Foedera*   Et, pur ce que, avant ces heures, gentz ount este desceuz **par cause qil** n'aveit nulle eschange overte.
(38) 1349 *Negotiations for the Ransom of David Bruce*   Item coment grant empeschement est a les grosses busoignes le Roi **par cause qe** monsieur E. de B. ne voet accorder a bones voies de paiz tieles come.
(39) 1377 *Fœdera*   et **a cause que** le dit Esmond le pier morust seisi de mesme le manoir en son demesne come de fee, mesme cest Esmond le fitz adonques esteant deinz age, notre seignur le Roi, laiel notre seignur le Roi q'ore est, seisit le dit Esmond le fitz en sa garde, **par cause que** fuisit trove en mesme le livre que le dit manoir fuist tenuz par an par tieux services, et prist les profitz de mesme le manoir par quatre ans come de sa garde.

4.3. Anglo-Norman and Middle English bilingualism

The examples above prove that the conjunctive phrase *a cause que/par cause que* appeared first in Anglo-French, most likely in the circle of London clerks. These people must have been perfectly bilingual (cf. Ingham 2005) and it looks that the phrase was calqued in their English as *by (the) cause (that)*. We find some evidence of the process in the 14th century trilingual (Latin, French, English) verse treatise *Femina* (Trinity College, Cambridge MS B.14.40), where *by cause þat* systematically corresponds to *a cause qe*, e.g.:

(40) c1415   *Femina* 24
    A vous ne di ne ceyntés,   To ȝow y say nat wexe wit chyld,
    A cause qe femme est par homme enceynte,   **By cause þat** womman ys by man wit chyld,
    Et ové une seinture [est] ele seinte.   And wit a seynture she ys ygurd.

(41) c1415   *Femina* 41
    Et donque dit homme par seynt George   And þanne seyþ man by seynt Gorge
    Qi trop ad bu du grece d'orge,   Þat over muche haþ dronke fat of bere,
    Qi luy covient d'aler a repose,   Þat hym byhovyþ go to reste,
    A cause qe ne puet faire altre chose.   **By cause þat** he may do noon oþer þynge.

Similarly, in the collection of letters and documents written by the Stonor family we observe a transition from French to English on the turn of the 15th century. In many letters of the 1370s-1380s the Stonors use the preposition *a/par cause de* and the conjunction *pur cause qe*:

(42) 1377 Trescher syre, ceste requeste vous pleise accomplier **a cause du** dit mon meistre, qi maintenant est deschayte de grevouse maladie.
(43) 1378 Trescher et tresame cosyn, molt vous merciouns de ceo qe vous avetz ease noz tenauntz de Aston **par cause de** nostre preyer, queux furent pris et areynez, pur quele chose molt sumes tenus a vous.
(44) 1380 par quey, treshonore seignour, le dit Richard et Marjorye sa femme vous prie enterement, si il soit a vostre voluntee qe le jour puet estre pro||longe tanke a le Chandelure, **pur cause qe** il ne at mye seme tot soun semaile de furment, et auxi pur ceste temps est pluviouse et bret jours.

In the next generations the English-speaking Stonors often use the English cognates:

(45) ?1462 bot I supposet ye wold not so, **for by cause of the penalte** of the pay|ment of the xl. s. yerly.
(46) ?1466 and that altho personys þat the seyde Richard had wrongfully take mony of **for cause of me** þat he shuld a restoryd ayen to hem in Ermyngton chyrche.
(47) 1477 I am wrothe with Kateryne, **by cause** she sendith me no writtynge.
(48) 1480 but as sone as y cam to Exeter then was y yn heven: and **be cause that** y am now in joy y do send you this letter.

(49) 1481 she was verry ffull off thought and ferd lest 3e had ben sore seke or gretly diseasid, **be cause** she cowd not here from 3our good Mastership many a day.

Numerous instances of *be cause(that)* are found in the 15th century documents of the Chancery, which definitely was a bilingual institution. Witness the following examples from the Signet of Henry V (1418-1419):

(50) þat our said seruant haue non hindrynge þer of now in his absence. but þat ye se þe more tendrely þerto **be cause þat** he is heer continuelly abydinge wiþ vs in our seruice.
(51) And þat ye se þe better to him / **by cause** he is here wiþ vs continuely in oure seruice.
(52) And doo yow to wite þat we haue yeuen vnder oure greet seel here þe chirche of Morton whiche as we were enfourmed voyded be þe deces of oon maister Richard Penelles and longed to oure yift **be cause of** þe beyng of oure Cousin Courrenays landes yn oure handes.

The phrase was commonly used in legal petitions:

(53) 1444 John Bolton   *Petition concerning the murder of Isabell, wife of Roger Bakeler*
And at the last **be cause** he cowde noghte haue his desir of her . he ther at the same tyme felonesly sloeth and murdred her and kutte her throte twyes. and twyes stikked her thurgh her pappes [*breasts*] and sides with a dagger wher vppon sche died...And ther vppon to procede in hast as hit ys forsaid (And yf any man desire here after to Rauisshe Any woman) and **for cause that** sche wolle noghte assente (vnto hym sle and) murdre her that any chartre to be made to any suche person for any suche murdre (be) voide and noght auaillable in lawe for the loue of ihesu and yn way of charite.

4.4. Middle English *by cause* > *because*

The English phrases *by cause of/that* appeared first in the 1370's. We find the earliest attestations in the Chaucerian corpus (see below). *Oxford English Dictionary*, even in its latest online version (www.oed.com) suggests much earlier dating, but this is definitely wrong. The same quotations in *Middle English Dictionary* have much more convincing dates. Compare:

(54) OED   **1356** Wyclif *Last Age* Ch. (1840) 31: þe synnes **bi cause of** whiche suche persecucioun schal be in Goddis Chirche.
MED   ?c1400 *Wyclif Last Age Chirche (1840) 31* [OD col.]: Þe synnes **bi cause of** whiche suche persecucioun schal be in Goddis Chirche.

(55) OED   **1305** *Deo Gratias* 37 in E.E.P. (1862) 125: þou hast herd al my deuyse, **Bi cause whi**, hit is clerkes wise.
MED   c1390 *In a Chirche* (Vrn) 36: I moste seie forþ my seruise..**Bi-cause whi** hit is clerkes wyse..Forte synge Deo Gracias.

Furthermore, *Cursor mundi* manuscript differences support the view that *because* had not appeared in English until the last quarter of the 14th century, as only the Fairfax MS copied c1400 has the phrase, while other earlier manuscripts have other causal conjunctions (*for, als*), e.g. line 20778:

(56) & at ho is þer in flesshe & bane for of alle wemmen ho is out-tane **be-cause** at god him-selue ho bare hir priuilage sulde be þe mare. mare þen ani oþer is *Fairfax*
Sais þer scho es in fleche & ban, For scho is of al wimmen out-tan, **Als** scho þar godd and lauerd bar, þat her priuelege war þe mar, Mar als scho þat makles es *Cotton*
Sais þar scho es in fless and ban; For scho es of all wimmen vte-tan, **Als** scho þat godd him-seluen bare, þat hir priuelege war þe mare, Mare als scho makeles es *Göttingen*
In flesshe & blode vp to be take **For** in erþe she had no make For she him bar of hir body Hir priuelage most be þe more for-þi *Trinity*

4.4.1. Preposition

The following examples illustrate the grammaticalisation cline from the phrase *by/for the cause of*, where *cause* was still a noun preceded by the definite article *the* (as in 57, 58) down to the complex preposition *because of*, with the univerbation of the preposition *by* (with the vowel reduced phonetically to *schwa*) and the noun *cause* (as in 61):

by/for the cause of
(57) (CMJULNOR):   Thus I sawe howe cryste has compassyon of vs **for the cause of** synne.
(58) c1450 *Godstow nunnery register*   to the abbesse and mynchons of Godestowe, all her right that she had or might have, **by the cause of** her dowery or mariage.

by/for cause of
(59) (CMBOETH):   Natheles the propre maner of every thing, dressynge hem to gode, disponith hem alle, for ther nys no thing doon **for cause of** yvel.
(60) (CMROLLTR): Bot a defference þat es by-twyxe a manes saule in flesche and ane Aungelle, **be-cause of** vnclennes.
(61) (CMCLOUD):   For oftymes, **bicause of** infeccion of þe original synne, it sauoreþ a þing for good þat is ful yuel, and þat haþ bot þe licnes of goode.
(62) 1475 *Paston Letters* And asfor suche money as I haue receyued of yours, non but for the wode at Sporle xx li., and of Pecok for your lyfelode in Flegge ix li. xv s. iij d., nor no more is like to haue this yere, as he telleth me, but for xx quarter barly **be-cauce of** suche charges as hath be leide vpon your lond this yere, as he sethe.

4.4.2 Conjunction

The evolution of the conjunction was similar. The first stage was the phrase *for/by the/this cause that*:

by/for the cause (that)
(63) c1385 Chaucer *CT.Kn.* A.2488   And **by the cause that** they sholde ryse Eerly, for to seen the grete fight, Vnto hir reste wenten they at nyght.
(64) (CMPRIV):   spede of oure mater that day, hit was by my seide lorde ajorned over yn to the morun Saterdey **for these causis that** a grete disputacion was be fore my lorde yn his chapell at Lambeth for prechyng of Bysshoppis.
(65) a1400 *Lanfranc* (Ashm 1396)   **Bi þe cause þat** cirurgians ben clepid algate to þis manere passioun, þerfore I haue studied to make a general chapitre of passiouns of ioinctis.

(66) a1425(c1385) Chaucer *TC* 4.1268   Soth is, the wo, the which that we ben inne, For aught I woot, for nothyng ellis is But **for the cause that** we sholden twynne.
(67) c1425 *Petition of John Staverne of Canterbury* bot he wald haue a maundement fro yowe **for the cause that** he shuld noght be haldyn parciall in the same matier.
(68) a1470 Malory *Works* 825/25   All was **for the cause that** ye and dame Brusen made me for to lye be you.

Then the definite article was eliminated, but the prepositions *be/for* continued to be spelt separately, regardless of what one may think of the medieval spelling as a diagnostic of word boundaries:

because that
(69) (CMMANDEV 30): In   Egypt þere ben but fewe Forcelettes or castelles **be cause þat** the contree is so strong of himself.
(70) (CMBRUT3): And at þat tyme Sir Andrew of Herkela, þat newe was made Erl of Cardoile, **for cause þat** he hade taken þe goode Erl of Lancastre, he hade ordeyned, þrou3 þe Kyngus commandement of Engeland.

The next stage was the hyphenation:

be-cause that
(71) a1475(1445) *Harley lyrics* 1706   **By-cause þat** 3oungþe ys from vs wente þan wol men do vs no ry3te.
(72) (CMROYAL): þat he is lorde and fadere, euery man oweþ hym drede and loue: drede **by-cause þat** he is lorde, and worshippe be-cause þat he is fader.

This, in turn, was followed by the complete univerbation:

because that
(73) (CMPRIV): And Sire, my lady of Southfolke is halfindell dysplesyd   **because that** my Cystere Barantyne is no better arayed, and leke wyse my Cyster   Elysabeth.
(74) a1400 *Lanfranc* (Ashm 1396) 114/19:   Al þe brayn is deemed cold & moist, **bicause þat** he schulde atempren spiritual fumosite þat comen of þe herte..& þe brayn is whijt, **bicause þat** he schulde þe bettere resseyue resoun & vnderstondynge.

Finally, the subordinating conjunction *that* was dropped, which allowed *because* to acquire the status of a subordinator on its own. We find here variant spellings, first separate and hyphenated, but towards the end of the Middle English period *because* is usually spelt as a single word (univerbation), thus finishing the last stage of grammaticalisation:

by cause – bi-cause
(75)   (CMPRIV): Me thynkythe þat wold hurte. Here colour is **fore cause** 3e can gett no lycens to fownde it at Castere, werfore, thow 3our wyll were trwe, they myth lawfully fown.

(76) a1425(?a1400) Chaucer *RRose* 4518 He may not out, and that is wrong, **By cause** the tour
is so strong.
(77) 1426-7 *Memorandum to Arbitrators* 8 þe seyd John Grys and hys sone and a seruaunt man of
hese by here bodyes tokyn and fro þe seyd dwellyng place by þe space of a myle to a peyre gal-
wes ledden, þere hem for to have hangyd; and **by-cause** hem fayled ropes convenient to here felonowse purpos þe seyd John Grys, hese sone, and hys man þere felonowsely slowen and mordered in þe most orrible wyse þat euer was herd spoken of in þat cuntre.
(78) (1461) *Paston* 2.254: And so whas I lefte stille at Cotton with xij men with me, **be-cauce** they
report and we a-bode there ij dayes we schulde be pult out be the heedes.

because
(79) (CMEDMUND): And **bycause** he was bore on Seynt Edmondis daye the kyng he was namyd Edmond.
(80) (CMPRIV): Hengston seide moche and strongely **because** y seide they hadde suche charters.
(81) a1425(c1385) Chaucer *TC* 4.125 **Bycause** he nolde payen hem here hire, The town of Troie shal ben set on-fire.
(82) c1450 *Alph.Tales* (Add 25719) 11/21: Hur susters þe nonnys..was passand fayn þerof, **be-cauce** sho wa so strayte vnto þaim at þai myght have a cauce to accuse hur in.
(83) (CMREYNAR): And fonde reynart his eme there standyng whiche had goten two pygeons as they cam first out of her neste to assaye yf they coude flee and **bicause** the fethers on her wyngis were to shorte they fylle doun to the ground.

There are also several ME examples of mere *cause* functioning as a conjunction, which might have occurred more frequently in the colloquial speech, similarly to modern clipped '*cause* (often spelt *coz*, as in Slade's song *Coz I Luv You*):

'cause
(84) ?a1439 Lydgate. *FP* 6.1918 Of o thyng most he dede hym dreede, **Cause** he hadde non heir to succeede.
(85) a1464 Capgr. *Chron.*(Cmb Gg.4.12) 109: In the xix 3ere of his regne went he to Rome, **cause** of devocion.

On the other hand, in the 15th century we find some instances of the two prepositions *for* and *by* combined into the conjunction-phrase *for-because*, which best proves that *because* was perceived as a single word at the time, *by* having thus achieved the status of a prefix:

for because
(86) ?c1450 *Knt.Tour-L.* The seuenthe foly of Eue was **for be-cause that** she beleued not that God saide to her that she shulde deye yef that she ete of the fruit. (French: La VII[e] folie de

Eve fut **pour ce qu**'elle ne creut pas ce que Dieu lui avoit dit que elle mourroit se elle mengoyt du fruit.)

(87) a1484 *Treat.7 Lib.Arts* And **for bi cause that** a smoth place and holl moist and hote is a goode place for sowne, therfor the consonauntis that bien gendred in suche placis bien cald.

(88) (CMMALORY): And **for bycause** I love and cherysshe my cousyn jarmayne, he is jolowse betwyxte me and hym.

(89) (CMMIRK): þen **for bycause þat** Sonday ys no day of fastyng, þerfor 3e schull begyn your fast at Aske-Wanysday.

In the 15th century *because* very quickly spread from London to other Middle English dialects, including Scots, for which we find many attestations in the latter half of the 15th century, e.g.

(90) 1463 *Extracts from the Council Register of the Burgh of Aberdeen* (SREC0B): The quhilk the saide Thomas reffoysit to do, **because that** the ferthing was brokin be the saide Theman, and nocht in the ply he gaf it him.

(91) 1474 (SREC0B): The same day, **because** thare was na dene of gilde chosin on the Friday next efter that the alderman was.

(92) c1490 Dunbar *Kind Kittok* 31 Scho come againe to hevinis 3et, quhen þe bell rang Sanct petir hit hir with a club, quhill a grit clour Raiß on hir heid, **becauß** the wyfe 3eid wrang.

In addition to the phrases with *cause* Middle English also had a phrase *by reason of/that*, which, however, was far less frequent and disappeared by the end of the 15th century:

(93) c1400(c1378) *P.Pl.B* 14.206 Þe riche is reuerenced **by resoun of** his richchesse.

(94) c1440(?a1400) *Morte Arth.* 174 Þe senatour was sett..At þe kyngez ownn borde..**Be resoun þat** þe Romaynes whare so ryche holden As of þe realeste blode.

4.5. *Because* in clauses of purpose

Apart from being the subordinating conjunction of cause, in the 15th century *because* came to introduce the clauses of purpose. In this case, however, the verb had to be preceded by a modal (*shulde, wolde*), as the subjunctive forms had by that time become identical with the indicative:

(95) a1393 Gower *CA* 2.343 **Be cause that** he **wolde** winne, He bad his fela ferst beginne.

(96) a1450(1391) Chaucer *Astr.*1.66 The firste partie of this tretis shal reherse the figures and the membres of thyn Astrolabie, **bi-cause that** thou shalt han the grette knowing of thyn owne instrument.

(97) c1450 *Alph.Tales* (Add 25719) 92/30: God hase sufferd þe to be tempid **becauce at þou sulde** know þine infirmyte.

(98) a1500(a1450) *Gener.(2)* (Trin-C O.5.2) 4279: He putte a ryng On his fynger, **be cause** she **shuld** it see.

(99) (a1470) Malory *Wks.*(Win-C) 1036/15: The kynge made grete clerkes to com before hym, **for cause** they **shulde** cronycle of the hyghe adventures of the good knyghtes.

5. Conclusion

In this paper I have traced the evolution of *because* in Middle English. Contrary to what we find in etymological dictionaries and reference books, the word-phrase is not a direct French loan but appears to have arisen among bilingual Anglo-Norman and Middle English speakers in the last quarter of the 14th century. The preposition *par/a cause de* and the conjunction *par/a cause que* are found in Anglo-French texts two centuries earlier than in Central French and they became the pattern for the Middle English hybrid phrase consisting of the native preposition *by* and the Romance noun *cause*. Before that Middle English used mostly the conjunction *forþy (þat)* and *for (that)*, which introduced both coordinate and subordinate clauses of cause and explanation. However, since French clearly distinguished the two types by marking them with coordinating *car* and subordinating *par ce que/par cause que*, Middle English bilingual speakers appear to have copied the distinction in their English. The novel phrase *by (the) cause that* rapidly underwent the process of grammaticalisation in all the dialects, achieving the stage of complete univerbation by the end of the 15th century.

References

Bonnard, Henri – Claude Régnier
    1997   *Petite grammaire de l'ancien français*. Paris: Magnard.
Campbell, Alistair
    1959   *Old English Grammar*. Oxford: Clarendon Press.
Dam, Johannes van
    1957   *The Causal Clause and Causal Prepositions in Early Old English Prose*. Groningen: Wolters.
Dardel, Robert de
    2002   *Grammaire de l'ancien français*. Paris: Klincksieck.
Fischer, Olga C. M.
    1992   "Syntax", in: Norman Blake (ed.) *The Cambridge History of the English Language*. Vol. II. Cambridge University Press, 207-408.
Guiraud, Pierre
    1963   *L'ancien français*. Paris: Presses Universitaires de France.
Hopper, Paul – Elizabeth Closs Traugott.
    2003   *Grammaticalization*. 2nd ed. Cambridge: Cambridge University Press.

Ingham, Richard
 2005 "Bilingualism and Syntactic Change in Medieval England". *Reading University Working Papers in Linguistics* 8: 1-25.
Kortmann, Bernd
 1997 *Adverbial Subordinators: A Typology and History of Adverbial Subordinators Based on European Languages.* Berlin – New York: Mouton de Gruyter.
Kurath, Hans – Sherman Kuhn (edd.)
 1956-2001 *Middle English Dictionary.* Ann Arbor: University of Michigan Press.
Kytö, Merja
 1993 *Manual to the Diachronic Part of the Helsinki Corpus of English Texts: Coding conventions and lists of source texts.* Helsinki: Department of English, University of Helsinki.
Lenker, Ursula
 2007 "*Forhwi* 'because': Shifting Deictics in the History of English Causal Connection", in: Ursula Lenker and Anneli Meurman-Solin (edd.), 193-228.
Lenker Ursula – Anneli Meurman-Solin (edd.)
 2007 *Connectives in the History of English.* Amsterdam – Philadelphia: John Benjamins.
Mitchell, Bruce
 1985 *Old English Syntax.* 2 vols. Oxford: Clarendon Press.
Molencki, Rafał
 2003 "The Etymology and Development of the Conjunction *as* in Middle English". *Linguistica Silesiana* 24: 25-39.
 2007 "The Evolution of *since* in Medieval English". In Ursula Lenker – Anneli Meurman-Solin (eds.), 97-114.
Rissanen, Matti
 1998 "Towards an Integrated View of the Development of English: Notes on Causal Linking", in: Jacek Fisiak and Marcin Krygier (edd.), *Advances in English Historical Linguistics* (1996). Berlin/ New York: Mouton de Gruyter, 389-406.
Traugott, Elizabeth Closs
 1992 "Syntax", in: Richard M. Hogg (ed.) *The Cambridge History of the English Language.* Vol. I. Cambridge University Press, 168-289.
Visser, Frederikus Theodor
 1963-1973 *An Historical Syntax of the English Language.* 3 vols. Leiden: E.J. Brill.

Primary sources

DOE = *Dictionary of Old English* – http://www.doe.utoronto.ca
Foedera Foedera conventiones, literæ, et cujuscunque generis acta publica, inter reges Angliæ et alios ... habita aut tractata, edited by Thomas Rymer – Robert Sanderson, additions and corrections by Adam Clarke and Frederick Holbrooke. London: Record Commissioners 1816-1869 Digitised by Siân Pilborough, Russell Kneath and Michael Beddow. Electronic edition © The Anglo-Norman On-Line Hub 2003-2004 (http://www.anglo-norman.net/texts/**foedera**)

Helsinki Corpus
1991 *Diachronic Part of the Helsinki Corpus of English Texts* prepared by Matti Rissanen and Ossi Ihalainen et al. University of Helsinki.

Helsinki Corpus of Older Scots
1995 http://icame.uib.no/olderscotseks.html

MED = *Middle English Dictionary Online* –
http://ets.umdl.umich.edu/m/mec

OED = *Oxford English Dictionary Online* – http://www.oed.com

Rothwell, William
2005 *Femina.* Trinity Colllege MS B.14.40
(http://www.anglo-norman.net/texts/**femina**.pdf)

16 The Word Pairs in *The Paston Letters and Papers* with Special Reference to Text Type, Gender and Generation
Akinobu Tani, Hyogo University of Teacher Education

1. Introduction

The language of *the Paston Letters and Papers* is considered to reflect "everyday" English better than that of literary texts (Davis (1954-5)), so that the collection is often used in linguistic studies of fifteenth-century English. At the same time, this epistolary collection gives us a fairly clear picture of the social relationships between the addressers and addressees, hence a good corpus for sociolinguistic studies. Thus Bergs (2005) analysed the morphosyntax of this collection in the framework of social network. Most linguistic studies of the Paston documents have centred on syntax such as Carstensen (1959), Davis (1972) and Stein (1998).[1] Therefore, this collection needs further analyses specifically in the area of lexis.

The Paston Letters and Papers are unique as well in that this collection contains composite texts, i.e. letters, legal texts and other texts. Such composite texts are considered to show variation in language use, especially in the case of lexis which seems to be more sensitive to text types or genres. This composite nature of the texts in this collection, in fact, can provide a good material for the comparison of text types because the same writers wrote in different text types.

Taking into account such composite nature of the texts, this study classified, for analysis, the collection into two major categories: 1) letters and 2) papers. The second category, in turn, consists of 1) legal texts and 2) others. The former includes indentures, petition, draft will, testament and so on, while the latter does memorandum, accounts, recipes etc. In addition to the three categories, this collection contains inventories, which, being lists in nature, are excluded from consideration in the present study.

The Paston documents by each family member were classified according to the above-mentioned text types, and their numbers of words were counted.[2] The result is shown below in Table 1. As the table shows, only some Paston family members left their writings in all three text types. Therefore, in examining word pairs (henceforth WPs) specifically in terms of text types or genres, focus is put on the analysis of the texts of those members who left writings in more than one text type.

---

1   The only exceptions would be Bergs (2005) and Tanabe (1999), both of whom studied one aspect of lexis, that is, composite predicates.
2   Edmond I, Walter and William IV were excluded from examination because the total numbers of words of the documents they left are too small for a proper analysis. Documents written solely in Latin or French were also excluded. The text used for analysis is Davis (1971).

218   Akinobu Tani

Table 1: Number of words in differet text types by family members

	legal	letters	others	total
William Paston I		5890	66	5956
Agnes Paston	3034	4680		7714
John Paston 1	11256	17804	993	30053
William Paston II	2310	9386	2961	14657
Clement Paston		3241		3241
Elizabeth Poynings	2699	1245		3944
Margaret Paston	3364	58736		62100
John Paston II	8352	39361	125	47838
John Paston III	3169	39508	609	43286
Edmond Paston II	1183	2611		3794
William Paston III		4492		4492
Margery Paston		2620		2620
Total	35367	189574	4754	229695

WPs or doublets in literary works have received due attention: for example, Mueller (1984) gives one chapter to examine Caxton's use of WPs. In contrast, this phraseology in non-literary writings has been left unexamined except for that in legal texts (Koskenniemi (1968) and Gustafsson (1984)). In this respect, the analysis of WPs occurring in *the Paston Letters and Papers* will shed more light on the use of WPs in utilitarian Middle English prose which is thought to be less influenced by the rhetoric in the contemporary age.

The purpose of the present study is to examine the WPs occurring in *the Paston Letters and Papers*, specifically whether there is any difference in their use in terms of text types, gender and generations, and, if there is, how their use is different. For this purpose, the WPs are analysed in terms of frequency and etymology. The analysis also discusses whether the use of WPs is affected by the social relationships between the addressers and addressees of the letters.

2. Frequency of WPs in *the Paston Letters and Papers*
2.1. Frequency of WPs in the letters and papers of each family member

First, the occurrences of WPs in the documents of each family member were counted and then their normalised frequency per 1000 words was calculated. The result is shown below in Table 2. The overall average frequency of WPs in *the Paston Letters and Papers* is 8.5 per 1000 words. This frequency is by far lower than that in Chaucer's prose or Caxton's *Reynard the Fox*, whose frequency of WPs per 1000 words is 16.2 and 17 respectively (cf. Tani (forthcoming a and b)).

As for the frequency of WPs in individual Paston members, there is a great divergence. The family members whose use of WPs is unique in frequency are William I and Elizabeth Poynings. William Paston I used as many as 21.32 WPs per 1000 words and Elizabeth as many as 19.27. Both used more than twice as many WPs as the overall average frequency of WPs in *the Paston Letters and Papers*. Overall frequency, however, should be considered with caution because of the composite texts contained in the Paston documents. Therefore, more detailed frequency analyses of WPs are discussed in the following sections.

Table 2: Frequency of WPs in the Paston family members

	# of WPs	WPs /1000 wds
William I	127	21.32
Agnes	56	7.26
John 1	436	14.51
William II	120	8.19
Clement	12	3.70
Elizabeth	76	19.27
Margaret	348	5.60
John II	408	8.53
John III	281	6.49
Edmond II	37	9.75
William III	26	5.79
Margery	26	9.92
Total	1953	8.50

2.2. Frequency of WPs according to text types

Different text types are considered to show different language use. Therefore, the frequency of WPs according to different text types was analysed. The result for each Paston member is shown in Graph 1:

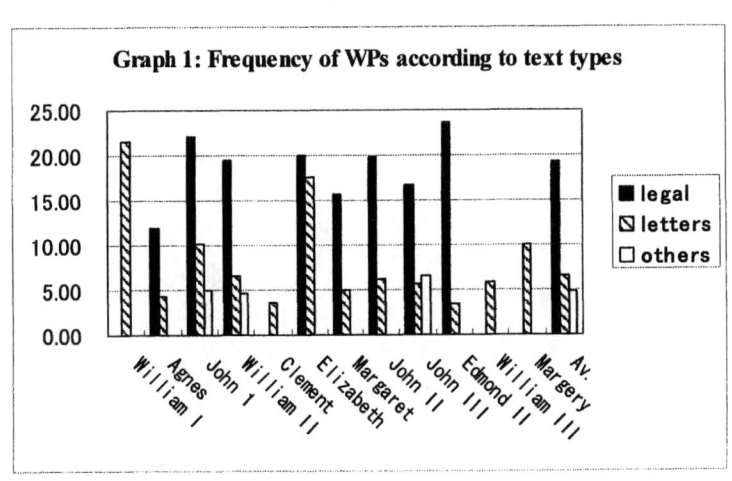

Graph 1: Frequency of WPs according to text types

From Graph 1, the general tendency of frequency of WPs in the different text types is evident: the frequency of WPs is much higher in legal texts than in letters and other documents. The average frequency of WPs in legal texts is 19.34 per 1000 words, which is followed by that in letters with the frequency of 6.57 and then by that in other documents with 4.84. This means that the frequency in legal texts is about three times as high as that in letters or other documents. The highest frequency of legal texts among the three text types is understandable considering the nature of this text type which requires precision of reference, along with the fact that the legal texts in the present-day English still abound in WPs (cf. Gustafsson, 1984). As for the low frequency in the letters in general, the more private or plain nature of these epistolary texts can be a cause since this low frequency in the letters of the Paston family makes a stark contrast to the findings of a pilot study of 20 signet letters of Henry V in *An Anthology of Chancery English*: i.e. 15.10 WPs per 1000 words. This means that there is a difference in frequency of WPs among "letters" depending on their nature and content, or possibly on their formality. One more interesting point is that the frequency in legal texts among different members is more uniform than that in letters which shows more variation.

As for the use of WPs by individual family members, William I and Elizabeth Poynings are atypical in using WPs with high frequency in letters. William I used no less than 21.56 WPs per 1000 words in letters in stark contrast to the average frequency of 6.57 in the whole letters of the Paston family.[3] Likewise, Elizabeth Poynings used as many as 17.67 WPs per 1000 words in letters. William I left letters addressed to only non-family members, which could make his style more formal with the result that WPs were more used in his letters. The following two examples from William I contain the more formal or Gallicised WPs:[4]

(1) And also þe seyd Walter <u>hath sued and yet pursuyth</u> Adam Aubré, on of þe seyd jnquisicion, in þe court of þe seyd Duc of Norffolk of hys manoir of Fornsete by <u>cause and occasion</u> of þe seyd matiers (Wiliam I, 12/157-160)
(2) his pretense of his title to þe priourie of Bromholm is <u>adnulled and voide</u> in yowr lawe (William I, 3/12-13)

Elizabeth Poynings left only two letters addressed to Agnes Paston, her mother, and to John Paston II, her brother. Of course, given the relationship between Elizabeth and Agnes or John II, it was possible that she wrote in a formal style. But the total number of words in the letters she left amounts to only 1245 words. Therefore, Elizabeth's frequency of WPs is considered to be distorted by the small text size of her letters, though she did use some formal WPs in her letters:

---

3   The uniqueness of William I's language is discussed by Iyeiri (2006) concerning negatives. She attributes his unique use of language to his early birth. But this is not the case with his use of WPs.
4   In the quotations henceforth, the WPs are underlined.

(3) [Sir Robert Fenys] . . . receyueth þe issuez and profitez of gret part of theym (Elizabeth, 207-8/7-8)

This distortion in the frequency of WPs in Elizabeth Poynings' letters also seems to apply to that in her legal texts.

2.3. Frequency according to gender

Frequency of WPs was examined to check whether there is any difference in their use between male and female members. The result is shown in Graph 2:

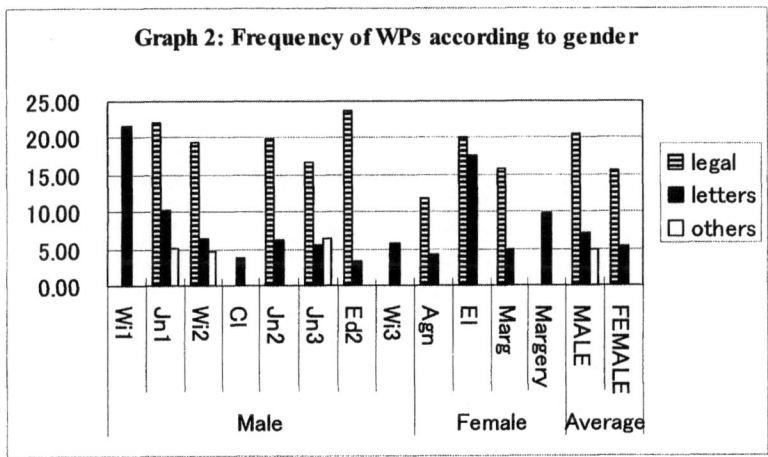

Graph 2: Frequency of WPs according to gender

[Bar chart showing frequencies for Male members (Wi1, Jn1, Wi2, Cl, Jn2, Jn3, Ed2, Wi3), Female members (Agn, El, Marg, Margery), and Averages (MALE, FEMALE), with categories: legal, letters, others]

The normalised frequency shows that male members used more WPs in all three text types than female members. The average frequency for male members is 20.59 for legal texts, 7.22 for letters and 4.84 for other documents, while that for female members is 15.72 and 5.4 for legal texts and letters respectively. The divergence in frequency between male and female members is greater in legal texts than in letters, presumably demonstrating the discrepancy in the knowledge of the law and legal phraseology necessitated in legal texts. Actually, male members were familiar with legal parlance through their education in the law. In contrast, in letters, individual difference is greater than gender difference.

Up to this point, I have discussed the frequency under the denomination of "gender." Yet this denomination "gender" is dubious in *the Paston Letters and Papers* because other factors such as education and literacy merge with this same factor. These factors, in fact, cannot be clearly separated. Therefore, it should be born in mind that the frequency difference between male and female members comes not only from gender but also from education and literacy. Unlike the female members in the Paston family, most male members had legal training at Cambridge or Oxford and some Inns of Court. As for the high frequency of WPs in the legal texts of Margaret, it is not certain to what degree her legal texts reflect her own language. In this respect, other female members must have counted on others for help like Margaret in preparing legal texts. Yet it is also true that Margaret was more exposed to legal expressions in everyday situations than any other female members as she managed the household in Norwich most of the time when John I, her husband, was away from home.

2.4. Frequency according to generations

We have three generations in the Paston family who left letters and papers:
    First generation: William I, Agnes
    Second generation: John I, Margaret, Elizabeth, William II, Clement II,
    Third generation: John II, John III, Margery, Edmond II, William III.
The frequency of WPs was analysed according to generations. The result is shown in Graph 3:

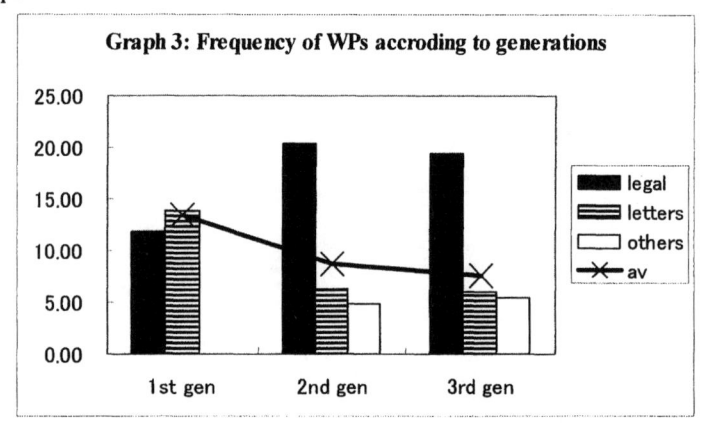

Graph 3: Frequency of WPs accroding to generations

The average normalised frequency in Graph 3 shows constant decrease from the first to the third generation. The first generation has William I and Agnes; the former left only letters yet using WPs with very high frequency and the latter left both legal texts and letters, yet using WPs with not so high frequency. This might have distorted the average given. Rather, because the average frequency was calculated using all the data of each generation, this trend of the average frequency through the generations can be considered to reflect the different degree of social aspiration shown by the different generations of the Paston family, with William I as the first generation trying hardest to rise, in the society, from humble origins to gentry.

3. Etymology of components of WPs

Here we examine the etymological makeup and order of components of WPs. Despite the warning by Davis (1974) and Burnley (1983) that mere etymological analysis is not useful, but that the stylistic values attached to words of different etymology should be taken into account, etymology can be a rough indicator of stylistic values attached to words, if examined with due care. The major etymological makeups and orders of components of WPs found in *the Paston Letters and Papers* can be summarised as follows;

1) OE+OE
(4) That no man be so hardy to <u>seye ne telle</u> oney false nouelté or tydyngys   (John I, 118/42)
2) OE+OF
(5) he hade <u>no wrytyng nor euidens</u> of no swyche thyng   (Margery, 255-6/4-5)
3) OF+OE
(6) my lord the Cardynall, hos sowle God <u>assoyle and forgeve</u>   (John I, 81/4-5)
4) OF+OF
(7) it were a gode frendely dede and <u>no jopardy nor hurt</u>   (William II, 170/7-8)

3.1. Etymology of WPs according to text types

The etymological makeup and order of components of WPs was examined in terms of text types. Their percentage was calculated and is shown in Graphs 4 and 5:

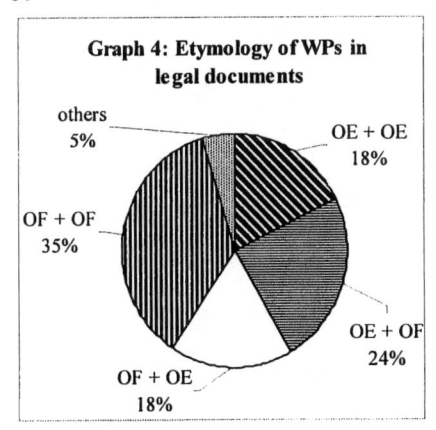

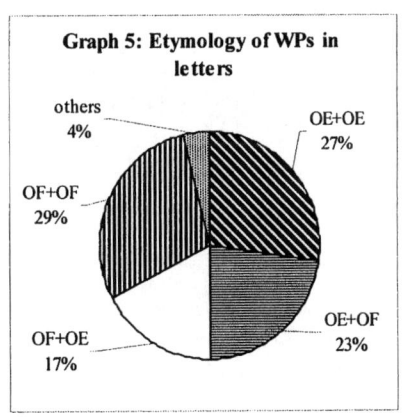

Graph 4: Etymology of WPs in legal documents

others 5%
OE + OE 18%
OE + OF 24%
OF + OE 18%
OF + OF 35%

Graph 5: Etymology of WPs in letters

others 4%
OE+OE 27%
OE+OF 23%
OF+OE 17%
OF+OF 29%

The two graphs show that there is little difference in the parts of OE+OF and OF+OE between letters and legal texts. The major differences lie in the parts of OE+OE and OF+OF. In legal texts, the WPs consisting of OF+OF account for 35 % and those of OE+OE 18%, while, in letters, the WPs consisting of OF+OF account for 29% and those of OE+OE 27%. In short, legal texts contain more OF components and fewer OE components. It is natural that legal texts contain more OF elements given the fact that French was the language of administration for about 300 years after the Norman Conquest. Many WPs consisting only of OF components are specialised legal phrases made up of mainly nouns:

(8) and also <u>an oyer and determyner</u> ayenst þe seid Lord Molens, . . .   (John I, 56/24-5)
(9) for the sustentacion of hem and of the seyd pourmen, c marke of <u>annuité and rent charge</u> yerly goyng owt of all maneres, londes, and tenementz. . . (John I, 123/8-10)

In addition to such WPs consisting only of OF components, legal texts also contain some conventional WPs, though limited in number:

(10)   . . . <u>to have and to hold</u> the seid maners   (Margaret, 381/9-10)
(11)   . . . then I <u>yeve and bequeth</u> all and euery part of my forsaid plate, juelx, and stuffe of housholde vnto my soon Sir Edward Ponyngis.   (Elizabeth, 213/160-161)

3.2. Etymology of WPs according to gender

Here we examine the etymological makeup and order of components of WPs in terms of gender. Their percentage was calculated and is shown in Graphs 6 and 7:

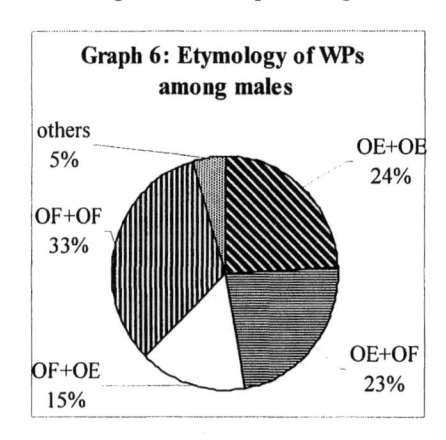

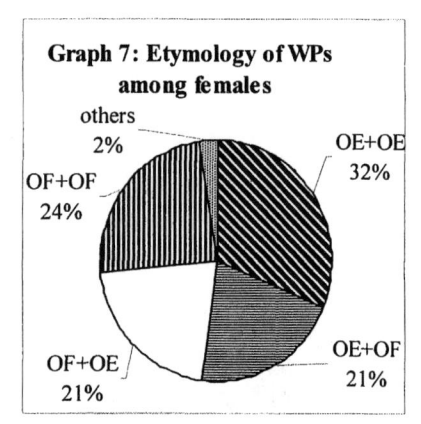

Graph 6: Etymology of WPs among males
- others 5%
- OE+OE 24%
- OE+OF 23%
- OF+OE 15%
- OF+OF 33%

Graph 7: Etymology of WPs among females
- others 2%
- OE+OE 32%
- OE+OF 21%
- OF+OE 21%
- OF+OF 24%

The difference in the etymological makeup of WPs between male and female members lies in the different ratio between OE+OE and OF+OF WPs. Male members use more WPs consisting of OF+OF and fewer WPs consisting of OE+OE WPs than female members. As mentioned in section 2.3, this result again is thought to result from not only gender but the education and literacy of males and females because these factors are inseparable. The overall pattern of etymology of WPs among males and females shows a similar pattern to that among different text types. The etymology of WPs, especially OE+OE and OF+OF, is closely linked with text types and "gender" at least in *the Paston Letters and Papers*.

3.3. Etymology of WPs according to generation

Here we examine the etymological makeup and order of components of WPs according to generation. As limited family members left legal texts, it is difficult to compare the etymology of WPs in legal texts among generations. This problem applies especially to the first generation which left only 36 examples of WPs in legal texts. Therefore, the etymological analysis of WPs according to generation focused on only letters, which all the family members left.[5] The WPs in the three generations were classified according to the etymological makeup and order of components of WPs. Then the percentage of each etymological meakup and order of WPs was calculated according to generation. The result is shown in Graph 8:

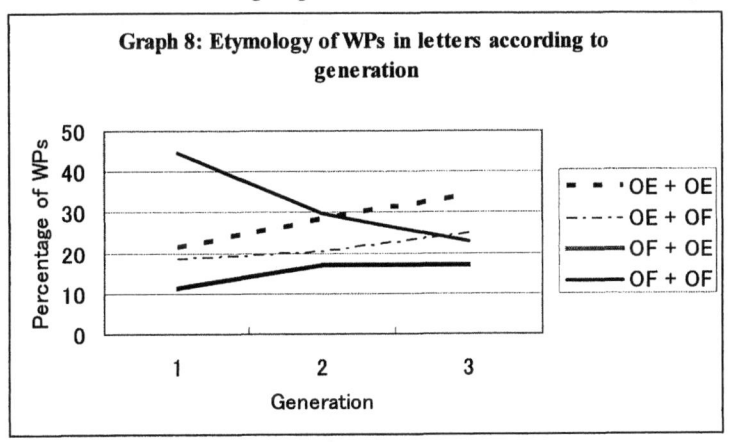

Graph 8: Etymology of WPs in letters according to generation

The result shows that, while the OF+OF WPs decrease through generations, other WPs, especially the OE+OE WPs increase in inverse relation. The first generation used more WPs which are thought more formal, i.e. more OF+OF WPs, than OE+OE WPs. But later generations used more informal WPs. The trend of etymology of WPs, especially OF+OF, through the generations shows similarity with that of frequency of WPs through the generations (cf. Graph 3). These two trends can be interpreted as reflecting the relation of the Paston family to the society: as mentioned before, the first generation tried hardest to settle in the society as gentry.

---

5   Graph2 in section 2.4 gives the data on legal papers despite the reason given here. That section, however, made the examination of WPs by using only the average frequency from all the data.

4. Use of WPs in terms of the social relationships between the addressers and addressees

As already mentioned, in the case of most Paston letters, the social relationships between the addressers and addressees are known. Therefore in this section, focus is placed on the examination of WPs in terms of such relationships to understand whether there is any difference in the use of WPs depending on such relationships. For this examination, only letters were examined because legal texts are not addressed to specific people like letters. The letters left by most Paston family members are addressed to other family members only. So the examination was made of only the letters by those members who left letters addressed to both family and non-family members. Thus the letters of Margaret, John I, John II and John III were analysed. These letters were then divided into 1) those addressed to someone socially equal including family members, 2) those addressed to someone socially higher, and 3) those addressed to someone socially lower. In the three categories, the letters addressed to someone socially lower was found only in those left by Margaret and John I. The WPs occurring in the letters of Margaret, John I, John II and John III were counted according to the aforementioned classification and their frequency was calculated and normalised in Graph 8:

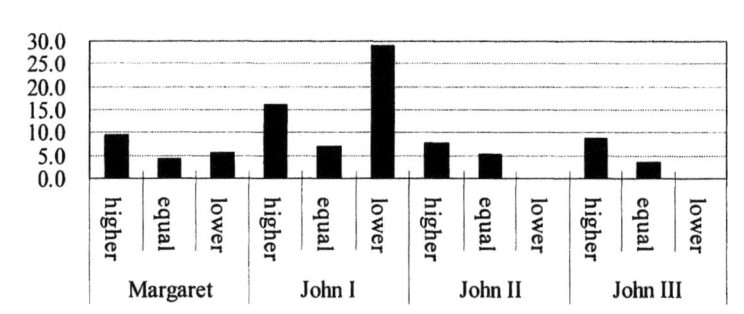

Graph 9: Frequency of WPs / 1000 wds in letters in terms of social relationships

The result shows that the letters addressed to the socially higher contain more WPs than those addressed to the socially equal in all the writers. Furthermore, the frequency of WPs in the letters addressed to the socially lower is higher than in the letters addressed to the socially equal. This latter result can be interpreted as showing that the Pastons used more WPs in the letters addressed to non-family members than in those addressed to family members which account for the majority of the letters addressed to the socially equal. As for the frequency of WPs in the letters addressed to the socially higher and lower, two different results were gained between Margaret and John I. The interesting and apparently contradicting result in John I is that the frequency of WPs in the letters addressed to the socially lower is much higher than that in the letters addressed to the people with higher social standing. This point is discussed in the next section.

4.2. John Paston I's use of WPs according to the addressees with different social standings

John Paston I's use of WPs is examined in terms of frequency and etymology because only Margaret and John I left such letters as addressed to people with the three different social relations, i.e. higher, equal and lower, and because his use is more conspicuous than that of Margaret. The number of WPs and their normalised frequency according to social relationships are shown in Table 2:

Table 3: Frequency in John I's letters addressed to people with different social standings

	# of WPs	Total wds	WPs / 1000 wds
equal	89	12871	6.91
higher	62	3861	16.06
lower	31	1072	28.92

The table shows that the normalised frequency of WPs is 6.91 in the letters addressed to the socially equal, while that in the letters addressed to the socially higher is 16.06. The latter frequency is similar to the one in the Chancery collection, i.e. 15.10 (cf. section 2.2) This similarity in the frequency of WPs may be attributed to formal nature of the letters in both the Chancery collection and the Paston letters addressed to the socially higher. As for the frequency of WPs in the letters addressed to the socially lower, we cannot deny the possibility that the frequency is distorted by the small size of the data, i.e. totally 1072 words. So at the moment, it is not certain why the frequency of WPs in the letters addressed to the socially lower is much higher than that in the letters addressed to the socially high in John I's letters.

Next, the etymology of WPs in John I's letters was analysed in terms of the social relationships between John I and his addressees. The result is shown in Table 4:

Table 4: Etymolgoy of WPs according to social relations in John I's letters

	OE+OE	OE+OF	OF+OE	OF+OF	others
higher	12 (19.35%)	5 (8.06%)	12 (19.35%)	25 (40.32%)	8 (12.9%)
equal	26 (29.21%)	14 (15.73%)	15 (16.85%)	29 (32.58%)	5 (5.62%)
lower	7 (22.58%)	7 (22.58%)	3 (9.68%)	13 (41.94%)	1 (3.23%)

The result is interpreted as demonstrating that fewer OF+OF WPs are used in the letters addressed to the socially equal than in those to the socially higher or lower.

In most cases, the socially equal means other family members while the socially lower means non-family members. In other words, between family members, the Paston members did not use so many OF+OF WPs which are considered to be more formal. In addition, in the letters addressed to non-family members whether socially higher or lower, the Pastons tended to use more formal WPs. This shows that the difference between family or non-family addressees also may affect the use of WPs.

5. Conclusion

The present study has discussed the WPs occurring in *the Paston Letters and Papers* in terms of frequency and etymology with special reference to text type, gender and generation. In addition, the social relationships between the addressers and addressees have been taken into account for analysis of WPs. This study has demonstrated that text types and "gender" affect the frequency and etymology of WPs.

Text types affect the frequency and etymology of WPs more than other factors such as gender and generation: 1) the frequency of WPs in legal texts (19.34 WPs per 1000 words) is much higher than that in letters (6.57 WPs per 1000 words), and 2) the difference between legal texts and letters appears in the different ratio between the OE+OE WPs and OF+OF WPs: legal texts contain fewer OE+OE WPs (18%) and more OF+OF WPs (35%) while letters contain more OE+OE WPs (27%) and fewer OF+OF WPs (29%).

"Gender" also determines the frequency and etymology of WPs: 1) male family members used more WPs than females in both letters (7.22 vs. 5.4 WPs per 1000 words) and legal texts (20.59 vs. 15.72 WPs per 1000 words), and 2) males used fewer OE+OE WPs (24%) and more OF+OF WPs (33%) while females used more OE+OE WPs (32%) and fewer OF+OF WPs (24%). But what is called "gender" is inseparable from such other factors as education and literacy. Therefore, the above findings of "gender" difference in frequency and etymology of WPs should be understood as resulting from such complex factors.

Generation difference can be also interpreted as being reflected in the use of WPs. The first generation of the Paston family used a greater number of WPs than the following two generations. Furthermore, the first generation used more formal WPs than the following generations as far as letters are concerned.

The present study has also made clear that the social relationships between the addressers and addressees of letters affect the frequency of WPs: 1) more WPs are used in the letters addressed to the socially higher than in the letters addressed to the socially equal, and 2) more WPs are used in the letters addressed to the socially lower than in the letters addressed to the socially equal. Yet we might have to reconsider the problem by taking into account the difference in the letters addressed to the family and non-family members.

From the discussion above, the use of WPs is considered to be very closely related with, or more properly, constrained by text types. Smith (2005) discusses that John II was "clearly part of Caxton's social network" through Sir John Fastolf, and that he owned some of Caxton's publications. This means that John II was familiar with Caxton's style or curial style, linguistic characteristics of which include ample use of WPs.[6] But John II's use of WPs in his letters and papers is not unique in terms of frequency and etymology when compared with other Paston members. This I interpret as demonstrating that text types dictate the use of WPs more than, for example, a person's taste for or familiarity with WPs. In addition to text types, gender and social relationships can affect the use of WPs.

In summary, the present study has demonstrated that the use of WPs is closely related with the social aspects of language use.

References

Bergs, Alexander
    2005   *Social Networks and Historical Sociolinguistics. Studies in Morphosyntactic Variation in the Paston Letters (1421-1503).* Berlin: Mouton de Gruyter.

Brewer, D. S. (ed.)
    1974   *Geoffrey Chaucer: The Writer and his Background.* London: Bell.

Brinton, Laurel J. – Minoji Akimoto (edd.)
    1999   *Collocational and Idiomatic Aspects of Composite Predicates in the History of English.* Amsterdam: John Benjamins.

Burnley, David
    1983   *A Guide to Chaucer's Language.* London: Macmillan.

Burnley, J.D.
    1986   "Curial Prose in England." *Speculum* 61: 593-614.

Carstensen, Broder
    1959   *Studien zur Syntax des Nomens, Pronomens und der Negation in den Paston Letters.* Bochum: H. Poppinghaus.

Davis, Norman
    1954-5   "The Language of the Pastons." *Proceedings of the British Academy* 40: 119-44.

---

6   As for curial style or prose, see Burnley (1986).

Davis, Norman (ed.)
  1971 *Paston Letters and Papers of the Fifteenth Century.* Oxford: Oxford UP.
Davis, Norman
  1972 "Margaret Paston's Uses of *do*." *Neuphilologische Mitteilungen* 73, 55-62.
Davis, Norman
  1974 "Chaucer and Fourteenth-Century English" in Brewer, D. S. (ed.), 71-78.
Fisher, John H. – Malcolm Richardson – Jane L. Fisher (edd.)
  1984 *An Anthology of Chancery English.* Knoxville: U of Tennessee P.
Gustafsson, Marita
  1984 "The Syntactic Features of Binomial Expressions in Legal English." *TEXT.* 4:1-3, 123-142.
Iyeiri, Yoko
  2006 "Decline of Some Middle English Features of Negation in the Fifteenth Century: A Study of *The Paston Letters*." in Sawada, Mayumi, Larry – Walker – Shizuya Tara (edd.), 249-64.
Koskenniemi, Inna
  1968 *Repetitive Word Pairs in Old and Early Middle English Prose.* Turku: Turun Yliopisto.
Mueller, Janel M.
  1984 *The Native Tongue and the Word: Developments in English Prose Style, 1380-1580.* Chicago: U of Chicago P.
Mugglestone, Lynda
  2005 *The Oxford History of English.* Oxford: Oxford UP.
Sawada, Mayumi – Larry Walker – Shizuya Tara (edd.)
  2006 *Language and Beyond: A Festschrift for Hiroshi Yonekura on the Occasion of his 65th Birthday.* Tokyo: Eichosha.
Smith, Jeremy
  2005 "From Middle to Early Modern English", in: Mugglestone, Lynda (ed.), 120-146.
Stein, Dieter
  1998 "Relative Sentences in Late Middle English: The Paston and the Cely Letters." in: Stein Dieter – Rosanna Sornicola (edd.), 67-77.
Stein, Dieter – Rosanna Sornicola (edd.)
  1998 *The Virtues of Language: History in Language, Linguistics and Texts: Papers in Memory of Thomas Frank.* Amsterdam & Philadelphia: J. Benjamins

Tanabe, Harumi
   1999   "Composite Predicates and Phrasal Verbs in *The Paston Letters*" in: Brinton, Laurel J. – Minoji Akimoto (edd.), 97-132.

Tani, Akinobu
   Forthcoming a "Word Pairs or Doublets in Caxton's *History of Reynard the Fox*: Rampant and Tedious?"
   Forthcoming b "Comparison of Word Pairs between Chaucer's Verse and Prose."

17 Discourse Strategies in Late Middle English Women's Mystical Writing
Fumiko Yoshikawa, Hiroshima Shudo University

1. Introduction

This paper mainly treats Julian of Norwich's *Revelations of Divine Love* and *The Book of Margery Kempe* from a diachronic pragmatic viewpoint.[1] The analysis is based on Virtanen (1995), which examines their sentence-initial adverbial phrases of time and of place in several Early Modern English travelogues, with references to the author and participants of the discourse. The two Late Middle English texts treated in this paper belong to another genre, so-called mystical writing. In some regards they are similar, but in others they are quite different. Both texts are biographical in content, but in *Revelations* the author appears in the first person and in *The Book of Margery Kempe* the main character, Margery herself, is referred to in the third person, often as 'this creature'. In many parts, the latter text can be said to be almost a travelogue, but the former is not. However, mystical works have some similarity to travelogues in another way. Both describe what they saw. In mystical writing, authors describe the visions they received, while in travelogues, authors describe scenes they saw on their journeys.

The same three discourse strategies as Virtanen (1995) investigated in six travelogues are examined in these two mystical works. They are temporal, locative, and participant/topic oriented strategies. In both Julian and Margery, as well as in Early Modern English travelogues (Virtanen (1995: 501)), temporal discourse strategies often serve as text segmentation. The textualisation in a chronological sequence is a characteristic of narrative. Virtanen (1995) focuses on clause–initial or sentence-initial adverbials of time as explicit markers of temporal discourse strategy, which serve as a cohesive device and also as a text-segmentation marker. We also follow her method.

Virtanen (1995: 509) concludes in the Early Modern English travelogue texts she investigated that the voyagers' texts typically followed the chronological order of events they experienced on their journeys, and that the clauses are often lead by adverbials of time. In addition, she states that locative adverbials also function to show the time sequence in accordance with the route of the traveller and that the discourse with such clause-initial locative adverbials is descriptive and makes the readers themselves feel as if they were following the tour. However, it is doubtful whether we will get the same result from the research on Middle English travelogues as Virtanen (1995). A rough overview of a well-known fourteenth

---

[1] I would like to express my sincere gratitude to Prof. Malcolm J. Benson, Prof. James M. Ronald and Dr. Yoshitaka Kozuka for reading this paper through and making many helpful suggestions. I am also grateful for valuable comments from the audience at the SHELL 2007 conference.

century travelogue, *Mandeville's Travels*,[2] shows that the text rarely involves clause-initial temporal adverbs. It seems to follow the route of John Mandeville's travels. In this regard, it is indeed based on the temporal oriented strategy, but when we examine the sentence-initial adverbial phrases, we find that the clauses are mainly connected by locative adverbials on cities, buildings and objects he saw in the course of his travels. The following[3] is the beginning of the fourteenth chapter in Hamelius's edition of British Museum MS. Cotton Titus C. XVI, as an example of clauses connected by sentence initial locative adverbials:

(1) <u>From this contree of the samaritanes</u> þat I haue spoken of before gon men to the playnes of GALILEE And men leuen the hilles on þat o partye. And GALILEE is on of the prouynces of the holy lond, And <u>in þat prouynce</u> is the cytee of NAYM & CAPHARNAUM & CHOROSAYM and BETHSAYDA. <u>In this BETHSAYDA</u> was seynt Peter & seint Andrew born And <u>þens</u> a .iiij. myle is CHROSAYM & .v. myle fro CHOROSAYM is the cytee of CEDAR whereof the psayter speketh : ET HABITAUI CUM HABITANTIBUS CEDAR, þat is for to seye : And I haue dwelled with the dwellynge men in Cedar. (Mandeville's Travel, Ch. XIV, Hamerius 1919, p. 73, ll. 7-17.)

We would need further discussion on the status of this text as a typical travelogue because there are many fictional elements in it. However, if we regard the example above as a Middle English travelogue, it is not necessarily appropriate to suggest that earlier travelogue texts are mainly connected by a temporal oriented strategy. Therefore, in the following sections, the three discourse strategies, temporal, locative, and participant/topic-oriented strategies, are examined in some excerpts from each of the two texts without any preconception about genre. There are other problems to be considered such as the amanuenses of these texts. It is certain that *The Book of Margery Kempe* was written by a male priest. It is not clear who inscribed Julian's *Revelations of Divine Love*, but if Julian herself wrote the text, we should consider gender-related differences in style. The discussion on the amanuenses must remain as a future work. All the excerpts shown are drawn from the Short Text of *the Revelations of Divine Love* (hereafter *Revelations*), edited by Beer (1978) and *The Book of Margery Kempe*, edited by Windeatt (2000).

2. Discourse Strategies in *Margery Kempe*

As was mentioned above, in this section, we examine the three types of discourse strategies seen in *The Book of Margery Kempe*; temporal, locative and participant/topic oriented strategies are discussed in order. This work consists of two books, but Book II was left out of the subject of this research because there is possibility that the analysis of differences between the two mystical texts treated

---

2 P. Hamelius (ed.). (1919). *Mandeville's Travels*. Early English Text Society, o.s. 153. London: Oxford University Press.
3 All the underlines in quotations are added by the present author.

in this paper might be more complicated by including Book II. The processes of making the two books in *The Book of Margery Kempe* and their aimed discourse are different. In his introduction, Windeatt (2000: 6) positions Book II as "a pendant, a postscript added after the first's completion, but mirroring the incidents and concerns of the longer book." According to the shorter Proem, the Book I was first written by a man who knew neither English nor German, and was rewritten in 1436 by a priest, who also dictated Book II (BMK, ll. 164-174). Windeatt (2000: 5, 6) calculates that the first version of Book I was made before Margery's trip to Danzig, which is dated to 1433. It also presumes that there are some chapters, such as Chapters 24, 25, and 62, added to the first version by the priest who became her second amanuensis. When we consider its provenance, even treating only the first book would suggest prudence.

This text shows many similarities to the travelogues which Virtanen (1995) treated. Virtanen (1995: 500) says that the travelogue texts she investigated largely follow the chronological order of events the traveller experienced on their journey. Margery declares in the preface that the text is not organised in chronological order but in which she remembered the events. This can be seen in quotation (2) below, and indeed the events represented in the text are sometimes out of time sequence, but the events described in each chapter do largely follow the chronological order as shown in quotation (3). Wårvik (1987) discusses the problems in pointing out factors behind the change of the use of discourse markers come from, a historical change or a stylistic difference. At least in *The Book of Margery Kempe* (hereafter *Margery Kempe*), the author or the scribe is very conscious that travelogue texts are often linearised in a chronological order and disclaims the adoption of that kind of text structure.

(2) A schort tretys of a creature sett in grett pompe and pride of the world, whech sythen was drawyn to ower Lord be gret poverte, sekenes, schamis, and gret reprevys in many divers contres and places, of whech tribulacyons sum schal ben schewed aftyr, not in ordyr as it fellyn, but as the creatur cowd han mend of hem whan it wer wretyn. (BMK, ll. 153-158)

(3) And <u>aftyr on the XII Day, whan iii kyngys comyn wyth her yyftys and worschepyd owyr Lord Jhesu Crist</u>, being in hys moderys lappe, this creatur, owyr Ladys handmayden, beheldyng al the processe in contemplacyon, wept wondyr sor. And <u>whan sche saw that thei wold take her leve to gon hom ayen into her cuntre</u>, sche mygth not suffyre that they schuld go fro the presens of owyr Lord, and for wondyr that thei wold gon awey sche cryed wondyr sore.

And <u>soon aftyr</u> cam an awngel and bad owyr Lady and Josep gon fro the cuntre o[f] Bedlem into Egypt. <u>Than</u> went this creatur forth with owyr Lady, <u>day be day</u> purveyng hir herborw wyth gret reverens, wyth many swet thowtys and hy medytacyons, and also hy contemplacyons, <u>sumtyme duryng in wepying ii owyres and oftyn lengar</u> in the mend of owyr Lordys Passyon wythowtyn sesyng, <u>sumtyme</u> for hir owyn synne, <u>sumtyme</u> for the synne of the pepyl, <u>sumtyme</u> for the sowlys in purgatory, <u>sumtyme</u> for hem that arn in poverte er in any dysese, for sche desyred to comfort hem alle. <u>Sumtyme</u> sche wept ful plentevowsly and ful boystowsly for desyr of the blys of hevyn and for sche was so long dyfferryd therfro. (BMK, Ch. 7, ll. 590-608)

The temporal adverb *than* (*then* in Modern English) is frequently used in *Margery Kempe*, and Virtanen (1995: 502) recognises the same tendency in the six Early Modern English travelogues. Virtanen (1995: 502) points out that this adverb indicates 'a minor textual boundary'. Another temporal adverbial phrase seen in quotation (3) *soon aftyr* (soon after) also seems to be a minor boundary marker. Lengthy temporal adverbial phrases such as 'aftyr on the XII Day, whan iii kyngys comyn wyth her yyftys and worschepyd owyr Lord Jhesu Crist' and 'whan sche saw that thei wold take her leve to gon home ayen into her cuntre' in the same quotation function as major textual boundaries. These longer temporal phrases often appear at the beginning of chapters. These major temporal adverbial phrases often indicate a deviation from the simultaneity or temporal adjacency, that is, a rather large time gap from the time described in the previous passage. Virtanen (1995: 502) comments that when two or more temporal adverbials are used at the beginning of a new textual unit, they appear in chronological order. It may be true indeed, but in quotation (3), the first adverbial phrase 'after on the XII Day' is a rough temporal marker and the second one 'whan iii kyngys comyn wyth her yyftys and worschepyd owyr Lord Jhesu Crist' seems to be more specific.

Temporal adverbial phrases also indicate 'duration, frequency, or adjacency' (Virtanen (1995: 501)). The phrase in the second paragraph in quotation (3), 'sumtyme duryng in wepying ii iwyres and oftyn langar' describes both duration and frequency, which means that it happened more than once and continued two hours or more. The adverb *sometime* (sometimes) can be also said to be a non-specific temporal adverb. Temporal adjacency in events is often unmarked in this text, as Virtanen (1995) notices in the Early Modern English travelogues.

As is seen in Early Modern English travelogues, locative adverbial phrases are sometimes used in *Margery Kempe* as devices to create cohesion in the text, but they are used much less often than temporal adverbial phrases.

(4) And so ovyr al wher-that-evyr the frerys led hem in that holy place, sche alwey wept and sobbyd wondyrfully, and specialy whan sche cam ther owyr Lord was nayled on the cros. Ther cryed sche and wept wythowtyn mesur, that sche myth not restreyn hirself. Also thei comyn to a ston of marbyl that owyr Lord was leyd on whan he was takyn down of the cros, and ther sche wept wyth gret compassyon, havyng mend of owyr Lordys Passyon. (BMK, Ch. 29, ll. 2317-2323)

(5) And therfor this creatur had gret desyr to be howselyd in that holy place wher owyr mercyful Lord Crist Jhesu fyrst sacryd hys precyows body in the forme of bred and yaf it to hys discipulys. And so sche was wyth gret devocyon, wyth plentevows teerys, and wyth boystows sobbyngys, for in this place is plenyr remyssyon. And so is in other iiii placys in the Tempyl. On is in the Mownt of Calvarye; another at the grave wher owyr Lord was beriid; the thridde

is at the marbyl ston that hys preciows body was leyd on whan it was takyn of the cros; the ferd is ther the holy cros beriid, and in many other placys of Jerusalem. (BMK, Ch. 29, ll. 2341-2350)

(6) Another day, erly in the morwenyng, thei went ageyn[es the] gret hyllys. And her gydes teld wher owyr Lord bare the cros on hys bakke, and wher hys modyr met wyth hym, and how sche swownyd, and how sche fel down and he fel down also. And so thei went forth al the fornoone tyl thei cam to the Mownt Syon. And evyr this creatur wept abundawntly al the wey that sche went for compassyon of owyr Lordys Passyon. In the Mownt Syon is a place wher owyr Lord wesch hys disciplys fete, and a lityl therfro he mad hys Mawnde wyth hys disciplys. (BMK, Ch. 29, ll. 2332-2340)

Quotation (4) is a paragraph from Chapter 29 of *Margery Kempe*. Here Margery is guided around Jerusalem by friars. The author or the scribe still organises the chapter in a chronological sequence in this chapter, but in these paragraphs the main cohesive devices are locative elements. Virtanen (1995: 504) exemplifies in Early Modern English travelogues that 'once a stop has been indicated, existential constructions tend to appear, to present sights and give information about them.' A similar textualisation is seen in quotation (4). First, it is shown that the party Margery joined was led to a holy place in Jerusalem by the friars, and at each significant point she cried out, wept and sobbed, though the clauses are not existential sentences but clauses with a preposed locative adverb *ther*. Next, they move to another holy place and again at the new stop she weeps. In quotation (5), the number of places she shed tears is counted up and the places are described in simple ways.

The last sentence in quotation (6) includes an existential construction, "In the Mownt Syon is a place wher owyr Lord wesche hys disciplys fete." In this clause, the larger place is shown as its theme at the beginning of the sentence, and then a particular spot is described as its rheme. Virtanen (1995: 503) indicates that a sentence-initial locative adverbial phrase sporadically appears in a text connected mainly by temporal adverbial phrases. She suggests that this is because in the text which has cardinally been made cohesive by temporal adverbial phrases, the locative adverbial phrases connect sentences temporally as well as spatially. In quotation (7), temporal and locative strategies are intricately interwound.

(7) And than owr Lord grawntyd hir hir bone. And so sche toke hir schip in the name of Jhesu and seylyd forth wyth hir felaschip, whom God sent fayr wynde and wedyr, so that thei comyn to Seynt Jamys on the sevenyth day. And than thei that weryn ayen hir whan thei wer at Bristowe, now thei made hir good cher. And so thei abedyn ther xiiii days in that lond, and ther had sche gret cher, bothyn bodily and gostly, hy devocyon, and many gret cryes in the mende of owr Lordys Passion, wyth plentyvows terys of compassyon.

And sithyin thei come hom ageyn to Bristowe in v days. And sche abood not long ther, but went forth to the Blod of Hayles, and ther was schrevyn and had lowde cryes and boystows wepyngys. And <u>than</u> the religiows men had hir in amongse hem and mad hir good cher, saf thei sworyn many gret othys and horryble. (BMK, Ch. 45, ll. 3645-3657)

Virtanen (1995: 504) summarises that when the traveller is described in the text with a locative discourse strategy the text is more narrative, and that when the traveller is not described with a locative discourse strategy it is more descriptive. From this viewpoint, *The Book of Margery Kempe* is narrative.[4] In fact, this text does not appear to be so descriptive with regard to what she saw on her journey. Even in paragraphs textualised by using locative discourse strategies such as in quotations (4) and (5), sentences beginning with a locative adverbial phrase do not give detailed information on the place introduced by the locative phrase, although this might be partly because she had become old by the time she asked the priest to write down this book and her memory had faded. Those locative phrases just show that at those Bible-related sites Margery cried out and wept tears heavily. On this point, it is widely different from the travelogues examined by Virtanen (1995). This feature might have characterised her text as mystic. Throughout the text, the author describes that she cried out, wept and sobbed in many places and in many situations, whether she was alone or accompanied by people, and tries to convince us that the tears were gifts from God.

What is summarised above is directly connected to participant/topic-oriented strategy. The main participant of this text is of course 'this creature', that is Margery herself. Virtanen (1995: 508) states that this participant/topic-oriented strategy can co-occur with temporal strategy and in fact both strategies co-occur in this text.

(8) <u>On a tyme beforn</u>, this creatur went to hir praerys for to wetyn what answer sche schuld yevyn to the wedow. Sche was comawndyd in hir spyryt to byddyn the wedow levyn hir confessowr that was that tyme, yf sche wold plesyn God, and gon to the ankyr at the Frer Prechowrys in Lenn and schewyn hym hir lyfe. <u>Whan this creatur dede this massage</u>, the wedow wold not levyn hir wordys, ne hir gostly fadyr neythyr, les than God wold yevyn hir the same grace that he yaf this creatur, and sche chargyd this creatur that sche schuld no mor comyn in hir place. And for this creatur told hir that sche had to fele lofe of affecyon to hir gostly fadyr, therfor the wedow seyde it had ben good to this creatur that hir lofe and hir affeccyon wer set as hir was. (BMK, Ch. 18, ll. 1432-1443)

The passage above, quotation (8), is connected with a temporal discourse strategy, and, at the same time, with intricately interwound references to the participants. Here the main characters are *this creatur* and *the wedow*, and they are cohesively connected in the forms of full noun phrases or pronouns. This type of strategy is observed throughout this text.

---

4   On the other hand, *Mandeville's Travels* should be regarded as descriptive.

3. Discourse Strategies in *Julian of Norwich*

Next, we examine Julian's discourse strategies using some excerpts from her Short Text. There might be some differences between her Short Text and Long Text, but here we analyse the Short Text as a pilot study.

First, with regard to temporal discourse strategy, it is not difficult to find a chronological sequence in this text.

(9) Ande <u>when I was thryttye wyntere alde and a halfe</u>, god sente me a bodelye syekenes in the whilke I laye <u>thre dayes and thre nyghttes</u>, and <u>on the ferthe nyght</u> I toke alle my ryghttynges of haly kyrke, and wenyd nought tylle haue lyffede tylle daye. And <u>aftyr this</u> y langourede <u>furthe two dayes & two nyghttes</u>; & <u>on the thyrde nyght</u> I wenede <u>ofte tymes</u> to hafe passede, and so wenyd thaye that were abowte me. (ST, Ch. II, p. 41, ll. 4-10)

In quotation (9) she autobiographically describes that she experienced a terrible sickness and that she was more dead than alive. As we saw in *Margery Kempe*, there is a rather long temporal adverbial phrase at the beginning of this chapter, and it is followed by other shorter temporal phrases such as 'on the ferthe nyght' and 'aftyr this'. There are also phrases to describe a duration (i.e. 'thre dayes and thre nyghttes' and 'furthe two dayes & two nyghttes'), and a phrase to describe frequency ('ofte tymes'). More precisely, she places a duration first ('furthe two dayes & two nyghttes'), then sets one day during that period ('on the thyrde nyght'), and describes the frequency within that day ('ofte tymes').

The explicit use of locative strategy is highly limited in *Revelations*, but we can see a kind of locative discourse strategy, for example, in her description of Christ's Passion.

(10) <u>Aftyr this</u> cryste schewyd me a partye of his passyone nere his dyinge. I sawe that swete faace as yt ware drye and bludylesse with pale dyinge, <u>sithen</u> mare de[de] pale langourande; and <u>than</u> turnede more dede to the blewe, & <u>sithene</u> mare blewe as the flesche turnede mare deepe dede. For alle the paynes that cryste sufferde in his bodye schewyd to me in the blyssede faace als farfurthe as I sawe it, and namelye in the lyppes. <u>Thare</u> I sawe this foure colourse, thaye that I sawe beforehande, freschlye & rud[dy], lyflye & lykande to my syght. (ST, Ch. X, p. 53, ll. 17-25)

Julian starts this chapter, as well as other chapters, with the temporal adverbial phrase 'aftyr this'. However, in the course of describing Christ's Passion, she speaks focusing on what she saw in this revelation and uses a locative adverb 'thare' at the beginning of the sentence. The previous sentence has also been organised by locative cohesive devices zooming in on Christ's body, getting closer to his face, and then to his lips. This is a reasonable and effective shift to describe her vision vividly. Virtanen (1995: 510) says that 'the locative discourse strategy has the effect of taking the reader on a tour.'

References to participants are steady throughout her text. One difference from *Margery Kempe* is that she narrates from the first-person viewpoint as stated above. A network of cohesion by referYoshikYoring to the participants is shown in quotation (11):

(11) In this our lorde brought vnto my mynde & schewyd me a perte of the fendys malyce & fully his vnmyght, and for that he schewyd me that the passyon of hym is ouercomynge of the fende. God schewyd me that he hase nowe the same malyce that he had before the incarnacyon, and als sare he travayles & als contynuelye he sees that alle chosene saules eschapes hym worschipfullye, and that es alle his sorowe. (ST, Ch. VIII, p. 50, l. 25-p. 51, l. 1)

Previous studies account for the means by which Julian makes her writing style intelligible. Stone (1970: 110) says:

It is basically in terms of sentence structure that R. M. Wilson gives Julian of Norwich the laurel as one of the greatest of the Middle English mystic writers[5]. His greatest praise is for her straightforward style (p. 99), in which rhetorical devices are subordinate and used as they "should be" to emphasize thought rather than to obscure it through overabundance.

In fact, from the viewpoint of textualisation, her text sounds more logical than Margery's. For example, she often explains things in an orderly sequence, as the reader of this paper would have already noticed in quotation (10). Two further examples are shown in quotations (12) and (13).

(12) In this lytille thynge I sawe thre partyes. The fyrste is that god made [it], the seconde ys that he loves it, the thyrde ys that god kepes it. (ST, Ch. IV, p. 44, ll. 12-14)

(13) God schewyd me thre degrees of blysse that ylke saule schalle hafe in hevene that wilfullye hase servyd god in any degree heere in erthe. The fyrste is the wyrschipfulle thankkynge of owre lorde god that he schalle resayfe when he es delyuerede fro payne. This thanke is so hy3e and so wyrschipfulle that hym thynke it fylles hym þow3 þare ware no mare blys: for me thought that alle the payne & travayle that myght be suffyrde of alle lyffande men myght nought [hafe] deserwede the thanke that a man schalle hafe that wylfullye has servydde god. For the seconde, that alle the blyssede creatures þat er in hevene schalle see that worschipfulle thankynge of oure lorde god, & he makys his servyce to alle that er in heuen knawen. And for the thyrde, that als new ande als lykande as it es resayvede that tyme, ryght so schalle itt laste withowten ende: I sawe that goodelye and swetlye was this sayde & schewyd to me, that þe age of euerylk [man] schalle be knawen in heuen and rewardyd for his wilfulle seruyce and for his tyme, and namelye the age of thame þat wilfullye and frelye offers thare 3ought vnto god es passande rewardede & wondyrlye thankkyd. (ST, Ch. IX, p. 51, l. 23-p. 52, l. 11)

---

5   Wilson, R. M., "Three Middle English Mystics", *Essays and Studies 1956*, N.S. 9. (London, John Murray, 1956), pp. 87-112.

4. A Comparison of Discourse Strategies Used by the Two Authors

As mentioned above, both texts are sometimes autobiographical and sometimes describe visions they received. With regards to the discourse strategies in autobiographical passages, they do not show much difference. For example, both Julian and Margery describe their illnesses, which almost killed them. Compare quotation (9), which we have already examined, with Margery's description in quotation (14).

(14) Afftyrward God ponyschyd hir wyth many gret and divers sekenes. Sche had the flyx a long tyme tyl sche was anoyntyd, wenyng to a be deed. Sche was so febyl, that sche myth not heldyn a spon in hir hand. Than owr Lord Jhesu Crist spak to hir in hir sowle and seyd that sche schulde not dey yet. Than sche recuryd ayen a lytyl while. And anon aftyr sche had a gret sekenes in hir hevyd and sithyn in hir bakke, that sche feryd to a lost hir witte therthorw. Aftyrwarde, whan sche was recuryd of alle thes sekenessys, in schort tyme folwyd another sekenes, whech was sett in hir ryth syde, duryng the terme of viii yer, saf viii wokys, be divers tymes. Sumtyme sche had it onys in a weke contunyng, sumtyme xxx owrys, sumtyme xx, sumtyme x, sumtyme viii, sumtyme iiii, and sumtyme ii, so hard and so scharp that sche must voydyn that was in hir stomak, as bittyr as it had ben galle, neythyr etyng ne drynkyng whil the sekenes enduryd, but evyr gronyng tyl it was gon. (BMK, Ch. 56, ll. 4609-4624)

There is really not much difference in their adoption of discourse strategies in these passages. Both organise their texts using a temporal strategy, although Margery uses temporal words many times. Excessive repetition is sometimes pointed out as one of the characteristics of her writing.[6]

However, in the passages describing their visions, the two authors show some differences. As we have already seen, Julian uses locative discourse strategies, for example, in quotation (10), which is Julian's description of her vision of Christ's Passion. Margery also describes experiencing Christ's Passion in her contemplation, as shown in quotation (15) below.

(15) And anon aftyr sche beheld how the cruel Jewys leydyn hys precyows body to the crosse, and sithyn tokyn a long nayle, a row and a boistews, and sett to hys on hand, and wyth gret violens and cruelnes thei drevyn it thorw hys hande. Hys blisful modyr beheldyng, and this creature, how hys precyows body schrynkyd and drow togedyr wyth alle senwys and veynys in that precyows body for peyne that it suffyrd and felt, thei sorwyd and mornyd and syhyd ful sor.

...

And than sche wept and cryid passyngly sor, that myche of the pepil in the chirche wondryd on hir body. And anon sche sey hem takyn up the crosse wyth owr Lordys body hangyng theron, and madyn gret noyse and gret crye, and lyftyd it up fro the erthe a certeyn distawnce, and sithyn letyn the crosse fallyn down into the morteys. And than owr Lordys body schakyd and schoderyd, and alle the joyntys of that blisful body brostyn and wentyn

---

6   See Stone (1970: 110).

asundyr, and hys precyows wowndys ronnyn down wyth reverys of blood on every syde. And so sche had evyrmor cawse of mor wepyng and sorwyng. (BMK, Ch. 80, ll. 6449-6479)

Margery describes her vision as vividly as Julian does, but Margery does not use a locative strategy here. Her text follows the course of the story of the Bible and it is bound by temporal adverbial phrases.

Also in quotation (10), Julian uses enumeration: 'Thare I sawe this foure colourse, thaye that I sawe beforehande,' in the first paragraph; and also in the second paragraph 'For I sawe in criste a doubille thyrste, ane bodylye, ane othere gastelye.' As is shown in this example, Julian gives her interpretation to revelations. Unlike Julian, Margery does not give such interpretation to her visions. Instead, Margery explains that those visions caused her to cry with copious tears. The last sentence in quotation (15) says 'And so sche had evyrmor cawse of more wepyng and sorwyng.' A similar difference as to whether the author gives her interpretation to the vision or not is also seen in the use of verbs of cognition. Both authors use the impersonal verb *think*, but Julian's *Revelations* shows more variations. In *Margery Kempe*, it is always used to express her perception.

(16) And than hir thowt owr Lord comendyd hys spiryt into hys Fadrys handys and therwyth he deyid. Than hir thowt sche sey owr Lady swownyn and fallyn down and lyn stille as sche had ben ded. Than the creatur thowt that sche ran al abowte the place as it had ben a mad woman, crying and roryng. (Ch. 80, ll. 6497-6501)

The first sentence in quotation (16) states that it seemed to Margery that Jesus Christ died at that moment. The second sentence says that it seemed to her that she saw the Virgin Mary swoon, fall down and lie still. The expression 'the creatur thowt' in the third sentence may possibly be a personal construction, but considering its parallel use with the aforesaid impersonal construction 'hir thowt', we would also be able to regard it as impersonal. She felt she ran around the place crying.

On the other hand, Julian uses this impersonal *think* not only to express her imperfect perception in revelations she received but also to give her interpretation of the revelations.

(17) And in this sodaynlye I sawe the rede blode trekylle down fro vndyr the garlande alle hate, freschlye, plentefully, & lyvelye, ryght as me thought that it was in that tyme that the garlonde of thornys was thyrstede on his blessede heede. (ST, Ch, III, p. 43, ll. 7-10)

(18) And eftyr, oure lorde brought vnto my mynde the langynge that I hadde to hym before. And I sawe that nathynge letted me bot syn; and so I behelde generallye in vs alle, and me thought, "3yf syn hadde nought bene, we schulde alle hafe bene clene and lyke to oure lorde, as he made vs". (ST, Ch, XIII, p. 59, ll. 32-36)

Quotation (17) is an example of *think* showing the uncertainty of her perception. Quotation (18) is an example of the use of impersonal *think* in a question, which gives her interpretation regarding the revelation. In these examples with impersonal constructions with *think*, there is initially no apparent difference between the two texts except for the choices of first-person or third-person point of view, but as we look more closely into the content of each text, they show such a difference as discussed with regard to these examples.

Virtanen (1995: 510) points out that the text producer's thought processes are sometimes reflected in evaluative elements. Evaluative adjectives such as *evil* and *good* are often taken as typical evaluative elements to be examined, but as is observed above, examining sentences with recognition verbs such as *seem* and *think* could also show the authors' thought processes. This is especially true in *Revelations*, because the author is always thinking of the reasons and the meanings of the revelations she received.

5. Concluding Remarks

This paper has compared two Late Middle English women's mystical works mainly from the viewpoint of the author's choice of discourse strategies to link sentences or clauses. The appearance of the participants in their clauses clearly shows narrative characteristics in both texts. Referring repeatedly to the author or to other major participants was one of their major cohesive devices. The use of temporal discourse strategies to make a chronological sequence was also common to both texts. This is also accentuated in the narrative. With regard to locative strategy, the two texts showed differences. In *The Book of Margery Kempe* a locative discourse strategy is sometimes used, while in Julian's *Revelations* it is rarely used. Though the typical characteristics in Middle English travelogue have not been clear, the difference on their use of locative discourse strategy could be regarded as a reflection of their stylistic differences; *Margery Kempe* has some characteristics of travelogues, while *Revelations* does not. At least in the description of one revelation, *Revelations* also shows an effective shift from temporal to locative strategies.

In the autobiographical passages, both texts look similar. However, even in the case where a resemblance in their choice of discourse strategies is recognised, it is difficult to say whence the resemblance comes, whether because of a consequence demanded by the content or because they both follow a writing style typical in that genre. In passages explaining their visions, they do show some differences, for example both show narrative characteristics in those passages and Margery's passages sound more prototypically narrative. Julian adds some logical explanations and her own interpretation to the visions. The similarities or dissimilarities in their discourse strategies might be keys to distinguish writing styles or to show separate genres, but it is too complicated to demonstrate such distinctions by this simple comparison of two texts. Examining the sentence-initial adverbials in further mystical works and comparing the results with those of works in related genres such as travelogues would render possible a fuller description of the relationship between discourse strategies and genres in Middle English related to mystical writing.

References

Beer, Frances (ed.)
    1978   *Revelations of Divine Love by Julian of Norwich*. Heidelberg: Carl Winter Universitätsverlag.

Colledge, Edmund –James Walsh (edd.)
    1978   *A Book of Showings to the Anchoress Julian of Norwich*, 2 vols. Toronto: Pontifical Institute of Mediaeval Studies.

Halliday, M. A. K. – Ruqaiya Hasan
    1976   *Cohesion in English*. London: Longman.

Hamelius, P.
    1919, 1923   *Mandeville's Travels*. 2 vols., Early English Text Society, o. s. 153, 154. London: Oxford University Press.

Meech, Sanford Brown (ed.)
    1940   *The Book of Margery Kempe*, Vol. I, Text, Early English Text Society, o. s. 212., Oxford: Oxford University Press.

Stone, Robert Karl
    1970   *Middle English Prose Style: Margery Kempe and Julian of Norwich*. The Hague: Mouton.

Virtanen, Tuija
    1995   '"Then I Saw to Antique Heddes": Discourse Strategies in Early Modern English Travelogues', in Andreas H. Jucker (ed.), *Historical Pragmatics: Pragmatic Developments in the History of English*, Amsterdam: John Benjamins, 499-513.

Wårvik, Brita
    1990   'On the History of Grounding Markers in English Narrative: Style or Typology?', in *Historical Linguistics 1987*. Edd. Henning Andersen and Konrad Koerner. Amsterdam & Philadelphia: John Benjamins, 531-542.

Windeatt, Barry (ed.)
    2000   *The Book of Margery Kempe*. Harlow: Longman.

Yoshikawa, Fumiko
    2008   'Julian of Norwich and the Rhetoric of the Impersonal', in *Rhetoric of the Anchorhold: Place, Space and Body within the Discourse of Enclosure*. Ed. Liz Herbert McAvoy. Cardiff: University of Wales Press.

Part III
Modern English and the History of English

18 A Broader and Sharper Characterisation of Grammaticalisation
Masachiyo Amano, Nagoya University

1. Introduction

There seem to be at least two types of grammaticalisation distinguished in the literature, as discussed in Hopper and Traugott (2003), among others. One is the type in which lexical items undergo phonological attrition gradually until they become functional morphemes dependent on free ones. It is often called cline-type grammaticalisation and schematised as in (1), which is called functionalisation here since it alters lexical categories into functional ones.

(1) Cline Type of Grammaticalisation (=Functionalisation)
    content item > grammatical word > clitic > inflectional affix
                                                                        (Hopper and Traugott 2003: 7)

The other is the type in which relatively independent constituents detached from the rest of clauses are gradually incorporated in the clauses. Let us state this type of grammaticalisation as in (2) and refer to it as grammatical reorganisation.

(2) Grammatical Reorganisation
    margin (topic, adjunct, etc.) > nucleus (subject, object, head, etc.)

A good example of grammatical reorganisation is given in (3), in which the topic in (3a) is reorganised as the subject in (3b).

(3) a. The new yacht of his, he has spent a fortune on it.
    b. The new yacht of his cost him a fortune.   (Ibid.: 28)

In grammatical reorganisation, margins gradually become essential constituents, or nuclei, of constructions, so that more rigid, often better organised, grammatical structures are historically created.[1]

The main purpose of the present paper is to give an additional support for assuming grammatical reorganisation as a type of grammaticalisation, thus extending the notion of grammaticalisation. It also restricts the class of grammaticalisation by recognising only the two processes in (1) and (2) as true grammaticalisation.

---

1   Although it is very difficult to see in what sense grammatical reorganisation creates better organised constructions, it often alters grammatically complicated constructions to simpler ones which have fewer margins but can convey the same amount of information in a more economical way. In other words, it makes constructions more informative.

2. More Examples of Grammatical Reorganisation

Since functionalisation is already well established as real grammaticalisation in the literature, often as the only type of grammaticalisation, no one will raise any objection to its reality.[2] Thus our primary task here would be to provide more examples of grammatical reorganisation to further motivate its status as another type of grammaticalisation.

A first example comes from an observation by Denison (1993:105). He points out that "at least some dative objects changed to direct objects as they lost the case marking in early ME, despite the fact that they were adjuncts in OE." Basically, dative objects in OE underwent two changes: some started to occur with the preposition *to*, as in (4), and others shifted to assume the status of direct object, as in (5).[3]

Dative object   >   *to*-PP
(4) (1340) *Ayenb.* 26.28
    ... uror to kueme kueadliche to þe worlde.
    ... for to please sinfully   to the world.
    '...to please the world sinfully.'   (Denison 1993:105)

Dative object   >   direct object
(5) c1225(?c1200) *St Juliana* (Bob) 13.131
    ne nulle   ich neauer mare him lihen   ne leauen
    nor not-will I   never   more him prove-false-to nor leave
    'nor will I ever more prove false to him or leave him'   (Ibid.)

If the change from dative adjunct to direct object is well motivated, we can take it as an example of grammatical reorganisation because it is a change from margin to nucleus. Denison also provides convincing evidence that motivates the change: objects which were dative in OE could be passivised as nominative subjects in the 13th century, as exemplified in (6) and (7).

---

2   In a sense functionalisation is a process that changes analytic expressions into synthetic ones, and thus it is rather difficult to observe functionalisation or discern the entire process of functionalisation in a typically analytic language like English. By contrast, grammatical reorganisation is much more likely to be observed in English. It seems to me that if grammatical reorganisation is not available to an analytic language, it does not have a means for evolution to be more informative.
3   The remarks in the text do not exclude the possibility that dative objects in OE changed other ways. Obviously, some of them co-occurred with the preposition *for* in compensation for the loss of dative case marking.

Passives with a nominative subject in the 13th century
(6) c1225(?c1200) *St Kath.*(1) 196
Þe king was swiðe icwemet, and wolde witen ...
the king was very   pleased and wished know ...   (Ibid.)
(7) (c1359) Chaucer, *CT.Sq.* V.666
Ne hadde he ben holpen by the steede of bras
not had he been helped   by the steed of bras
'had he not been helped by the steed of bas'   (Ibid.)

Since only true direct arguments are able to be nominative subjects of passives, examples such as (6) and (7) are not allowed without grammatical reorganisation of dative adjuncts as arguments.

Another example of grammatical reorganisation is provided by a historical change of the grammatical status of *to*-prepositional phrases, which is also observed by Denison (1993:107), as summarised in (8).

(8) Grammatical Status of *to*-phrases
　　a.　*To*-phrases as Goal adjuncts: common in OE
　　b.　*To*-phrases as true Benefactives: more common since the 14th century

We have to admit that there are a large number of *to*-phrases in present-day English which are adjuncts, but it might also be true that many goal adjuncts were reanalysed as benefactive arguments, as attested by the following examples:[4]

(9) *Or* 147.27
　　& [Dioclitianus &   Maximianus] leton þa onwealdas
　　and Dioclitianus and Maximianus   left   the jurisdiction/dominions
　　to Galeriuse &   to Constantiuse
　　to Galerius and   to Constantius   (Denison 1993:107)
(10) *Or* 148.3
　　& for þæm he forlet   his agnum willan   Italiam &   Affriam to
　　and for that he relinquished his own   volition Italy   and Africa to
　　Galeriuse
　　Galerius
　　'and for that reason he relinquished Italy and Africa to Galerius of his own
　　volition'   (Ibid.)
(11) a1425(a1382) *Wbible(l)* Gen 29.19
　　Betir is that Y ȝyue hir to thee than to another man
　　better is that I give her to you than to another man   (Ibid.)

4　It seems to me that the relevant reanalysis took place to *to*-phrases appearing especially in constructions which alternate with double object constructions. However, it did not take place to *for*-phrases appearing in constructions which alternate with apparent double object constructions. For a more detailed discussion, see Amano (2002).

In these examples, the *to*-phrases were clearly reanalysed as benefactive arguments, a sort of nucleus, without any morphological or phonological change, leading us to the conclusion that there has happened a grammatical reorganisation to the *to*-phrases.

We have already seen an example in which a margin shifted to subject position in the history of English. It would be worthwhile here to turn to another example which showed a similar shift. The expletive *there* in existential or presentational constructions is clearly functioning as subject in present-day English, because it undergoes Subject-Auxiliary Inversion like ordinary subjects when it appears in interrogative sentences. Breivik (1983, 1991), however, argues that the ancestor of *there* was inserted in sentence-initial position as an instantiation of the verb-second phenomenon in earlier English. Thus it was an adverbial just like *nu* in the verb-second sentence of (12).[5]

(12) Nu   sceal beon aefre on Iiabbod.
     Now shall be   ever on Iian abbot.   (*Anglo-Saxon Chronicle*, A 565, Schmidt 1980:131)

If this is the case, it means that *there* did not occupy the subject position in OE or ME existential or presentational constructions. Thus we might conclude that *there* was grammatically reorganised as a nucleus by present-day English.

It is impossible to give an exhaustive list of grammatical reorganisations that have taken place throughout the history of English, but the examples discussed so far might be enough to motivate the claim here that grammatical reorganisation has been a major historical process underlying many shifts of phrases from margin to nucleus. We deal with a completely different type of grammatical reorganisation to further enhance its validity and clarify what is actually meant by grammatical reorganisation here.

3. A Different Type of Grammatical Reorganisation

It is said that clause combining was rather simple in OE; coordination was the main means for syntactically connecting clauses and subordination was a later development. Of course, we do not intend to claim that there was no subordination in OE, but that it was still underdeveloped or rather scarce. Basically based on this observation, the present section shows that the development of subordination was driven by grammaticalisation.

---

[5] Although we do not make clear exactly where adverbials were inserted in verb-second sentences in OE or ME, one idea would be to adopt the claim proposed by many generative linguists who are studying historical changes of English within the standard theoretical framework developed by Noam Chomsky and his students. They argue that adverbials in examples like (12) were inserted in the specifier of complementiser projection and the finite verbs shifted to the complementiser from Tense.

Hopper and Traugott (2003) present a "cline of clause combining" consisting of three cluster points, as in the following:[6]

(13) a. "Parataxis," or relative independence, except as constrained by the pragmatics of "making sense" and relevance.
   b. "Hypotaxis," or interdependence, in which there is a nucleus, and one or more clauses which cannot stand by themselves, and are therefore relatively dependent. However, they are typically not wholly included within any constituent of the nucleus.
   c. "Subordination," or, in its extreme form, "embedding," in other words, complete dependency, in a margin is wholly included within a constituent of the nucleus.

(Hopper and Traugott 2003: 177)

(14) parataxis   >   hypotaxis   >   subordination
     −dependent   +dependent   +dependent
     −embedded   −embedded   +embedded   (Ibid.: 178)

For expository purposes, let us suppose that only two clauses, A and B, are involved in the change. In parataxis, exemplified in (15), clause A and clause B are simply juxtaposed sometimes under one intonation contour and both A and B form grammatically independent nuclei which are only connected pragmatically or semantically. In hypotaxis, exemplified in (16), clause B has almost lost the status of nucleus and is acquiring the status of margin. Subordination, exemplified in (17), is a final stage of the change, in which clause B has totally changed into a margin adjoined to the preceding noun phrase.

(15) You keep smoking those cigarettes, you're gonna start coughing again. (Ibid.: 180)
(16) Bill Smith, who is our president, would like to meet with you. (Ibid.: 182)
(17) I think the guy who just walked out of the store resembles the photo in the post-office window. (Ibid.: 183)

In all the examples of grammatical reorganisation given in the preceding sections, a margin acquires the status of nucleus, so it might appear that the change in (15)-(16) is a different type of change from grammatical reorganisation.

It seems to me, however, that the change in question is a type of grammatical reorganisation, because the syntactic combination of the two clauses has come to be reorganised in a more systematic way. First of all, we should notice that parataxis does not involve any grammatical means for clause combination. It is true that the second clause is a nucleus in (15); but since the two clauses are nuclei independent from each other at least grammatically, clause B is not a nucleus constituent of clause A. Actually, it is not even a margin constituent of clause A. As

---

6 To avoid any misunderstanding, we do not use the term 'cline' for the change stated in (13)-(14). If we have to adopt it, we apply it only to the traditional type of grammaticalisation in (1), though (1) is referred to as functionalisation here to again avoid a possible misunderstanding.

compared with this, hypotaxis is a more systematically grammaticalised combination, because clause B in (16) is adjoined to clause A or made one of its constituents by an overt grammatical means, i.e., nonrestrictive relativisation. At the final state of subordination, clause B is syntactically incorporated or embedded in clause A by restrictive relativisation. Thus the grammatical relation between the two clauses is firmly established and clause B is clearly a margin constituent of clause A.[7]

If the considerations just above are basically correct, it may be claimed that clause B is grammatically reorganised in the sense that it has gradually changed into a constituent more deeply incorporated into clause A through a particular grammatical means. Thus it seems that the change of a constituent from margin to nucleus is not necessarily a characteristic property of grammatical reorganisation. What is critically important to it will be a grammatical means that connects clause B with clause A. Accordingly, as pointed out by Hopper and Traugott (2003) in a slightly different context, we might say that (18b) is a grammatically reorganised form of (18a).

(18) a. I came, I saw, I conquered.
 b. I came and I saw and I conquered.

This is simply because the three clauses involved are connected by a particular grammatical means, i.e. coordination, in (18b), but they are just juxtaposed in (18a). It might naturally be claimed that grammatical reorganisation should be restated in a much simpler way than (2), for instance, as in (19).

(19) loosely connected constituents   >   rigidly connected constituents

This characterisation is not incompatible with (2), since in all examples discussed so far all margins have become more closely connected with the rest of the sentences while changing into nuclei. Thus (19) might be a good idea, but we leave it an open question here, because it is very difficult to see what consequences (19) will have for the claim here.

4. Subjectification and Phonological Attrition

In many traditional studies, grammaticalisation has been very frequently associated with coexisting phenomena such as phonological attrition, semantic bleaching, or subjectification. However, in no examples of grammatical reorganisation illustrated above can we see such phenomena accompanying them. Thus it might

---

[7]   Clause B does not seem to be incorporated or embedded in clause A in (16), because it has often been referred to as appositive clause in traditional grammar, and this sentence is semantically and probably syntactically equivalent with *Bill Smith, our president, would like to meet with you.*

be objected that grammatical reorganisation has nothing to do with real grammaticalisation. In this section, we will first address the problem of subjectification, and then that of phonological attrition.[8]

Although there are many examples in which grammaticalisation co-occurs with subjectification or semantic bleaching, it might be relevant to consider the development of parenthetical clauses in present-day English.

(20) a. I think that the coup was planned by the CIA.
    b. Do you think that the coup was planned by the CIA?
                                           (Thompson and Mulac 1991: 322)
(21) a. I think Commander Dalgeish writes poetry.
    b. Commander Dalgeish writes poetry, I think.   (Ibid.)

While *think* is the main verb in the two examples of (20), it serves as a parenthetical verb in those of (21), qualifying the main assertions expressed by the rest of the sentences. If we apply the definition of subjectification given in (22), the change of *think* from main verb to parenthetical one will be one of the clearest cases of subjectification.

(22) Subjectification
It is a gradient phenomenon, whereby forms and constructions that at first express primarily concrete, lexical objective meanings come through repeated use in local syntactic contexts to serve increasingly abstract, pragmatic, interpersonal and speaker-based functions. (Traugott 1995: 32)

However, a question which arises here is exactly in what sense parentheticals are grammaticalised. If they are classified as functional categories compared with main clauses, we can claim that their development is a result of grammaticalisation in the sense of functionalisation. Indeed, the distribution of parentheticals suggests that they are adverbials, as shown in (23).

(23) a. That stuff, you can't deny, is quite poisonous in these amounts.
    b. That stuff is, you can't deny, quite poisonous in these amounts.
    c. That stuff is quite poisonous, you can't deny, in these amounts.
                                                                  (Downing 1973)

But their adverbial status does not mean that they are functional, since adverbials form an open class.

---

8   We do not directly deal with semantic bleaching here. Of course, subjectification and semantic bleaching are different grammatical phenomena that should be discussed separately. It seems to me, however, that they also have some important similarities; if subjectification includes "losing concrete, lexical meanings" as stated in (22), it may be counted in as an instance of semantic bleaching because semantic contents are lost through subjectification.

Thus what is actually happening here seems to be degrammaticalisation rather than grammaticalisation. In other words, this is a change from nucleus to margin; the main clauses, as nuclei, are shifting to adverbials in the course of development of parentheticals. Alternatively, the rigidly connected constituents are now being detached from the rest of the sentences to be more loosely connected during this change. We might conclude that subjectification does not necessarily lead to grammaticalisation. Therefore, it does not raise any problem for the claim here if grammatical reorganisation takes place without being accompanied by subjectification or semantic bleaching.

Grammatical reorganisation is not accompanied by phonological attrition, either. But this also does not undermine its status as grammaticalisation, because even functionalisation, which is more likely to co-occur with phonological attrition, has happened without it in English. Here is the list of possible cases of functionalisation.[9]

Examples of Functionalisation in English
(24) a. Complementiser *that* from pronoun *that*
 b. Complementiser *for* from preposition *for*
 c. Infinitive *to* from preposition *to*
 d. Definite article *the* from demonstrative pronoun *that*
 e. Indefinite article *a(n)* from cardinal number *one*
 d. Introduction of semantically empty preposition *of* in derived nominals
 e. Introduction of semantically empty auxiliary *do* in negation and interrogation
 f. Negative head *not* from a negative adverb
 g. Expletive *there* from adverbial *there*
 h. Modal auxiliaries from preterit verbs

Even a cursory examination will reveal that all the cases in (24) have taken place in English without any substantial phononogical attrition,[10] though semantic bleaching or subjectification is sometimes observed.

Thus we might conclude this section by claiming that grammaticalisation, whether functionalisation or grammatical reorganisation, often occurs in English without subjectification or phonological attrition. This observation suggests that grammaticalisation can be a purely syntactic or grammatical process that makes language more informative by providing it with routinisation of expressions

---

9 Needless to say, (24) is never intended to be an exhaustive list. Of course, I will try to make a complete list. It should be noticed here that some cases of the list has arisen in English through a combinatory force of both functionalisation and grammatical reorganisation. We will discuss such a case in more detail below.
10 It should be noticed that phonological attrition is different from the so-called levelling, which historically affects inflectional affixes to reduce their phonetic contents. Phonological attrition is a process that reduces the phonetic contents of the base or root of a relevant word.

5. Combinatory Pressures from the Two Types of Grammaticalisation

This section demonstrates that although functionalisation and grammatical reorganisation are independent historical processes, they sometimes operate jointly to produce grammaticalised forms. Here we take up the emergence of possessive genitives with *'s* in English, though there are a number of other such examples.

There seem to be two rival groups of researchers in the literature concerning the origin of *'s* in present-day English. One includes Baugh and Cable (1978), Janda (1980), Taylor (1996), Amano (2003) etc., who claim that *'s* has derived from the *his*-genitive in late ME or early ModE. Some examples of the *his*-genitive are given in (25).

(25) a. Felyce hir fayrnesse   (*PPL.* B xii 47)
   b. Gwenayfer his love   (*Lawman* B 22247)
   c. at þare ditch his grunde   (*Lawman* B 1589)   (Mustanoja 1960: 160)

The other includes Allen (1997), Fischer (1992), Rosenbach (2002), etc. who claim that *'s* has derived from the genitive case in OE or are just critical about the proposal by the first group. Here we adopt the proposal by the first group and show that the development of *'s* was driven by a combinatory pressure from the two types of grammaticalisation.

By using a hypothetical example, let us suppose that the relevant change was from (26) to (27), assuming the DP analysis proposed by Abney (1987).[11]

(26) God his name: [$_{DP}$ God [$_{DP}$ [$_{D'}$ [$_D$ his] [$_{NP}$ name]]]]
(27) God's name: [$_{DP}$ God [$_{D'}$ [$_D$'s] [$_{NP}$ name]]]

While *God* is adjoined to DP in (26) and thus treated as a margin somehow like a topic, whereas it is located in the Specifier of DP in (27) and thus treated as a nucleus like a subject. In addition, while the head D is a pronoun, *his*, in (26), it is reduced to a clitic, *'s*, in (27). If these observations are basically correct, it will follow that the two different types of grammaticalisation were involved in the change from (26) to (27), as stated in (28).

(28) a. Functionalisation: ponoun *his* > clitic *'s*
   b. Grammatical reorganisation: *God* as topic > *God* as specifier

There remain many problems to be worked out and solved in a future study, but it seems to me that the historical changes stated in (28) are basically on the right track.

---

11   For the details of the change, the reader is referred to Amano (2003).

6. Conclusion

We have tried to discover some characteristic properties of grammaticalisation in English and made the three points. First, grammaticalisation in English should be restricted to the two types: functionalisation and grammatical reorganisation. Second, neither phonological attrition nor subjectification plays an important role in English grammaticalisation, implying that it is a purely syntactic phenomenon. Third, some cases of grammaticalisation in English have been driven by the combination of pressures from both functionalisation and grammatical reorganisation.

Although the number of examples of grammaticalisation discussed here is limited, it seems that many examples we have not addressed are compatible with the characterisations of functionalisation and grammatical reorganisation, though many critical problems are left open.

References

Abney, Steven
  1987   *The English Noun Phrase in its Sentential Aspect,* Ph.D. dissertation, MIT.
Allen, Cynthia
  1997   "The Origins of the 'Group Genitive' in English," *Transactions of the Philological Society* 95, 111-31.
Amano, Masachiyo
  2002   "On the Syntactic Status of Indirect and Direct Objects in English," *The Journal of School of Letters* 48, Nagoya University, 89-113.
  2003   "On the Historical Role of the *His*-Genitive in the Development of *'S,'* *The Twentieth Anniversary Publication of the Modern English Association*, Published for the Association by Eichosha, 95-108.
Baugh, Albert and Thomas Cable
  1978   *A History of the English Language,* Routledge & Kegan Paul, London.
Breivik, Leiv
  1983   *Existential* There: *A Synchronic and Diachronic Study*, Bergen, Department of English, University of Bergen.
Breivik, Leiv
  1991   "On the Typological Status of Old English," in Dieter Kastovsky (ed.) *Historical English Syntax*, 31-50, Mouton de Gruyter, Berlin.

Bybee, Joan, Revere Perkins and William Pagliuca
　1994　　*The Evolution of Grammar: Tense, Aspect, and Modularity in the Languages of the World*, University of Chicago Press, Chicago.
Denison, David
　1993　　*English Historical Syntax*. Longman, London.
Downing, Bruce
　1973　　"Parenthesization Rules and Obligatory Phrases," *Papers in Linguistics 12*, 1-47.
Fischer, Olga
　1992　　"Syntax," in N. Blake (ed.) *The Cambridge History of the English Language*, vol. II, 1066-1476, 207-408, Cambridge University Press, Cambridge.
Hopper, Paul and Elizabeth Traugott
　2003　　*Grammaticalization*, Cambridge University Press, Cambridge.
Janda, Richard
　1980　　"On the Decline of Declensional Systems: The Overall Loss of OE Nominal Case Inflections and the ME Reanalysis of *-es* as *his*," in E.C. Traugott, R. Labrum, and S. Sheperd (eds.), *Papers From the 4th International Conference on Historical Linguistics*, 243-53, John Benjamins, Amsterdam.
Mustanoja, Tauno
　1960　　*A Middle English Syntax*, Société Néophilologique, Helsinki. Reprinted by Meicho Fukyu Kai, Tokyo, 1985.
Roberts, Ian and Anna Roussou
　2003　　*Syntactic Change: A Minimalist Approach to Grammaticalization*, Cambridge University Press, Cambridge.
Schmidt, Deborah
　1980　　*A History of Inversion in English*, Ph.D. dissertation, The Ohio State University, Ohio.
Taylor, John
　1996　　*Possessives in English: An Exploration in Cognitive Grammar*, Clarendon Press, Oxford.
Thompson, Sandra and Anthony Mulac
　1991　　"A Quantitative Perspective on the Grammaticalization of Epistemic Parentheticals in English," in Traugott, Elizabeth Closs and Bernd Heine, eds. *Approaches to Grammaticalization*, 2 vol., 313-29, Benjamins, Amsterdam.
Traugott, Elizabeth Closs
　1995　　"Subjectification in Grammaticalization," in Dieter Stein and Susan Wright, eds., *Subjectivity and Subjectivisation in Language*, 31-54. Cambridge University Press, Cambridge.

Wyld, Henry
    1936   *A History of Modern Colloquial English*, 3rd ed., Basil Blackwell, Oxford.

19 'Parts of the Body' and 'Parts of Clothing' – A Semantic Analysis
Magdalena Bator, Adam Mickiewicz University

1. Introduction

The present paper concentrates on the semantic analysis of lexical items belonging to two semantic fields, i.e., 'parts of the body' and 'parts of clothing'. In the first field we have also included words denoting hair, e.g., *fringe*. In the second, names of accessories and various elements of clothes, such as *bag* or *sole*. 42 items have been selected. They underwent semantic changes, such as extension, narrowing or transfer of meaning. The words have been examined from the Old English period until today. In Modern English we have analysed the items which have survived both in Standard English as well as in local dialects.

The data collected for the present study come from the *Oxford English dictionary* (*OED*), the *Middle English dictionary* (*MED*) and Wright's *English dialect dictionary* (*EDD*).

2. Extension of meaning

The words which underwent the extension of meaning constitute the largest group. It contains 17 items, 9 of them originally denoted various parts of clothing, and later extended their meanings to parts of the body, 8 words originally referred to body parts and later assumed additional senses connected with parts of clothing. It is not possible to examine all of them in the context of this paper. Thus, only a few instances will be analysed to illustrate the process. The whole list of items collected for the present study has been included in the Appendix.

The word *girdle*, first appeared in the written records in 1000 (*The holy gospels in Anglo Saxon*), meaning 'a belt worn round the waist to secure or confine the garments; also employed as a means of carrying light articles, esp. a weapon or purse' (*OED*: s.v. *girdle*). It was also used in *Orrmulum* (1200), Chaucer (1386), Barret (1598), Steele & Addison (1709), Shelley (1819), etc. According to the *MED*, throughout the 15th c., *girdle* was also used with reference to jewellery, denoting 'a necklace; a baldric; a belt about the neck or shoulders from which a shield is suspended' (e.g., *Mandeville's Travels*, Chaucer). In the 20th c., the word assumed the sense 'corset' and appeared in *Delineator* (1928), *Daily Mail* (1932), *Time to be born* (Powell, 1942), Roosenburg (1957), etc.

At the beginning of the 13th c. the word adopted the sense 'the part of the body round which the girdle is fastened', however, this meaning occurred exclusively in phrases, e.g., *beneath the girdle*, *up to the girdle*, etc. and it became obsolete in the 1st half of the 18th c. From the beginning of the 16th c. *girdle* has also been used with reference to 'various parts in the structure of animal bodies;

chiefly of the bony supports for the upper and lower limbs, which in Vertebrata are respectively called the shoulder and pelvic girdle'.

Mantle, another word originally belonging to the field 'parts of clothing', entered also the field of 'parts of the body'. It is a borrowing from Latin *mantellum*, which entered the English language in the Old English period. It first appeared in Ælfred (eOE), with the sense 'a loose sleeveless cloak'. Throughout history the word firstly extended its meaning in the field of 'clothes', e.g.,

'a kind of blanket or plaid formerly worn in rural Ireland and the Scottish Highlands' (1488-1688);
'a long loose cloak of the kind which the apostles were commonly depicted as wearing' (1496-1586);
'a blanket made of softened skins or fur, used by North American Indians, members of various South African peoples, etc., both as a cloak and a covering for a bed or floor' (1612-1953);
'a coarse apron; a working apron' (1825-1970)[1].

In the 15th c. the referential field of *mantle* extended to 'body parts'. In 1425 it first occurred with the sense 'a lobe of a liver'. However, this meaning became obsolete in the same century. Only in the 19th c. the loanword reappeared with the sense 'a kind of a tissue', and was recorded in e.g., Bower (1884), *Journal of anatomy and physiology* (1901), *Brain* (1967), Clowes (1961), Mountcastle (1974), etc.

Next item which broadened its meaning from 'parts of clothing' to 'parts of the body' is *poke*. Various sources do not agree on the etymology of the word. According to the *OED*, *poke* is either of Anglo-Norman or French origin. The *MED* considers it a derivative from OE *pohha*, while the *EDD* suggests Scandinavian origin. *Poke* was first recorded in *Havelok* (1300) with the meaning 'a bag, a small sack'. This sense, which, according to the *EDD*, is still present in the local dialects of Scotland, the Shetland Islands, Northern Ireland, Cumberland, Durham, Westmoreland, Yorkshire, Cheshire, Lancashire, Derbyshire, Nottinghamshire, Rutland, Lincolnshire, Northamptonshire, Warwickshire, Gloucestershire, Huntingdonshire, East Anglia, Suffolk, Norfolk, Kent, Sussex, Devonshire and Surrey, was extended to 'a pocket in a person's clothing' (1616-1930). In the 14th c. the word adopted the sense 'the stomach', with which it appears until the Present-Day English. The *EDD* records this meaning in the dialects of Lancashire and Somerset as late as at the end of the 19th c. It should be mentioned that from the beginning of the 15th c. *poke* appears also with the denotation 'a long, full sleeve', e.g., *Political Poems* (1402), *Higden* (1432-50), Phillips (1706).

The process of extension of meaning in the other direction, i.e., from the field 'parts of the body' to 'parts of clothing' has also been very common. The

---

[1] Sense (4) was used chiefly in the dialect of East Anglia, but also Suffolk and Essex.

shift usually involved the extension of meaning from a particular part of the body to the piece of garment covering that part of the body. This was the case with such lexemes as *arm, finger, knee, leg, neck*, etc. This process was observed in 8 of the analysed words.

Arm originally denoted 'the upper limb of the human body, from the shoulder to the hand'. It first appeared in *Lindisfarne Gospels*. Later it extended its meaning to:

> the fore limb of an animal (1607-1847);
> the leg of a hawk from the thigh to the foot (1575-1706);
> the flexible limbs or other appendages of invertebrate animals; as the locomotive and prehensile organs of cuttle-fish, the tentacula of the hydroid polyps, the rays of star-fish, etc.' (1822-1870).

The first record of *arm* denoting 'the part of dress covering an arm; a sleeve' comes from the 14th c., (*Cleanness*), i.e., according to the *MED*, from the dialect of Cheshire. However, according to the *OED*, the denotation started to be used more frequently in the 18th c.

Similarly, the word *finger*, which from 950 occurred with the meaning 'one of the five terminal members of the hand', in the 16th c. adopted the sense 'that part of a glove which is made to receive a finger' and with such a denotation it occurred in Cooper (1565), Marquis of Worcester (1655), *Chester Glossary* (1884), etc.

Another example belonging to this group is *heel*, from OE *hela*. It was first recorded in *Lorica Glossary*, with the meaning 'the projecting hinder part of the foot, below the ankle and behind the hollow of the foot'. From ca. 1000 the word also referred to the part of the body of animals and birds. In the 16th c. *heel* started to denote 'the part of a stocking that covers the heel' and 'the thick part of the sole of a boot or shoe which raises the heel'. With such senses it was recorded by e.g., Holinshed (1577), Shakespeare (1596), Wood (1671), Steele (1709), Macaulay (1849), Caulfeild (1882), Barker (1950), etc.

More examples of words which extended their meanings from the field 'parts of the body' to 'parts of clothing' have been included in the Appendix.

3. Narrowing of meaning

The process of the narrowing of meaning appears in fewer items (5). First of the words, i.e., *lug* appeared in English at the end of the 15th c., denoting 'one of the flaps or lappets of a cap or bonnet, covering the ears'. It was recorded among others in *Accounts of the Lord High Treasurer of Scotland* (1495), *Complaint Scotland* (1549), Ramsay (1737), Goldie (1822), etc. Additionally, from the early 16th c., *lug* was also recorded with the sense 'an ear', and with such a denotation it appeared in *Extracts from the council register of the Burh of Aberdeen* (1507), *Complaint Scotland* (1549), Greene (1592), Jonson (1625), Shirley (1659), Burns

(1786), Scott (1824), etc. The former sense became obsolete in the first half of the 19th c., while the latter, according to the *EDD*, became limited to the dialects of Scotland, Northern Ireland, Northumberland, Cumberland, Westmoreland, Durham, Yorkshire, Lancashire, Cheshire, Derbyshire, Nottinghamshire, East Anglia, Norfolk, East Suffolk and Cornwall. Moreover, outside Scotland, *lug* appears with the meanings 'the lobe of an ear' and 'a large ugly ear'. It is interesting to note that in Scotland the word *ear* went out of use, except in combinations, and *lug* became the only word in use with the sense 'an ear'.

Another word which underwent the narrowing of meaning is *nab*. Its origin is uncertain, the *MED* suggests that it is a borrowing from Scandinavian (cf. ON *nabbi*). In the 16th c. the lexeme appeared with the meaning 'the head of a person or animal' as well as 'a hat'. The former sense was used by such authors as Copland (1536), Harman (1567), Fletcher (1640), Grose (1785), Joyce (1922), etc., while the latter appeared for instance in Head (1673), Fielding (1730), Byng (1784), etc. According to the *OED*, the denotation referring to 'part of clothing' disappeared from the written records at the end of the 18th c. It has not been recorded by Wright in his *EDD*.

Similarly, the word *pallet*, from Anglo-Norman *palet*, originally was used within both fields, i.e., 'parts of the body' and 'parts of clothing'. *Pallet* denoted 'a piece of armour for the head, a helmet; a type of headpiece or skullcap' and 'the head'. Both senses were recorded from the 14th c. However, only the latter sense survived. The *OED* records it as late as 1879 (Beattie). The *EDD* localises the word, meaning 'the head', in Scottish dialects throughout the 19th c. The sense referring to clothing disappeared from the records in the 1st half of the 17th c.

Finally, the word *vizard* from the time of its appearance in the English language, i.e., from the 16th c. denoted both 'a mask; something worn to protect the face and the eyes' as well as 'the face'. The former meaning was especially common until the 18th c. Throughout the history it was used in Dekker (1600), Washington (1692), Steele (1711), Scott (1821), Thackeray (1851), etc. The latter sense appeared in Howell (1568), Breton (1603), Fletcher (1625), etc. However, the sense referring to 'the face' became obsolete at the end of the 17th c. According to the analysed dictionaries, the sense referring to 'parts of clothing' has survived into the Present-Day-English.

4. Transfer of meaning

The group of words which underwent the transfer of meaning consists of only 3 words, i.e., *hure, belly* and *poll*.

The first word *hure*, from OF *hure*, represents transfer of meaning from the field 'parts of clothing' to 'parts of the body'. It entered the English language in the 13th c. (*Beket*), denoting 'a covering for the head, a cap'. Both the *OED* and the *MED* record the word with such a sense until the late 15th c. However, the word re-surfaced in the early 19th c. with the meaning 'the head of a boar, wolf, or bear', which may suggest that after its disappearance from the written records, the lexeme may have been retained in the local dialects to re-appear four centuries later in the written sources.

The second word, *belly*, first occurred in *Lindisfarne Gospels*, denoting 'a bag, skin-bag, purse'. The sense appeared in the written records until the end of the 11th c. (see Wright-Wülcker). In the 13th c. *belly* was used with reference to 'the body', e.g., *Sinners Beware, Death*. However, in the next century this sense shifted to 'that part of the human body which lies between the breast and the thighs, and contains the bowels; the abdomen; the stomach'. It first appeared in Hampole (1340). Later it occurred also in Wyclif (1380), Chaucer (1395), *Promptorium Parvulorum* (1440), Shakespeare (1600), Bristed (1803), Marryat (1834), etc. In the 15th c. the sense started to be used also with reference to animals, e.g., *Cookery* (1440), Coverdale (1535), Milton (1667), Johns (1862), etc. It is interesting to note that although the original sense became obsolete in the 11th c., the word re-occurred in the field 'parts of clothing'. In 1599 (Jonson) *belly* was used to denote 'the part of a garment covering the belly'. However, this sense did not remain long in the language, its last record comes from 1601 (Cornwallyes).

Poll, from Du. *polle*, entered the English language in 1290 (*Saints' Lives*), meaning 'the human head'. It was used in *Early English alliterative poems* (14th c.), *Promptorium Parvulorum* (1440), Hudson (1584), Shakespeare (1597), de la Grey (1639), Hunt (1820). According to the *EDD*, in the 17th c. the use of the sense was limited to the local dialects of Scotland, the Shetland Islands, Northumberland, Cumberland, Durham, Yorkshire, Lancashire, Cheshire, Derbyshire, Suffolk, Hamptonshire, Dorset, Somerset and Devonshire. At the same time the word appeared with the sense 'the top or crown of a hat or cap' (*OED*). The meaning was recorded in Pitts (1704), Burton (1875), etc.

5. Words belonging to both fields at the same time

A number of words from the analysed corpus were in use side by side in both of the examined fields. One of the words is *sole*, from OF *sole*. It was recorded in English from the beginning of the 14th c., denoting 'the under surface of the foot; that part of it which normally rests or is placed upon the ground in standing or walking' and 'the bottom of a boot, shoe, etc.; that part of it upon which the wearer treads'. The former appeared in Wyclif (1382), Du Wes (1532), Spenser (1590), Topsell (1607), Dryden (1697), Tennyson (1842), etc. The latter was recorded by Palsgrave (1530), Tusser (1573), Shakespeare (1602), Lovell (1661), Beloe (1791), Beresford (1806), etc. Neither of the senses has become obsolete.

Several words belonging to one of the semantic fields analysed in the present paper had single or short-lived occurrences with senses from the other field. For instance, the word *ear*, whose main meaning is 'the organ of hearing in men and animals' (from 825) in 1830 (Sherwood) was also recorded with the sense 'the part of a cap coming over the ears'. Similarly, *gullet*, from OF *golet*, entered the

English language in 1380 (Wyclif), meaning 'the passage in the neck of an animal by which food and drink pass from the mouth to the stomach; the esophagus' and from the 17th c. 'the throat, neck' (Evelyn). In the 1st half of the 15th c. *gullet* was also recorded with the sense 'a piece of armour for the neck; the part of a hood which envelops the neck', e.g., *Morte d'Arthur* (1400), Lydgate (1426) and *Robin Hood and the Monk* (1450), which was the last appearance of the sense.

6. Conclusions

To conclude, the data collected for the present study shows that the extension of meaning from the field 'parts of clothing' to 'parts of the body' can be explained on functional grounds. The analysed words change their meanings, however, the function of the denoted items remains unchanged, e.g., *girdle* both when referring to the part of the body as well as to the part of garment presents 'supportive function'; *mantle* in both semantic fields denotes 'covering items', while *poke* meaning both 'a bag' and 'stomach' denotes 'carrying' containers. However, the extension of meaning in the other direction, i.e., from 'parts of the body' to 'parts of clothing' is based on the place on the human body, to which a particular item refers, i.e., words denoting particular body parts after adopting additional meanings refer also to the garment covering that particular part of the body.

Moreover, when it comes to the process of narrowing, only one of the analysed words, i.e., *vizard*, retained the sense referring to clothing. All the other words discarded one of the meanings and remained in the field of body parts. Words which underwent transfer of meaning, although not numerous, mostly shifted from the field of 'parts of clothing' to 'parts of the body'.

References

Lehrer, Adrienne
    1974   *Semantic fields and lexical structure. North Holland Linguistic Series* 11. Amsterdam: North-Holland Publishing Company.

Lyons, John
    1977   *Semantics*. Vols. 1-2. Cambridge: Cambridge University Press.

MED Online – Middle English dictionary. Available:
    http://ets.umdl.umich.edu/m/mec (date of access: April 2007).

Murray, James, Henry Bradley, William Craigie and Charles T. Onions (eds.)
    [1989]   *The Oxford English Dictionary*. (2nd edition.) Oxford: Clarendon Press.

OED Online – *Oxford English Dictionary*. Available:
    http://oed.com (date of access: February 2007)

Öhman, Suzanne
  1951   *Wortinhalt und Weltbild*. Stockholm: Kungl. Boktryckeriet P.A. Norstedt & Söner.
  1953   "Theories of the linguistic field". *Word* 9: 123-34.
Onions, Charles T., G.W.S. Friedrichsen and Robert Burchfield (eds.)
  1966   *Oxford Dictionary of English Etymology*. Oxford: The Clarendon Press.
Orton, Harold et.al. (eds.)
  1962-1971 *Survey of English dialects*. London and New York: Routledge.
Spence, Nicol Christopher William
  1961   "Linguistic fields, conceptual systems and the Weltbild". *Transactions of the Philological Society* 1961: 87-106.
Stern, Gustaf
  1931   *Meaning and change of meaning, with special reference to the English language*. Göteborg: Elanders Boktryckeri Aktiebolag.
Ullmann, Stephen
  1957   *The principles of semantics*. Oxford: Basil Blackwell & Mott Ltd.
Wright, Joseph (ed.)
  1898-1905 *The English dialect dictionary*. Oxford: Oxford University Press.

Appendix

The Appendix lists all the words collected for the present paper, together with the meanings[2] (relevant for this study).

arm (1) 'the upper limb'; (2) 'a sleeve';
bag (1) 'a purse, small sack'; (2) 'loose clothes'; (3) 'the udder, dug'; (4) 'fold of skin';
belly (1) 'a bag, skin-bag'; (2) 'the body'; (3) 'the abdomen';
breech (1) 'a garment covering loins and thighs'; (2) 'the buttocks';
breek = breech;
cap (1) 'a covering for the head'; (2) 'the head';
collar (1) 'the part of garment round the neck'; (2) 'necklace'; (3) 'strip round the neck (of birds, animals, etc.)';
crown (1) 'ornament for the head'; (2) 'the top of a hat'; (3) 'the head'; (4) 'the top of the skull';
dock (1) 'the fleshy part of animal's tail'; (2) '(of human beings) the buttocks';
ear (1) 'the organ of hearing'; (2) 'the part of a cap over the ears';
famble (1) 'a hand'; (2) 'a ring';

---

2   The meanings were taken from the *OED*, the *MED* and the *EDD*.

fillet (1) 'a head-band'; (2) 'a muscle';
finger (1) 'a part of a glove'; (2) 'one of the five terminal members of the hand';
flag (1) (slang) 'an apron'; (2) 'the tail of a setter or Newfoundland dog, also of a deer, horse, etc.';
flipper (1) 'a limb used to swim with'; (2) 'a rubber attachment to the foot';
fringe (1) 'an ornamental bordering, e.g., worn by the Hebrews'; (2) 'a portion of hair';
girdle (1) 'a belt worn round the waist'; (2) 'the part of the body round which the belt is worn';
gullet (1) 'esophagus, the throat, neck'; (2) 'a part of the hood';
heel (1) 'a part of a stocking'; (2) 'a part of the sole'; (3) 'the hinder part of the foot';
hip (1) 'the projecting part of the body on each side formed by the lateral expansions of the pelvis and upper part of the thigh-bone'; (2) 'a projecting part of a dress';
hure (1) 'a cap'; (2) 'the head of a boar, wolf or a bear';
knee (1) 'the part of the limb, the joint'; (2) 'the part of garment covering the knee';
lap (1) 'a part of a garment, a flap, lappet'; (2) 'the part of a robe, which serves as a pocket'; (3) 'a part of the ear, liver, the lobe';
lappet (1) 'a loose or overlapping part of a garment'; (2) 'a fold of skin, flesh, etc.';
leg (1) 'the limb'; (2) 'the part of garment covering the leg';
limb (1) 'any organ or part of the body'; (2) 'a part of the body distinct from the head or the trunk'; (3) 'the pieces of a suit of armour';
lug (1) 'one of the flaps or lappets of a cap or bonnet covering the ears'; (2) 'an ear, the lobe of an ear';
mantle (1) 'a loose sleeveless cloak'; (2) 'a kind of a tissue';
nab (1) 'the head'; (2) 'a hat';
nerve (1) 'a sinew or tendon'; (2) 'the penis'; (3) 'a piece of material used to ornament a garment';
pallet (1) 'a piece of armour for the head'; (2) 'the head';
poke (1) 'a bag, a small sack'; (2) 'a long wide sleeve'; (3) 'the stomach, e.g., of a fish';
poll (1) 'the human head'; (2) 'the top of a hat or a cap';
prat (1) 'the buttocks'; (2) (slang) 'a pocket';
shank (1) 'the part of a leg from the knee to the ankle'; (2) 'a kind of fur'; (3) 'a (part of) stocking';
shoulder (1) 'the part of the human body including the upper joint of the arm and a portion of the trunk'; (2) 'the part of a garment which covers the wearer's shoulder';
sole (1) 'the under surface of the foot'; (2) 'the bottom of a shoe';

thigh (1) 'the upper part of the leg'; (2) 'the part of a garment covering the thigh';
thumb (1) 'the short thick inner digit of the human hand'; (2) 'that part of a glove which covers the thumb';
tuft (1) 'a small cluster or plexus of capillary blood-vessels, e.g., of the kidney'; (2) 'a turban'; (3) 'an ornamental tassel on a cap';
visor (1) 'the front part of a helmet'; (2) 'a mask'; (3) 'the face';
vizard (1) 'a mask'; (2) 'the face'.

20 The Evolution of English Ordinals: Integrative Explanation in Historical Linguistics
Charles Elerick, The University of Texas at El Paso

1. Understanding Language Change as Grammar Change

An important goal of diachronic linguistics is to understand the nature of language change and to investigate how languages change. An understanding of how languages do, and do not, change extends our understanding of language itself. Accordingly, there is a close relationship between synchronic linguistics, involving the construction of formal representation of a language at a given time and diachronic linguistics, which, if ideally pursued, would involve the construction and scrutiny of a set of formal grammars that represent successive stages of a language. The promise of this approach to the diachronic study of language, initially suggested by Kiparsky (1965), extended by King (1968), and elaborated by Lightfoot (1995), has borne significant fruit. An important development in the meantime has been the emergence of language acquisition as integral to the discipline of linguistics, and this development has served to extend the ideal agenda of historical linguistics. We now know that to do historical linguistics means to look at $G_n > G_{n+1} > G_{n+2}$ ... such that G_{n+1} and subsequently G_{n+2} are understood to be the principled outcome of the language acquisition dynamic. This dynamic induces speakers with internalised G_{n+1} to acquire that grammar on the basis of available output produced by speakers with internalised G_n. Such an approach cannot in fact be totally implemented because of the unattainable idealisation that is implicit in this model. But such a model for understanding language change does guide the principled study of fragmentary aspects of successive grammars. In addition to the close attention to principles of language acquisition, diachronic linguistics has also increasingly integrated attention to factors of language variation and bilingualism. In the present study, I will investigate the instructive evolution of the English ordinals, including most importantly those that correspond to cardinal forms that end in /n/ (*seven/seventh*, etc.), as an exercise in integrative diachronic explanation.

2. The History of English Ordinals in Brief

In the continental precursor of OE, the Ingvaeonic variety of West Germanic, ordinal forms such as **sefenþa, *nigonþa* 'ninth', **tenþa* 'tenth' lost the nasal segment preceding the /þ/. These appear in OE as *sefeoþa, nigoþa, teoþa*. The ordinal forms corresponding to 13-19 also evidence the loss of the nasal before the ordinal formative. The Old English ordinal array also included forms that showed preserved PIE /t/ after a fricative i.e., *fifta, siexta, enleofta,* and *twelfta*.

The following passage from Ælfric's *De Temporibus Anni* with its explanation of the Zodiac (ca. 1000) provides an invaluable record of the ordinal forms of OE in the consistency of a unified document.

þære sunnan gear is þæt heo beyrne ðone micelan circul *Zodiacum*, & gecume under ælc þæra twelf tacna. Ælce monað heo yrnð under an ðæra tacna.

An ðæra tacna is gehaten *Aries*, þæt is Ramm.
Oðer, *Taurus*, þæt is fearr.
Ðridda, *Gemini*, þæt sind getwisan.
Feorða, *Cancer*, þæt is Crabba.
Fifta, *Leo*.
Sixta, *Uirgo*, þæt is mæden.
Seofoða, *Libra*, þæt is pund oþþe wæge.
Eahteoðe is *Scorpius*, þæt is ðrowend.
Nigoðe is *Sagittarius*, þæt is Scytta.
Teoðe is *Capricornus*, þæt is buccan horn oððe bucca.
Endlyfte is *Aquarius*, þæt is wætergyte oþþe se ðe wæter gyt.
Twelfte is *Pisces*, þæt sind fixas.

In the Middle English period the inherited forms that show the loss of the nasal persist and then forms that show the nasal reappear and are used in competition with the n-less forms. During this same period, -nd(e)# ordinals of North Gmc. origin gained currency and competed with the array of variable West Gmc. forms.

Ordinals that show a restored nasal ("seventh", "ninth", etc.) are used exclusively in ModE. The loss and subsequent reassertion of ordinals with nasals is not the outcome of dialectal shift. It is rather the result of a bookend process that first sees the nasal segments lost before fricatives, a universal phonological tendency, and the subsequent restoration of nasals as part of a larger reformulation of the cardinal-ordinal morphological configuration. The innovation of /þ/ forms *fifth, sixth, eleventh,* and *twelfth* that replace the inherited /t/ forms that are still present in ME, *fifte, sixte, ellefete,* and *twelfte,* reflects an extension of the process of paradigm regularisation.

3. The loss of nasals before fricatives as a recurring phonological process

The loss of nasal segments that precede a fricative is a common synchronic rule. This is attested in contemporaneous competing forms and of course can also lead to diachronic outcomes that involve the lexicalisation of reflex forms that show the loss of the nasal segment.

The data from Latin and Romance displayed below reflects the operation of a general nasal deletion rule of the form **[C, +nas]** → Ø / ___ **[-son, +cont]**

The Evolution of English Ordinals 271

Classical Latin   **Popular Inscriptional Form**

cōnfēcī 'I made'   cōfēcī 'I made'
tōnsor 'barber'   tōsor 'barber'
īnferī 'nether dwellers'   īferī 'inhabitants of the nether world'

Diachronic loss of nasals before fricatives in Romance.
Lat. mēnse 'month'   >   Sp. mes   'month'
Lat. mēnsa 'table'   >   Sp. mesa 'table'
Lat. spōnsa 'promised one' > Sp. esposa 'wife'
Lat. mōnstru- 'monster' > Ital. mostro 'monster'

4. Nasals before Fricatives in Germanic

In Ingvaeonic varieties of West Germanic, i.e., OE, Old Saxon, and Old Frisian, nasals were lost before fricatives in the prehistoric period. (Robinson, p. 250) Comparative Gothic-English and NHG-English data illustrates the effect of the loss of nasals in English which were preserved in Gothic and which persist in NHG.

Gothic	English
tunþus	tooth
munþs	mouth
fimfta	fifth
unsis	us

NHG	English
Gans	goose
fünf	five
Mund	mouth
anderer	other

The loss of nasals before fricatives in OE and other Ingvaeonic varieties must be understood as an instance of grammatical change that can be assumed to have proceeded in approximately the following manner.

A) One or more speakers whose output is specified by G_1 innovate a post-acquisition performance modality involves the relaxation of the oral closure attending the articulation of consonantal nasal segments preceding fricatives. It is not clear where the boundary between sub-linguistic performance modalities and phonological rules lies but it is clear that the output of speakers who (sometimes) display lenition of nasal consonants supports the acquisition of grammars by new speakers that include a rule of the form

(opt) [C, +nas] → Ø / ___ [C, +cont].

This simple rule supports variable output over the underlying /gō:ns+/ which is heard sometimes as [gō:ns] and sometimes as [gō:s].

B) Children hearing such output might internalise a grammar that continues the optional status of nasal deletion, operating over underlying forms that include /n/.

C) At some point one or more children internalise a grammar that specifies /gō:ns+/ and the nasal deletion rule as non-optional and which results in the outputs [gō:s], etc. The obligatory deletion of nasals before fricatives spreads to more new speakers. Instances of /n/ in lexical forms that have no surface manifestation will persist as long as there are supporting alternations in the (pre-historic) OE lexicon.

D) At some point new speakers of pre-historic OE and its closely related varieties begin to internalise grammars that specify lexical forms / gō:s+/, etc. with no nasal, and which do not include the corresponding nasal deletion rule. It is not clear how late this occurred but it could not have been later than the appearance of the form *munþ* 'month', as the result of the syncope, cf. OE *monaþ* (attested in Aelfric, above) and NHG *Monat*. Significantly, this reappearance of nasal + fricative serves in effect as a phonotactic license for the later development of ordinal morphology, which is central to this paper.

5. Middle English Ordinal Forms-Innovation and Competition

In Middle English ordinal forms corresponding to cardinals with bases ending in /n/ which also showed /n/ before the ordinal formative /þ/ reappeared. The emergence of ordinals showing /n/ and their competition with forms that continue the OE pattern with loss of /n/ is well documented in the OED. The oldest attested forms with restored /n/, listed to the right in the chart below, appear in the very late 12th century and the last attestations of forms without /n/ date from the 16th century. These latter are rare and may represent the conscious use of an archaic form. Note also that the earliest attestation of the nasal-restored **þrittenþe** is nearly a century later than the last attestation of the form without /n/, a clear anomoly. Also, The OED offers a very late earliest attestation for the /n/ r estored form **fourteenth**, also clearly anomolous. Looking at the big picture, the 14th century saw ordinal forms with restored /n/ established and corresponding ordinal forms without /n/ pass out of currency. This data is consistent with the findings of Kroch (1994) that in the Middle English period doublets coexisted for about 300 years and that some of that extension appeared to reflect artificially of usage.

1st attestation of restored /n/ forms		Last attestation of forms without /n/	
1290	seuenþe	1550	sevethe.
1300	nynþe	1325	niþe
1150	tenðen	1337	teþe
1325	enleuenþe	1380	elleuefþe
1380	þrittenþe	1297	þritteþe
1579	fourteenth	1300	fourteothe
1382	fiftenthe	1440	fyftethe
1220	sixtenðe	1387	sixteþe
1300	seuentenþe	1400	seuenteþe
1258	eʒtetenþe	1305	eiʒteteoþe
1382	nyntenþe	1450	nyentethe

In addition to the ME ordinals of West Germanic origin seen above, other competing ordinal forms of N. Gmc. provenance showing –nd(e)# were widely attested in the same period. Representative instances include *zeuende* (1340) (note Southern [z], indicating the geographic spread of -nd forms.); *seuend* (1400); *nigenda* (c1275) *neʒende* (1333) *neghend* (1425) *nynde* (1440) *tende* (c1200) *teynd* (1460) *Þrittennde* (c1200) *threttend* (1447) fiftende (c1200). Closely related ordinal forms showing word-final obstruent devoicing are also attested in the latter ME period and even later in orthographic context that supports the reading of "t" as a stop. Examples include *Þe seyuent day* (1375); *Þe elleuynt* 1400); *The levint*, (1552) The *ellewint* (1588). A study by Taylor (1994) shows that competing forms were at their greatest extent in exactly this period and one of the reasons in this lexical domain was the incorporation of northern forms into written English.

6. The ME innovation of /þ/ and /nþ/ ordinals as grammar change

As in the case of the disappearance of nasals before fricatives in OE, the emergence of ordinals with /n/ must be explained as the result of grammar change. Concretely, **seuenþe** did not replace **sevenþe** but rather the grammar that specified **seuenþe** as output was replaced by a grammar that specified **sevenþe** and similarly **fifte** and its reflex **fifth**, etc. So again, the diachronic process by which ordinals with innovative nasals and ordinals with innovative /þ/ appeared in the Middle English period must be understood as being the result of the language acquisition process. An explanation of this diachronic outcome must be based on a principled and credible acquisitional scenario that represents the process by which learners of English innovated the replacement forms. But unlike the simple diachronic phonological process by which learners in the pre-historic period of OE innovated internalised grammars that lexicalised the effect of a natural phonological rule that resulted in the loss of nasals before fricatives, the reemergence of /n/ forms involves a morphological and paradigmatic phenomenon. Also, and as an additional complicating factor, the cognitive and linguistic development of notions of number and the terms that express them represents a special case within the general framework of language acquisition, as will be discussed below.

An additional dimension of language change that is relevant to the ordinal issue must be understood before proceeding. An innovation in grammar, $G_n > G_{n+1}$ the essential motor of language change, involves one of two developments. An acquisitional scenario can involve an output of G_n that is the same as that of G_{n+1} with the same output proceeding from grammars that are not identical. The acquisitional account of the pre-historic loss of nasals before fricatives assumes such a development. A second type of change involves a *saltus*, the appearance of previously un-modeled innovative output, necessarily proceeding from a G_{n+1} that is different from G_n. The innovation of /nþ/ ordinals in ME is an instance of such a diachronic development in which a new speaker spontaneously and without benefit of input produces the form in question. Lightfoot (77ff.) has discussed this type of development, differentiating between gradual and "catastrophic" grammar change, the latter exemplified by the innovation of –**nþ** ordinals in Middle English discussed here.

7. The special status of number terms in language

Number terms are special is two ways. There are special cognitive/linguistic dimensions that attend their acquisition. Also, they are arrayed in a lexical matrix that promotes various phonological morphological effects, abetted especially by serial performance, i.e., counting. The cognitive and linguistic development of *numerosity* and number terms, especially cardinals, has been widely studied. Numerocity, a term used widely but only recently by developmental psychologists, refers to the complex cognitive-linguistic development by which the cognitive foundation and number terms are acquired in a strictly ordered two-part sequence, a development that is fairly well understood. In their 1997 study, Bloom and Wynn argue convincingly (p.513f) that the cognitive and linguistic developments that eventually merge and support the use of number concepts and terms are distinct, parallel, even initially unrelated. These distinct developments are as follows.

1) The acquisition of "numerosity" as a cognitive category.
performance, i.e., counting. The cognitive and linguistic development of *numerosity* and number terms, especially cardinals, has been widely studied. Numerocity, a term used widely but only recently by developmental psychologists, refers to the complex cognitive-linguistic development by which the cognitive foundation and number terms are acquired in a strictly ordered two-part sequence, a development that is fairly well understood. In their 1997 study, Bloom and Wynn argue convincingly (p.513f) that the cognitive and linguistic developments that eventually merge and support the use of number concepts and terms are distinct, parallel, even initially unrelated. These distinct developments are as follows.

2) Counting, i.e., one, two, three, four... knowing that *four* follows *three* and represents some numerosity but not which one. Following Gelman and Gallistel (1978) Bloom and Wynn assume that counting reflects a child's access to innate knowledge of enabling principles.

3) The match up between numerosity, specific numerosities, and the names for those specific numerosities results as an acquisitional response to the complex of syntactic and semantic clues that the language presents. We should especially note the reference to a "complex" of clues and for this study add "morphological" to "syntactic" and "semantic."

So the first essential fact regarding the acquisition of number terms is that it is internally and systemically referenced as opposed to externally referenced, i.e., the referents of number terms, unlike most lexical entities, are not primarily "objects" in the material universe but rather exist as constructs relative to other cognitive-linguistic entities that together define the system. Understanding the complex development that the acquisition of cardinal number terms represents is doubtless the point of departure for studying ordinals.

Another indication that insights into the nature and acquisition of cardinals are important for understanding ordinals is the concept of "subitising." Bloom and Wynn (p.530) point out that humans can apprehend quantity in small sets, those with up to three members, without counting. This is reflected in the fact that children learn the meaning of these numerosities and the corresponding terms first and early. Consistent with this is the occurrence in English and other languages of ordinal forms such as *first*, *second*, *third*, which are more morphologically distanced from the corresponding cardinals. Accordingly, for this reason the history of the ordinals corresponding to *one*, *two*, and *three* is not integrated into this study.

The acquisition of ordinals has been much less carefully studied than has been the acquisition of cardinals. This is probably because the acquisition of ordinals takes place later and is seemingly less interesting as a reflection of essential cognitive-linguistic development. In fact, the cognitive development that is reflected by the acquisition of ordinals involves the concept of the ordered set, an increment of cognitive prowess over the simpler notion of set, which is itself recognised to be a demanding cognitive accomplishment.

The second special characteristic attending number terms mentioned above is their relationship to each other in a lexical matrix. Between the cardinal array and the parallel series of ordinals there obtains a set of double relationships. Specifically, *seven*, to take a random example, is simultaneously the next in a series after *sixth*, preceding *eighth,* and the cognitively and also the morphologically marked member of the pair *seven/seventh*. In other words, the form *seventh* resides in two lexical "gravitational fields", so to speak, or more graphically:

four	→	fourth
		↓(↑)
five	→	fifth
		↓(↑)
six	→	sixth
		↓(↑)
seven	→	seventh
		↓(↑)
eight	→	eighth
		↓(↑)
nine	→	ninth, etc.

The effect of this matrix of paradigmatic influence can be seen in variously in Germanic, to stay within that language family. Prokosch (p. 286ff.) notes these examples. Initial /f/ in *four*, etc. reflects regressive influence from the /f/ of the Proto-Germanic etymon of *five* . OHG *sibunto* (for *sibundo*) 'seventh' reflects progressive influence from *sehsto* 'sixth'. NHG *zweite*, replacing MHG *anderer*, shows cardinal > ordinal influence.

Such diachronic outcomes confirm that the operation of such a matrix of influence is of palpable significance in the acquisitional process. In the same way that children serialise *one, two, three*... as a first step in the acquisition of cardinals, serialisation and its effect is a significant dimension in the organisation of the ordinal array.

8. 1st language acquisition and the innovation of ordinal forms in the ME period

During the ME period an ordinal series starting with *fourth* which is characterised by transparent and non-allomorphic relationships to the corresponding cardinal (except for *five/fifth*) and by the consistent morpheme /þ/ was innovated. This diachronic outcome can be, in fact must be, understood as the result of the dynamic of 1st language acquisition and therefore as quite principled.

A general understanding of the acquisition of derived forms within an unmarked > marked lexical paradigm is provided by Clark (p.109ff) and her findings will be shown to support aspects of the acquisitional scenario by which the /nþ/ ordinals were established in the ME period. Working specifically with nouns, she establishes (p. 145) that as children acquire items based on forms that they already know, base plus derivational affix, for example, this proceeds on the basis of just a few principles, which are obviously inter-twined.

- Transparency: New items are more easily acquired when the constituent elements and their meaning are known.
- Regularisation: There is a tendency to reject multiple forms, i.e., allomorphy.

The Evolution of English Ordinals

- Simplicity: The formal and semantic match-up involves the least complication is the most highly valued.
- Frequency: When choosing between transparent options, children choose the transparent option that is most frequent.

New learners of English in the late 11th century heard ordinal forms in the "fourth" and higher sequence that presented three complications.

- Some of the forms had a morpheme for [Ordinal] with /t/ and others had a morpheme with /þ/.
- Some ordinals were extensions of bases that were identical to the corresponding cardinal base while others showed alternating bases, several involving the alternating presence or absence on /n/.
- Children in most if not all of England heard competing ordinal forms (of Northern origin) showing /d/, or /nd/ in the case of ordinals that corresponded to cardinal bases ending in /n/.

In this way at the beginning of the ME period, children heard, approximately [sVvVn]; [sVvVþə] ~ [sVvVndə] and other similar sets of alternations. Returning to Clark's framework, her principles of Regularisation and Simplicity, predict that this represented an unstable situation. Employing Clark's insights and assuming the effect of the matrix of paradigmatic influence, which, as seen above, shapes number term forms, we can understand the evolution of ME ordinals as the outcome of the complex dynamic of language acquisition. One important note is in order. Morphemic innovation of the extent that is in fact attested by the diachronic outcomes is unusual. Normally, children experiment with regularising innovation (*go/goed*) but end up acquiring the modeled forms (*go/went*). The case of ME innovation of ordinal forms represents a significant departure from the expected suppression of innovative morphology. The combination of the lesser frequency of ordinals, the three-way competition of ordinal forms, and the cited number-term matrix factor serve to support the acquisition of the regularising forms.

I hypothesise as an early development in ME the innovation of the attested /nþ/ forms, which are the output of an innovative grammar that has a morpheme specification rule of the form

cardinal + [ORD] → /x.....y+þə/

The attestation of ME shows fairly clearly that the inclusion of the ordinal forms corresponding to *five* and *six* were not immediately included and so one would hypothesise a grammar that specified these forms separately.

With the innovation of /sVvVnþə/ the next "generation" of learners would hear [sVvVn]; [sVvVþə] ~ [sVvVndə] ~ [sVvVnþə]. Clark's principles of Regularisation and Simplicity predict that this situation would represent an acquisitional challenge and that the value placed on simplicity of parsing and production would favor the acquisition of grammars that included a rule that supported [sVvVnþə] even if other rules that supported one or more alternate ordinal forms were also internalised, as attested forms indicate. The fact that alternate forms persisted in the speech community suggests that in the internalised grammars of individuals a range of alternate rules and/or lexical captures persisted for many generations.

During this period, the principles of Transparency and Simplicity favoured the spread of the rule specifying ordinals of the **-nþ** type and the frequency of their occurrence, both at the output of grammars that specifies this as the only possibility and as the more frequently used forms by speakers whose grammars supported alternative forms. At this point, Clark's principle of Frequency ("When choosing between transparent options, children choose the transparent option that is most frequent.") becomes a dominant factor effecting the standardisation of /nþ/ forms. These are both the transparent and most frequent forms and therefore the single option for new speakers acquiring the rules that underlie these forms.

At about the same time and as part of the larger process, learners of English started to internalise grammars that specified the /þ/ formative for ordinals corresponding to *five* and *six* as well as *eleven* and *twelve*. This again is the result of the operation of both the principles of Simplicity and Transparency advanced by Clark and the effect of the matrix of paradigmatic influence that abets those principles. The outcome is a stable system that has endured for half a millennium. The stability of the simple and transparent ordinal paradigm of English is as much an illustration of linguistic principle as is its reorganisation in the period of Middle English.

References

Bloom, P.- K. Wynn
    1997   *Linguistic cues in the acquisition of number words. Journal of Child Language* 24: 511-533.

Clark, Eva
    1994   *The Lexicon in Acquisition.* Cambridge, UK: Cambridge University Press.

Gelman, R. & Gallistel, C. R.
    1978   *The Child's Understanding of Number.* Cambridge, MA: Harvard Univ. Press.

King, Robert D.
    1968   *Generative Grammar and Historical Linguistics.* Englewood Cliffs, NJ: Prentice Hall.

Kiparsky, Paul
 1965 *Phonological Change*. MIT Dissertation.
Kroch, Anthony
 1994 *Morphosyntactic Variation*. In K. Beals et al. (eds) *Papers from the 10th Regional Meeting of the Chicago Linguistic Society I*. 199-144. Chicago: University of Chicago.
Lightfoot, David
 1999 *The Development of Language: Acquisition, Change, and Evolution*. Oxford: Blackwell.
Prokosch, E.
 1939 *A Comparative Germanic Grammar*. Philadelphia, PA: Philadelphia, Linguistic Society of America, University of Pennsylvania.
Robinson, Orrin W.
 1992 *Old English and its Closest Relatives*. Stanford, CA: Stanford Univ. Press.
Taylor, Ann
 1994 *Variation in past tense formation in the history of English*. Stanford, CA: In R. Ivorski et al. (edd), *University of Pennsylvania Working Papers in Linguistics*. University of Pennsylvania.

21 Aspect and Modality: the Blurring of Categories[1]
Sylvie Hancil, University of Rouen

It has long been established that the progressive from (PF) can be associated with subjective meanings, underlining the speaker's attitude towards a situation. Since Wright's (1994, 1995) work, it has been possible to rely on a useful set of linguistic parameters to identify the behaviour of the subjective, in particular modal, PF. The purpose of this study is to offer a diachronic analysis of the modal values of the periphrasis in a nearly half-a-million-word corpus of private letters,[2] a genre that is very close to spoken discourse, from the 15th to the 20th century. We shall try to quantify the empirical evidence that takes into account the various types of linguistic parameters collocating with the subjective PF, which will lead us to focus on the study of some specific examples.

1. Evolution of the number of PF with temporojuncts and subjuncts

Fig. 1: PF with temporojuncts and subjuncts

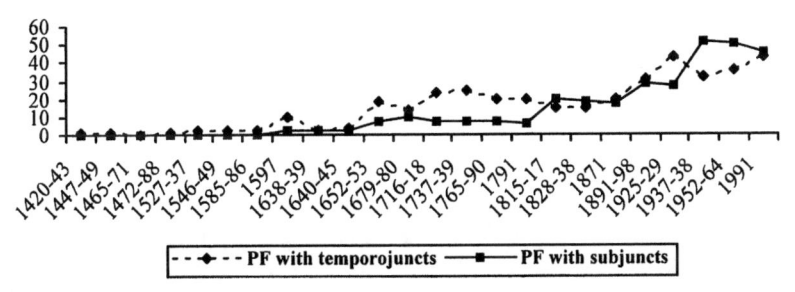

Fig. 1 shows the evolution of the number of PF collocating with temporojuncts (temporal adjuncts and conjuncts) and subjective markers (hence subjuncts[3]). In the 16th-century private letters, the occurrences of PF are very rare (1 or 0 per period) but whenever they occur, they are supported by temporojuncts. The number of these markers rapidly increases till the early 18th century and decreases for a century, which corresponds to the point in time when the periphrasis acquires its aspectual function. Even though the raw number of PF with temporojuncts increases again afterwards, the corresponding percentage goes down to 23.7% in 1937 and does not exceed 40% in 1991. The percentages have been constantly under 50% since the late 1890s. This suggests that the PF has become less and

---
1 I would like to thank Agnès Celle, Steven Schaefer and Nicholas Smith for their helpful comments and suggestions on an earlier draft of this paper.
2 The list of the letters used for the study is given in the references.
3 See section 2.4 for a detailed description of subjuncts.

less dependent on the explicit marking of temporal linking structure since it carries the temporal parameter within itself. The conversational implicature of a temporal parameter associated with the PF has therefore become conventionalised over time. No PF collocates with a subjunct in the data until the late 16th century in the *Letters of John Chamberlain* (3 occurrences). The first collocation of subjuncts with the PF in the private letters that we examined occurs one century before the date of the first instance recorded in Wright's (1995) study, based on prose comedies. One possible reason for this is that private letters are stylistically closer to colloquial discourse than prose comedies in this period. The number of subjuncts regularly goes up in the 17th century, reaches a plateau in the 18th century and then increases dramatically from the early 19th century onwards. The beginning of this dramatic increase coincides with the time when the PF acquires its maturity rate.[4] It is worth noting that it is in the early 19th century that the rate of subjective PF outnumbers that of aspectual PF for the first time. This crucial period is followed by a period of instability for almost a century, in which temporal PF become more numerous again than subjective PF. The tendency is emphatically reversed from 1937 onwards, even though the temporal support of the PF seems to increase and reach the same proportional rate as that of explicit markers of subjectivity. The increase of the use of subjuncts with the PF at the expense of the use of temporojuncts with the PF corresponds to an increasing dependence of the construction on the linguistic marking of the speaker's attitude. By increasingly marking the speaker's interpretation in the linguistic context surrounding the PF, the latter is more and more associated with a subjective meaning. Indeed, the subjective interpretation of the PF is pragmatically inferred from the linguistic environment signposting the speaker's attitude. Since 1937, the number of PF collocating with subjuncts has decreased significantly, a trend that shows a growing independence with respect to the linguistic marking of subjectivity since the PF starts conveying the notion of subjectivity in itself more and more: the conversational implicature of subjectivity thus becomes increasingly conventionalised.

2. Grammatical context of the subjective PF

We shall now turn to the study of the linguistic parameters collocating with the subjective PF, relying on a classification developed in Strang's (1982) and Wright's (1994) which includes verb type, clause and tense type, subject type and subjuncts.

---

4   The maturity rate corresponds to the rate reflecting the fact the PF becomes obligatory in all the aspectual contexts.

2.1. Verb type

The classification of verb types associated with subjective PF is based on Bouscaren and Deschamps's (1991) study, which takes into consideration the cognitive representation of a given verb in an utterance, and associates it with a specific topological structure. Three categories are distinguished. The first category includes Activity and Accomplishment verbs; they are topologically represented with a heterogeneous interior, showing the distinct occurrences of the activity, and two separate boundaries, the first being closed to represent the beginning of the activity, and the second boundary indicating a potential boundary which is in brackets: [...( ]). If the verb is an Activity, the second boundary is not taken into account; if the verb is an Accomplishment, the second boundary is present. The second category comprises Achievement and Punctual verbs, i.e. instantaneous events, so they are topologically represented with two merged boundaries: I. The third category regroups Stative verbs, which are topologically represented by two open boundaries and a homogeneous interior:]_[since there is no distinctive stage in Stative verbs, contrary to process-type verbs. It is well known that the first category favours the use of the PF in the majority of cases. Let us see if it is still the case for subjective PF.

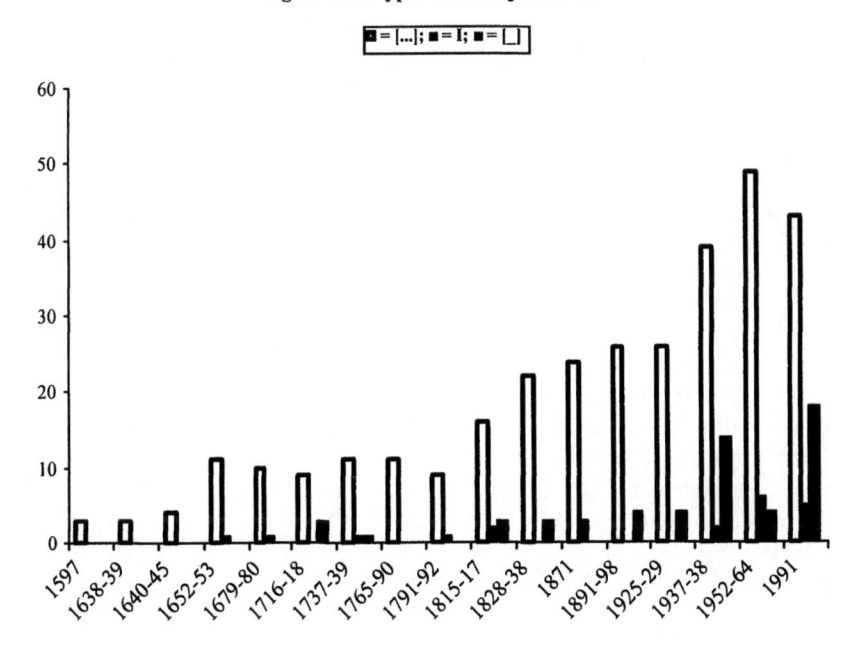

Fig. 2: Verb types with subjective PF

The subjective PF cooccur primarily with Activity and Accomplishment verbs, namely the first topological category (see Fig. 2). The first occurrence of a verb with merged boundaries is recorded in *The Letters of Dorothy Osborne* in 1652-53:

(1)　Your fellow Servant kisses your hands and say's if you mean to make love to her olde woman this is the best time you can take, for shee **is dyeing**. (*Letters of Dorothy Osborne*, 26 Feb 1653, p.22)

The first occurrence of stative verbs is identified in the *Letters of Lady Montague* in 1717, namely almost one century before the examples offered by Denison (1998: 146):

(2)　By his saying, – He went down to admire the beauty of the vines, and her charms ravished his soul –, I understand a poetical fiction, of having first seen her in a garden, where he **was admiring**[5] the beauty of the spring. (*Letters of the Right Honourable Lady Mary Wortley Montague*, letter XXX, April 1717)

The examination of the data also shows a decrease in the dependence on the temporal marking of the verb after 1937. The number of verbs topologically represented with two separate boundaries and a heterogeneous interior decreseases significantly from 83.1% to 68.6% between 1937 and 1991. Even though the number of mental Activity and Stative verbs was almost non-existent in the 18th century, it subsequently increases significantly but it stabilises at around 30% after 1952 (31.8% in 1952 and 33.3% in 1991). Consequently, the results do not support the hypothesis (see Wright 1994) that mental states are the preferred candidates for indicating subjectivity with the PF but rather confirm Killie's (2004) findings for prose fiction in the early modern English. Fitzmaurice (2004) has recently discussed a few occurrences of activity verbs with the subjective PF, although her study does not attempt a quantitative analysis of this usage in her corpus.

2.2. Clause and tense type

Table 1 shows the evolution of clause and tense types associated with subjective PF. Out of the 17 periods under examination, almost 65% show a preference for the use of the subjective PF in present-tense main clauses, this choice being categorically preferred from 1871 onwards. The diversification of tenses and clauses becomes effective from the early 19th century, when the perfect and the past start to compete for second place. The past has lagged behind the present in both clause types since the mid-twentieth century. The hypothesis that the present-tense main clause is the ideal place for the occurrence of the subjective PF (Wright 1994) is largely confirmed by the data.

5　The occurrence of the PF with a mental stative verb is fully analysed in section 3.2.2.

Table 1: Clause and tense type of the subjective PF

Period Clause & tense type	1597	1638-39	1640-45	1652-53	1679-80	1716-18	1737-39	1765-90	1791-92	1815-17	1828-38	1871	1891-98	1925-29	1937-38	1952-64	1991
MC PR	2	2	3	2	0	4	2	3	2	5	4	10	11	21	27	28	25
MC PA	0	0	0	0	0	0	2	1	3	2	0	2	3	2	5	5	5
MC PFPr	0	0	0	1	0	0	1	0	0	6	6	4	4	5	3	2	4
MC PFPA	0	0	0	0	0	0	0	1	0	0	0	1	1	0	0	0	0
SC PR	0	1	1	3	3	1	5	3	2	3	6	3	9	13	11	15	10
SC PA	0	0	0	2	1	2	0	1	1	0	3	4	2	1	3	7	6
SC PFPr	0	0	0	1	2	0	1	1	0	1	1	2	0	4	4	1	1
SC PFPA	0	0	0	1	0	0	0	0	1	2	2	0	0	0	0	0	1

2.3. Subject type

Fig. 3 : Subject type of the subjective PF

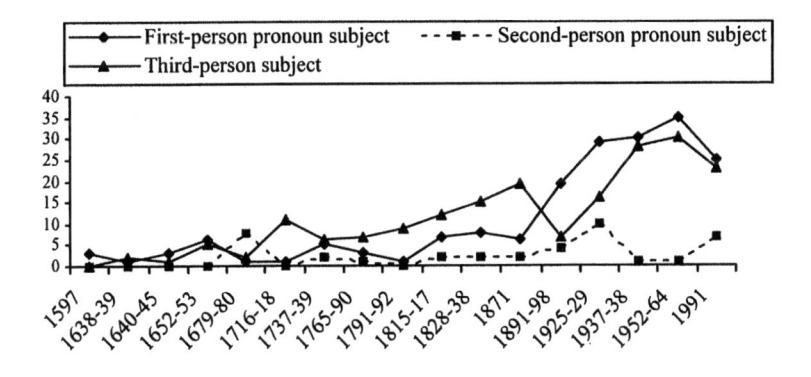

Fig. 3 illustrates the distribution of the subject type collocating with the subjective PF. Since it first occurred in the late 16th century, the subjective PF has co-occurred with different kinds of subject, depending on the period considered. From 1597 till 1652, the dominant subject is the singular first-person pronoun, followed by the third-person subject, with an exception in the data from 1638, in which the second-person pronoun leads by a small margin. In 1679, the second-person pronoun is clearly the dominant pronoun. From 1716 till the early 19th century, the third-person subject, especially the singular third-person pronoun, is the most frequent with the subjective PF, the first-person pronoun subject coming second. The tendency is reversed from the late 19th century onwards: the singular first-person pronoun is the leading subject, even though third-person subjects, i.e. singular NPs, are numerically ranked second and have been more and more employed since 1937. It follows from this that Wright's (1994) hypothesis that subjective PFs preferrably occur with first- and second- person pronoun subjects is not borne out by the data. In a later paper, she (as Fitzmaurice 2004) mentions that third-person subjects also occur with subjective PF (although the extent to which this occurs is not estimated).

2.4. Subjuncts

To fully understand the nature of subjective PF and its evolution, it is important to distinguish several categories of subjuncts:[6] epistemic markers, deontic markers, and markers of Affect.

2.4.1. Epistemic markers

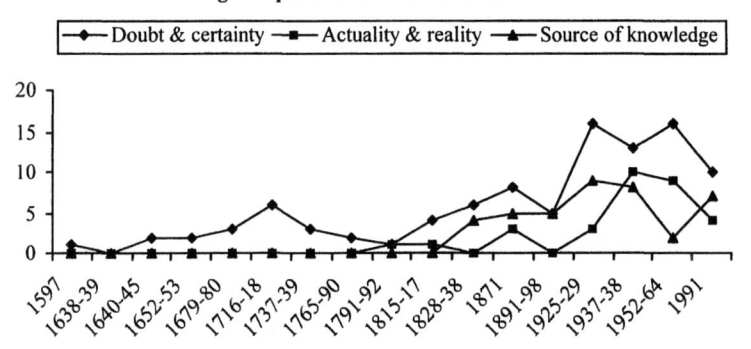

Fig. 4: Epistemic markers with the PF

Fig. 4 takes into account the distribution of the various types of epistemic markers collocating with PF, namely doubt and certainty, actuality and reality, and source of knowledge.[7] They are rare till the early 19th century, then their number varies between 10 and 16 till the late 19th century, before surging to 31 in 1937 and slowly decreasing to 21 in 1991. The markers of doubt and certainty lead the epistemic category and are the first to co-occur with the PF. Markers of actuality and reality start being used from 1791, and markers of source of knowledge from 1828. Here are some examples:

- doubt and certainty:
(3) I went with him and Miss Mitford to Chiswick, and thought all the way that I must **certainly** be dreaming.(Elizabeth Barrett Browning, To Mrs Martin, Dec 7 1836)

---

6 The category of subjuncts elaborated by Wright (1994) mainly focussed on epistemic markers of doubt and certainty, deontic markers and markers of amount.
7 The subcategories of epistemic markers are based on Biber et al.'s (2002) classification of stance markers.

- actuality and reality:
(4) **In fact** this is only to say I'm longing to see you (*The Letters of Virginia Woolf, 1936-1941*, p.182)
- source of knowledge:
(5) and I think it very likely that, after I had gone, **she would tell you the story**, as if on good authority, that I am constantly hearing, of the (alleged) immoral life of Miss E. T. and Mr. Irving.(*The Selected Letters of Lewis Caroll, To his cousin Dorothea Wilcox*, p. 238-9)

2.4.2. Deontic markers

Fig. 5: Deontic markers with the PF

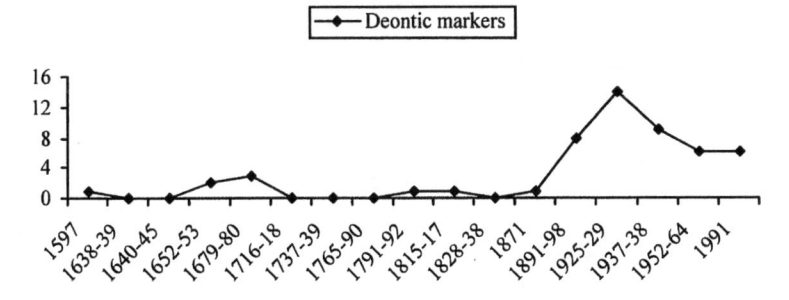

Deontic markers with PF (see Fig. 5) are extremely rare till the late 19th century, reaching a peak in 1925 (14 occurrences) and varying between 6 and 9 instances, as exemplified in (6), which includes an imperative, and in (7), which comprises the deontic use of a semi-modal:

(6) In the mean time pray **bee finishing** that little which rests still to be done there (*Letters of Pepys*, 1679-80, p.129)

(7) **I am having to** re-number the later chapters, and will let you have the list as soon as I have compiled it. (*Selected letters of Edith Sitwell, To Elizabeth Salter*, 1952-54, p. 403)

2.4.3. Markers of Affect

The category of the markers of Affect includes markers of appreciation, indicators of moral assessment, markers of punctuation and markers of amount.

Fig. 6 shows that, compared to epistemic and deontic markers, markers of Affect are, by far, the most frequently-occurring type with the PF (cf. Figs. 4 and 5). In contrast to the other two categories which start being more used in the early 20th century, the category of markers of Affect reaches a first peak in 1815 (27 occurrences), which coincides with the time when the PF acquires a maturity rate ; the second peak is achieved in the early 20th century (63 occurrences), before slowly decreasing. Up to the late 18th century, it is not possible to identify a leading category among the markers of Affect, because of the low number of occurrences.

288 Sylvie Hancil

Fig. 6: Markers of Affect with the PF

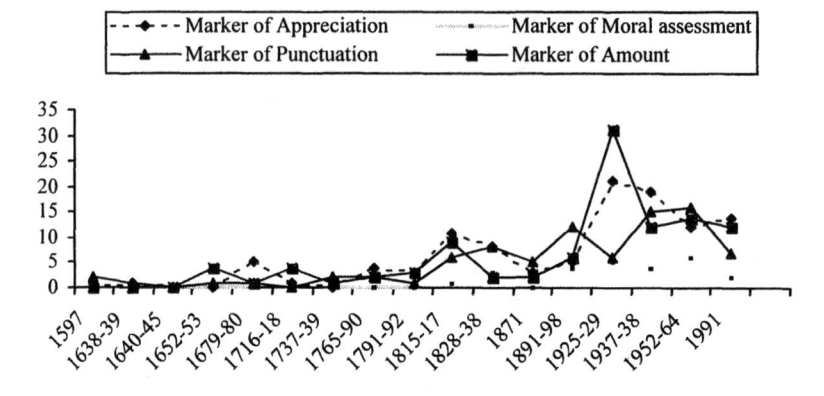

- - ♦ - - Marker of Appreciation   ⋯⋯■⋯⋯ Marker of Moral assessment
———▲——— Marker of Punctuation   ———■——— Marker of Amount

[chart with x-axis labels: 1597, 1638-39, 1640-45, 1652-53, 1679-80, 1716-18, 1737-39, 1765-90, 1791-92, 1815-17, 1828-38, 1871, 1891-98, 1925-29, 1937-38, 1952-64, 1991; y-axis 0 to 35]

Out of the eight periods distinguished from the early 19th century, markers of appreciation are the most popular in 50% of the cases, markers of punctuation coming second in 37.5% of the cases, markers of amount lagging behind (12.5% of the cases), as illustrated below:

- appreciation:

(8) for I was so very wise as to lie down upon the grass last Monday, when the sun was shining **deceitfully**, though the snow was staring at me from the hedges, with an expression anything but dog-daysical!(Elizabeth Barrett Browning, To Mrs. Boyd, 1828)

(9) In order to try and get a resident's permit for the car you are so **generously** letting me have temporary use of, I need a mass of bumf for the Regional Council in due course (BNC, HD4, sn 223)

- moral assessment:

(10) **Odd** that you should be going to the Roman Wall: thats an old dream of ours (*The Letters of Virginia Woolf, 1936-1941*, p.164)

(11) I expect this sort of thing is **fearfully bad for the character**; I'm feeling wooden yet enraged (*The Letters of Virginia Woolf, 1936-1941*, p.154)

- punctuation: colon (example (12)) ; dash (example (13)) ; exclamation mark (example (14)):

(12) One of Julians essays came this morning. War and Peace — the letter to Morgan—I thought there were 2 others: perhaps they weren't being typed (*The Letters of Virginia Woolf, 1936-1941*, p. 166)

(13) I cannot give you all the intimate details of our private affairs that I would — we are even now cleaning off the mud for tea at Tilton (*The Letters of Virginia Woolf, 1936-1941*, p. 178)

(14) I am very cross with the police for shooting poor Mr. Noble, whom I had been *hoping* to contact ! (*Selected letters of Edith Sitwell, To Sacheverell Sitwell*, p. 373)

- amount:
(15) I suppose she thought I was **just** leaving this neighbourhood (Amberley papers, p. 508)
(16) We have been wanting **very much** to hear of your Mother, & are happy to find she continues to mend (Jane Austen, mil. 457)
(17) I had an audience next day of the empress mother, a princess of great virtue and goodness, but who picques herself too much on a violent devotion. She is **perpetually** performing extraordinary acts of penance, without having ever done any thing to deserve them. (Lady Montagu, 1716-18, Letter IX, Sep 14)

Among the markers of amount, strengtheners are the most often employed, minimisers lagging behind and approximators being almost non-existent (see Fig. 7).

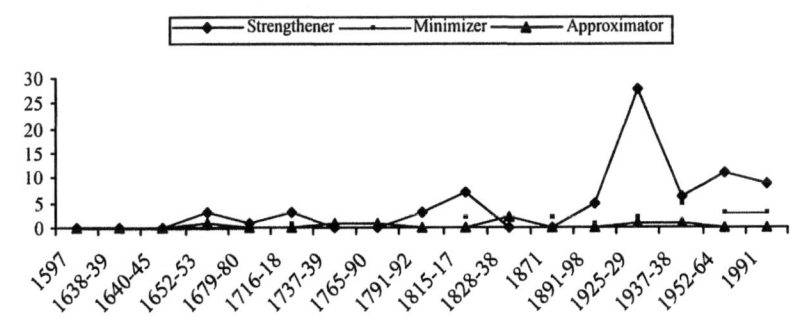

Fig. 7: Markers of Amount with the PF

3. Qualitative analysis[8]

Due to limitations of space, we shall focus our attention on the analysis of a few examples illustrating qualifying modality and examples used as part of a politeness strategy.

3.1. The PF and qualifying modality

Among the various examples of qualifying modality, (18) is an interesting example since it combines two types of qualifying modality. The writer Lewis Caroll, through the combination of the PF and the use of the adverbial *constantly*, not only shows his irritation at being recurrently disturbed by strangers but also shows it is perfectly abnormal to be disturbed when one wants to preserve one's anonymity:

(18) It looks, no doubt, an inordinate piece of vanity, to have supposed that is was because of books of mine that you had wished to know me: but I may plead, as an excuse, the actual fact

---

8   I would like to acknowledge permissions from the editors and publishers of *My Darling Pussy* and the *Selected Letters of Edith Sitwell* to quote examples from these books. A special thanks, too, to Lynette Hunter for giving permission to use her electronic edition of *The Letters of Dorothy Moore*.

that people are *constantly* doing it: for years I have suffered from applications, from perfect strangers, who persist in ignoring my « anonymous » position – some seeking autographs, some interviews, some personal acquaintance. (*The Selected Letters of Lewis Caroll, To Mrs. A. S. Walford*, p. 231)

(19) illustrates another form of commentary from the same writer. Lewis Caroll encourages his friend Lord Salisbury to raise an important question before Queen Victoria. The author does not use the PF of the verb *throw away* with an aspectual value in mind. Rather, Lewis Caroll scans the topological structure of the predicative relation <she, throw away, an opportunity> and locates it in relation to his attitude, i.e. his disappointment and his disagreement. Lewis Caroll uses the adverb of degree *how* combined with the adjective *vast* to explicitly underline the queen's mistake of refusing cooperation.

(19) Is there any one living, whose opportunities, and whose fitness for the task, can for a moment be compared with *yours*? Oh, pardon the boldness with which I say all this: it is not for myself, it is for thousands and thousands of my fellow-subjects that I am urging it: but do, do, if by any possibility you can, bring this vital question to the notice of the queen, and indice her – as probably only you can do – to see **how vast an opportunity,** for doing good, **she is throwing away** ! (*The Selected Letters of Lewis Caroll, To Lord Salisbury* p. 277-8)

These interpretations in (18) and (19) echo Pullum and Huddleston's (2002: 165) comment on this type of PF which « extends the situation in order to be able to focus on clarifying its nature ».

3.2. The PF and politeness strategy: cases illustrating the combination of epistemic and deontic modalities

The use of PF as part of a politeness strategy is also worth examining since it can be shown to be a combination of epistemic and deontic modalities. Our purpose is to identify which characteristics of the PF allow for such an interpretation, using Culioli's theory of enunciation (see Groussier 2000), Bouscaren and Deschamps's (1991) topological structure of verbs, and Brown and Levinson's (1987) concept of face.

3.2.1. The PF with mental Activity verb *wonder*

Typical examples involve the use of the verb *wonder* in the PF, as illustrated in (20):

(20) **I am wondering** if you could *possibly* allow me to show him, perhaps give him a copy, of that glorious work, just discovered, the poem to Mary, that you sent me. I ask this, because Kenneth is a tremendous prop of the Arts, and people listen more, almost, to what he says, than to anyone, and it will rouse excitement about the book before it appears. (*Selected letters of Edith Sitwell, To Roy Campbell*, p. 387)

By definition, the verb *wonder* expresses doubt and indicates the wish to know. The use of this verb means that the speaker scans all the occurrences of doubt without stopping. Consequently, the topological structure of *wonder* corresponds to that of an activity verb, with two separate boundaries, a heterogeneous interior, and no ending point: [...[. The Aktionsart of *wonder* does not contain the notion of an ending point. The latter has to be linguistically constructed, as in *wonder something*. The direct object complement *something* represents the potential ending point, which can be reached if the addressee provides the speaker with the relevant answer. In (31), it is the subordinate clause introduced by *if* which plays the role of *something*, namely a goal to be achieved.

By using the PF at the moment of speech in a polite situation, the speaker deliberately indicates that the ending point of the topological structure of the predicative relation < I, wonder, if you could *possibly* allow me something > has not been reached yet. This reasoning is in accordance with Groussier's (1991) findings. Consequently, the use of the PF is a way for the speaker to distance himself from the validation of the predicative relation <you, allow, something> by evaluating the chances of validity of the predicative relation. This operation can be related to epistemic modality.

Moreover, with the PF, as the ending point of the topological structure associated with the interior of the *if*- clause is not taken into account, the speaker suggests that the conditions of validity of the predicative relation <you, allow, something> are dependent on the subject of the utterance *you*, namely the addressee. The speaker here is concerned with a situation involving deontic modality. By putting the condition of validity of the predicative relation <you, allow, something> in the hands of the addressee, the speaker relaxes the constraint he is imposing on the addressee and the potential effect of the speaker's act on the addressee's negative face is toned down. By respecting the addressee's need for independence, the speaker uses a strategy of negative politeness. However, we could also say that because the addressee is considered as a key element in the decision, the speaker highly values the addressee's point of view and shows consideration to his positive face. In this sense, the use of the PF in this situation also partakes of positive politeness and represents an act of what Kerbrat-Orecchioni (1997) calls a Face-Enhancing Act, underlining the solidarity and cooperativeness between the participants.

3.2.2. The PF with mental stative verbs
Occasionally we find the PF used with verbs expressing mental states, as shown below:

(21) I've had it in my mind, for ever so long, « Enid would like to hear about your adventures at Eastbourne, » **and I've been *meaning* to write you a letter**. But I *am* so busy, dear child ! *Sylvie and Bruno Concluded* takes up (when I'm in the humour for it, which I generally *am*, just now) 6 or 8 hours a day. And there are letters that *must* be written.

(The Selected Letters of Lewis Caroll, To Enid Stevens, p. 240)

(22) I have worked very hard on my speech & think it is alright. But how I missed your wise & loving help in its preparation. **I was always wanting** to ask you 'What do you think of this?'
(My Darling Pussy, 25 March 1929, p. 127)

The use of the PF is a way for the speaker to pretend that he is fragmentising the homogeneous topological structure of the stative verb, which allows him to turn it into a heterogeneous topological structure. The speaker can then make as if he were in the process of indulging a mental activity. By focussing on the past mental activity and not the actual goal of this activity (« write a letter » in (21) or « ask something » in (22)), he represents himself as not fully responsible for being late in the achievement of his goal. The use of the PF helps the speaker to turn the addressee's attention away from the missed goal. By underlining the positive side of the situation, the speaker shows solidarity with the addressee, thereby displaying positive politeness. By downplaying the non-existence of the validation of the goal, the speaker minimises the imposition on the hearer to reply to the letter or question, thereby indicating negative politeness.

4. Conclusion
The diachronic study of the PF in a corpus of private letters from the 15th to the 20th century has provided evidence that this written genre has moved towards an increased marking of subjectivity throughout the modern period, which testifies to the increasing discursivisation of the genre. The quantification of the empirical evidence of the different types of subjuncts contributes to a better understanding of the interaction, and even the blurring, of aspect with modality. Even though it is commonplace to say that all grammars leak (in the Sapirian sense) to explain the presence of some rhetorical occurrences of the PF, there exist a number of examples, especially relating to politeness strategy, which show that this is not a sufficient explanation. It would be opportune to pursue the research in this direction further to better understand the cognitive processes which can be held responsible for the acquisition and the development of subjective values of the PF.

References

Data sources

Bamford, Francis (ed.)
    1936   *Dear Miss Heber, an Eighteenth Century Correspondence,* London: Constable.

Beer, Barrett L. — Sybil M. Jack (edd.)
    1974   *The Letters of William, Lord Paget of Beaudesert, 1547-1563*, Camden Miscellany vol. XXV, Camden fourth series, Vol. 13, London: Royal Historical Society.

British National Corpus
    1994   Personal letters, web version.

Bruce, John (ed.)
    1844   *Correspondence of Robert Dudley, Earl of Leycester, During His Government of the Low Countries, in the Years 1585 and 1586.* Camden Original Series, 27. London: Camden Society.

Carpenter, Christine (ed.)
    1998   *The Amburgh Papers*, Woodbridge: Boydell Press.

Chapman, Robert W. (ed.)
    1952   *Jane Austen's letters to her sister Cassandra and others*, London: Oxford University Press. Computerised version.

Cohen, Morton N. (ed.)
    1996   *The selected Letters of Lewis Caroll*, London: Papermac.

Countess of Cork and Orrery (ed.)
    1903   *The Orrery Papers*, London: Duckworth and Company.

Davis, Norman (ed.)
    1971   *Paston letters and papers of the 15th century, Part I, Paston family*, Oxford: Clarendon Press. Computerised version.

Greene, Richard (ed.)
    1998   *Selected Letters of Edith Sitwell*, London: Virago Press.

Grocott, Desmond (ed.)
    2006   *Letters of the Right Honourable* Mary Wortley Montague. Computerised version.

Hanham, Alison (ed.)
    1975   *The Cely Letters 1472-1488.* Early English Text Society, 273. London, New York and Toronto: Oxford University Press.

Hemlow, Joyce et al. (edd.)
    1972   *The Journal and Letters of Fanny Burney (Madame d'Arblay)*, vol.1, 1791-1792, Letters 1-39, Oxford: Clarendon Press.

Hoyle, Richard W. (ed.)
    1992   *Letters of the Cliffords, Lords Clifford and Earls of Cumberland, c. 1500-1565,* Camden Miscellany XXXI, Camden fourth series, v. 44, Royal Historical Society, London: Camden Society.

Hunter, Lynette (ed.)
    2004   *The letters of Dorothy Moore 1612-1664.* Computerised version.

Kenyon, Frederic G. (ed.)
    2004   *Letters of Elizabeth Barrett Browning 1806-51,* Vol. 1, 2004. Computerised version.

Lewis, Thomas Taylor (ed.)
   1854   *Letters of the Lady Brilliana Harley, Wife of Sir Robert Harley, of Brampton Bryan, Knight of the Bath*, Camden Original Series, 57. London: Camden Society.
McClure, Norman E. (ed.)
   1939   *Letters of John Chamberlain*, Vol.1, Philadelphia: the American Philosophical Society.
Moore, Stuart A. (ed.)
   1965   *Letters and Papers of John Shillingford, Mayor of Exeter 1447-50.* Camden New Series, 2. New York: Johnson Reprint Company.
Moore Smith, G. C. (ed.)
   1928   *The letters of Dorothy Osborne to William Temple*, Oxford: Clarendon Press.
Nicolson, Nigel (ed.)
   1980   *Leave the letters till we're dead, The letters of Virginia Woolf,* Vol. 6: 1936-1941, London: Hogarth Press.
Russell, Bertrand — Patricia Russell (edd.)
   1937   *The Amberley Papers*, vol. 2, *The Letters and Diaries of Lord and Lady Amberley*, London: Hogarth Press.
Taylor, Alan J.P. (ed.)
   1975   *My Darling Pussy, The Letters of Lloyd George and Frances Stevenson 1913-41,* London: Weidenfeld and Nicolson.
Truesdall Heath, Helen (ed.)
   1955   *The Letters of Samuel Pepys and his family, circle,* Oxford: Clarendon Press.`

Books and articles

Biber, Douglas et al.
   2002   *Longman Student Grammar of Spoken and written English*, Harlow: Longman.
Bouscaren, Janine — Alain Deschamps
   1991   "Réexamen de la typologie des verbes anglais", *Cahiers Charles V,* 13, Travaux de linguistique énonciative, Université Paris VII, 7-23.
Brown, Penelope — Stephen C. Levinson
   1987   *Politeness: some universals on language.* Cambridge: Cambridge University Press.

Denison, David
  1998 "Syntax". *The Cambridge history of the English language*, vol. 4, *1776-1997*, ed. Suzanne Romaine, 92-329. Cambridge: Cambridge University Press.

Fitzmaurice, Susan
  2004 "The meanings and uses of the progressive construction in an early eighteenth-century English network", In Anne Curzan and Kimberly Emmons (edd.), *Studies in the History of the English Language II: Unfolding Conversations,* Berlin: Mouton de Gruyter, 131-174.

Groussier, M.arie-Line
  1991 "A propos de l'*attitudinal past* de Quirk et al.", *Cahiers de Charles V* 13, Université Paris VII, 103-18.

Groussier, Marie-Line
  2000 "On Antoine Culioli's theory of enunciative operations", *Lingua* 110, 157-182.

Kerbrat-Orecchioni, Catherine
  1997 "A multilevel approach in the study of talk-in-interaction", *Pragmatics* 7-1, March 1997, 1-20.

Killie, Kristin
  2004 "Subjectivity and the English progressive", *English Language and Linguistics* 8, 25-46.

Pullum, Geoffrey — Rodney Huddleston
  2002 *The Cambridge Grammar of the English Language,* Cambridge: Cambridge University Press.

Strang, Barbara M. H.
  1982 "Some aspects of the history of the *be + ing* construction., in J. Anderson (ed.), *Language Form and Linguistic Variation*, (1982), Amsterdam: John Benjamins, 427-474.

Wright, Susan
  1994 "The mystery of the modal progressive", in D. Kastovsky (ed.), *Early Modern English,* (1994), Berlin: Mouton de Gruyter, 467-485.
  1995 "Subjectification in experiential syntax," in Dieter Stein and Susan Wright (edd.), *Subjectivity and subjectivisation, Linguistic perspectives,* 1995, Cambridge: Cambridge University Press, 151-172.

22 The Verb *prevent* and its Changing Patterns of Complementation in the History of English

Yoko Iyeiri, Kyoto University

1. Introduction

Burchfield (1998: 622) states that "[t]here are three competing constructions when the verb *prevent* is followed directly or indirectly by a gerund in *-ing*" and gives the following: (a) *prevent* + possessive + *-ing* (*The Oxford English Dictionary* = *OED* 1841-) (e.g. *Either the fire-guard or his mother prevents his reaching the fire*, H. T. Lane, 1928);[1] (b) *prevent* + object + *-ing* (*OED* 1689-) (e.g. *Two women climb up the iron bars, which are meant to prevent people or animals falling under the tram*, J. Berger, 1972); and (c) *prevent* + object + *from* + *-ing* (*OED* 1711-) (e.g. *Sleeman had tried to prevent a widow from committing suttee*, R. P. Jhabvala, 1975).[2] As for the rise and fall of these patterns, he refers to (a) only, and says that it "is beginning to fall into disuse" in current English.[3] Furthermore, Weiner and Delahunty (1994: 159) regard (b) as informal, while Grattan regarded it as a vulgarism in the 1960s (see Kruisinga 1967: 110). Considering these accounts, it is most likely that "*prevent* + possessive + *-ing*" is on the decline on the one hand and that "*prevent* + object + *-ing*" is increasingly acknowledged on the other hand, in contemporary English.

The purpose of the present study is to investigate various patterns of complementation of the verb *prevent* from a historical perspective, by analyzing the quotations in the second edition of the *OED* on CD-ROM. This paper will deal with several hundred years during the Modern English period to see how various patterns in the past affect the present-day usage of *prevent*. Here, the present-day usage means the usage of British English only, since it is widely known that there is a significant difference between British and American English, in the latter of which "*prevent* + object + *-ing*" is extremely limited even on informal occasions.[4]

---

1   I have quoted only the first of the examples provided by Burchfield (1998: 622) under each pattern.
2   Burchfield (1988: 622) gives incorrect dates for the first quotations of (b) and (c) in the *OED*, which I have modified. The dates given by the *OED* are, however, not absolute in any case, since they can easily be antedated. Visser (1963-1973, §2103), for instance, gives an example of 1696 for (a), while Visser (1963-1973, §2092) gives an example of 1592 for (b). Furthermore, even the text search of the *OED* yields an example of 1600 for (a), an example of 1614 for (b), and an example of 1641 for (c).
3   In the interest of consistency throughout this paper, I have changed the order of the three patterns. Pattern (a), for instance, appears last in Burchfield (1998: 622).
4   Mair (2002: 112-115) displays the statistical data from the four corpora of LOB, FLOB, Brown and Frown, and proves that "*prevent* + object + *-ing*" is expanding in current British English and that its use is extremely limited both in the 1960s and the 1990s in American English. Frown (American English), however, gives the following single instance of this

2. The establishment of gerundial constructions in the History of English

Whereas Present-day English shows the vacillation among the three types of gerundial constructions as mentioned above in the Introduction, there is a stage prior to this in the history of English. As Figure 1 below (see also Appendix 1) reveals, the establishment of the use of gerunds after *prevent* is attested only in the seventeenth-century:[5]

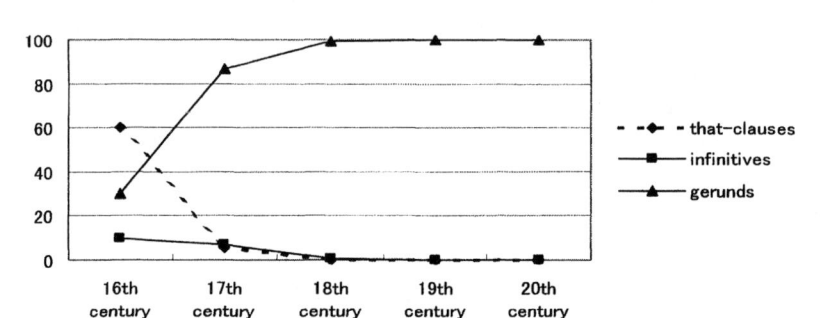

Figure 1: Various types of complementation of *prevent* in the *OED* (%)

The above graph elucidates the constant increase of the use of gerunds after *prevent*. During the sixteenth and seventeenth centuries, however, there are still examples of *prevent* followed by *that*-clauses and infinitives, as in:

(1) Doth it not stand her in hand to *preuent that* the number of catholiks do not increase?
 (1600 W. Watson, *Decacordon*, 303)[6]

(2) To *preuent* those Thracian theeves *that* they should not hide themselues within their peakish holes ... and ordinarie couert musets. (1600 Holland, *Livy*, xxxviii. xlix., 1015)

(3) To *prevente* the same [bone] *to be* ... putrefacted and corrupted.
 (1597 A. M. tr., *Guillemeau's Fr. Chirurg*, 33 b/2)

Whether the *that*-clauses as in (1) and (2) above are a genuinely nominal one is an open question. They may be a final clause with the sense of 'so that', but this does not matter. The important point is that examples of this kind are increasingly

---

construction: *but sometimes quite small groups can prevent it being lost*. It is also relevant to mention that *The Columbia Guide to Standard American English* (Wilson 1993: 343) admits all of the three patterns under consideration. For a thorough survey of previous studies on the American usage of *prevent*, see Tajima (1995: 3).

5 As for the dates of texts from which examples are quoted, I have followed the datings of the *OED*. For practical reasons, I have regarded "c1500" as "1500", and so forth. Duplicated examples are counted only once.

6 Unless otherwise stated, the italics in the citations are mine.

restricted in use in the history of the English language, whatever the nature of the *that*-clause is.

Thus, the historical expansion of the use of gerunds after the verb *prevent* is fairly clear. It is predominant from the seventeenth century onwards. Other verbs also experience the changeover of patterns during the early Modern English period, although tendencies are not always as transparent as in the case of *prevent*. I have, for instance, investigated the historical development of the verb *prohibit*, which also exhibits the use of *that*-clauses, infinitives, and gerunds in the sixteenth and seventeenth centuries. With this verb also, gerunds become the dominant form in the course of the seventeenth century, although infinitives linger to a much larger extent than in the case of *prevent* until around the nineteenth century (Iyeiri 2002). As for other adversative predicates, Fanego (1996) discusses *forbear* among other verbs. Unfortunately, she does not investigate *that*-clauses, but about the use of infinitives and gerunds she argues that they are still in competition during the period 1640-1710 and that gerunds are dominant after 1710.

Incidentally, that the early Modern English period is a key period in terms of the development of complementation patterns is also shown by predicates which eventually establish the use of infinitives instead of gerunds. A significant decline of the use of *that*-clauses is witnessed with the verb *forbid* by the eighteenth century, although in this case, it is *to*-infinitives that were established in history after the decline of *that*-clauses (see Iyeiri 2003: 155-158)[7].

3. Three types of constructions with gerunds in later Modern English

As discussed above in Section 2, the established use of gerundial constructions is evidenced only from the seventeenth century, before which the patterning of complementation of the verb *prevent* is still unstable. The following discussion focuses upon the several hundred years from the seventeenth century. This is the second stage of the development of *prevent*, where three different types of gerundial constructions compete. As mentioned in the Introduction, this competition has not been completed even in contemporary English, which yields: (a) *prevent* + possessive + *-ing*; (b) *prevent* + object + *-ing*; and (c) *prevent* + object + *from* + *-ing*. Historical examples illustrating the three patterns include:

---

7   A notable extension of the use of gerunds is also evidenced for some time with *forbid* side by side with the decline of *that*-clauses, although it is *to*-infinitives that ultimately survived the history of English.

(4) He built a house without his Camp for all strangers ..., whereby he *prevented their sneaking into his Camp.* (1656 *North's Plutarch* Add. Lives, 43)

(5) A free Confession ... easily *prevents a little Error growing* to a great Evil.
(1718 J. Fox, *Wanderer*, 147)

(6) Nothing but an invincible Resolution ... could have *prevented me from falling* back to my Monosyllables. (1714 Addison, *Spect.*, No. 556, 3)

The relationship among the three patterns is relatively well discussed in respect of Present-day English. As mentioned above, Burchfield (1998: 622) states that "*prevent* + possessive + *-ing*" is beginning to decline in current English. This is confirmed by Heyvaert et al. (2005: 84), who provide the table below:

Table 1: Diachronic evolution of the use of *-ing* forms after *prevent*

	prevent + possessive + *-ing*	*prevent* + object + *-ing*	*prevent* + object + *from -ing*
Kirsten 18th century	(25) 30%	(8) 10%	(49) 60%
Kirsten 19th century	(48) 53%	(5) 6%	(37) 41%
Van Ek 1950-1964	(2) 5%	(14) 38%	(21) 57%
COBUILD corpus	(32) 6%	(120) 23%	(367) 71%

(from Heyvaert et al. 2005: 84)[8]

Table 1 is based upon the analysis by Heyvaert et al. (2005) of the COBUILD corpus (around 1990 and after) as well as the data provided by Kirsten (1957) and those by van Ek (1966). Although the dataset is a collection of various materials which may be inconsistent from the stylistic perspective, the table most explicitly reveals the dramatic decline of the "*prevent* + possessive + *-ing*" construction in the twentieth century. It is perhaps safe to conclude that the pattern is indeed on the decline in recent years.

One thing that is not so evident in Table 1 is whether "*prevent* + object + *from* + *-ing*" is expanding at the cost of "*prevent* + object + *-ing*." As far as Table 1 is concerned, the construction with the preposition *from* is most likely on the increase in contemporary English, but at the same time, there are other studies which make contentions to the opposite effect. Mair (2002: 112), for instance, investigates "*prevent* + object + *-ing*" and "*prevent* + object + *from* + *-ing*" in the LOB and FLOB corpora, providing the following data:

---

[8] In the interest of consistency throughout this paper, I have slightly modified the presentation of this table from Heyvaert et al. (2005: 84). Needless to say, all the figures including percentages remain the same.

Table 2: Frequencies of *prevent* + object + *-ing* and *prevent* + object + *from* + *-ing*

	prevent + object + *-ing*	*prevent* + object + *from -ing*
LOB (1961)	7	34
FLOB (1991/1992)	24	24

(from Mair 2002: 112)[9]

Unlike Table 1 above, Table 2 hints at the possibility that the pattern "*prevent* + object + *-ing*" (rather than "*prevent* + object + *from* + *-ing*") is on the increase in Present-day English. It was not as frequent as the construction with the preposition *from* in 1961, while it is already as frequent in 1991/1992. The question is where the difference between the data of Heyvaert et al. (2005) and those of Mair (2002) arises.

The ultimate answer to this question can be given only after further analyses of Present-day English are conducted, but the historical data of the *OED* yield an important suggestion in this concern. And this is what the present study is interested in discussing. There is a clear difference in terms of the pace in the historical development of the three constructions at issue, depending upon whether the "possessive" or the "objective" before the gerund is a personal pronoun or not. In the following, I have given the raw frequencies of the three gerundial patterns found in the *OED*, Figure 2 (see also Appendix 2) showing the case of personal pronouns and Figure 3 (see also Appendix 3) the case of nouns.[10] Examples of "*prevent* + *her* + *-ing*" (nine examples in all) are all excluded from this analysis, since it is impossible to tell whether *her* in this case is possessive or objective.

Figure 2: The case of personal pronouns in the *OED*

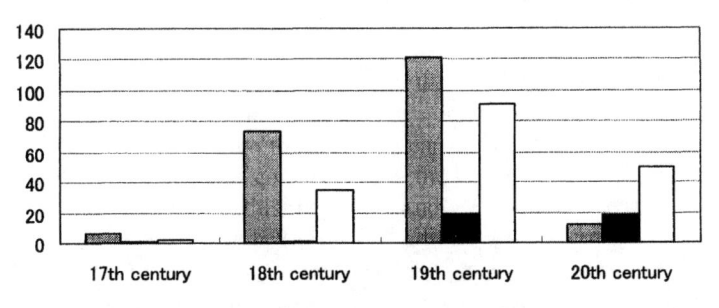

▨ prevent + possessive + –ing ■ prevent + object + –ing ☐ prevent + object + from + –ing

---

9   In the interest of consistency, I have slightly modified the presentation of this table from Mair (2002: 112). Needless to say, the frequencies under each pattern have not been changed.
10 Pronouns other than personal pronouns are included in Figure 3, considering the fact that they have lost the case distinctions which personal pronouns retain.

Figure 3: The case of nouns in the *OED*

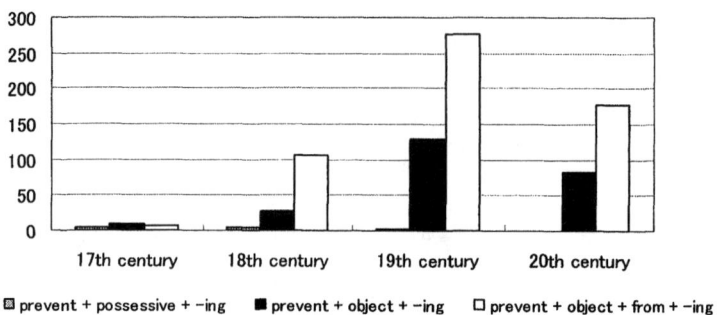

▨ prevent + possessive + -ing   ■ prevent + object + -ing   ☐ prevent + object + from + -ing

Since the number of quotations per century is not constant, it is not wise to compare and contrast the raw frequencies of different centuries under the same type of constructions. In other words, attention has to be paid to the relationship among the three patterns in each century, which reveals that the tendencies of personal pronouns (Figure 2) and those of nouns (Figure 3) are quite contrastive. The most outstanding distinction between the two graphs is that "*prevent* + possessive + *-ing*" as illustrated by (7) is relatively well preserved in the case of pronouns, while the same construction recedes much earlier in the case of nouns:

(7) Their Leaves ... may be tied in knots, which will *prevent their spindling*.
(1707 Mortimer, *Husb.*, II. 145)

As a matter of fact, it is the predominant pattern until the nineteenth century in the case of personal pronouns, and even in the twentieth century, it is observed to an unignorable extent.

This is most likely a reflection of the general tendency of using possessive pronouns rather than objective pronouns before gerunds, a tendency not restricted to the verb *prevent* but observed across the board in the history of English. Denison (1998: 269) states that "with personal pronouns a preference for the genitive [i.e. possessive] form was often vociferously expressed in the prescriptive tradition" and refers to Dekeyser (1975: 180-181), who gives the proportions ranging from 2.3% to 6.7% for nongenitive pronouns in the nineteenth century. Furthermore, even today, Quirk et al. (1985: 1063) state that "[i]n general, the genitive is preferred if the item is a pronoun, the noun phrase has personal reference, and the style is formal", although, according to Visser (1963-1973, §1102), the use of objective pronoun was increasingly frequent "from about the middle of the nineteenth century." In addition, there are grammatical reference guides which even state that the use of the possessive is the norm (e.g. Wood 1981: 136).

Thus, the statistical data provided by Heyvaert et al. (1998) and Mair (2002) need further subdividing to present a clearer picture of the development of gerundial constructions with *prevent* in the twentieth century. In other words, nouns and pronouns need to be treated separately. Mair (2002) analyzes nouns and personal pronouns together. On the other hand, Heyvaert et al. (1998) restrict their analysis to personal pronouns, but comparing their data with those presented by Kirsten (1957) and van Ek (1966), who investigate nouns and pronouns inclusively.[11]

Once the division is made between the cases of personal pronouns and nouns, some interesting points are revealed about the relationship between "*prevent* + object + -*ing*" and the construction with the preposition *from*. It seems to be relatively stable in the case of nouns from the nineteenth century onwards (see Figure 3), "*prevent* + object + -*ing*" occurring about half as frequently as the construction with *from*. By contrast, a much more radical change is taking place when the subject of the gerund is a personal pronoun (see Figure 2), in that the relative frequency of "*prevent* + object + -*ing*" to that of "*prevent* + object + *from* + -*ing*" seems to be rising. The question is whether the expanded use of "*prevent* + object + -*ing*" in the case of personal pronouns is caused by the decline of the older possessive construction alone or also at the cost of the decline of the construction with *from*. This is not an easy question to answer, but Figure 4 (see also Appendix 4), which indicates the changing proportions of the three patterns to the total, will provide a hint:

Figure 4: Changing proportions of the three patterns of *prevent* when the subject of –*ing* is a personal pronoun (*OED*) (%)

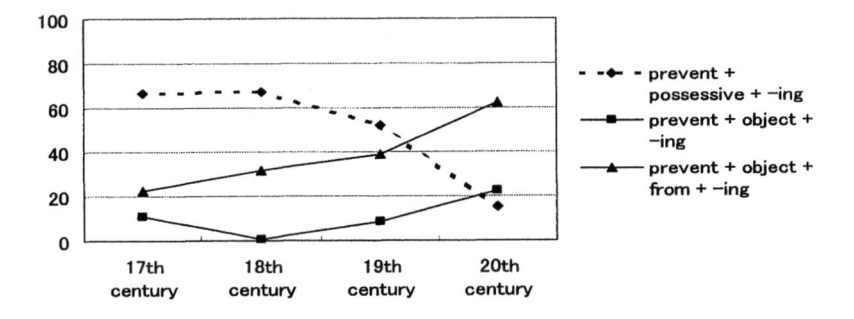

---

[11] Kirsten (1957) does not state this, but I have confirmed this point by double-checking some of the works investigated by him.

Figure 4 suggests that the rise of "*prevent* + object + *-ing*" was most plausibly triggered by the drop of the possessive construction from the eighteenth century to the nineteenth century. By contrast, the construction with the preposition *from* also seems to be on the constant increase from the seventeenth century. In fact, it is on the increase even in the twentieth century. In other words, the gap caused by the decline of the possessive construction is filled not only by "*prevent* + object + *-ing*" but also by "*prevent* + object + *from* + *-ing*." Still in other words, the decline of the possessive construction is likely to be the key factor in the expansion of "*prevent* + object + *-ing*", at least as far as the *OED* data are concerned.

Incidentally, the proportion of the "objective + *-ing*" construction with a personal pronoun is not as low as Dekeyser (1975: 180-181) states about the general tendency of gerunds, in the nineteenth century, as far as the case of *prevent* is concerned. He gives the proportions ranging from 2.3% to 6.7% for the objective case as opposed to the possessive one, while the proportion of the "objective + *-ing*" construction in Figure 4 is about 8.6%, which means that the proportion will be even larger when the construction with *from* is excluded. This may be a matter of differences due to different verbs. Otherwise, stylistic factors may be involved, which is beyond analysis in the present paper as it draws materials from various types of texts. As mentioned above, it is well-known that the possessive is more favoured in formal style than in informal one. See Quirk et al. (1985: 1063) and also Huddleston and Pullum (2002: 1192).

4. Is "*prevent* + object + *-ing*" an elliptical form of "*prevent* + object + *from* + *-ing*"?

Whereas the discussion by Heyvaert et al. (2005) is based upon the assumption that the use of the objective (pro)nouns in the form of "*prevent* + object + *-ing*" is a way to indicate the subject of the *-ing* form, there is also a widely-prevalent view that the pattern is a short form of "*prevent* + object + *from* + *-ing*." In other words, it is also considered to be a form produced through the ellipsis of *from*. The *OED* (s.v. *prevent*) assumes thus, which is quoted by Visser (1963-1973, §2092). Among more recent studies, Dixon (1991: 194) gives the same contention.

As I discuss later in this section, both factors are perhaps relevant, but for the moment, I would like to take the side of Heyvaert et al. (2005), since their argument seems to be better justified. Figure 4 above clearly reveals that the initial rise of "*prevent* + object + *-ing*" was triggered by the decline of "*prevent* + possessive + *-ing*." The graph also shows the constant rise of both "*prevent* + object + *-ing*" and "*prevent* + object + *from* + *-ing*" in the history of English. It is more likely that "*prevent* + object + *-ing*" develops at the cost of the decline of the possessive construction than at the cost of the decline of the construction with *from*.

Furthermore, this view is consistent with what Rohdenburg (1996: 151) calls the Complexity Principle, which runs as follows: "[i]n the case of more or less explicit grammatical options the more explicit one(s) will tend to be favored in cognitively more complex environments." If "*prevent* + object + *-ing*" is the short form of "*prevent* + object + *from* + *-ing*" and if the Complexity Principle holds for this case, the form with *from*, which is the more explicit option, will be favoured by nouns, since nouns are more complex than pronouns from a cognitive perspective, according to Rohdenburg (1996: 152-159). In other words, if ellipsis is the key factor in the development of "*prevent* + object + *-ing*", it would take place more rapidly with pronouns than with nouns, since pronouns are less complex than nouns. However, the historical development of "*prevent* + object + *-ing*" displays the opposite tendency. The construction develops much more quickly with nouns than with pronouns (see Figures 2 and 3 above). Thus, the assumption that "*prevent* + object + *-ing*" is the short form of the pattern with *from* is refuted. In other words, one needs to consider another factor in relation to the expanded use of "*prevent* + object + *-ing*", i.e. the decline of the "possessive + gerund", which is in fact more relevant.

This does not mean, however, that the omission of *from* is wholly irrelevant to the expanded use of "*prevent* + object + *-ing*", especially in the context of contemporary English. In the end, the almost complete obliteration of the possessive construction results in the situation in which only "*prevent* + object + *-ing*" and "*prevent* + object + *from* + *-ing*" are available. In other words, the expansion of one form is possible only at the cost of the other. Given the similarity between the two forms, it is not surprising that language users regard the former construction as a short form of the latter. The significant point is that this widely-held view can further accelerate the use of "*prevent* + object + *-ing*", perhaps in colloquial contexts first and then in other contexts later, although I do not know at this stage to what extent this has indeed taken place.

5. Conclusion

The present study has investigated varying patterns of complementation of the verb *prevent* from a historical point of view. In Present-day English, there is a well-known variation among the three gerundial patterns: (a) *prevent* + possessive + *-ing*; (b) *prevent* + object + *-ing*; and (c) *prevent* + object + *from* + *-ing*. These are, however, not the only forms attested in the history of English. There is a stage prior to this vacillation, where complement finite clauses and infinitives are also attested with the verb *prevent*. After the decline of these complementation patterns (i.e. finite clauses and infinitives) in early Modern English, the use of gerunds was firmly established with *prevent*, and here the second stage of vacillation was launched in the sense that the above-mentioned three types of gerundial complementation were in competition.

Of the three patterns, *"prevent* + possessive + *-ing"* is on a gradual decline in current English, although it is still observed especially with personal pronouns today. In fact, it is most significant in the analysis of the historical development of *prevent* to make a separate treatment between the cases of nouns and personal pronouns, since there is a clear distinction in terms of the variation of the three gerundial patterns between the cases. With nouns (rather than personal pronouns), the decline of the possessive form occurs much earlier, while with personal pronouns it lingers much longer, almost hindering the expansion of *"prevent* + object + *-ing."*

Finally, whether *"prevent* + object + *-ing"* is a short form of *"prevent* + object + *from* + *-ing"* was discussed. The historical survey of the present study strongly suggests that the objective form of the former construction arises at the cost of the decline of the possessive form of *"prevent* + possessive + *-ing"* rather than from the ellipsis of the *"prevent* + object + *from* + *-ing"*, and this conjecture is consistent with what Rohdenburg (1996) calls the Complexity Principle. In the contemporary setting, however, the inference that the omission of *from* is involved in the development of *"prevent* + object + *-ing"* cannot entirely be denied, since it is not surprising if language users consider this way once the decline of the possessive construction is much in progress, leaving the situation in which only the pattern with the objective case with or without *from* are available. This can lead to a further stage of the development of the complementation patterns of *prevent*, which is outside the purview of the present discussion.

Appendices

1. Various types of complementation of *prevent* in the *OED* (%)

	that-clauses	infinitives	gerunds
16th century	60.0	10.0	30.0
17th century	5.8	7.2	87.0
18th century	0.3	0.7	99.0
19th century	0.1	0	99.9
20th century	0	0	100

2. The case of personal pronouns in the *OED*

	prevent + possessive + *-ing*	*prevent* + object + *-ing*	*prevent* + object + *from* + *-ing*
17th century	6	1	2
18th century	74	1	35
19th century	122	20	91
20th century	12	18	50

3. The case of nouns in the *OED*

	prevent + possessive + *-ing*	*prevent* + object + *-ing*	*prevent* + object + *from* + *-ing*
17th century	4	9	8
18th century	4	27	106
19th century	3	130	278
20th century	1	82	177

4. Changing proportions of the three patterns of *prevent* in the *OED* (%)

	prevent + possessive + *-ing*	*prevent* + object + *-ing*	*prevent* + object + *from* + *-ing*
17th century	66.7	11.1	22.2
18th century	67.3	0.9	31.8
19th century	52.4	8.6	39.1
20th century	15.0	22.5	62.5

References

Burchfield, Robert W.
    1996   *The New Fowler's Modern English Usage.* Oxford: Clarendon Press.

Denison, David
    1998   "Syntax", in: *The Cambridge History of the English Language, vol. IV: 1776-1997*, ed. Suzanne Romaine, 92-329. Cambridge: Cambridge University Press.

Dekeyser, Xavier
    1975   *Number and Case Relations in 19th Century British English: A Comparative Study of Grammar and Usage.* Antwerpen: Uitgeverij de Nederlandsche Boekhandel.

Dixon, Robert M. W.
    1991   *A New Approach to English Grammar, on Semantic Principles.* Oxford: Clarendon Press.

Fanego, Teresa
    1996   "The Development of Gerunds as Objects of Subject-Control Verbs in English (1400-1760)." *Diachronica* 13: 29-62.

Heyvaert, Liesbet — Hella Rogiers — Nadine Vermeylen
    2005   "Pronominal Determiners in Gerundive Nominalization: A 'Case' Study." *English Studies* 86: 71-88.

Huddleston, Rodney — Geoffrey K. Pullum
    2002   *The Cambridge Grammar of the English Language.* Cambridge: Cambridge University Press.

Iyeiri, Yoko
 2002 *"Prohibit ni kakawaru Kobun no Rekishiteki Hensen nitsuite"* (History of the English Verb *to prohibit*). *Eigoshi Kenkyukai Kaiho* (The Bulletin of the Japanese Association for Studies in the History of the English Language) 8: 1-4.
 2003 " 'God forbid!': A Historical Study of the Verb *forbid* in Different Versions of the English Bible." *Journal of English Linguistics* 31: 149-162.

Kirsten, Hans
 1957 "Bemerkungen zu *to prevent* + Gerundium." *Zeitschrift für Anglistik und Amerikanistik* 1: 327-328.

Kruisinga, E.
 1967 "Syntactic Groups with Verbal *-ing*." *English Studies* 12: 58-66, 110.

Mair, Christian
 2002 "Three Changing Patterns of Verb Complementation in Late Modern English: A Real-time Study Based on Matching Text Corpora." *English Language and Linguistics* 6: 105-131.

Quirk, Randolph — Sidney Greenbaum — Geoffrey Leech — Jan Svartvik
 1985 *A Comprehensive Grammar of the English Language*. London: Longman.

Rohdenburg, Günter
 1996 "Cognitive Complexity and Increased Grammatical Explicitness in English." *Cognitive Linguistics* 7: 149-182.

Rudanko, Juhani
 1989 *Complementation and Case Grammar: A Syntactic and Semantic Study of Selected Patterns of Complementation in Present-day English*. Albany, NY: State University of New York Press.

Tajima, Matsuji (ed.)
 1995 *Computer Corpus Riyo niyoru Gendai Eibei Gohou Kenkyu* (Present-day British and American English Usage: A Corpus-based Study). Tokyo: Kaibunsha.

Van Ek, Jan A.
 1966 *Four Complementary Structures of Predication in Contemporary British English: An Inventory*. Groningen: J. B. Wolters.

Visser, Frederikus Th.
 1963-1973 *An Historical Syntax of the English Language*. 4 vols. Leiden: E. J. Brill.

Vosberg, Uwe
 2003 "Cognitive Complexity and the Establishment of *-ing* Constructions with Retrospective Verbs in Modern English", in:

Insights into Late Modern English, ed. Marina Dossena and Charles Jones, 197-220. Bern: Peter Lang.

Weiner, E. S. C. — Andrew Delahunty
    1994   *The Oxford Guide to English Usage*. 2nd edition. Oxford: Oxford University Press.

Wilson, Kenneth G.
    1993   *The Columbia Guide to Standard American English*. New York: Columbia University Press.

Wood, Frederick T.
    1981   *Current English Usage*. Revised by Roger H. Flavell and Linda M. Flavell. London: Macmillan.

23 The Subjunctive in Nineteenth-Century English Dramas
Namiko Kikusawa, Kyoto University, Graduate School

1. Introduction

The subjunctive, a set of forms chosen typically to express doubt, wishes, unreality, etc., has been losing ground from ME times onwards, being replaced by the indicative and the modal auxiliary periphrasis. In LModE (=Late Modern English), the distinctive subjunctive is observed with: 1) the verb *be*; 2) the third person singular of the present tense without the ending *–(e)s*; 3) the verb *were* of the first and the third person singular (Denison 1998: 161). It is argued about the LModE period that there was a partial revival of the subjunctive in formal styles because of the influence of prescriptive grammars. On the other hand, there are opinions which assert the continuing decline of the subjunctive. However, studies based upon the examination of actual texts have not been done sufficiently.

Therefore, I decided to investigate the situation of the subjunctive and the subjunctive substitutes in LModE from both historical and sociolinguistic viewpoints. I chose drama texts written in the nineteenth century as materials for this study. Dramas are interesting from the standpoint of sociolinguistics. In dramas, many types of characters in different social classes appear speaking in various situations. In this research, I am going to analyse the subjunctive expressions from three points of view: 1) chronological change; 2) formality of the play; 3) how social classes affect the speeches of characters in the drama. I am going to argue that the subjunctive is a symbol of gentility and formality in LModE.

In the present study, eight dramas will be considered. I am going to count the number of the distinctive subjunctive and show the ratio to the total of the finite verbs in the texts. Apart from the distinctive subjunctive, I will also regard the non-standard form *was* (in place of *were*) uttered by each character in the dramas. The abbreviations of the titles of each drama will be as follows:

Susan = Douglas Jerrold (1803-1857): *Black-Eyed Susan* (1829)
Money = Edward Bulwer-Lytton (1803-1873): *Money* (1840)
Game = George Henry Lewes (1817-1878): *The Game of Speculation* (1851)
Acres = Tom Taylor (1817-1880) and Augustus William Dubourg (1830-1910): *New Men and Old Acres* (1869)
Harold = Alfred Tennyson (1809-1892): *Harold* (1876)
Silver = Henry Arthur Jones (1851-1929) and Henry Herman: *The Silver King* (1882)
Earnest = Oscar Wilde (1854-1900): *The Importance of Being Earnest* (1895)
Super = George Bernard Shaw (1856-1950): *Man and Superman* (1903)

2. Previous studies

As for the LModE period, it has been indicated that there was a partial revival of the subjunctive in formal styles owing to the influence of prescriptive grammars. Strang (1970: 209) points out that the decline "reversed sporadically only by the tendency to hypercorrection in 18c and later teachers and writers." According to Rissanen (1999: 228), the eighteenth-century grammarians' favorable attitude to the morphological distinction between subjunctive and indicative forms enhanced the use of the subjunctive. Some scholars such as Jespersen (1924: 318) and Harsh (1968: 84) emphasise the revival of the subjunctive in the nineteenth century. Harsh (1968: 84), by his research on drama texts, shows a slight upswing in frequency of the subjunctive in the late nineteenth century.

On the other hand, there are also opinions which disapprove such revivals. Turner (1980: 272), and recent studies of Denison (1998: 160-164) and Görlach (1999: 83) argue that the subjunctive continued to lose ground in LModE.

Thus, many remarks have been made about the subjunctive in LModE, but there are very few suggestions based upon the examination on actual texts.

3. The subjunctive in prescriptive grammars

The LModE period was the time when grammar attracted the public attention and thus prescriptive grammars had a large influence on society. Then, how was the treatment of the subjunctive in prescriptive grammars? As the summaries by Traugott (1972: 180) and Visser (1966: §837) note, all the grammarians agreed that the subjunctive was rare. Dr Johnson, in *A Dictionary of the English Language* (1755: 'Of the VERB'), states that the subjunctive is "wholly neglected" by his contemporary writers, being used only by the "purer" authors. Nevertheless, grammarians of the LModE period set strict rules on the use of the subjunctive. They emphasise the importance of the distinction between the use of the indicative and that of the subjunctive. They especially make efforts to preserve the present subjunctive. Let us look at some examples:

(1) It [the subjunctive] seems to be used with propriety only when some degree of *doubt* or *hesitation* is implied; [. . .]we should say, in pursuing a person, *We should overtake him though* he run; not knowing whether he did run or no; whereas, upon seeing him run, we should say, *We shall overtake him though* he runneth, or *runs*. (Priestley 1769: 90)[1]

(2) [. . .], in English the several expressions of Conditional Will, Possibility, Liberty, Obligation, etc. come all under the Subjunctive Mode: The mere expressions of Will, Possibility, Liberty, Obligations, etc. belong to the Indicative Mode: It is their Conditionality, their being subsequent, and depending upon something preceding, that determines them to the Subjunctive Mode. (Lowth 1769: 38)

---

[1] In this paper, as for the citations from the works of prescriptive grammarians, all the italics are of their original.

(3) It is a general rule, that when something contingent or doubtful is implied, the subjunctive ought to be used: [. . .]. Conjunctions that are of a positive and absolute nature require the indicative mood. (Murray 1806: 193)

The three grammarians, who are the representatives of the eighteenth-century grammars, say almost the same thing: When doubt or hesitation is implied, the subjunctive should be used; when expressing the matter of fact, the indicative. This idea is adopted by nineteenth-century grammarians. Furthermore, the attitude toward the differentiation between moods might have hardened in the nineteenth century. Some grammarians make sarcastic remarks about the 'wrong' usages:

(4) There is a great necessity for care as to this matter [=the distinction between moods]; for the meaning of what we write is very much affected when we make use of the modes indiscriminately. (Cobbett 1823: 140)

(5) No speaker of good English, expressing himself conditionally, says, Though thou *fallest* or Though he *falls* but, Though thou *fall*, and Though he *fall*; (Brown 1845: 54, from Visser 1966: §837)

Thus, prescriptive grammarians insisted on the distinction between the use of the (present) subjunctive and that of the indicative throughout the eighteenth and nineteenth centuries.

4. Occurrences and frequencies

This section will deal with the brief survey of the occurrences and frequencies of the subjunctive in this research. Table 1 shows the distribution of the subjunctive examples divided into categories and the ratio to the total of the finite verbs in each drama text. The data is classified in the same way as Denison (1998). As the purpose of this study is to reveal the chronological decline (or revival) of the subjunctive, phrases which are still commonly used in PDE (i.e. the optative subjunctive such as *bless you* and formulas such as *had better, would rather*, etc.) are omitted.

In Table 1, seven prose dramas are placed in chronological order, and six of them, from *Susan* to *Earnest* are relatively casual dramas. They are melodramas or comedies. *Super* has more formal taste which reflects the philosophy of G. B. Shaw. *Harold* at the right side is separated from the other dramas because it is a verse drama and its data looks quite different from the others. As we can see, the frequency of the subjunctive decreases in order of times toward the end of the nineteenth century. However, we should note that the frequency of the subjunctive in *Super* is larger than those of the four preceding dramas. Also, the frequency in *Harold* is outstandingly high. In *Harold*, the subjunctive is observed in main

Table 1: Occurrences and frequencies of the subjunctive in the eight dramas

Title Clausal type	Susan (1829)	Money (1840)	Game (1851)	Acres (1869)	Silver (1882)	Earnest (1895)	Super (1903)	Harold (1876)
Main 1[2]	0	4	0	0	0	0	0	7
Main 2	0	0	0	0	0	0	1	1
Temporal	0	0	0	0	0	0	0	5
Rejected comparison	2	0	0	1	2	0	4	0
Final	0	1	0	0	0	0	0	4
Consecutive	0	0	0	0	0	0	0	0
Concessive	1	0	0	0	0	0	1	0
Conditional	12	15	8	5	7	4	19	30
Nominal	3	1	1	0	0	0	1	8
Total	18	21	9	6	9	4	26	55
Frequency (%)	1.11	0.76	0.40	0.21	0.22	0.15	0.41	2.36

clauses and even in temporal and final clauses. Therefore, Table 1 implies that two points are concerned with the frequency of the subjunctive: 1) the date when the drama was written; 2) the literary genre of dramas. These tendencies are clearly observed in conditional clauses which will be considered in Section 5.

5. Close analysis

In this section, from the categories displayed in Section 4, I am going to pick up two points which are of special interest: 1) the chronological change of the verb forms in conditional clauses; 2) the choice between the subjunctive form *were* and its substitute form *was*.

5.1 Conditional clauses

In LModE, the main event which happened in conditional clauses is the disuse of the present subjunctive. Denison (1998: 298) states that nowhere is the present subjunctive obligatory. According to Denison (1998: 297), the alternatives of the present subjunctive in LModE are modal auxiliary periphrasis and the present indicative. The data of this paper, however, does not support his view. As for PDE, Quirk et al. (1985: 1012) point out that the present indicative appears more frequently in conditional clauses and that the only case where the present subjunctive could occasionally occur is in formal styles.

First, let us look at the data of conditional clauses found in the dramas under consideration. The eight dramas provide: 50 occurrences of the present subjunctive, 50 cases of the past subjunctive, 218 instances of modal preterit inflections (including 12 cases of *was*), 17 examples of the modal auxiliary periphrasis, 242 occurrences of the indicative, and 203 cases of indistinguishable forms. Table 2 below shows the distribution of verbal types in the conditional clauses:

---

[2] Main 1 = Main clauses without protases; Main 2 = Main clauses with protases.

Table 2: The distribution of verbal types in the conditional clauses of the eight dramas (%)

Verbal types \ Title	Susan (1829)	Money (1840)	Game (1851)	Acres (1869)	Silver (1882)	Earnest (1895)	Super (1903)	Harold (1876)
Present subjunctive	13.3	10.0	3.1	1.0	0	0	2.5	35.4
Past subjunctive	6.7	3.6	9.2	3.9	6.7	6.3	6.9	12.3
Modal preterit inflection[3]	31.7	30.0	27.7	28.4	26.0	29.7	30.4	15.4
Periphrasis	3.3	2.7	1.5	1.0	2.0	3.1	2.0	1.5
Indicative	33.3	37.3	26.2	35.3	23.0	32.8	34.3	15.3
Indistinguishable	11.7	16.4	32.3	30.4	42.0	28.1	24.0	20.0

As for the seven prose dramas (*Harold* will be discussed later), the major change is in the ratio of 'Present subjunctive', which declines chronologically, although there is a slight upswing in *Super*. Then, by what form is the present subjunctive replaced? Judging from the fact that the ratio of 'Past subjunctive', 'Modal preterit inflection' and 'Periphrasis' in Table 2 neither increase nor decrease, it is natural to conclude that the substitute of the present subjunctive is the indicative. Although the ratio of 'Indicative' itself does not increase, most of the data in 'Indistinguishable' are probably those of the indicative having either plural subjects or those of the second person singular. From Table 2, we can see that the total number of 'Indicative' and 'Indistinguishable' grows larger. It has been generally agreed that modal auxiliaries are one of the substitutes for the present subjunctive in conditional clauses. However, looking at my data, it would be more appropriate to state that the subjunctive is supplanted 'exclusively' by the indicative.[4]

As mentioned in Section 3, prescriptive grammarians in LModE period made efforts to preserve the present subjunctive. For instance, Lindley Murray states:

(6) It may be considered as a rule, that the changes of termination are necessary, when these two circumstances concur: 1st, When the subject is of a dubious and contingent nature; and 2nd, When the verb has a reference to future time. (Murray 1806: 195)

He states that the present subjunctive should be used when two circumstances happen together: 1) when expressing doubt or contingency; 2) referring to future time. In my research, in the dramas written in the first half of the nineteenth century, this rule is kept. For example:

(7) If the prisoner *be* executed, he is a murdered man. (*Susan* 200)[5]
(8) [. . .], if he ever *marry* again, I think he will show his respect to the sainted Maria by marrying a black woman. (*Money* 165)

---

3   Modal preterit inflection = Preterit verb forms used to show the contrast not of time but of modality.
4   González-Álvarez (2003: 305) also observes the same point. She compares the data of the seventeenth century with those of the nineteenth century and argues that modal auxiliaries do not act as the main subjunctive substitutes in conditional protases.
5   In citations from drama texts under consideration, all the italics are mine.

In (7), the event in which the prisoner is executed is still uncertain and it is a future matter. Therefore, the subjunctive form *be* is used. Also, the form *marry* in (8) implies that it is doubtful for the speaker if 'he' would marry in the future. On the contrary, as illustrated below, in dramas written in the latter half of the nineteenth century, to express uncertain future, the indicative is often employed. [6]

(9) [...] and if he *is* moved in this bitter weather, it will kill him (*Silver* 77)

In (9), the mother begs her landlord not to force her and her child outside. Her anxiety is still an uncertain matter. However, the indicative form *is* is used. Thus, it has been implied by this research that the present subjunctive declined and was replaced by the indicative in spite of the rule set by the grammarians.

Another significant point seen from Table 2 is the characteristics of literary genre. There is a big flow in my data where the subjunctive decreases chronologically. However, *Super* and especially *Harold* are outside of this main stream. The reason seems to be the level of formality of the play. As seen from Table 2, the verbs in the conditional clauses of *Super* contain 2.5% of the present subjunctive, although in the other dramas written in the late nineteenth century, the ratio is zero %. Examples found in *Super* include:

(10) How if a time *come* when this shall cease to be true? (*Super* 164)
(11) But if Hell *be* so beautiful as this, how glorious must heaven be! (*Super* 152)

Harold, as illustrated below, displays as much as 35.4% of the present subjunctive in the total of conditional clauses. It deserves attention that there is a big difference in the frequency of the subjunctive between prose dramas and verse dramas.

(12) Except it *be* a soft one, / And undereaten to the fall. (*Harold* 614)
(13) If the king *fall*, may not the kingdom fall? (*Harold* 637)

As so far revealed, the frequency of the present subjunctive in conditional clauses is influenced by two factors: 1) dates when the works were written; 2) the formality of the play.

5.2 The choice between *were* and *was*
Another interesting point concerned with subjunctive substitutes observed in this study is the use of *was* instead of *were*. The data of this paper provide 32 instances of *was* mainly in *as if* constructions and conditional clauses. In this paper, I am going to examine the choice between *were* and *was* from the viewpoints of literary genre, the personality of each character, and the situation in which they speak.

---

[6] It is, however, sometimes difficult to know how the character in the drama truly thinks about the matter.

Curme (1931: 427) and Visser (1966: §880; §890) point out that *was* as a subjunctive substitute tends to be employed in writing since the seventeenth century. According to Visser (1966: §880), such *was* is condemned by prescriptive grammarians in the eighteenth and nineteenth centuries. For example, William Cobbett in his work says:

(14) If I *be*; If I *were*; If he *were*; and not if I *was*, if he *was*. (Cobbett 1823: 139)

Cobbett clearly indicates that the use of *was* is wrong. On the other hand, the form *was* gradually comes to be regarded as an optional form to represent modality in PDE.

The numbers of *were* and *was* uttered by each character in the dramas under consideration are displayed in Table 3.[7] The data is categorised according to the character's vocation and social classes they belong to.

Table 3: The numbers of *were* and *was* spoken by each character

Title	Name	vocation	class[8]	were	was
Susan	Doggrass	Smuggler	L	2	1
	Dolly	Factory girl	L	1	2
	Gnatbrain	Unknown	L	3	0
	Hatchet	Smuggler	L	1	0
	William	Seaman	L	2	3
Money	Blount	Knight	U	1	0
	Clara	Companion	M	3	0
	Evelyn	Secretary	M	3	0
	Graves	Executor	M	1	0
	Sir John	Knight	U	1	1
Game	Earthworm	Creditor	M	1	0
	Hawk	Speculator	M	3	1
	Noble	Clerk	L	1	0
	Prospectus	Creditor	M	1	0
Acres	Brown	Merchant	M	1	1
	Bunter	Self-made man	L	0	6
	Mrs. Bunter	Bunter's wife	L	1	1
	Fitz-Urse	Cousin of Lilian	M	0	4
	Lilian	Esquire's daughter	U	2	0
	Lady Matilda	Esquire's wife	U	1	0
Silver	Corkett	Clerk	L	0	1

---

7   Since no occurrence of *was* is observed in *Harold*, the data is not shown in Table 3. Also, the data of *Game* will not be included in the following discussion because the amount of data is too limited.
8   U=Upper; M=Middle; L=Low.

	Cripps	Locksmith	L	0	1
	Denver	Laborer	L	1	0
	Jaikes	Servant	L	0	1
	Nelly	Denver's wife (teacher)	L	7	0
	Olive	Skinner's wife	L	1	0
Earnest	Algernon	Playboy (of wealthy family)	M	2	4
	Lady Bracknell	Lord Bracknell's wife	U	0	2
	Cecily	Mr. Cardew's grand daughter	M	0	1
	Chasuble	Canon	M	1	0
	Gwendolen	Lord Bracknell's daughter	U	1	0
	Jack	Mr. Cardew's adopted child	M	0	1
Super	Ann	Ward of Ramsden and Tanner	M	4	0
	Ana	Elderly lady	M	1	0
	The Devil	Devil	?	1	0
	Don Juan	Legendary person	?	2	0
	Hector	Rich American	M	0	1
	Mendosa	Robber	L	2	0
	Octavius	Poet	M	1	0
	Ramsden	Elderly gentleman	M	1	0
	Tanner	Revolutionist	M	7	0
	Violet	Sister of Octavius	M	2	0

Broadly speaking, the use of *was* is quite limited in *Money* and *Super*, and in the other five prose dramas, there is a rivalry between *were* and *was*. In details, the dramas *Susan, Money, Acres, Silver, Earnest* and *Super* can be divided into three types: in Type 1), there is a clear distinction between the characters who use *were* and those who employ *was*; in Type 2), the same person utters both *were* and *was*; and in Type 3), there is only one occurrence of *was* exceptionally, although in the rest of the text, the form *were* always appears to represent modality.

5.2.1 Type 1: Class and intelligence (*Silver* and *Acres*)

In *Silver*[9], Nelly, Olive, and Denver employ *were*, not a single case of *was*. Conversely, *was* is exclusively used by Corkett, Cripps, and Jaikes. Except for Nelly, the number of examples of each character is only one, however, this division of persons by the use of *were/was* clearly coincides with the level of 'intelligence' of each character in the drama. All the persons who utter *were* in *Silver* are described as 'smart' people. For example, Nelly earns her living by teaching and Denver succeeds in business of silver in America. Especially, the data of Nelly (seven out of seven occurrences of *were*) evidently shows that she is intelligent enough to speak properly. One of the examples is shown in (15).The three people who em-

---

9   In *Silver*, the examples exhibited in Table 3 are observed in pp. 158, 161, 162, 163, 168, 172, 174, 176, 178, 192.

ploy *was* are a servant and villains of the city. As illustrated in (16), their speech often contains mistakes of grammars, and thus they are depicted as typical 'unintelligent' citizens in the low class. There are similar cases in Jane Austen's works where *was* is "deliberately" used to represent the character's carelessness (Phillipps 1970: 157).

(15) NELLY. [. . .] and calling out, 'Will! Will! come back to me, come back to me, if it *were* but for a moment! (*Silver* 82)
(16) CRIPPS. [. . .] in stead of keeping us hangin' about the place as if we *was* suspicious characters. (*Silver* 87)

Although the examples of *Acres*[10] cannot be divided as explicitly as those of *Silver*, a certain 'class-distinction'[11] is observed: The upper-class characters, Lilian and Lady Matilda, use *were*; *Was* is employed by the low-class persons especially Mr. Bunter, a self-made man. Though Firz-Urse belongs to the middle class, he is portrayed as an airhead who is often made fun of by Lilian. This could be the reason why he utters four out of four instances of *was*. Examples found in *Acres* include:

(17) LILIAN. Oh, if I *were* only a gentleman farmer! (*Acres* 262)
(18) BUNTER. Sometimes I feel as if she *was* insulting of me, [. . .]. (*Acres* 289)

5.2.2 Type 2: The state of mind (*Susan* and *Earnest*)

The second type is represented by *Susan* and *Earnest*. In these dramas, the same person uses both *were* and *was* almost equally, and the choice seems to be affected by the character's state of mind.

In *Susan*, as illustrated below, the examples of William provide two occurrences of *were* and three cases of *was*:

(19) WILLIAM. I feel as if I *were* driving before the gale of pleasure for the haven of joy. (*Susan* 172)
(20) WILLIAM. Your honours, I feel as if I *were* in irons, or seized to the grating, to stand here and listen --- (*Susan* 192)
(21) WILLIAM. Damn it, I feel as if half of me *was* wintering in the Baltic, and the other half stationed in Jamaica. (*Susan* 174)
(22) WILLIAM. I've come fifteen knots an hour, yet I felt as if I *was* driving astern all the time. (*Susan* 176)
(23) WILLIAM. If they are drafted aboard of us, all I wish is that I *was* boatswain's mate for their sake. (*Susan* 178)

---

10 In *Acres*, the data shown in Table 3 are found in pp. 254, 255, 262, 266, 270, 274, 284, 285, 289, 295, 299, 301, 303, 304, 308.
11 With this viewpoint, the data of *Money* could also be explained. As seen from Table 3, *Money*, a story which depicts the upper-class society, provides rather high frequency of *were*.

In the lines of William, *were* appears when he is calm or when he is in public. The case (19) is spoken tenderly to the sailors and (20) is delivered at court to the majesty. On the contrary, as for (21), (22), and (23), he is saying to himself in private circumstances. Especially, the examples (21) and (22) are uttered when he is emotional because, coming back from the long voyage, he is shocked to know that his wife is not waiting for him. Although it is sometimes difficult to decide whether a character is calm or emotional, William seems to have a tendency to use *were* when he is composed and when in public, and to utter *was* when he talks passionately or when he is in private situations.

The examples of Algernon in *Earnest* are not as clear-cut as those of William in *Susan*. However, Algernon is liable to employ *were* when he is tranquil and *was* when he is upset. As illustrated below, the speech of Algernon displays two occurrences of *were* and four cases of *was*:

(24) ALGERNON. Modern life would be very tedious if it *were* either, and modern literature a complete impossiblity! (*Earnest* 258)
(25) ALGERNON. If I *were* in mourning you would stay with me, I suppose. (*Earnest* 281)
(26) ALGERNON. You look as if your name *was* Ernest. (*Earnest* 257)
(27) ALGERNON. If it *wasn't* for Bunbury's extraordinary bad health, for instance, I wouldn't be able to dine with you at Willis's tonight, [. . .]. (*Earnest* 258)
(28) ALGERNON. But seriously, Cecily... (*moving to her*) if my name *was* Algy, couldn't you love me? (*Earnest* 285)
(29) ALGERNON. If it *was* my business, I wouldn't talk about it. (*Earnest* 293)

The sentences (24) and (25) are uttered when Algernon, being calm, enjoys arguing with Jack. On the contrary, in (26), (28), and (29), he is disturbed. In (26), he is surprised to know that his close friend's real name is Jack for the first time. The example (28) shows his shock at Cecily's words that she cannot love a man unless his name is Ernest. In (29), he is in desperation because he was ditched by Cecily.

5.2.3 Type 3: Exceptional cases (*Money* and *Super*)

In *Money* and *Super*, *were* predominantly appears to represent modality. However, each drama has one exception which cannot be explained from the viewpoints discussed in sections 5.2.1 and 5.2.2. As the following examples illustrate, in *Money*, the only one example of *was* is spoken by Sir John, and in *Super* by Hector:

(30) SIR JOHN. I would not have said this for the world, if I *was* not a little anxious about my own girl. (*Money* 195)
(31) HECTOR. I feel as if I *was* stealing his money. (*Super* 124)

The interpretation of this phenomenon is difficult, but at least it is clear that both Sir John and Hector are portrayed as 'out of place' persons in each story. Sir John is the meanest character in *Money*. Hector is, as Shaw himself explains (*Super* 120-121), an American whose personality looks strange for the other British characters. The solitude of these two gentlemen might be one of the reasons for the use of *was*.

5.2.4 Generalisation

By the data of occurrences of *were* and *was* displayed so far, though they are limited, I found that two factors are concerned with the choice between *were* and *was*: 1) the genre of dramas; 2) the dispositions of characters. As for 1), the present study has revealed that in dramas having formal tastes such as *Super* and *Harold*, the form *were* exclusively appears. As for 2), it has been shown that the choice between *were* and *was* is affected by the character's social class, the level of education and the state of mind. In short, *were*, the 'correct' subjunctive form in prescriptive grammars, represents gentility and formality. On the contrary, *was*, the 'incorrect' form condemned by grammarians, symbolises lowliness and casualness.

6. Conclusion

In sum, from the historical viewpoint, the subjunctive decreases chronologically. In such situation, the choice between subjunctive and non subjunctive forms depends upon the character's social class, intelligence, and the state of mind in the dramas which I examined in this paper. Also, the possibility has been shown that the frequency of the subjunctive is affected by literary genre, which means the more formal the drama is, the more subjunctive expressions are preserved. I conclude that the subjunctive is a symbol of gentility and formality in LModE.

References

Primary sources

Booth, Michael R. (ed.)
    1969-1976 *English Plays of the Nineteenth Century*, Vol. 1, Vol. 3. Oxford: Clarendon Press.
    1995 *The Lights o' London and Other Victorian Plays*. Oxford: Oxford University Press.

Byrne, Sandie (ed.)
    2002 *George Bernard Shaw's Plays*. 2nd ed. New York and London: W. W. Norton & Company.

Jackson, Russell (ed.)
    1982   *Plays by Henry Arthur Jones*. Cambridge: Cambridge University Press.

Oxford Standard Authors (ed.)
    1953   *Poetical Works: Including the Plays*. London: Oxford University Press.

Raby, Peter (ed.)
    1995   *The Importance of Being Earnest and Other Plays*. Oxford: Oxford University Press.

Secondary sources

Alford, Henry
    1884   *The Queen's English*. A reprint series of books relating to the English Language. Vol. 21. Ed. Takanobu Otsuka. Tokyo: Nan'un-do, 1968.

Araki, K. and M. Ukaji
    1984   *Eigoshi IIIA*. [*The History of the English Lanugage IIIA.*] Eigogaku Taikei. 10. Tokyo: Taishukan Shoten.

Bailey, Richard W.
    1996   *Nineteenth-Century English*. Ann Arbor: University of Michigan Press.

Beal, Joan C.
    2004   *English in Modern Times 1700-1945*. London: Arnold.

Cobbett, William
    1823   *A Grammar of the English Language*. Rpt. ed. Oxford: Oxford University Press, 2002.

Curme, George O.
    1931   *Syntax*. Boston; London: D. C. Heath.

Denison, David
    1998   "Syntax", in *The Cambridge History of the English Language, IV: 1776-1997*. Ed. Suzanne Romaine. Cambridge: Cambridge University Press, 92-329.

Fowler, H. W.
    1926   *A Dictionary of Modern English Usage*. Oxford: Clarendon Press.

González-Álvarez, Dolores
    2003   "*If he come* vs. *if he comes, if he shall come*: Some Remarks on the Subjunctive in Conditional Protases in Early and Late Modern English", *Neuphilologische Mitteilungen* 104: 303-313.

Görlach, Manfred
 1999 *English in Nineteenth-Century England.* Cambridge: Cambridge University Press.
 2001 *Eighteenth-Century English.* Heidelberg: C. Winter.

Harsh, Wayne
 1968 *The Subjunctive in English.* Alabama: University of Alabama Press.

Jespersen, Otto
 1924 *The Philosophy of Grammar.* London: George Allen & Unwin.

Johnson, Samuel
 1755 *A Dictionary of the English Language: in which the words are deduced from their originals: and illustrated in their different significations by examples from the best writers: to which are prefixed, a history of the language, and an English grammar.* 2 vols. Rpt. ed. New York: AMS Press, 1967.

Kikusawa, Namiko
 2007 "The subjunctive in Nineteenth-Century English Dramas." Unpublished MA thesis. Kyoto University.

Lowth, Robert
 1769 *A Short Introduction to English Grammar: With critical notes.* Ed. Takanobu Otsuka. A reprint series of books relating to the English language. Vol. 13. Tokyo: Nan'un-do, 1968.

Murray, Lindley
 1806 *English Grammar, Adapted to the Different Classes of Learners.* A reprint series of books relating to the English language. Vol. 19. Ed. Takanobu Otsuka. Tokyo: Nan'un-do, 1971.

Phillipps, K. C.
 1970 *Jane Austen's English.* London: André Deutsch.
 1984 *Language and Class in Victorian England.* London: Basil Blackwell.

Priestley, Joseph
 1769 *The Rudiments of English Grammar.* Ed. Takanobu Otsuka. A reprint series of books relating to the English language. Vol. 14. Tokyo: Nan'un-do, 1971.

Quirk, Randolph — Sidney Greenbaum — Geoffrey Leech — Jan Svartvik
 1985 *A Comprehensive Grammar of the English Language.* London: Longman.

Rissanen, Matti
 1999 "Syntax", in *The Cambridge History of the English Language, III: 1476-1776.* Ed. Roger Lass. Cambridge: Cambridge University Press, 187-331.

Strang, Barbara M. H.
   1970   *A History of English*. London: Methuen.

Suematsu, Nobuko
   2004   *Jane Austen no Eigo: sono Rekishiteki Shakaigengogakuteki Kenkyu* [*Jane Austen's English: Historical and sociolinguistic perspectives*]. Tokyo: Kaibunsha.

Traugott, Elizabeth Closs
   1972   *A History of English Syntax: A Transformational Approach to the History of English Sentence Structure*. New York: Holt, Rinehart and Winston.

Turner, John F.
   1980   "The Marked Subjunctive in Contemporary English", *Studia Neophilologica* 52: 271-277.

Visser, F. Th.
   1963-73   *An Historical Syntax of the English Language*. 4 vols. Leiden: E. J. Brill.

24 On the Development of *because*: A Corpus-based Study
Ji Won Lee, Seoul National University, Graduate School

This paper follows the rise and development of the causal connective *because* in Middle and Early Modern English. The causal marker of native origin, *forþam þe*, used since the beginning of English, decreased in number and ultimately became obsolete by the end of Middle English period. Causality being a basic quotidian concept, it is logical to assume that the decline of the traditional connective is tied to the introduction of the new form, *because*. In this light, the paper addresses the rise and decline of markers of reason. By aid of data from the Helsinki Corpus, the study investigates the formation and stabilisation of *because* to its present form in a diachronic perspective. In the process, grammaticalisation of *because* is discussed.

1. Introduction

This paper is about the rise and development of the causal connective *because*. In order to express causative relationship, we use *because* on a daily basis. But we did not have this expression in English until the second half of Middle English period (1150-1500). Furthermore, it even looked slightly different (*by cause that*) when it first came into English.

Old English had a native connective *forþam þe*[1], which has approximately the same meaning and function as *because*. *Forþam þe* existed until the 15th century but its occurrences sharply decreased entering the second half of 13th century (see section 2 below). In its place, a causal marker of Anglo-Norman origin[2], *because*, was adopted in the 14th century. Study revealed that *because* underwent transformation before it was realised into current form (PDE *because* <ModE *be cause (that)* < ME *by cause (of, that)* < Anglo-Norman *par cause de, à cause que*).

In the following sections the paper addresses the formation and stabilisation of *because* as an English vocabulary. In doing so, a process called grammaticalisation is discussed. The Helsinki Corpus of English Texts (HC) is used for diachronic research, along with the Word Smith Concordance Program. Oxford English Dictionary (OED) also served as a valuable tool. We begin with the native causal connective *forþam þe*.

---

1   *Forþam þe* is used here as a representative form of all the variations preposition *for* + dative and instrumental demonstrative pronoun (*ðon, þam, ðam, ði* etc.) + subordinating particle (*þe, þat*) construction takes to express causality.

2   For detailed explanation on the origin of *because* refer to Molencki paper in this book.

2. The native causal connective *forþam þe*

Forþam þe was the causal connective used during the Old and the Early Middle English period. Its internal construction can be broken down to *for* followed by various forms of dative or instrumental demonstrative pronoun *ðan, þan, þi, þam* and subordinating particle *þe/ðat.* As spelling was not yet fixed in the earlier times, as many as 74 different written forms were found in the HC. Its primary meaning in the sentence is the same as today's *because* in that it marks the relationship of reason and consequence. Here are examples from the M1 (1150-1250) period[3] of the HC:

(1) Þerefter wæx suythe micel uuerre betuyx þe king & Randolf eorl of Cæstre: noht *forþi ðat* he ne iaf him al ðat he cuthe axen him, alse he dide alle other. (After this waxed a very great war betwixt the king and Randolph, Earl of Chester; not *because* he did not give him all that he could ask him, as he did to all others.) (*Peterborough Chronicle* AD 1140)

(2) Mi feader & Mi moder *for-þi þt* ich nule þe forsaken; habbe forsake me. (My father and my mother, *because* I haven't forsaken you, have forsaken me.)(*ST Juliana* M2/HC)

Table1 below shows the occurrences of *forþam þe* in all periods of the HC. The number drops noticeably in the M2 (1250-1350) period and no instance is found entering the Early Modern English period:

Table1: Occurrences of *forþam þe* in the HC (per 100,000 words)

O1	O2	O3	O4	M1	M2	M3	M4
46	149	122	154	76	2	2	3

The new form *because*, on the other hand, gains frequency starting from the M3 (1350-1420) period. Table2 below is where the occurrences of *because* is summarised:

Table2: Occurrences of *because* in HC (per 100,000 words)

M3	M4	E1	E2	E3
19	31	98	121	72

It is interesting to note that just as there were many forms of *forþam þe, because* did not emerge fully fixed in form. In the next section, such morphological diversity and the significance of it will be discussed in terms of grammaticalisation.

---

3 Time division here follows the convention of the Helsinki Corpus: O1 (-850), O2 (850-950), O3 (950-1050), O4 (1050-1150), M1 (1150-1250), M2 (1250-1350), M3 (1350-1420), M4 (1420-1500), E1 (1500-1570), E2 (1570-1640), E3 (1640-1710).

3. The new causal connective *because*
3.1. The emergence of *because*

According to OED, *because* was originally a phrase consisting of preposition *by* and substantive *cause*. The dictionary reads that *because* was followed by the preposition *of*, or subordinator *that* or *why* to express cause or purpose. *For cause* was equivalent to *because* thus *for because* is said to be found as an interim form. Results obtained from searching the ME and EME section of the HC is provided in 3.1.1, starting with the internal construction of *because*.

3.1.1. *Because*: its form

Data from the HC rendered ample variations of *because* which reflected its change in form over the course of time. Evidence for two points is provided in this subsection. First, since *because* was initially a phrase (*by* + *cause*), two word construction is frequent in the earlier period but statistics lean toward dominance in merged form (*because*) later on. Second, *because* with preposition *by* is prevalent at the incipient developmental stage but ones with *be-* is much more frequently found in the later period of the corpus.

Table3 shows frequencies of merged (*because*) and separate (*by cause*) construction of *because*. The hyphenated form *be-cause that* can be regarded as an interim form on the way to the merged one. In the M3 (1350-1420) period, preposition + noun form prevails at 91%. The percentage drops to 45 in the M4 sub-period and in the EME period, *because* is mostly a one word construction.

Table3: Occurrences of merged and separate construction of *because*

	preposition separated	preposition hyphenated	preposition merged	total
M3	28(91%)	1	5	34
M4	30(45%)	17(26%)	19(29%)	66
E1	10	0	177(95%)	187
E2	8	0	222(97%)	230
E3	0	0	124(100%)	124

Data analysis from another angle reveals that prepositional elements are headed towards unity as well. The original preposition *by* prevails in the earlier periods but increasingly *be-* becomes dominant. Table4 shows the change:

Table4: Spelling variations of the prepositional elements

	be-	*by-*	*bi-*	total
M3	9	22(65%)	3	34
M4	28(42%)	36(54%)	2	66
E1	114(61%)	41(22%)	32	187
E2	222(97%)	7	1	230
E3	124			124

In Table4 above, *because* in combination with the preposition *by* accounts for 65% of the total make up in the M3 (1350-1420) period. But in the subsequent period, the percentage drops to 54. When it enters the EME period, *be-*, presumably the phonetically reduced form of *by*, occupies majority of the construction. Finally in the E3 period, the spelling of *because* is unified to current usage. Although the knowledge of the arbitrariness of medieval spellings may cast doubts on the validity of this study, general trend is strong enough to conclude that the transformation of *because* into current form is reflected in the data.

3.1.2. Because: because that and because of
In PDE, *because of* is a prepositional phrase followed by a noun attributed as the cause. The ratio of prepositional phrasal use (*because of*) to subordinating conjunctional use of *because* in the HC data is shown in Table5. The proportion of the prepositional phrase decreases with time resting at 7% (8/124☐0.065) in the E3 period. The earlier form *because that* shows the most remarkable change in frequency in that it occupies 56% (19/34☐0.558) of the *because*-related marker slot in the M3 (1350-1420) period but occurring only once in the E3 (1640-1700) period.

Table5: Occurrences of *because*-related grammatical markers

	because that	because	because of	total
M3	19	1	14	34
M4	10	41	15	66
E1	16	156	15	187
E2	7	207	16	230
E3	1	115	8	124

History of the English language tells us that subordinating particle *that* (*þe*, *þat*) came after the connective to mark its function in a sentence, one prominent example being *forþam þe*, the predecessor of *because*. Same rule seems to have applied to *because* since it came with the subordinator in its early forms (19 compared to 1 in the M3 period). But frequency drops at a considerable rate and by the E3 period, the situation is completely reversed (115 appearing without as opposed to 1 with the subordinator).

3.1.3. The interim form *for because*
As mentioned in 3.1, the interim form *for because* was found in the HC. Examples (3) and (4) are from the M4 (1420-1500) and E2 (1570-1640) period respectively. And (5) is the OED's example of the interim construction from the M4 period.

(3) Þen *for bycause* þat Sonday ys no day of fastyng, þerfor ȝe schull begyn your fast at Aske-Wanysday. (Then *because* Sunday is no day of fasting, therefore you shall begin your fast at Ash Wednesday.)(Mirk's *Festial* P82 M4/HC)

(4) And the Angel of the LORD called vnto Abraham out of heauen the second time, And said, By my selfe haue I sworne, saith the LORD, *for because* thou hast done this thing, and hast not withheld thy sonne, thine onely sonne, That in blessing I will blesse thee, and in multiplying, I will multiply thy seed as the starres of the heauen, and as the sand which is vpon the sea shore. (The angel of the LORD called to Abraham from heaven a second time and said, "I swear by myself, declares the LORD, that *because* you have done this and have not withheld your son, your only son, I will surely bless you and make your descendants as numerous as the stars in the sky and as the sand on a seashore.)(*The Old Testament* Authorized Version E2/HC)

(5) *For because that* Saturne is of late so sterynge. (*Because* Saturn is lately so strange)(1400/*Mandeville*/OED)

For because construction was rare, appearing 4 times in the M4 (1420-1500) period, 7 times in the E1 (1500-1570) period and once in the E2 (1570-1640) period before it was no longer found. Relative rarity of the interim construction compared to *forþam þe* and *because* may indicate that the transition was met without resistance from the public and that the new causal marker caught on quickly. We discuss the grammaticalisation of *because* in the next section.

3.2. Grammaticalisation of *because*

Fischer et al. (2000: 286) defines grammaticalisation as "a process whereby a lexical item, with full referential meaning, developments into a grammatical marker". According to Hopper and Traugott (2003: 1), "grammaticalisation refers to that part of study of language change that is concerned with such questions as how lexical items and constructions come in certain linguistic contexts to serve grammatical functions or how grammatical items develop new grammatical functions".

The case we have here is a grammatical item (PP *by cause*) becoming a more grammatical item (Conjunction *because*). In 3.2.1 some trees are shown to exemplify this development. And in 3.2.2, mechanisms of grammaticalisation are discussed in full. We commence with the tree structure analogy.

3.2.1. Tree structure analogy

In the introduction, *because* is said to have developed from a phrase, *by* + *cause* + (*that*). Tree on the left below is the internal make of *because* when it was first adopted. The appended *that* functions as a marker of subordination (see 3.1.2 above). Tree on the right below shows the grammaticalised structure of *because*, in which case it appears both as a PP (for example, *because of*) and as a conjunction. Look at the trees below:

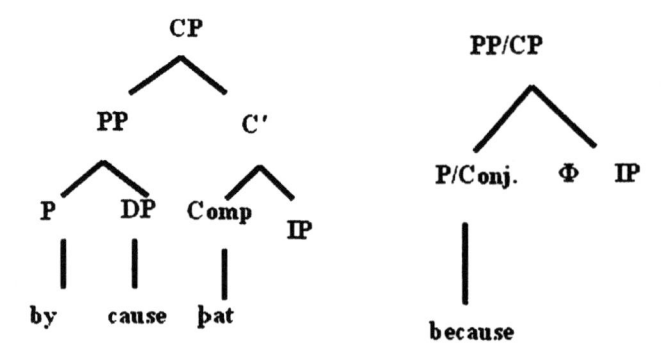

```
        CP                          PP/CP
       /  \                         /    \
      PP   C'                   P/Conj.  Φ   IP
     /  \    \                     |
    P   DP   Comp                  |
    |   |    |    IP            because
    |   |    |
    by cause þat
```

The tree structure of *by cause þat* is analogous to that of its predecessor, *forþam þe*. Consider the following:

Figure2: The tree structure analogy between *forþam þe* and *because that*

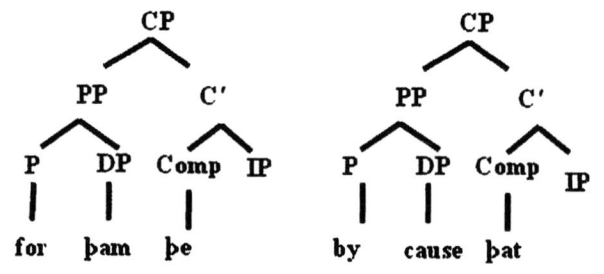

```
       CP                        CP
      /  \                      /  \
     PP   C'                   PP   C'
    / \    \                  / \    \
   P  DP   Comp  IP          P  DP   Comp  IP
   |  |    |                 |  |    |
   for þam þe                by cause þat
```

Both *forþam þe* and *because* are in the form of a preposition followed by a substantive and a subordinating particle. With the exception of the subordinating particle *þe* and *þat*, trees bear striking resemblance. But knowing that even *forþam þe* had more occurrences of *þat* than *þe* in the ME period, it is fair to assume that *because* developed imitating the structure of *forþam þe*. For reference, occurrences of *þe* and *þat* with *forþam þe* are given below in Table6. The subordinating particle is varied in appearance but can be grouped around few characteristic patterns. *Þe* (413 and *ðe* 156) is by far the dominant marker of subordination. But its numerousness is accounted for in the OE period only. Out of the 569 cases with the use of *þe* (and *ðe*) for the *forþam þe* constructions, the ME portion in the total frequency is only 48 instances (8.4%). But *that* and its equivalents (*ðat, þatt, þt*) are better choice for the ME turnouts: 48 instances out of 96 (50%) employ *that* as subordinating particle in the ME period. Table6 below summarises the finding:

Table 6: Occurrences of the subordinating particle with *forþam þe* (absolute figures)

Type	Number of Tokens

Table 6: Occurrences of the subordinating particle with *forþam þe* (absolute figures)

Type	Number of Tokens		
	Total	OE	ME
þe	413	378	35
ðe	156	143	13
þatt	21	-	21
þæt	14	14	-
þat	11	-	11
þt	11	-	11
ðæt	10	9	1
ðætte	4	4	-
ðat	3	-	3
þet	1	1	-
þætte	1	1	-
that	1	-	1

One objection to the tree structure analogy is the seemingly reversed analytic to synthetic development of *because*. Against the gradual typological change of English towards analyticity in the Middle English period, *because* here is seen to become even more synthetic (*by cause* → *because*). But it may be that the loan word status of *because* has overridden the general development trend. This should be an interesting topic for further study. For now, we move on to features of grammaticalisation noted in the formation of *because*.

3.2.2. Mechanisms of Grammaticalisation

In Heine (2003: 578-9), grammaticalisation is said to involve four interrelated mechanisms:

i. desemanticisation: loss in meaning content
ii. extension: use in new contexts
iii. decateorialisation: loss in morphosyntactic properties characteristic of the source forms, including the loss of independent word status
iv. erosion: loss in phonetic substance

In the following, the four mechanisms of grammaticalisation are tested against the development of *because*.

One feature previously covered is (iv) erosion, loss in phonetic substance: phonetically, current causal connective *because* starts with *be-*, the reduced version of *by*. Table 4 in 3.1.1 above demonstrated that *by-* accounted for 65% of the total prepositional element in the M3 (1350-1420) period but later, more grammaticalised version employed *be-* 97% of the time in the E2 (1570-1640) period. This explains the gradual phonetic erosion of the preposition in the course of grammaticalisation.

Decategorialisation (iii) refers both to loss in morphosyntactic properties of the source form and loss of independent word status. First, in terms of loss in morphosyntactic property, look at the following examples, which exemplify the use of *because* with the noun *cause* still strongly exhibiting its nominal property, appearing with a determiner:

(6) Thus I sawe howe cryste has compassyon of vs *for the cause of* synne, and ryght as I was before with the passyon of cryste fulfilled with payne and compassion. (M3/HC)
(7) Be þe *cause* þat þei scholde rise Erly, Vnto her reste went þei att nihte. (1386/OED)
(8) Thei had in hem no shame nor drede *by the cause* thei wer so used. (1450/OED)

In the examples above, the definite article is placed before *cause*. Examples such as (6), (7) and (8) are found only until the earlier phase of grammaticalisation but are practically non-existent in the EME period (1500-1700). This means *cause* in *because* lost its nominal characteristics and the cohesion between *be-* and *cause* has become stronger. In addition, prepositional element *be-* indicate that the original preposition *by* has lost its word status and is attached to *cause* thereby forming *because*, which testifies another trait of decategorialisation.

Desemanticisation (i) and (ii) extension seem to go hand in hand with the development of *because*. In order to explain the loss of meaning content in *cause* and the use of *because* in a context where the dictionary meaning of *cause* is not the norm, direct reason relationship given by Quirk et al. (1985: 1103) is provided as evidence. In a monumental grammar reference book of Quirk and his colleagues, causal relationship marked by *because* can be divided into three basic categories:

Direct reason relationships
- Cause and effect: inherent objective connection in the real world
- Reason and consequence: speaker's inference of a connection
- Motivation and result: the intention of an animate being that has a subsequent result

Cause-effect, reason-consequence pairs are easier to accept as having directly stemmed from the root word *cause* in *because* construction. But the third category motivation-result makes a person think a little deeper for the connection. OED in fact lists this third sense as *because*'s obsolete meaning (*for the purpose that, in order that*). Here is the example:

(9) They axed him *because* they might acuse hym. (1526 Tindale *Matt. xii. 10*/OED)

This extended use of *because* to account for motivation-result relationship can be attributed to desemanticisation (the semantically blurred sense of the literal phrase *by (the) cause*) and extension (the expanded meaning of the noun *cause*).

Another principle of grammaticalisation applicable to explaining the development of *because* is layering, which according to Hopper (1991:22) is "more than one form available in a language to serve similar or even identical functions".

One definite evidence of this principle is the fact that *forþam þe* and *because* existed in parallel over a certain period of time:

(10) But *forþi þat* þou schalt not erre in þis worching, and wene þat it be oþerwise þen it is, I schal telle þee a lityl more þer-of, as me þinkeþ. (M3/HC)
(11) In Egypt þere ben but fewe Forcelettes or castelles *be cause þat* the contree is so strong of himself. (M3/HC)

And a rather developed stage of layering is exemplified by the occurrences of the interim construction *for because that* (see 3.1.3 (3), (4) and (5) above), all be it fewer in number.

Fischer et al. (1992: 288) listed as parameters of grammaticalisation, 'increase in cohesion' and 'decrease in variability'. In terms of cohesion, the readers are referred to Table3 (Occurrences of merged and separate construction of *because*). As for the decrease in variability, Table 4 (Spelling variations of the prepositional elements) explains the facts well.

In this section, the development of *because* was accounted for in terms of grammaticalisation. It was interesting to observe that *because* largely followed the general mechanism and featured principles of grammaticalisation. Empirical data from the HC served as a valuable source to elucidate the process. The frequency alone cannot explain much but data findings combined with the analysis helped answer questions on the development of a connective.

4. Conclusion

This paper attempted to address the development of the causal connective *because*. Studies to date have mainly focused on the syntactic structure of the connected clause or semantics of causality but not the connective itself. The value of this paper is on the effort to explain the internal construction of *because* per se.

In a historical perspective, the paper followed the steps *because* took from its initial appearance to stabilisation. Findings revealed that the development of *because* reflected features such as increase in cohesion, decrease in variability and other mechanism of grammaticalisation. The tree structure analogy of *forþam þe* and *because* showed that *because* syntactically imitated its predecessor *forþam þe*. The unique status of *because* as a loan word justified its seemingly backward evolution.

The study of one causal connective provided an opportunity for close individual analysis. The value of this study will be augmented if the explanatory adequacy gained here can be expanded to answer for other grammatical markers and broader linguistic phenomenon as well. And in doing so, evidence from the computerised corpora will render results to be more convincing.

References

Fischer, Olga – Ans van Kemenade – Willem Koopman – Wim van der Wurff
2001 *The Syntax of Early English.* Cambridge: Cambridge University Press.

Fisiak, Jacek – M. Krygier (edd.)
1998 *Advances in English Historical Linguistics.* Berlin: Mouton de Gruyter.

Heine, Bernd
2003 "Grammaticalization" in: *The Handbook of Historical Linguistics.* Oxford: Blackwell.

Hopper, Paul
1991 "On Some Principles of Grammaticalization", in: Traugott and Heine (edd.), 17-35.

Hopper, Paul – Elizabeth Closs Traugott
2003 *Grammaticalization.* Cambridge: Cambridge University Press.

Quirk, Randolph – Sidney Greenbaum – Geoffrey Leech – Jan Svartvik
1985 *A Comprehensive Grammar of the English Language.* London-New York: Longman.

Rissanen, Matti
1998 "Towards an integrated view of the development of English: Notes on causal linking", in: Jacek Fisiak and M. Krygier (edd.), 389-406.

Traugott, Elizabeth Closs –Bernd Heine (edd.)
1991 *Approaches to Grammaticalization Vol I: Focus on Theoretical and Methodological Issues.* Amsterdam-Philadelphia: John Benjamins.

25 Joseph Wright's *English Dialect Dictionary* Computerised: A Platform for a New Historical English Dialect Geography
Manfred Markus, University of Innsbruck

1. Introduction

This paper is a revised version of a plenary speech delivered at the 2007 SHELL conference in Nagoya. Given the relatively non-specialist audience of a plenary, my aim was to provide an overview of Joseph Wright's famous *English Dialect Dictionary* (*EDD*) and of the Innsbruck project concerned with it (SPEED, for "Spoken English in Early Dialects"), but also to give evidence of its value for a new historical English dialect geography.

Dialect geography is a widely neglected field of English historical linguistics, and even the Cinderella of Late Modern English studies. No wonder – the (positivist) method of collecting and attributing dialect words without any theoretical concepts as a basis may be exciting for dialectology specialists, but average linguists, whether university staff or students, seem to have mostly bypassed dialects. Indeed, compared to other, more modern branches of English linguistics, dialectology and, even more, dialect geography provide linguistic knowledge that seems eclectic, non-systematic and overloaded with detail.

The computer age now allows for selective accessibility of a huge mass of data at one's fingertips and the evaluation of detailed observations for finding features, patterns and structures. This new method should have, and doubtless will have, an effect on the linguistic exploitation of a dictionary like Wright's *EDD*, so that dialectology and dialect geography, lexicography, computer science, historical linguistics, particularly of Late Modern English, and the history of linguistics can meet and will profit from their cooperation.

In more concrete terms, this paper suggests taking Wright's *EDD* off the dusty shelf and reflecting on the use of the digitised version of the dictionary in historical English dialect geography.

2. Portrayal of Wright and his dictionary (descriptive part)

One of the great linguistic achievements of the nineteenth century, slumbering on library shelves until recently, deserves to be brought back to life by the computer. This is Joseph Wright's *English Dialect Dictionary*, the most comprehensive English dialect dictionary ever produced. Within the Innsbruck project SPEED, Wright's compilation of dialect words used between 1700 and 1900 allows for the retrieval and analysis of many linguistic aspects of Late Modern English to be associated with dialect words, both in Britain and – to a lesser extent – in some English-speaking countries overseas.

2.1. Wright as a person and scholar

Joseph Wright himself should be of interest as a person and scholar. Extremely poor and illiterate in his youth, he profited from the Education Act of 1870 and turned out to be a real Victorian self-made man and an extremely talented philologist. In spite of his late start in academic education, and a long stay abroad (mainly at Heidelberg in Germany), he was finally most successful as a professor of Comparative Philology at the University of Oxford. Time forbids me to present details of this "dishwasher" career here, but I have done this in earlier papers on Wright (cf. Markus 2007b, Markus and Heuberger 2008). In the biography on Wright written by his widow Elizabeth Mary Wright and published in two volumes in 1932, a warm and affectionate picture of Wright's personal life and admirable achievement was painted. Elizabeth Mary was herself a historical linguist[1], so that her detailed description of Wright the scholar and of his academic achievements testifies to her knowledge and competence as a professional. The two volumes are difficult to obtain in the world's public libraries but they make enchanting reading, enriched by authentic documents, such as letters by J. Wright, and a few illustrative photos.

One of the major topics of the book is, of course, the making of the *EDD*. Wright's work of compiling the six volumes (1898-1905) was preceded and accompanied by other publications on dialects, in particular, *A Grammar in the Dialect of Windhill, in the West Riding of Yorkshire* (1892), and his very valuable *English Dialect Grammar* (1905). While in the former book Wright simply used his home dialect in West Yorkshire, the dialect grammar, in the wake of Ellis' previous activity in the phonetics and phonology of early English (1869-89), tried to come to terms with the features of English dialects in general.

2.2. The *English Dialect Dictionary* and its background

Wright is best remembered through his comprehensive dictionary. With its six volumes, it comprises more than 5,000 pages and is based on more than 1,000 sources and more than 12,000 queries. The compiler seems to have been a remarkable "manager", motivating and occupying over 600 helpers. The result was more than 60,000 lemmas and perhaps about as many references to phrases, compounds, derivations and "combinations" (somewhere between compounds and phrases).[2]

But the *EDD* is not only "the most comprehensive" (as Wright claims with some pride in the preface), but also most substantial in that the entries, beyond the

---

[1] She not only co-authored with him several historical English grammars, from Old English to Modern English, but also published a very substantial book of her own, *Rustic speech and folk-lore* (1914).

[2] At present we are only able to count the tags: 24,680 in sum (7,647 *phras.*, 3,578 *comp.*, 11,210 *hence* [= derivations], and 2,245 *comb.* [= combinations]). However, single tags very often announce several cases in point.

basic dialect attribution of lemmas, also include considerable information on word classes, spelling or lexical variants, frequency of usage, semantic and pragmatic subtleties, the variable pronunciations of a word, etymology, sociolectal parameters (such as slang), sources (e.g. literary ones) and time periods to which any of the dialect features, and not just the lemma as a whole, can be attributed. The dictionary refers to the period from 1700 to Wright's own time, i.e. (roughly) 1900 and, thus, makes a major contribution to our knowledge of Late Modern English.

2.3. Computerisation of the EDD

The digitisation of this admirable work is, of course, the decisive step forward. In its paper version, the *EDD* would probably be used as sparingly in the future as it has been in the past. Within the first phase of our Innsbruck SPEED project, Wright's dictionary has been scanned, processed by OCR, parsed, (partly) proofread and equipped with a dialectologically helpful query mask/interface. The details of our work and organisation have been described in earlier papers (cf, e.g., Markus 2007b; Markus and Heuberger 2007). Suffice it to say this: we are presently a team of six; some of the work (such as proofreading) has been outsourced to China; we are trying to cooperate with colleagues, particularly at the Universities of Bamberg and Leeds, as well as specialists abroad (e.g. the *OED* team of Oxford University Press); and finally, the project is government-funded. At present (December 2007), we are correcting manually or semi-automatically those parts of the dictionary's structure or spellings that have proved inaccessible to the parsing and OCR routine.

2.4. Late Modern English

We understand that the SPEED project has a chance of filling a gap not only in English dialectology but also in the branch of historical linguistics concerned with Late Modern English. The *Third Late Modern English Conference*, which coincidentally took place in Leiden/Netherlands just before the SHELL Conference in Nagoya[3], can perhaps be seen as a mirror of the research situation in view of the – generally rather neglected – latest phase of historical English. There was a strong emphasis on the historiography of "linguistic" contributions in the 18th and 19th centuries, in the wake of the method practised by Görlach and Bailey in their three books on these centuries (Bailey 1996; Görlach 1999 and 2001). Focussing on bibliographical data (overviews of dictionaries etc.) and on the now generally-rejected "prescriptivism" from the 18th century[4], the question of the basic features of Late Modern English was only tentatively raised. The *Cambridge History of the English Language,* vol IV (1776-1997), in both the introduction (by

---

3   30 August to 1 September 2007. I took part in it.
4   Two of the (excellent) plenaries (by Joan Beal and Raymond Hickey) were related to this issue, not to mention the many section papers.

Romaine, the editor) and the chapter on vocabulary (by Algeo), is very valuable as an introduction to Late Modern English, yet not much concerned with dialects in the old (and Wright's) regionalectal sense of the word, but more with sociolects as a result of the Industrial Revolution (cf. Romaine ed. 1998).

Generally, some useful introductions and special analyses have recently been published, e. g. by Beal (2004[5]), Dossena & Jones eds. (2003), and Kytö et al. eds. (2006). However, unlike the earlier phases of the English language, Early Modern English has hardly been subject to the combination of corpus-driven analysis and ensuing synthesis. The electronic version of Wright's dictionary may well prove the basis for starting to fill this gap.

2.5. Historical dialect geography

The substantial material of the *EDD* may also prove very useful in view of historical dialect geography. This is a field that the German Rolf Kaiser, in the preface to his book on that field (1937), called "ein Stiefkind der anglistischen Philologie" ('a stepchild of English Studies'). But Kaiser's book itself deals with Middle English words only. And Hoad, in a much later (short) paper on dialect geography, again with reference to Middle English (1994), likewise complains about the scholarly neglect of the affinity of words to dialect areas.

While there seems to be a wide popular interest in the regional positioning of words, the striking lack of scholarly concern craves an explanation. Three main reasons come to mind: (1) In the 18th century the normative attitude was so dominant among opinion leaders (the prescriptivism mentioned above) that there was more interest in standards than in the deviant features of dialect words. (2) The 20th century, by and large, favoured the analysis of the language system (cf. de Saussure and Chomsky's "competence"), which naturally implies criticism of, or disinterest in, the complexity of dialect usage. (3) As reflected by the *Cambridge History* (Romaine 1998), 19th-century industrialisation and urbanisation reduced the relevance of rural language features.

Today, the kind of new interest taken in dialect geography seems to depend very much on the kind of approach that we care to adopt. Probably not many wish to return to 19th-century positivism, to what Walters (1988, 23) called "This tradition of description (and sometimes description alone)", which, he said, "has left dialect geography largely out of touch with developments in the study of language" (as to the developments, he then mentions structuralism and the generative framework). Probably this methodological scepticism is also appropriate in view of present-day dialectology as a whole. In the meantime, the methodological discussion on dialectology has been carried on explicitly or implicitly by Viereck and Ramisch (1991 and 1997), Dossena and Lass (edd. 2004) and also by the work in

---

5   For a review of this book, see Markus 2007a.

the wake of the *Survey of English Dialects* (SED), for example, by Upton and Widdowson (2006).[6]

3. Interpretative part

The issues just discussed may profit from the use of the computerised version of Wright's *EDD*, which is now (Dember 2007) available in both a pdf- and a (widely proofread) txt-version.[7] One feature of dialect language, however, which has so far remained unmentioned is its spoken quality. This is so dominant and all-embracing a feature of dialect that detailed discussion of it has to be postponed until another occasion[8]. Instead, this chapter deepens and evaluates the points raised in the previous one and tries to show in what way Wright's dictionary may contribute to a solution of the problems involved.

3.1. Characteristics of a new dialect geography: overview

In his quotation referred to above, Walters (1988) implicitly suggests a more modern method for dialectology than the merely "descriptive" one. In more concrete terms, this postulate could be branched into a feature-oriented, explanatory and interdisciplinary as well as intra-disciplinary method.

The first point means that in the case of phonology too much focusing on phones or phonemes, rather than on more abstract characteristics (features[9]), will keep us away from an understanding of the principles of dialectal variation; examples will be given below. An explanatory approach to dialect features implies that our observations should not remain eclectic, but should be connected and quantified to allow for theoretical conclusions; moreover, the complexity and often overwhelming number of dialect data should trigger strategies of visualisation, such as charts and maps specially designed for purposes of demonstration. Finally, an inter- and intradisciplinary approach means that dialectology and, in particular, dialect geography should be open to cooperation with neighbouring academic disciplines, such as geography and cultural/economic history, and that linguistic levels (phonology, phonotactics, prosody, morphology, lexicology, phraseology, etymology, etc.) should not be dealt with in isolation, but as a combination of factors contributing to scholary insights.

---

6   Some of the various concepts of how to come to terms with word geography and dialect distribution will be tested in a workshop on 15 ICEHL in Munich (August 2008), convened by Upton and my Innsbruck project team.
7   So far our own proofreading and that of Chinese helpers has been limited to the essential parts of the entries, which we have called "heads" (see 4.1. below).
8   A paper on this particular aspect is forthcoming (Markus 2008c).
9   Even though the phonology of Chomsky and Halle (1948) has, for all I know, not come to be a textbook in most present-day university courses, its methodological principles have had an impact on later synchronic approaches and should not be totally ignored in (diachronic) dialectology; cf the still valuable introduction by Schane 1973.

In order to test the validity of these programmatic statements, the following discussion will go into detail, first on two or three examples of feature-orientation.

3.2. Feature-orientation

A convincing phonological theory that lends itself to explaining the behaviour of some consonants in English dialect is the scale of "consonantal strength" as propagated by scholars such as Vennemann and Lutz (cf. Lutz 1991). According to this theory, some consonants are "weaker" than others and, as a result, liable to be changed or elided under the "pressure" of conditioning factors. The eroding effect of history is such a factor. As is well known, the plosives and fricatives, i.e. the stronger consonants, have been relatively stable in the history of English, whereas those consonants that are based on a lesser degree of articulatory obstruction ("weak"), such as the half-vowels, nasals and liquids, have been subject to various "rules" of change.

English dialects, as we find them in Wright's dictionary, reflect principles similar to those immanent in the history of English. The liquids, for example, have been partly affected by loss or reduction in post-nuclear position, which means that after the nucleus of a syllable (the vowel), they have often been subject to processes of assimilation or simplification. This paper is not concerned with individual dialects. But many of them equally reveal loss of /l/ or /r/ respectively. Since the "non-rhotic" form (loss of /r/) is a well-known feature of the standard of British English, the survival of post-vocalic /r/ in some British dialects as opposed to the non-rhotic dialects is really the point at issue. Here are examples from the *EDD* for the role of variants with deletion or "insertion" of /l/ and /r/ respectively, depending on the dialect:

HOLD, *v.* Var. dial. uses in Sc. Irel. Eng. and Amer.
I. Gram. forms. 1. *Present Tense*: (1) **Ald**, (2) **Haad**, (3) **Haald**, (4) **Had(d**, (5) **Hald**, (6) **Haud**, (7) **Haul**, (8) **Hauld**, (9) **Hawld**, (10) **Heeld**, (11) **Ho**, (12) **Hod**, (13) **Hode**, (14) **Hohd**, (15) **Hole**, (16) **Holld**, (17) **Holt**, (18) **Houd**, (19) **Houl**, (20) **Hould**, (21) **Houle**, (22) **Howd**, (23) **Howld**, (24) **Hud**, (25) **Hull**, (26) **Hyld**, (27) **Oald**, (28) **Od**, (29) **Ole**, (30) **Owd**. [For further instances see II. below.]

HORN, *sb.* and *v.* Var. dial. uses in Sc. Irel. Eng. and Amer. Also written **hooan** n.Yks.; **hoarn** Nhb.[1]; hoorn n.Yks.[2]; and in form **orn** w.Yks [h)orn, œən.] 1. *sb*.

Variants 2, 4, 6, 12, etc. of *HOLD* (down to 30) show loss of the post-nuclear liquid. This type of reduced consonant cluster, however, competes with the other possible option, loss of the final plosive (cf 15, 19 etc.). One form (11: *ho*) is due to the loss of even both consonants. In the short quotation from the entry HORN, rhotic forms coexist with non-rhotic ones, as is also testified by the phonetic transcription at the end. Summing up the two cases, there is a pervasive tendency of post-nuclear liquids to get lost, but the variants as a whole present a mixed picture of causal factors for the behaviour of post-nuclear consonants.

The variants of *HOLD* and *HORN* also illustrate pre-nuclear behaviour of consonants. I am talking about h-dropping. The first variant and the last four of *HOLD*, as well as the spelling variant *orn* from West Yorkshire in the second entry, are examples of this common deviant pronunciation, which only came to be ostracised in the 19th century (cf. Markus 2002).

Given the commonplace nature of h-dropping, this paper suggests focussing on two "by-products" of h-dropping that seem particularly common in dialect: *h*-insertion and insertion of /j/.

H-insertion is known from historical English, for example, from Late Middle English (Markus 2002), where it obviously occurred as a result of hypercorrection. English dialects, as represented by Wright, give evidence of the former confusion about pre-vocalic aitches. Table 1 provides a few examples, with the meanings and a tentative explanation of the motivation added (under "note"):

Table 1: A few examples of *h*-insertion from the *EDD*

h-spelling	proper form	meaning	note
hairif	airup	'goose-grass, meadow-sweet'	*hair* = folk etym.
haever	eaver	'darnel or rye-grass'	*haver* ('oats'): folk etym.
hagnail	agnail	'loose skin at the fingernail'	*hag*: folk etym.
harrywig	earwig	'insect forticula auricularia'	folk etym.
hei	aye	'always'	emphasis?
hard-haddled	hard-addled	'very rotten'	prefer. of alliteration

Joseph Wright in his *Dialect Grammar* (1905) used the general argument that words with an inserted initial /h/ are more emphatic than without it (as in *hit* for *it*). But our six examples in Table 1 only testify to the validity of this argument in perhaps one of the cases: *hei* for *aye*. The other examples suggest mainly folk etymology as a motivating factor for word formation, and in one case alliteration. The question deserves further detailed study.

An even more fascinating repercussion of h-dropping is j-insertion, again in front of word-initial vowels, as in *yable* instead of *able*. Such a non-etymological fricative /j/, usually spelt as <y>, is quite common in the *EDD*, cf Table 2:

Table 2: Insertion of /j/ in the *EDD*: a few examples

variant with <y>	normal form	dialect (Wright)
/jek/	*ache*	Nw. & e.Som.
/jeÙ/	*age*	Me.Nhb., n.Cum.
/jal, jel/ et al.	*ale*	North Eng, parts of Scotland
/jal/	*all*	Ne.Yks.
/ja*prən, ja*pərən, je*pən/	*apron*	m.Yks., Snw.,Yks., Wil.
/ja:m, jeəm/	*arm*	Wil., Dor.
/ja*gər/	*eager*	Nnw.,Yks.
/jiə(r)/	*ear*	Se.Lan., s.Oxf., Sus.,Cor.

This survey paper does not allow for a lengthy discussion of the origin of non-etymological /j/ before vowels. But it seems fair to assume that the variants with initial <y> are based on forms with inserted *h*. In case /h/ was (still) a fricative, rather than a mere aspirant, /j/ is its voiced – and if /h/ was velar, palatalised - equivalent. Given this fairly close phonetic proximity between /h/ and /j/, the assumption of the transfer from *hable* to *jable*, both variants of *able*, does not seem far-fetched.

Unfortunately, there is no evidence that word-initial /h/ was at any stage since Old English still articulated with friction (/X/).[10] Nor would Old Norse have encouraged dialectal pronunciation with friction, because there, just like in other Germanic languages, early proto-Germanic [X] had survived in initial position as a mere aspirant.[11] The question of the causes for *j*-insertion, thus, has to be left open now – perhaps until the search interface of the *EEDD* can provide us with a broad enough basis of dialect words with inserted *j* (probably in the course of 2008).[12]

3.3. Inter- and intradisciplinary approach: three examples
The fascinating way dialectology is connected with other disciplines will be illustrated in the following by three philological examples: connection with classical rhetorics, poetics and cultural studies/history.

3.3.1. Classical rhetorics
Classical rhetorics has systematically described the way sounds and syllables in a word may depend on the metrical needs, i.e. the necessity of adapting the shape of

---

10 Cf. the general remarks on Proto-Germanic /X/ and its development in the Germanic vernaculars in Krahe 1963, 97-98.
11 For details see Ranke and Hofmann 1967, § 16,2 (p. 399).
12 In another article focussing on this question (Markus 2008c.) I will consider the loss of word-initial /j/ in Old Norse as a possible factor for *j*-insertion in English dialects; cf. Ranke and Hofmann 1967, § 19,2 (p. 42).

a word to the metrically available slot.[13] For example, *aphaeresis* is the loss of a sound or syllable at the beginning of a word (as in U.S. English *gator* < *alligator*). *Synaeresis*, also called *syncope*, is the contraction in the middle of a word (*e'er* < *ever*). *Apocope* is the clipping of a word at its end (*Marge* < *Margery*).[14]

To select only the first two cases for illustration, examples of aphaeresis and synaeresis are easy to find in Wright's works. For the former, we may borrow a short list of words from the *Dialect Grammar* (1905, § 232). For the latter, a passage quoted from the *EDD*, entry FALL, may serve to show that the rules of rhetorics allowing word-length flexibility lead to the same outputs as the "rules" of the dialect colouring of words:

Aphaeresis:
bout (about), quaint (acquaint), gree (agree); cause (because), leven (eleven), tice (entice), demic (epidemic) (cf. Wright, *Grammar* 1905, § 232)

Synaeresis:
3. Pp. (l) Faan, (2) Faen, (3) Falled, (4) Fa'n, (5) Fao*h'lu'n, (6) Faud, (7) Faun, (8) Fawd, (9) Fawn, (10) Felled'n, (11) Fellen, (12) Foan, (13) Foean, (14) Fo@ln, (15) Foen, (16) Fon, (17) Fone, (18) Fown, (19) Fuo*h'lu'n, (20) Vaa*l(d, (21) Valled.

Many of the variants of the past participle *fallen* have lost their intervocalic /l/ and, as a result, a syllable. This observation of a case of synaeresis takes us back to the phonotactic "weakness" of the liquid /l/, discussed above. As surprising as this proximity between dialect and rhetorics may seem, they obviously have a common basis. But it has to be admitted that, without further empirical evidence, this basis can only be described tentatively: the two frames of reference both direct us to generally human aspects of language: strategies of simplification, tendencies towards "smoothness" of sound sequences and the "beauty" of sound patterns (such as rhythm).

3.3.2. Poetics

The suggestiveness of such statements will perhaps give way to clarity in view of the examples listed in Table 3. They are meant to show that some typical features in dialect word formation are "poetical": i.e. they tend to use patterns that we would otherwise associate with poetry, and poetry (at least, lyrics) has to do with simplicity, "smoothness" and "beauty".

---

13 Cf. Lausberg 1998, § 481-493, under the cover term Lat. *barbarismus*.
14 Strictly speaking, the technical term *clipping* is appropriate in view of processes of word formation and, thus, refers to the loss of morphemes rather than sounds or syllables.

Table 3: Poetic types of word formation in dialect

Type of WF	word	meaning
repetition	bleak-bleak	the cry of the hare
	sowie-sowie	call to sheep
	too-too	very good
rhyme	hag-a-bag	stout linen fabric
	honka-donka	heavy boots
	tee-hee	foolish laughter
	hiddie-giddie	topsy turvy
alliteration/ablaut	Bible-back	person with broad shoulders
	blaitie-bum	lazy fellow
	blue bonnet	a man's cap; hence a Scotsman
	snick-a-sneeze	term used to threaten children
	lea-laik	a shelter for cattle
	gibble-gabble	confused talk
asson./consonance	eastie-wastie	unstable person
	corse-house	house with a corpse

These examples gleaned from Wright's *EDD* may suffice to encourage further quests for poeticisms in dialect.

3.2.3. Cultural history/studies

The third example of the recommended cooperation between dialectology and other (philological) disciplines uses a word class, namely interjections, as an opportunity to topicalise the relationship of man to animals as revealed in dialect language. Interjections, apart from their being a means of emotional self-expression, are sometimes also used to address a person or even animals.[15] Since rural life up to the 19th century brought man more into contact with animals than our predominantly urban life today (apart from pets), the question of which animals were addressed by means of interjections seems to make sense.

With the help of a txt-version of the *EDD* and of WordSmith as a concordance program, one can easily find out what the interjections ("int.") in the *EDD* mainly refer to. Here is an overview of the most frequently addressed animals (Table 4):

---

[15] For a detailed discussion of interjections as a part of speech, see Ameka 1992 and Nübling 2004.

Table 4: Reference to animals (WordSmith)

reference to	# of occurr. as colloc. of interjections
horse*	51
pig*/swine	22
dog*	21
cattle, cow*, calf, calves	20
sheep	10
geese, goose	10
hen*, poultry	8
duck*	7
cat*	5
total	153

It does not come as a surprise that the horse is addressed most variably; it was man's best friend as a helper. The cat, it seems, did not have its present-day rank as a pet; pigs, cattle and dogs rank much higher. Needless to say, the interjections themselves would deserve a closer look, along the lines suggested by Sauer (in this volume). For example, interjections tend to be short and to have onomatopoeic or pragmatic functions. A query for *int.* in the *EDD* delivered 1,037 hits, which seem worth classifying. But again, as in the case of many other questions raised on Late Modern English dialects, a real analysis will only be possible when the *EDD* is accessible via the interface that my Innsbruck project team is presently elaborating, since only then will detailed combined queries be feasible (e.g. "Which are the main dialects involved?", "Do dialects have more interjections than the standard?").

4. Structure of the *EDD's* entries and the query mask

4.1. The main parameters of the entries

The text of Figure 2 shows a typical entry of the *EDD*, first as an image, which the user of the query panel can always go back to, and then as a machine-readable text, after applying OCR.

Figure 1: A typical entry of the EDD

BOLLARD, *sb.* Dor. Naut. [bo·ləd.] A wooden or iron post on a ship, or quay, for securing ropes.
    Dor. Standing by a bollard a little farther up the quay, HARDY *Trumpet-Major* (1880) xxxiv; Tuesday's gale hev loosened the pier; the bollards be too weak to make fast to, *ib. Ethelberta* (1876) II. xlv. Naut. SMYTH *Sailor's Word-bk.* (1867) 115.
    [Bollard (with shipwrights), one of the large posts set into the ground on each side of a dock, to which blocks are fixed, for the convenience of getting the ship into it, ASH (1795).]

BOLLARD, sb. **Dor.** Naut. [bo'l@d.] **A wooden or iron post on a ship, or quay, for securing ropes.**
Dor. Standing by a bollard a little farther up the quay, Hardy Trumpet-Major (1880) xxxiv; Tuesday's gale hev loosened the pier; the bollards be too weak to make fast to, ib. Ethelberta (1876) II. xlv. Naut. Smyth Sailor's Word-bk. (1867) 115.
[Bollard (with shipwrights), one of the large posts set into the ground on each side of a dock, to which blocks are fixed, for the convenience of getting the ship into it, Ash (1795).]

The different colours, here represented by different formats, stand for the eight main parameters of such a typical entry: headword, part of speech (mainly word class), dialect, usage label, phonetic transcription in brackets, definition, citations and comment. Since the first five parameters, down to phonetics, are the most important and also fairly stable, we have subsumed them under "head", whereas the rest, which are very variable in length, layout and structure, form the "body".

The multiple ways of variation in these basic parameters have been described before in publications by members of the Innsbruck project team (cf. Markus and Heuberger 2008, Onysko, Markus and Heuberger 2008), and cannot be discussed here in detail for lack of space. Suffice it to say that some of the parameters, particularly those of the "body", have turned out to be extremely multi-functional so that we had to create sub-parameters for the parser, i.e. functions hidden within the eight main fields of the entries. All in all, we ended up with more than a hundred parameters or functions. Only very few of these will be sketched in the following.

4.2. Reference to dialects
In line with Wright, we have parsed dialect on three levels, namely counties, regions, and nations (such as Dorsetshire/North Wales/U.S.), with possible Boolean linkage between them and the options on each of the three levels. Our query routine will also allow for some "fuzzy logic", for example, by storing phrases of the kind "in various parts of x" separately and making them optionally accessible. We have tagged such phrases as "partial/fuzzy". The words or features marked by these phrases may be of interest in view of combined queries where exact dialect attribution is not vitally important, for example, when one asks for words of a certain lexical field (everything on cattle) or of a certain etymology. To illustrate: if I am interested in patterns of Scandinavian elements of word formation, the question of where exactly in Scotland or the North of England these elements occurred, may be negligible. In view of such cases it would be a mistake if fuzzy statements in the dictionary had been totally excluded from our database.

Wright not only refers to dialect in the "head" (to mark the dialect affinity of the lemma as a whole), but he may also localise some point in the "body". For example, a special meaning of an otherwise common word is affiliated with a county, or a compound or phrase coined with the help of the lemma is attributed to dialect. Whatever a dialect code refers to, we have stored it both in relation to its referent and as a tag related to the lemma of the entry concerned (for further detail see Onysko, Markus and Heuberger 2008).

This double strategy also had to be pursued in view of the basic source codes that Wright uses. Thus, *Yks.1* will be stored as a source code which stands for a certain glossary identified in Wright's reference list, but also for the dialect of Yorkshire, so that a user searching for Yorkshire will also find the passages identified by the source code "Yks.1".[16]

4.3. Parts of speech

A common understanding of the term "part of speech" is that it is a synonym for *word class*. But Wright uses the term in a wider sense, overlapping with what modern lexicographers mean by "usage label". Accordingly, we have categorised all the markers in this field that do not really refer to word class in one of the three options: frequency, syntax or pragmatics. The phrase "improperly used as inf.", for example, is doubtless a piece of information on syntax. Some of Wright's partly lengthy phrases containing pragmatic information (long before the birth of *pragmatics*) may demonstrate the advantage of the classification according to modern linguistic terms:

> also used as a familiar term of address
> also used as a fencing term
> also used as a term of contempt
> also used as a term of endearment   to (X)
> also used as an epithet of contempt
> and in gen. colloq. use
> euphonic
> in colloq. use

4.4. Other parameters: definitions, phonetics, etymology

In the slot usually filled by a definition Wright frequently gives explanations of a non-semantic (e.g. syntactic) kind. Moreover, many entries in the dictionary have several listed meanings, or a listed meaning refers to a compound, derivation or phrase previously itemised. This changing content of the slot of *definition* results from the fact that Wright's *EDD* not only topicalises words but also other features of dialects: phonemes, patterns of morphology, phrases, etc. However, the com-

---

16   A more detailed study on the sources of Wright's dictionary is forthcoming (Markus 2008b).

plexity of "definition" in Wright has recently been dealt with in a publication of my project team (Onysko, Markus and Heuberger 2008) so that it seems unnecessary to go into detail now.

Another sub-routine of our query machine allows for phonetic/phonological searches. The *EDD* does not give a phonetic transcription for all lemmas, but only for what Wright considered to be special cases, mainly cases deviant in some way from the standard. The transcription itself is not exactly that of the International Phonetic Association, but still very close to it. The main point of deviation is that word accent is not marked before the stressed syllable, but after the stressed vowel (by a raised dot). Wright has transcribed words in the *EDD* very consistently so that users will be able to study all kinds of phonological, phonotactic and prosodic features.

Mention should finally be made of etymology. As a 19th century philologist, Wright was naturally interested in the origin of words and, therefore, frequently added their etymological background in a bracketed *comment* at the end of entries. Our query interface will allow for finding all etymological codes used in the dictionary so that, for example, all lemmas can be retrieved (or all compounds, or derivations, or phrases) that have a Scandinavian etymological background and deal with, say, navigation. There will be lots of possibilities.

4.5. Possibilities of combined searches: the query mask

Figure 2: The query mask of the *EEDD*

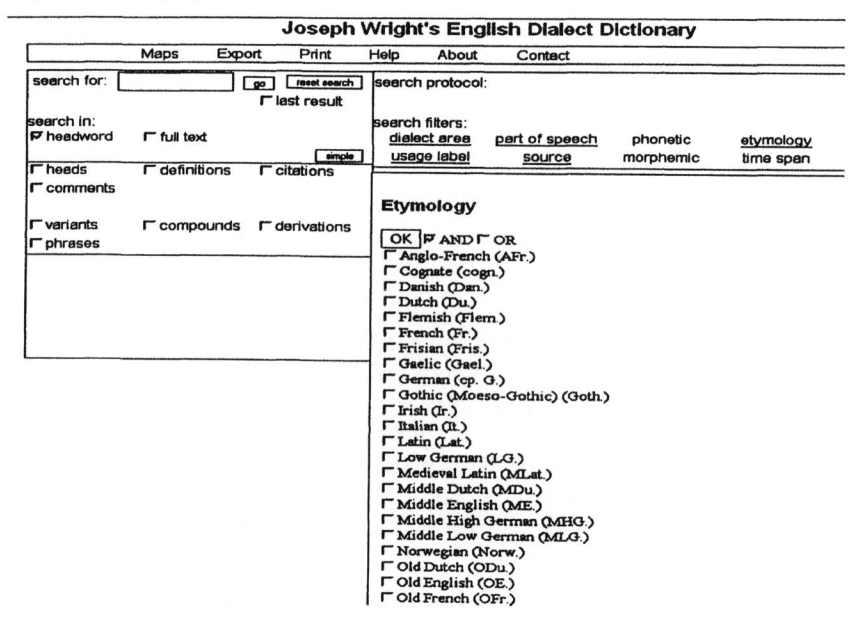

A glimpse at the screenshot of our (yet provisional) query panel may suggest the various possibilities that the *EEDD* offers. The panel is split into two halves: on the left, different parameters/sections of the entries and (at the bottom end) different lexical units, from variants to phrases, can be searched by a click on GO, either for browsing or as the basis for specific queries. A specific search may be defined by a string, to be typed in the search box on the top left, or it may be implemented by a specific filtering constellation (on the right of the panel), for example, by clicking on several etymologies (with activated AND or OR) and a dialect area. The screen in Figure 2 shows the open window on etymology, but when it is covered by the next window, e.g. on dialects, the program and the search protocol on top will have recorded the previous commands until the complex query is carried out. It will, thus, be easy to the user to raise fairly sophisticated questions such as: give me all the lemmas connected with a Dutch OR Frisian OR Low German etymology AND an occurrence in, say, East Anglia.[17]

5. Conclusion and outlook

Petyt (1980: 81) is one of the few who have found it necessary to describe Wright's works on English dialects as far from perfect:

> it soon became obvious that EDD and EDGr had deficiencies. The Dictionary had aimed to include 'all dialect words', but soon after its publication letters and articles began to point out areas which were undercovered and items which should have been included ... More serious than the omissions is the vagueness of reference.

Any dialect-based study, however, is bound to be incomplete, just as any systematic linguistic approach to language usage is necessarily inexhaustive (since based on a paradox of terms). Notwithstanding this, Wright can really be seen to have done an admirable job, for which we can only be grateful since he did an enormous amount of field-work for us. And whatever is non-precise in the dictionary ("fuzzy") will be, with the help of our search interface, subject to quantification so that future complaints about general imperfections will really be unfounded.

Unlike field-work dialectologists, then, users of the *EEDD* do not have to be concerned with collecting data, but can all the more concentrate on evaluating and interpreting it. It is our aim in the Innsbruck project to allow for all kinds of good questions in the query routine, not only data directly connected with the lemmas, but also data hidden in any of their parameters. To give a final example of the hidden treasures: in the field of *citations*, and occasionally also in the fields of the "head", Wright meticulously refers to his sources, among these also literary sources (Chaucer, Shakespeare, Dickens, etc.). On that basis, it will be possible to

---

17 East Anglia had traditional commercial contact with the Low Countries.

trace literature pertaining to a certain dialect or to dialects generally within a certain time.[18]

There will not only be more questions which can then be raised and answered[19]. We are also hopeful of promoting the aim of visually presenting dialect features in an innovative way, whether in the form of tables, charts or maps. With maps, for example, our aim is to provide different types of maps relevant for dialect distribution in the form of overlays, as provided by those of Google Earth. As a result, the user can "switch on" different dimensions that may have had an influence on dialect development, such as geography and urbanisation in combination with the county or nation outlines.[20] One of our team members, Christoph Praxmarer, is concerned with optimising the technique of such dialect overlay maps.

While the electronic version of Wright's dictionary is as yet only available in a beta version, it seems, in conclusion, fair to say even now that dialect geography will not be the same, but allow empirical access to a great many features of the language and culture of dialects. Our main aim is to develop a "speedy" instrument which may give answers to questions that nobody has so far dared to raise.

References

Ameka, Felix
    1992   "Interjections: The universal yet neglected part of speech". *Journal of Pragmatics* 18, 2/3: 101-117.

Bailey, Richard W.
    1996   *Nineteenth-Century English*. Ann Arbor: The University of Michigan Press.

Beal. Joan C.
    2004   *English in Modern Times*. London: Arnold.

Dossena, Marina — Charles Jones (edd.)
    2003   *Insight into Late Modern English*. Bern etc.: Peter Lang.

Dossena, Marina — Roger Lass (edd.)
    2004   *Methods and Data in English Historical Dialectology*. Bern, etc.: Lang.

Ellis, Alexander J.
    1869-1889   *On Early English Pronunciation, with special reference to Shakspere and Chaucer, containing an investigation of the correspondence of writting with speech in England from An-*

---

18   For a more detailed study of the sources of Wright's *EDD*, cf. Markus 2008b.
19   For a good introduction to the traditional method of English dialectology, see Francis 1983.
20   One of our team members, Christoph Praxmarer, is concerned with optimising the techniques of such dialect overlay maps.

glo-Saxon period to the present day. Part. 1-5. London: EETS ES 2, 7, 14, 23, 56.

Francis, W. Nelson
1983　　Dialectology. An Introduction. New York: Longmans.

Görlach, Manfred
1999　　*English in Nineteenth-Century England. An Introduction.* Cambridge: Cambridge University Press.
2001　　*Eighteenth-Century English.* Heidelberg: Universitätsverlag C. Winter.

Hoad, Terry
1994　　"Word geography: previous approaches and achievement". In Laing, Margaret, and Keith Williamson eds. *Speaking in our tongues. Proceedings of a colloquium on medieval dialectology and related disciplines.* Bury St Edmunds: D.S. Brewer. pp. 197-203.

Kaiser, Rolf
1937　　*Zur Geographie des mittelenglischen Wortschatzes.* Palaestra 205. Leipzig: Meyer & Müller.

Krahe, Hans
1963　　*Germanische Sprachwissenschaft. I: Einleitung und Lautlehre.* Berlin etc.: de Gruyter.

Kytö, Merja —Mats Rydén —Erik Smitterberg (edd.)
2006　　*Nineteenth-century English: Stability and Change.* Cambridge etc.: UP.

Lausberg, Heinrich
1998　　*Handbook of literary rhetoric: a foundation for literary study.* Transl. of the German original, 3rd ed. (1990). Leiden etc.: Brill.

Lutz, Angelika
1991　　*Phonotaktisch gesteuerte Konsonantenveränderungen in der Geschichte des Englischen.* Tübingen: Max Niemeyer Verlag.

Markus, Manfred
2002　　"The Genesis of H-dropping Revisited: An Empirical Analysis". In *Of Dyuersitie and Chaunge of Language: Essays Presented to Manfred Görlach on the Occasion of His 65th Birthday.* Eds. Katja Lenz and Ruth Möhlig. Heidelberg: C. Winter Universitätsverlag: 6-26.
2007a　　Review of Joan C. Beal. *English in Modern Times. 1700-1945.* Oxford: Oxford University Press: 2004. *Anglistik* 18. 154-157.
2007b　　"Wright's *EDD* Computerised: Architecture and Retrieval Routine", Online publication Conference Dagstuhl 3 Dec. 2006: http://drops.dagstuhl.de/opus/volltexte/2007/1052/pdf/06491.MarkusManfred.Paper.1052.pdf

2008a "Wright's *English Dialect Dictionary* Computerised: Towards a New Source of Information". Online publication of ICAME Helsinki 2006: http://www.helsinki.fi/varieng/journal/volumes/02/markus/
2008b (forthc.) "Joseph Wright's *English Dialect Dictionary* and its sources". In Proceedings of the Third Late Modern English Conference at Leiden, 29 August to 1 September 2007.
2008c (in progress). "Features of Spokenness in Wright's E*nglish Dialect Dictionary*".

Markus, Manfred, and Reinhard Heuberger
2007 "The Architecture of Joseph Wright's *English Dialect Dictionary*: Preparing the Computerised Version". *International Journal of Lexicography* 20: 355-368.

Nübling, Damaris
2004 "Die prototypische Interjektion: Ein Definitionsvorschlag". *Zeitschrift für Semiotik* 26, 1/2: 11-45.

Onysko, Alexander — Markus, Manfred — Reinhard Heuberger
2008(forthc.) "Joseph Wright's *English Dialect Dictionary* in Electronic Form: A Critical Discussion of Selected Lexicographic Parameters and Query Options". In Proceedings of ICAME Stratford-upon-Avon 2007.

Petyt, K.M.
1980 *The Study of Dialect. An Introduction to dialectology.* The Language Library. London: André Deutsch,

Ranke, Friedrich — Dietrich Hofmann
1967 *Altnordisches Elememtatbuch*. 3rd ed. Berlin: Walter de Gruyter.

Romaine, Suzanne (ed.)
1998 *The Cambridge History of the English Language, IV: 1776-1997.* Cambridge: UP.

Schane, Sanford A.
1973 *Generative Phonology*. Englewood Cliffs, N.J.: Prentice-Hall.

Upton, Clive, and J.D.A. Widdowson
2006 *An Atlas of English Dialects*, 2nd ed. London etc.: Routledge.

Viereck, Wolfgang — Heinrich Ramisch
1991/1997 *The Computer Developed Atlas of England*, vol. 1 (1991) and vol. II (1997). Tübingen: Niemeyer.

Walters, Keith
1988 "Dialectology". In *Linguistics: The Cambridge Survey. IV. Language: The Socio-cultural context*. Ed. Frederick J. Newmeyer. Cambridge etc.: UP. pp. 119-139.

Wright, Elizabeth Mary
  1914   *Rustic Speech and Folk-Lore*. 2nd ed. London etc.: OUP.
  1932   *The Life of Joseph Wright*, 2 vols. London.
Wright, Joseph
  1892   *A Grammar in the Dialect of Windhill*, in the West Riding of Yorkshire. E.D.S.
Wright, Joseph
  1898-1905 *The English Dialect Dictionary*. 6 vols. Oxford: Henry Frowde.
  1905   *English Dialect Grammar*. Oxford etc.: Henry Frowde.

26 Recursion in Language Change[1]

Fuyo Osawa, Tokai University

1. My claim

In this paper, I redefine recursion, which has been discussed in Hauser, Chomsky and Fitch (2002) from a historical perspective. Recursion is essential in human languages and this process has a developmental nature, which causes diachronic syntactic changes in English. In my hypothesis, recursion is defined as embedding an element within another instance of the same status through a relevant functional category. In this sense, recursion should be differentiated from mere repetition or pairing. Both nominal structures and clause structures concern this. I claim that this type of recursion is unique to human languages. I suggest that a language may go through developmental stages from a flat to embedded structure. Then the word 'evolution' should be used with respect to functional systems.

I prove this by referring to the development of nominal structures in the history of English; in Old English a functional category D was absent, that is, Old English had only NPs, and nominal structures were flat, not hierarchical. Later, NPs developed into hierarchical DPs due to the emergence of a functional category D within former nominal structures. As a result, embedding of a nominal phrase within another nominal phrase through a relevant functional category, in this case D, was made possible. There is a parallelism between nominal phrases and clause structures in this development.

2. The nominal structures in Present-day English

According to the DP analysis (Abney (1987), Longobardi (1994) among others), nominals in Present-day English are assumed to be a projection of a head D, not a head N. NPs are inherently predicative and thus cannot occur in argument positions, while DPs are referential and thus occur in argument positions. NPs are not referential; referential nominals may be paraphrased as "those that are understood as denoting a particular entity in the universe of discourse." For more details, see Rapoport (1995: 154). As Longobardi (1994: 628) argues, a common noun is kind-referring, not referential.

The role of picking out a particular referent is assumed to be taken care of by a functional D in Present-day English; the role of a functional D is to change predicative nominals into arguments.

Nominal phrases in Present-day languages are assumed to constitute a DP layer as shown below (cf. Carstens (2000), Alexiadou (2004: 34)):

---

[1] This work was supported by Grant-in-Aid for Scientific Research of Japan Society for the Promotion of Science No.18520392.

(1)
```
         DP
        /  \
       /    D'
            / \
           D   FP1
               / \
                  FP2
                  / \
                     nP
                    /  \
                her/his  n'
                        / \
                       n   NP
```

The parallel internal structure between noun phrases and clauses has been widely accepted (cf. Ritter (1991)).

(2) a. the enemy's destruction of the city
    b. the enemy destroyed the city
(3) a. John's proof of the theory
    b. John proved the theory

FP1 in (1) corresponds to AgrP in the clause structure, and nP corresponds to vP. NP is the equivalent of VP. FP2 is a Number Projection, which hosts numerals. Possessors are base-generated in the Spec of nP. NP is a lexical domain, corresponding to VP. Thus, paralleling V-to-I or C movement, there is N-to-D raising, which is an instance of head movement (cf. Ritter (1991), Longobardi (1994)). Genitives and possessives are paralleling the clausal subject.

3. Absence of DPs in Old English

I assume that in Old English a functional category D is absent, that is, Old English has only NPs, and hence, the related syntactic phenomena are absent. There are many pieces of evidence for the absence of the functional D-system. In Old English, we can find examples in which determiners would be required in Present-day English as shown in (4) and (5):

(4) fram beaduwe
    from battle-dat.
    'from the battle'   (Mitchell and Robinson (1992:107))
(5) heo   on   flet   gecrong
    she   on   floor   fell
    sweord   wæs   swatig
    sword   was   bloody
    'she fell to the ground and the sword was bloody'   (Beowulf, 1568,1569)

(6) Her   Martianus   and   Valentinus   on-fengon   rice
    here Mauricius -nom. and   Valentinian-nom. seized   kingdom-acc.
                                  (AS. Chronicle Parker MS, from Sweet (1953: 73))
    'At this point Mauricius and Valentinian seized the kingdom'

In Old English: personal pronouns were used as anaphors and then, the meaning of the sentence 'He killed him' was indeterminate whether the object referred to the subject or not (cf. Gelderen (2004)):

(7) ac   he   hyne   gewyrpte
    but   he   him-acc.   recovered
    'he recovered himself.'   (Beowulf 2976)

Since a D-system is the locus of binding properties of nominals and pronouns, this absence will follow easily if we assume the lack of a D-system in Old English.

There are many researchers (cf. Wood (2003), Alexiadou (2004)) who assume a DP layer, which is something like (1) in Old English. Evidence for the assumed DP layer in Old English seems to come from word order in nominals. For example, Wood (2003) gives a very detailed analysis of word order in Old English nominals and claims that demonstratives, possessives and adjectives are strictly ordered, and then, there must be some functional layers above NP. Thus, when possessive pronouns appear together with other adjectives, possessive pronouns usually precede them, and when possessives appear with demonstratives, possessives precede demonstratives.

(8) (i)   possessive pronoun + adjective + head noun
    (ii) possessive pronoun+ demonstrative + adjective + head noun

(9) is showing a pattern (8)(ii):

(9) his   sio   gode   modor
    his   that   good   mother   (Orosius 270.26, cited from Wood (2003: 110))

However, there are many pieces of evidence against this, including word order variation within nominals. Indeed, different word orders are available for most of the cases. So, the possessive +noun order is observed, while the noun + possessive order is also found. The demonstrative +possessive +adjective +noun order co-existed with the possessive + demonstrative + adjective +noun order. See Alexiadou (2004: 41). For that matter, we should note that, although the adjective + noun order is dominant in late Old English, the noun+ adjective order is also attested in the Old English texts.

The sentence (11) is showing a pattern (10)(ii'), although (10)(ii') is said to be rare in Old English:

(10) (i') noun + possessive
    (ii')demonstrative +possessive +adjective +noun
(11) in   þis   user   circlice   stær
    in   this-acc. our   ecclesiastical history
    'in this ecclesiastical history of ours'

(Bede 282.23, cited from Wood (2003: 115))

Although I admit that late Old English has already shown a tendency toward word order fixation, it is important that we can still observe a wide variety of orders in nominal phrases. What I could suggest here is that the presence of a few pronominal elements before the head nominal and the word order do not give crucial evidence for the presence of a DP layer and, especially, for the presence of a D-head.

4. The emergence of DPs

As discussed above, if Present-day English nominals are a projection of a D, it follows that a functional D appeared in English in the course of its development. I claim that what triggered the emergence of DPs is the demise of case morphology (cf. Osawa (2000a), (2000b), (2003a), (2007)).

The task of a D is to decide a referential status of an argument nominal and change predicative nominals into arguments. This role is assumed to be taken care of by either a functional D or morphological case. In the absence of a D-system, the task of identifying the referentiality of a nominal is taken care of by morphological case on the head nouns in Old English. Case affixes attached to head nouns can associate the nominals to their predicate verbs and then turn NPs into arguments. This affixation is a purely morphological process. That is, nouns can become arguments of predicates if they are case-marked in Old English.

The leveling of inflectional endings had already begun in Old English and by the early Middle English period many Old English inflectional distinctions were lost. Morphological case could not perform the task of identifying the referential role of nouns and turning them into arguments any more, and subsequently a functional D-system has developed to do the same job in English.

5. Group genitive constructions

In this section I take up the issue of group genitive constructions as independent syntactic evidence for the non-presence of a D-system, its flat structure in Old English, and its subsequent appearance.

In Present-Day English, the group genitive is a construction where the genitive ending -'s is apparently affixed to the last element of a noun phrase as is shown by (12) and in the tree (13).

(12) the king of England's hat

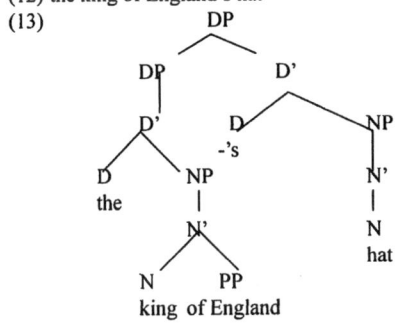

(13)
```
                    DP
                   /  \
                 DP    D'
                 |    /  \
                 D'  D    NP
                /|  -'s   |
               D  NP      N'
              the |       |
                  N'      N
                 / \     hat
                N   PP
              king of England
```

Genitive -'s in Present-day English is supposed to be a head determiner according to the DP analysis. The genitive marker -'s is not an inflection on the last noun, but is attached to the whole DP in the specifier position. Thus, the whole DP is integrated into another DP in group genitive constructions.

This group genitive construction is not observed in Old English, however; instead Old English used the following constructions to express the corresponding notion:

(14) (i) [N1-gen. + N-Head + N2-gen.]   'split genitive'
     (ii) [N1-gen. + N2-gen. + N-Head]
(15) Ælfred-es sweostor cynning-es   (i)
     'King Alfred's sister'   (AS.Chronicle Parker MS 82. 2. 888)
(16) Ælfred-es cynning-es godsunu   (ii)
     'King Alfred's godson'   (AS.Chronicle Parker MS 82. 10. 890)

In pattern (14)(i), which is called a split genitive, a head noun is placed between two genitive-marked nouns, and in pattern (14)(ii) two genitive-marked modifying nouns precede a head noun. It is said that the split type construction is not so rare and is used more often than the (ii) type (cf. Ekwall (1943: 2)).

In later Old English, the genitive inflection on N2 in pattern (14)(i) began to drop, while in pattern (14)(ii) the genitive ending on N1 began to drop and this form, i.e. the pattern (17)(ii') became common in Middle English (see Nakao (1972: 220-221), Ono and Nakao (1980: 291-292)):

(17) (i') [N1-gen. + N-Head + N2- Ø]
     (ii') [N1- Ø + N2-gen. + N-Head]

(18) þurh   Iulianes   heste   ðe   amperur
     by   Julian-gen.   command   the   emperor
                                            (The Ancrene Riwle 109, 11)
(19) Davið kingess kinn   (Ormulum i. 8)

(18) and (19) are showing (17)(i') and (17)(ii') each. Then, the latter pattern (17)(ii') is replaced by the following one:

(20) (iii) [N1 of N2] –gen.+ Head

In (20)(iii), an *of*-N2 is placed before a head noun, and the genitive inflection is attached to the last noun of a phrase, which is supposed to be a preceding form of the group genitive construction. This construction first appeared in Chaucer and became common in the 15th century.

(21) the god of slepes heyr   (Chaucer Book of Duchess: 168)

This genitive ending was reanalyzed as a head determiner and the group genitive construction was established as such around the middle of the 15th century. Thus, we can conclude that group genitive constructions have been made possible due to the emergence of a D-system (cf .Nakao (1972: 221), Hamasaki (1993)).

Based on the above facts, I propose the following structure for the nominal phrases such as (15) *Ælfred-es sweostor cynning-es* as one possibility (cf. Miyamae (2005)):

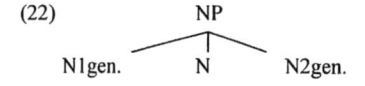

(22)   NP
            ┌────────┼────────┐
         N1gen.   N   N2gen.

I claim, although tentatively, that the Old English nominals have a partially flat, non-configurational structure like this, in parallel with the clause structure which I turn to soon. Just as another clause is integrated into a higher clause, so too another DP can be integrated into the specifier of one DP.

Although the DP analysis accounts for the group genitive constructions nicely, this analysis for Old English nominals runs into difficulties when we try to explain the derivation of split genitives like (15). The two modifying NPs are dispersed around a head noun. Splitting noun phrases like this is characteristic of non-configurational languages (cf. Hale (1982), (1983)), in which the specifier or complement status does not depend on the structure unlike configurational languages like Present-day English. How can we account for these two genitive endings and the word order variation shown in above examples, if we analyse that *–es* is not a case inflection, but a head-determiner, D, which occurs at the end of the entire phrase?   If it is a case inflection, it is supposed to occur at the end of each noun. One may say that the split structures in (14)(i) or (14)(ii) can be derived from a layered structure (1) without positing a flat structure. It may be possible theoretically. However, the operations become too complicated in that case.

6. Parallelism between clauses and nominal phrases

I propose the following structure for Old English clauses, which is the projection of a lexical V, i.e. VP, without IP/TP:

(23)
```
        VP
       / \
        V'
       /|\
    (NP) V (NP)
```

Fischer and van der Leek (1983) also propose a partially flat structure for Old English impersonal constructions. In (23) the two NPs are unordered with respect to each other, and the parenthesis show that NPs are optional. This structure accommodates the subject-less constructions, i.e. impersonal constructions given in (24) and (25):

(24) norþan   sniwde
     from the north snowed
     'snow came from the north'   (Seafarer 31)
(25) siððan   him   hingrode
     afterwards him-dat. hungered
     'he hungered afterwards'   (ÆCHom. I.11.166.12)

I assume that Old English did not have IP/TP. It is well known that Old English did not have modal auxiliaries, *do*-support and the subject requirement[2]. It is still possible to argue that IP/TP was operative in Old English as many researchers do. However, it is plausible to conclude that Old English lacked IP/TP, since syntactic phenomena depending on this projection were not observed in Old English. Concerning the invisible elements, I follow the proposals made by Thráinsson (1996) and Fukui and Sakai (2003). We must be careful when we posit the invisible or inactive elements in languages. Fukui and Sakai (2003: 329) argue that "if the functional categories are present in a language, but they are not active, what does their existence mean exactly?" Their "Visibility Guideline for Functional Categories" (Fukui and Sakai (2003: 327)) is along similar lines with Thráinsson (1996). Thráinsson (1996) argues that languages may vary with respect to the functional categories they have, and proposes the real Minimalist Principle: "Assume only those functional categories that you have evidence for."

---

2   I define the subject as a structural requirement due to the presence of a relevant functional category T. A finite T has an [EPP] feature requiring it (= T) to have a specifier with person/number properties. To satisfy this [EPP] feature, the nominal must be attracted into the specifier position. This [EPP] feature is usually satisfied by nominative elements. However, the relation between nominative case marking and the [EPP] feature satisfaction is obscure in the more recent Minimalist framework (cf. Chomsky (1995: 55), (2005: 18-19)).

It would be better to state my general background assumption here. That is, functional categories are not operative from the beginning of languages, but over a period of time a functional category emerges and the new, emergent functional category brings about new syntactic phenomena. Languages typically start as lexical-thematic, without any functional categories (i.e. DP, IP/TP, and perhaps CP), and the emergence of a new functional category is the characteristic mark of a transition from one stage to the next.

The development of infinitival constructions is an instantiation of the same process as we have observed in the previous sections. I assume that Present-day English infinitives are non-finite clauses, the projection of a non-finite Infl, although infinitival IPs may be classified into different types. I argue that these infinitival constructions having a clausal structure were made possible due to the emergence of a functional category, in this case an Infl. Before the emergence of Infl, Old English precursors had no clausal properties and then Old English had no syntactic embedding which means that another clause occupies the argument position of main clauses.

The ancestors of Present-day infinitivals are derived nominals. There are some who assert that the nominal property of 'infinitives' in Old English is overestimated. However, their nominal origin is clear from the presence of case inflections, although these are reduced to only two, *-an* (nominative/accusative), and *-enne* (dative) in the available Old English texts. Furthermore, as a nominal, its gender was neuter. These nominal forms were used as arguments of a verb. In Old English *I can write, can* was a full lexical verb meaning *know*, and *write* (Old English *writan*) was its object argument. So, the correct gloss of this sentence is 'I know writing.' This sentence had no two clauses, i.e. no syntactic embedding. Their nominal status is also shown by the fact that '*to* + *-enne*' could have both active and passive interpretations in Old English. The spread of passive infinitives is a striking feature of Middle English (cf. Fisher et al. (2000: 99-100)), although there is a different view on this. Likewise, perfect infinitives like 'I am glad to have met the king' did not develop well until the Middle English period (cf. Ono and Nakao (1980: 420), Nakao (1972: 308), Fischer et al. (2000: 100)).

Then, I argue that old English had no infinitival clauses. There are a few pieces of syntactic evidence for the non-presence of infinitival clauses in Old English. ECM constructions were absent in Old English except in direct translation from Latin. Given that the complement to ECM verbs is an instantiation of an Infl, the absence of the ECM constructions in Old English is ascribed to the absence of an Infl in the relevant structure.

(26) *I believe* [$_{IP}$ him to have killed John].

So-called raising constructions are also analysed as an instantiation of embedding in present-day English:

(27) *Mary seems to be happy*

It is widely accepted that the matrix subjects in these sentences are raised from the subject positions of the lower clauses by subject-raising:

(28) _e_   seems   [IP *Mary* to be happy]

These NPs obligatorily move from the subject positions of the lower clauses into the higher clauses. Hence, the presence of the subject raising constructions provides a strong piece of evidence for the presence of lower IPs. These subject-raising constructions are, however, not found in Old English and are rare even in early Middle English (Traugott (1972), Kageyama (1975)). Although some point out that there are a few instance of subject-raising (Allen (1984: 464), Anderson (1988: 14)), the examples they refer to need not contain an embedded clause (see Denison, (1993: 220)).

As mentioned above, the presence of a non-finite Infl in Present-day infinitives is well established in the literature. Hence, the conclusion drawn from these facts is that an Infl emerged in the relevant nominal structure. Infinitival constructions, which are an instantiation of embedding of IPs, were made possible due to the emergence of a functional category Infl into the earlier nominal precursors. After the emergence of Infl, the integration of another IP into a higher IP was made possible (cf. Osawa (2003b)).

Thus, there is a parallelism between the development of the clause structure, i.e. the development of syntactic embedding and a DP structure: just as another clause is integrated into a higher clause, so too another DP can be integrated into a higher DP. Present-day English clauses have a configurational structure with full-fledged functional projections. IP contains another IP. This development of clause structure, which has been referred to as a change from parataxis to hypotaxis in more traditional terms, is described as a change from flat to embedded structure.

7. Recursion from a historical perspective

The use of recursion in natural language has long been recognised implicitly. However, recursion was explicitly formalised by Chomsky (1957) for the first time. Unlimited extension of language is possible through the device of embedding sentences within sentences. This notion has been an important issue in syntactic theory ever since. Recently, this recursion is further refined and clarified from a viewpoint of language evolution in Hauser, Chomsky and Fitch (2002).

Hauser, Chomsky and Fitch (2002) argue what is special about language, and propose that a distinction should be made between the faculty of language in the broad sense (FLB) and in the narrow sense (FLN). FLN only includes recursion and is the only uniquely human component of the faculty of language. This FLN constitutes core syntax. This recursion is supposed to be the mechanism of forming a hierarchical structure by Merge and Move indefinitely. More recently, movement is integrated into Merge operation as internal Merge. So, Merge is an only syntactic operation within the Minimalist approach. Other aspects of language such as the lexicon are excluded from FLN. Language is perfect in that there is a perfect mapping between sound and meaning. Language exists in the only possible form that is usable.

There are many critical analyses of what is meant by this 'recursion only', for example, Pinker and Jackendoff (2005), Parker (2006) to name just a few. As Parker (2006) points out, the problem with Hauser, Chomsky and Fitch (2002) is the vagueness of their notion of recursion. "Hauser, Chomsky and Fitch (and the ensuing rejoinders too) are strikingly vague. What is meant by the term 'recursion'? (Parker 2006).

I investigate the plausibility of their argument about recursion from a historical perspective, referring to Parker's criticism, and propose a new definition of recursion, which is different from Hauser, Chomsky and Fitch (2002) in some points.

Apart from referring to the vagueness, the main points of Parker's criticisms are that recursion is not unique to languages of humans, and the presence of (human) languages without recursion shows that recursion may not even be necessary to human communication. To sum up, recursion is neither uniquely human nor uniquely linguistic, and thus should not be characterised as a property of the faculty of language in the narrow sense (FLN). I will discuss the above points and show that the criticisms appear to be not implausible. However, it does not mean that their proposal should be abandoned. Rather, with some refinements, I argue that this 'recursion only' fits in with the diachronic development of human languages.

The notion of recursion may originate in mathematics, but the definition varies from person to person. It means phrase structure rules to someone; it is the same as repetition to others; or there are some who emphasise the embedded nature of recursive structures. Although I am sympathetic to the last position, this idea needs more clarification.

First, is recursion not unique to languages of humans, as argued? It is true that the notion of simple hierarchy may be attested among animals. A simple repetition of elements can be observed in communicative behaviours of animals. For example, chimpanzees are said to arrange certain symbols in the correct order (cf. Eysenck and Eysenck (1981)). However, the association of any element to another one in a given hierarchy based on the structure can be possible only in human languages. Recursion is not reduced to the simple repetition of elements.

I clarify the notion of recursion as syntactic embedding using a functional projection. More specifically, recursion is defined as embedding an element within another instance of the same status through a relevant functional category. The above mentioned historical facts are realisation of this process. This is an essential part of humanity, since this is an integration of another concept within one. Conceptual integration is unique to human beings.

Secondly, as Parker (2006) argues, we cannot deny the presence of human languages without recursion. Parker (2006) mentions the Amazonian language Pirahã, which does not make use of recursion (cf. Everett (2005)). Although Pirahã uses juxtaposition instead of recursive embedding, Pirahã speakers can express the same conceptual structures as English speakers. Pirahã is a full human language without recursion. Parker (2006) states that this would indicate that recursion cannot be the defining property of human language and then, their proposal cannot be correct.

However, if we draw on the emergence theory of language change (cf. Osawa 2003a), we can find a way out of this. As stated above, my general background assumption is that functional categories are not operative in earlier languages, but over a period of time a functional category emerges and the new, emergent functional category brings about new syntactic phenomena. I propose that this applies to both diachronic change and synchronic variation. In other words, both diachronic language change and synchronic language variation are due to differences in functional categories between languages; whether in a given language functional features such as tense or agreement are realised as functional categories which have their own projection like DP and IP/TP, or these features are expressed in a different way, for example morphologically (affixation, etc.). Synchronically, some languages have highly developed functional category systems like Present-day English, while other languages have very limited ones or may have none at all. The latter is the case with Pirahã, which lacks determiner, complementiser and relative tense systems (cf. Everett (2005)). I would also suggest that Modern Japanese is another example, since Japanese is often assumed to lack functional categories (cf. Fukui (1995)), although arguably. This means the absence of D, C and I/T, and hence, related syntactic phenomena. It is a well-established fact that Japanese does not have the equivalents of English articles such as *a* or *the* (cf. Fukui (1995)). Thus, noun phrases can occur freely without being accompanied by anything, irrespective of differences in nouns such as countable, or mass, and singular or plural.

There may be a strong objection against the claim that Japanese has no IP/TP, since Japanese has a morpheme *–ta*, which is assumed to denote a past tense, then, is assumed to suggest the presence of TP. Although *–ta* sometimes denotes that events happen in the past, this *–ta* does not form a syntactic category, as Fukui (1995: 109) argues. Note that TP is a syntactic category which is projected in the clause structure: this should be differentiated from a semantic notion of 'past time'. The presence of IP/TP has many syntactic effects such as the subject requirement known as the EPP, modal auxiliaries, *do*-support, subject-verb agreement, and subject-auxiliary inversion. All of these properties are lacking in Japanese. *Do*-support and modal auxiliaries are simply lacking in Japanese. Subject-verb agreement is likewise absent in Japanese as well, since in this language there are no devices to express φ-features. Hence, Japanese is supposed to lack syntactic embedding like infinitivals.

If Japanese has no IP/TP, it follows that Japanese has no syntactic embedding such as infinitivals. This means that Japanese has no recursion which is defined as a syntactic embedding using a functional projection. Although this needs more elaborate discussion, I do not go into further details in this paper because of space limitation.

Diachronically, English is a good example, as we have observed so far. English started without a functional system, and later functional categories emerged, finally reaching a stage where functional categories have fully developed Hence, the presence of a language without recursion is not incompatible with the position that recursion is essential in human language, as long as recursion is defined as the syntactic embedding using a relevant functional category. This argument is not so easily verified, if we consider the newness of available Old English texts. However, as we have observed so far, it cannot be denied that there is a strong tendency from a flat to embedded structure in the English language.

Finally, concerning the problem that recursion is not uniquely linguistic, Parker (2006) points out that recursion is observed in a human non-linguistic activity such as music. However, Parker (2006) herself admits, it is very difficult to ascertain "if a piece consisting of repeated phrases should be analysed iteratively or recursively" in music. Although the organisation of music includes iteration, it is definitely different from the recursion defined above.

I would like to point out that I do not assert that a language with more elaborate functional categories is more developed or evolved than a language of a flat structure, with less functional projections. The above discussion does not suggest any value judgment. The word 'development' only refers to the functional projections. I assume that the total expressive power of language is the same over time (except the size of the lexicon, which may be influenced by the size of a society). I claim that language is a self-contained system in which without functional categories any notion can be expressible by using some other devices, if it is necessary. Every language is always perfect at a certain stage in that it is usable. Still, language changes over a period of time as we have observed in this paper, since there is some potential inherent in languages.

I claim that a language may go through developmental stages from a flat to embedded structure. Then the word 'evolution' is used with respect to functional systems. It cannot be denied that language has developed for human communication, but this does not explain the whole evolutional path of human language. The contribution of adaptation may be limited. I wish to stress that there is some potential inherent in languages whereby every change targets syntax (cf. Osawa (2003a)).

8. Concluding remarks

In this paper, I have argued that recursion is defined as embedding an element within another instance of the same status through a relevant functional category. The development of both nominal constructions and clausal constructions are realisation of this process. Recursion in this sense is unique to human languages, and has a developmental nature.

References

Abney, Steven Paul
    1987   The English Noun Phrase in its Sentential Aspect. Doctoral dissertation, MIT.
Abraham, Werner – Samuel D. Epstein – Höskuldur Thráinsson – C. Jan-Wouter Zwart (edd.)
    1996   *Minimal Ideas: Syntactic Studies in the Minimalist Framework*. Amsterdam: John Benjamins.
Alexiadou, Artemis
    2004   "On the Development of Possessive Determiners", in: Eric Fuß – Carola Trips (edd.), 31-58.
Allen, Cynthia
    1984   "On the Dating of Raised Empty Subjects in English", *Linguistic Inquiry* 15:461-465.
Anderson, John M.
    1988   "The Types of Old English Impersonals", in: John Anderson – and Norman Macleod (edd.), 1-32..
Anderson, John M. – Norman Macleod (edd.)
    1988   *Edinburgh Studies in the English Language I.* Edinburgh: John Donald.
Benson, Larry D. (ed.)
    1988   *The Riverside Chaucer.* 3rd *The Book of the Duchess.* Oxford: Oxford University Press.
Blake, Barry – Kate Burridge (edd.)
    2003   *Historical linguistics 2001.* Amsterdam: John Benjamins.
Carstens, Vicki
    2000   "Concord in Minimalist Theory", *Linguistic Inquiry* 31.2:319-355.
Chomsky, Noam
    1957   *Syntactic Structures.* The Hague: Mouton.
    1995   *The Minimalist Program.* Cambridge, MA.: MIT Press.
    2005   "Three Factors in Language Design", *Linguistic Inquiry* 36.1 :1~22

Day, Mabel (ed.)
    1952   *The English Text of the Ancrene Riwle* (Cotton MS. Nero A. XIV). EETS. o.s. 225.
Denison, David
    1993   *English Historical Syntax.* London: Longman.
Earle, John – Charles Plummer (edd.)
    1892-1899 *Two of the Saxon Chronicles, Parallel: with Supplementary Extracts from the Others.* Oxford: Clarendon.
Ekwall, Eilert
    1943   *Studies on the Genitive of Group in English.* Lund: Gleerup.
Everett, Daniel L.
    2005   "Cultural Constraints on Grammar and Cognition in Pirahã: Another Look at the design features of human language", *Current Anthropology* 46(4): 621-646.
Eysenck, Hans J. – Michael W. Eysenck
    1981   *Mindwatching: Why We Behave the Way We Do.* New York: Anchor Press.
Fischer, Olga – Frederike van der Leek
    1983   "The Demise of the Old English Impersonal Construction", *Journal of Linguistics* 19: 337-368.
Fischer, Olga – And van Kemenade – Willem Koopman – Wim van der Wurff
    2000   *The Syntax of Early English.* Cambridge: Cambridge University Press.
Fitch, Tecumseh – Marc D. Hauser – Noam Chomsky
    2005   "The Evolution of the Language Faculty: Clarifications and Implications ", *Cognition* 97.2:179-210.
Fukui, Naoki
    1995   *Theory of Projection in Syntax.* Stanford: CSLI publications.
Fukui, Naoki – Hiromu Sakai
    2003   "The Visibility Guideline for Functional Categories: Verb Raising in Japanese and Related Issues", *Lingua* 113.4-6:321-375.
Fuß, Eric – Carola Trips (edd.)
    2004   *Diachronic Clues to Synchronic Grammar.* Amsterdam: John Benjamins.
Gardinaletti, Anna – Maria T. Guasti (edd.)
    1995   *Small Clauses* [Syntax and Semantics 28] New York: Academic Press.
Gelderen, Elly van
    2000   *A History of English Reflexive Pronouns.* Amsterdam: John Benjamins.
Gordon, Ida L. (ed.)
    1960   *The Seafarer.* London: Methuen.

Hale, Kenneth L.
  1982 "Preliminary Remarks on Configurationality", *NELS* 12:86-96.
  1983 "Warlpiri and the Grammar of Non-configurational Languages", *Natural Language and Linguistic Theory* 1: 5-47.
Hamasaki, Koichiro
  1993 "Eigoshi ni Okeru DP Kouzou no Kakuritsu ni Tsuite (On the Establishment of a DP Structure in the History of English)", in: *Studies in Modern English* Editorial Board (ed.), 213-223.
Hauser, Marc D. – Noam Chomsky – Tecumseh Fitch
  2002 "The Faculty of Language: What Is It, Who Has It, and How Did It Evolve?", *Science* 298:1569-1579.
Kageyama, Taro
  1975 "Relational Grammar and the History of Subject Raising", *Glossa* 9:165-181.
Klaeber, F. (ed.)
  1950 *Beowulf and the Fight at Finnsburg.* Lexington: Heath.
Longobardi, Giuseppe
  1994 "Reference and Proper Names: A Theory of N-movement in Syntax and Logical Form", *Linguistic Inquiry* 25: 609-665.
Mitchell, Bruce – Fred C. Robinson
  1992 *A guide to Old English.* Oxford: Blackwell.
Miyamae, Kazuyo
  2005 "Why Has a Functional D Emerged?", *Tsuda Journal of Language and Culture* 20: 86-98.
Nakao, Toshio
  1972 *Eigoshi II* (A history of English II). Tokyo: Taishukan.
Ono, Shigeru – Nakao Toshio
  1980 *Eigoshi I* (A history of English I). Tokyo: Taishukan.
Osawa, Fuyo
  2000a "The Historical Emergence of DP in English", *English Linguistics* 17.1: 51-79.
  2000b The Rise of Functional Categories: Syntactic Parallels between First Language Acquisition and Historical Change. Doctoral dissertation, University College London.
  20003a "Syntactic Parallels between Ontogeny and Phylogeny", *Lingua* 113. 1:3-47.
  2003b "The Rise of IPs in the History of English", in: Barry Blake – Kate Burridge (edd.), 321-337.
  2007 "The Emergence of DP from a Perspective of Ontogeny and Phylogeny: Correlation between DP, TP and Aspect in Old English and First Language Acquisition", in: Elisabeth Stark – Elisabeth Leiss – Werner Abraham (edd.), 311-337.

Parker, Anna R.
 2006 "Evolving the Narrow Language Faculty: Was Recursion the Pivotal Step?", *Proceedings of the 6th Evolution of Language Conference.*
Pinker, Steven – Ray Jackendoff
 2005 "The Faculty of Language: What's Special about It?", *Cognition* 95.2: 201-236.
Rapoport, Tova R.
 1995 "Specificity, Objects, and Nominal Small Clauses", in: Anna Gardinaletti – Maria T. Guasti (edd.), 153-178.
Ritter, Elizabeth
 1991 "Two Functional Categories in Noun Phrases: Evidence from Modern Hebrew", in: Susan Rothstein (ed.), 37-62.
Rothstein, Susan (ed.)
 1991 *"Prospectives on Phrase Structures* [Syntax and Semantic 26] New York: Academic Press.
Stark, Elisabeth – Elisabeth Leiss – Werner Abraham (edd.)
 2007 *Nominal Determination: Typology, Constraints, and Historical Emergence.* Amsterdam: John Benjamins.
Studies in Modern English Editorial Board (ed.)
 1993 *Kindai Eigo no Shosō (Aspects of Modern English).* Tokyo: Eichosya.
Sweet, Henry
 1953 *Sweet's Anglo-Saxon Primer,* revised throughout by Norman Davis. Oxford: Clarendon.
Thorpe , Benjamin (ed.)
 1844 *The Sermones Catholici or Homilies of Ælfric I.* London: Ælfric Society.
Thráinsson, Höskuldur
 1996 "On the (Non)-Universality of Functional Categories", in Werner Abraham – Samuel D. Epstein – Höskuldur Thráinsson – C. Jan-Wouter Zwart (edd.), 252-281.
Tarugott, Elizabeth C.
 1972 *A History of English Syntax: A Transformational Approach to the History of English Sentence Structure.* New York: Holt, Rinehart and Winston.
White, Robert (ed.)
 1878 *The Ormulum with Notes and Glossary.* Oxford: Clarendon.
Wood, Johanna
 2003 Definiteness and Number: Determiner Phrase and Number Phrase in the History of English. Doctoral dissertation, Arizona State University.

27 Multilingualism in English Literature: Applicable to the Study of the History of English?[1]

Young-Bae Park, Kookmin University, Seoul

In this paper I will faithfully try to follow the main stream of the theme, 'Language and Style in English literature in relation to the history of English', in particular, the multilingual status in English literature in terms of the history of the English language and to talk about how this situation could be applicable to the study of the history of English from the particular point of view, that is, language contact which is a cultural as well as a sociolinguistic viewpoint. I will focus my talk primarily on medieval English periods, extending to Early Modern English periods if necessary in this paper.

English has been in continuous contact with other languages, through either migration or invasion, colonisation, or cultural or economic domination, and language contact has had an enormous influence on the shape of the English language in one way or the other.

Before I present a multilingual status in English, it is necessary to foreground the multilingual background that English has enjoyed since its very inception as a language. Multilingualism, as we know, has already existed in Old English period. We can clearly see from the description of the island of Britain at the opening of the *Peterborough Chronicle*: 'The island of Britain is eight hundred miles long and two miles broad. There are five languages: English, British,[2] Welsh, Scottish, Pictish and Latin. The first inhabitants of this island were the Britons'. The scribes copied *fif gepeode* - five languages - and then divided the list into six. He had mistaken what should have been one language - *Brito-Welsh* - for two. The Old English words *brittisc* and *wilsc* referred to the same people.

As the Anglo-Saxons settled in eastern England, and took control, there was some movement of population. It is known, for example, that in the fifth century a large number of Britons moved to Armorica, and this movement is reflected in the

---

1   The earlier version of this paper was read at the 48th Congress of English Summer Seminar of the English Research Association of Hiroshima(ERA) held at Hiroshima University on 8 August 2007. I am very grateful to Professor Yoshiyuki Nakao who invited me to the ERA annual meeting and allowed me to contribute this revised version to the SHELL2007 proceedings organised by Professor Michiko Ogura, currently Head of *The Society of Historical English Language and Linguistics* (SHELL). I owe to Professor Ogura who gladly accepted my paper for the proceedings. All aberrations in this paper are mine, of course.

2   It is likely that the name *British* originally belonged to a dominant Celtic-speaking tribe, and that it was later used generally. From the fourth century BC Britain and Ireland together were known as the *Pretanic* Islands, and this name survives in the Welsh form *Prydain*. It was adopted by the Romans in the Latin name *Britannia*, and from this in turn we derive the English name *Britain*.

name *Brittany*. The size of the native population has been estimated at about a million (Hodges, 1984:42), and the emigrants can have formed only a small proportion of the total. People in positions of power would speak *Englisc*, there would be strong incentives for Celtic speakers to learn the new language. Speakers who then spoke *Englisc* would be in contact with the native population, and the result of this contact is that the native population learned English.

In Old English period (450 AD to 1100 AD) a number of phenomena existed that we might mistakenly think of as post-colonial and post-modern: English was fragmented, had multiple norms, varied considerably, was used in multilingual settings and evinced a fair degree of borrowing in contact with other languages. English existed in a multilingual setting amidst Celtic languages (forerunners of Cornish, Irish, Manx and Scots Gaelic). There may well have been cases of bilingualism as English gradually spread amongst the Celtic populace, though there is no clear textual evidence for this.[3] There was also in all likelihood contact with Latin, which enjoyed prestige in British cities during the Roman period (starting in 43 AD), and later in the context of the Roman Catholic Church. Extensive influence from Old Norse (forerunner of Danish and Norwegian) occurred with the Viking invasions and settlement of the 8th to the 11th centuries AD. Fisiak (1995:58) suggests that towards 1000 AD there were signs of a written standard emerging out of the monasteries in and around Winchester 'which was written and read from Canterbury to York'. In the light of Crystal's (2004:54-6) account, entitled 'The rise and fall of West Saxon', it is tempting to characterise the fate of West Saxon as 'the first decline' (of a standard English variety).

From the end of the eighth to the eleventh century, the people of England were in close contact with the invaders and settlers from Denmark and Norway. This contact was to have important consequences for the English language in different ways. The Danes and Norwegians are referred to collectively by several names, including *Norsemen* or 'Norsemen'. The generic term now used for their language is *Old Norse*, although this term can refer specifically to Norwegian.

In terms of the English Language Complex (ELC) typology adopting McArthur's term (2003:56), the following phenomena already existed in the Old English period: regional dialects, ethnic dialects (initially amongst the different Germanic tribes), social dialects (presumably between kings and lords as against the serfs), and an incipient standard. The extent of bilingualism (Celtic-English and English-Norse) in this period is unclear, and can best be described as incipient. However, in subsequent centuries gradual bilingualism and shift did occur. We

---

3 Even in Great Britain, bilingualism was common in Old English times (Old English and Scandinavian), and Middle English times (English and French) without, as far as we know, having produced a language that could be identified as a pidgin (Traugott and Pratt 1980: 373). Bilingualism has continued for centuries in Wales between Welsh (a Celtic language) and English, and is now growing under nationalist pressures.

may therefore speak of language-shift Englishes (with Celtic or Scandinavian substrates) in the post-Old English period.

The early part of the period (c.1100 AD to 1500 AD) was dominated by the linguistic consequences of the Norman Conquest, with French being the language of the new upper classes and English being associated with their subjects. In the course of time there was convergence between the two languages, one assumes after a period of bilingualism, amongst segments of the populace (Crystal 2004:124-5). This convergence, admittedly, shows up much more in English than in Anglo-Norman. The radical difference between Old and Middle English has given rise to considerable debate over the reasons for this change. One line of reasoning holds that Middle English could be said to be a creole (Bailey and Maroldt 1977: Domingue 1975), insofar as a former Germanic language emerged in the post-Conquest period as a Germanic-Romance hybrid. Whilst the consensus these days seems to be that it is not a creole on most conceptions of creoleness (Thomason and Kaufmann 1988: 306-15), we could just as well ask whether Middle English at some stage involved convergence between Old English and a language-shift variety (Norman English). The ongoing bilingualism, with incipient shift from Celtic languages to English, made the contact situation fairly complex. The conquest of Ireland by Henry II in 1164 brought French (of the nobility) and English (of their soldiers and retainers) to Ireland. However, English did not really spread in Irland at this time; rather the colonisers became bilingual (and eventually shifted to Irish).

As regards Bailey & Maroldt's interpretation of Middle English as a creolised language based on Old French, I briefly quote Milroy's much less radical creolist approach (1984:11-12). He believed that Middle English had at some point been subjected to creolisation, but that none of the extant ME texts had been composed in a creole language. In reality, in the ME texts to have survived, the Franco-English contact was reflected in especially (a) the replacement of much of the lexicon of the subordinate language with the lexicon of the other; (b) gross morphological simplification; and (c) a preference for fixed SVO word-order (Milroy ibid.). Other scholars to have seen complete or partial relexification; morphological simplification (e.g. the loss of gender distinctions); and/or a predilection for SVO order as creole-like tendencies include Poussa (1982:70), Domingue (1977:90-93) and Romaine (1994:174). In my survey of the scholarly literature and relevant background evidence there is little or nothing to support the creolisation hypothesis.[4]

---

4   Mackey (1982) suggests some diagnostics for determining that a variety is a creole. Focusing on simplification in inflection as a defining criterion of creolisation, we know that it can be caused by extensive contact with similar languages or dialects, or by the absence of a norm or standard, or by both. There is no doubt, however, that there was simplification in ME and that contact with Scandinavian and French is the most likely reason for it.

In this period (c.1500-1700) a new standard English emerged. In considering a variety of views on the topic, Fisiak (1995:81-7) concludes that a written standard arose in the 15th century but that this had no spoken correlate. The standardisation of the pronunciation of English began in the 16th century but was not completed until the 18th (Dobson 1956; Strang 1970). The growth of a standard (written and oral) was a slow and unplanned event. English was after all - like many vernacular languages of Europe - still vying for status with French and Latin at the time. However, once the ideology of a standard (Milroy and Milroy 1991:22-8) came into force, and with the increasing role of print and (much later) radio broadcasting, standard English has almost come to have a life and power of its own. Once based on spoken (regional) dialects, the ideology of standardisation has overturned that relationship, presenting the standard as the primordial entity from which other dialects deviate. This centralising ideology has important ramifications for the status of new varieties of English that developed or were developing beyond the south of England and beyond the British Isles. However, as Crystal (2004:514-34) stresses, the technological and cultural practices of the post-modern era seem to support an opposing tendency towards decentralising the norms of English.

Up to now I have very briefly outlined a multilingual external history of English from Old to Early Modern English periods, thinking that a monolingual history of English is an oversimplification, even if it is a necessary one from a system-internal point of view. This is not to suggest that historians of English have been blind to the significant periods of contact in the Old, Middle and Early Modern English periods; but that the striking fact of English being involved from its very inception in complex contact situations has not been put on centre stage. The thrust of this argument has now been addressed by Crystal's engaging and comprehensive *Stories of English*, which appeared in 2004. Crystal accords full respect to 'new standards, non-standards, informalities and identities . . . the real stories of English, which have never, in their entirety, been told' (2004:14).

What about the linguistic conditions and literary achievements in medieval England? Both poetry and prose have survived in manuscript form since Old English times though hardly huge amounts of either. For instance, Toronto University's *Dictionary of Old English Corpus* shows that the entire body of Old English material from 600 to 1150 in fact consists of only 3,037 texts (excluding manuscripts with minor variants), amounting to a mere 3 million words.[5] A single prolific modern author easily exceeds this total: Charles Dickens' fiction, for example, amounts to over 4 million. Three million words is not a great deal of data for a period in linguistic history extending over five centuries, However, that scholars

---

5   The Corpus is a comprehensive database of Old English with at least one copy of every known text represented. Healey (2005:434-480) explicitly states the full-text corpus, the web corpus, the electronic dictionary of Old English, a number of hotlinks in the entry, the publication of microfiche via a paper copy from 1986 on, etc.

have been able to find evidence of even four major dialect areas in Old English times is quite an achievement, under these circumstances. In reality, there would have been many more. East Anglia is an example of a major gap. There would have been many dialects in this area, from what we know of early patterns of settlement, but there are no Old English texts which represent them. Doubtless thousands of manuscripts were destroyed in the Viking invasions.

As regards the linguistic or more precisely sociolinguistic conditions in early English times, the Latin influence on English vocabulary began even before there was such a language as English, while Latin was in contact with the Germanic dialects on the continent. These words largely suggest the cultural sophistication of the Romans, e.g. *street, wine, butter, pepper, cheese, silk, copper, pound, inch, mile*. Once the Romans settled in Britain, other words were adopted that reflect the Romanisation of the islands, including some well-known and still used place names. For instance, *caster* became *ceaster* 'fortified settlement, town' and survives in place names such as *Lancaster, Exeter, Manchester, Doncaster*, and *Chester*.

The Christianisation of Britain (from the sixth century) brought with it the adoption of another series of Latin words, e.g. *bishop, candle, creed, font, mass, monk, priest*. It has been ascertained that over 400 words from Latin were in Old English before the Norman Conquest, though most of them have not survived until today. This was, however, the first wave of Latin influence on English.

By contrast, the contact between Old English and Old Norse was much more intimate. The 1400 Old Norse-based place names in England bear witness to the strength of Scandinavian settlements. The amalgamation of the two races was largely facilitated by the close kinship existing between them. Apart from continuing to observe certain native customs, the Scandinavians adapted themselves on the whole to the English way of life - that is, they assimilated. Since the ways of life and the respective languages of the English and the Scandinavians were not as different at that time as they are now, some linguists claim that they were mutually intelligible. The result was a linguistic fusion, which is almost without parallel in the world, although, in fact, the subsequent fusion of Danish and Norwegian in the Norway of the late Middle Ages shows many similarities. It is more commonly the case that one language takes over in a situation like this, or that they coexist, functioning side by side in some sort of diglossic distribution. Moreover, many of the more common words of the two languages were either identical or extremely close in form, and if we did not have Old English literature from the period before the Scandinavian invasions it would be impossible to say of many words that they were *not* of Scandinavian origin. In certain cases, however, there are reliable criteria for recognizing a borrowed word.

How intimate was the contact between Old Norse and English? Some commentators have suggested that Old Norse was largely responsible for the simplification of English morphology, that is, the shift in English from a synthetic to an analytic type, which proceeded apace in the Middle English period. It seems highly unlikely that Old Norse could change the typology of English when Old Norse itself was almost identical in type. Thomason and Kaufman (1988) provide persuasive evidence that Old Norse did not influence the structure of Old (and then Middle) English. They suggest that Norse influence on particular pursuits such as farming was extensive, but that it was not the trigger of the major structural changes in English in the Middle English period.

We need to distinguish at this point two phases of contact with French after the Norman Conquest. The first involves the Scandinavianised French of the Norman elite. This language would not have been more developed or more prestigious than that of the English; neither was Norman culture more international or more literate in character: probably the only technical advantages it enjoyed were military organisation and wider use of stone as a building material. Norman French was imposed by a ruling caste; but since Latin continued in its spoken form in the Church, and as the written language of scholarship, the linguistic situation after 1066 may be described as *triglossic*.

A feature of the medieval English period is that there were, comparatively speaking, very few works in English. This does not mean, however, that there was a lack of literary activity or even indeed that there has been a wholesale destruction of manuscripts. The example of Bede (673-735) shows that from the beginning of the medieval period written works were produced in considerable numbers. Such works were usually written in Latin, which was felt to be the most suitable medium of communication. Latin was an international language at that time and Bede's audience would have been smaller if he had written in Old English.[6] Ironically it may have been the Danish invasions in the ninth century which inspired the production of works in Old English. We know that King Alfred made or had made translations of several Latin prose works. So it may be that many of the scriptural poems at least were written to educate people in much the same way as Alfred's translations. Furthermore, the use made by Ælfric of Old English poetry in the late tenth century suggests that the alliterative poetic form still retained for him its vigour and appeal. Yet although Old English is far richer than most other contemporary vernacular literatures, it is abjectly poor in comparison with the output of Latin literature. Even if we could date most Old English poetry to the latter three centuries of the OE period, it would still mean that about 30,000 lines have to be distributed over 250 years; the amount is insufficient to talk seriously of any literary tradition.

---

6 The creative work of Bede in the writing of the first really scholarly history in post-classical Western Europe is well enough known. But his great Church History of the English People [*Historia Ecclesiastica Gentis Anglorum*], though written in Latin, is very English(Wrenn1967: 11) Wrenn states that the Latin writings from Britain proper, though often of real historical importance, can, with the outstanding exception of the work of the Venerable Bede, scarcely claim to be literature in any strict sense of the word (op. cit. 57-73 passim).

Unlike the Old English literature a relatively large quantity of Middle English literature survives, especially after 1250. Printing presses developed in very late ME, which helped to preserve texts from this period. Considering the low level of literacy, the amount of literature surviving is in fact astonishing.

During the Middle English period three major literary languages were used, Latin, French and English, the last of which lagged far behind the first two. Apart from a few religious admonitory texts, literature from 1150 to 1250 was generally written in French under the patronage of the court - works like the *Ormulum*, a translation of some of the Gospels read at Mass, made by the monk Orm about 1200. There is *Ancrene Riwle* - advice given by a priest to three religious ladies living not in a convent but in a little house near a church.[7] This is rather charming, and it seems that, for a time in the literature of England, there is an awareness of woman as woman - a creature to be treated courteously and delicately, in gentle language.

In the twelfth and thirteenth centuries we also find songs and histories in Latin, some of the latter throwing a good deal of light on the changing *mythology* of England. Thus the old Greek gods belong to European mythology still, and so do the old Greek warriors who gained so much of their strength and skill from the gods - Agamemnon, Ulysses, Aeneas, and so on. These heroic figures began to appear in the Latin writings of England after the Norman Conquest, and so did Brutus (the legendary grandson of Aeneas), who was presented in Geoffrey Monmouth's *Historia regum Britanniæ* (History of the Britons, written about 1140) as the father of the British race. (This work was translated into French by Wace, and his translation was translated - about 1200 - into English by Layamon. Layamon's work is in verse and it is called, after the mythical founder of the British, quite simply *Brut*.) But - and this is interesting - a far greater hero than any of Greece or Rome emerges in the figure of King Arthur. This is interesting and curious because Arthur belongs to the mythology of a race - the Welsh or true Britons - that the Anglo-Saxons drove out of England and that the Normans, invading their borders, struck with a heavy fist. Why this renewed interest in the shadowy British king and his Knights of the Round Table? Well, Geoffrey Monmouth himself had been brought up in Wales and lived close to the myth; but even Norman writers seemed fascinated by it. It possibly seems to me that the Anglo-Saxons - a defeated race - were drawn closer to the race they had themselves defeated, and helped to spread the Arthurian myth throughout England. It is more likely that the Normans, through their invasions of Wales, became interested in the Welsh and their culture. Anyway, the myth of King Arthur is as powerful today as ever it was - we can see this not only from films and children's books but

---

7   This work is named *Ancrene Wisse* only in the Corpus manuscript. Editors have adopted the name *Ancrene Riwle* for other versions preserved in four other thirteenth-century manuscripts. There are also later texts and adaptations, and translations into both French and Latin. For details, *cf.* Wada (2002); Park (2000 revised version); Kubouchi (2006).

also from the curious rumour that circulated in England in 1940 - that Arthur had come again to drive out the expected invader, that Arthur would never really die. Soon another powerful - but not quite so powerful - myth was to arise among the English - that of Robin Hood and his followers, the outlaws who would not accept Norman rule but lived, free as the green leaves, in the forest.

A text like Layamon's *Brut* (c.1200) is extant in two copies, although at least one other manuscript is known to have existed. The French text on which the *Brut* is based, Wace's poem of the same name, survives in about thirty manuscripts. Wace used as his source Geoffrey of Monmouth's of which almost two hundred manuscripts are known, and about fifty of them are from the twelfth century. Clearly it is much more likely that a later writer would have known and been influenced by Geoffrey's Latin work or even Wace's French version than by Layamon's poem.

From the linguistic point of view, French influence is most obviously marked in the spelling. The introduction of French spelling conventions gives the superficial impression that English changed very rapidly in the years following the Norman Conquest. For example, new conventions were used for the [š] sound, producing spellings such as <fisshe, fishe, fische> and eventually <fish>. An aspect of Norman spelling which can be confusing for the modern reader is that no distinction was made between the letters <u> and <v>. Both characters were used for the vowel [u] and for the consonant [v]. The angled shape of <v> was sometimes used at the beginning of a word, and the rounded shape of <u> elsewhere. Up to the seventeenth century we consequently find *us* written <vs> and *give* written <giue>.

According to Knowles (1997) the length and nature of the contact between English and French resulted in the large-scale borrowing into English of French words and expressions, and even grammar and other features of usage. There are two routes from French to English: through speech and through writing. Early borrowings are consistent with what one might expect from a relatively stable situation in which French is the language of the rulers, and English the language of the ruled. English speakers coming into contact with French-speaking superiors would need to learn some key French expressions. By the fourteenth century, French was the language of the national enemy, and as the upper classes adopted English they retained many of the linguistic habits of French. At about the same time, written English began to assume some of the functions formerly carried out in French, and English-speaking clerks would borrow features of written French into English.

During the transition period, many people would know at least two languages. Bilinguals talking and writing to each other would be able to switch from one language to the other in the course of a conversation or written text.[8]

Early French loans reflects the contact between rulers and ruled. The Peterborough *Chronicle* entry for 1137 contains the words *chancellor, prison* and *justice*, and the proclamation of Henry III (1258) has *sign* and *seal*. From the beginning English and French elements are mixed, the *Chronicle* entry has *sotlice* (French *sot* 'foolish' + English *lice* 'ly'), and the Proclamation has *crowning* (French *crown* + English *ing*). It was John Wallis (1653) who first observed that animals with English names(e.g. *ox, pig, sheep*) took on French names (cf. *beef, pork, mutton*) when served up as meat on the lord's table. Eventually words were borrowed from a wide range of different areas: government, law, hunting, sport, social relations, ships, etiquette, morals, fashion, etc. The rate of borrowing peaked in the fourteenth century - ie. at the time of the shift from French to English - and began to decline in the last quarter of the century (Dekeyser 1986).

Perhaps the change which is of the greatest historical interest in the history of English concerns the second person pronouns. Originally English made a distinction between *thou*, used to address one person, and the plural *ye* for more than one person. These were subject forms, e.g. *thou art my friend, ye are my friends*, and contrasted with *thee* and *you* used for the object or after a preposition, cf. *I saw thee/you; I gave it to thee/you*. Two types of change take place in this system. First, the ambiguity of French *vous* is recreated in English, and *you* takes over the functions of *ye*, so that it becomes grammatical to say *you are my friends*. This is perfectly normal in Modern English, but originally must have been as strange as **him is my friend*. We also sometimes find 'I gave it to *ye*,' and this is still common in some varieties of English.

In view of the transfer of French vocabulary, expressions and grammar into English, one might also expect a significant influence on pronunciation. However, English texts were written by clerks familiar with English and not by aristocratic learners of English. French influence leaves no traces until it affects not only the way native speakers pronounce their words but also the way they spell them. There have been many changes in English pronunciation which have been traced back to the late medieval period (Wyld 1920) and which could well have begun as

---

8 As a good example, Knowles (1997:55-59) quotes the following extracts from a letter from Richard Kyngston, dean of Windsor, to Henry IV on 13 September 1403. "Please a vostre tresgraciouse Seignourie entendre que a-jourduy apres noone . . . q'ils furent venuz deinz nostre countie pluis de cccc des les rebelz de Owyne, Glyn, Talgard, et pluseours autres rebelz des voz marches de Galys, et ount prisez et robbez deinz vostre countie de Hereford pluseours gentz, et bestaille a graunte nombre." One thing to notice from the quotation is just how many words used in the French have since been borrowed into English: *noon, countie, rebel, march, rob, number. Please* is used grammatically as a French word, but it actually has the English spelling.

features of a prestigious foreign accent: loss of the [r] sound after a vowel, changing [ø] to [f], and simplifying consonant clusters, such as [wr, kn, hw] as in *wrong, knee, what*.

Finally, I must mention Geoffrey Chaucer (1340-1400) and some of his works including his masterpiece *The Canterbury Tales*, giving literature something it had never seen before in the history of English literature and its significance for the study of the history of English.

Chaucer's language is a variety of Middle English. The word 'middle' implies a historical perspective, which sees it as transitional between the highly inflected Germanic language, Old English, and the relatively uninflected, syntactically ordered, standard literary language of today. But Chaucer is also modern in that the language he uses is, for the first time in the history of English literature, recognisably the language of our time. At least it *looks* like it; to listen to it is still to hear what sounds like a foreign tongue. To look at it and listen to it at the same time is perhaps the only way really to appreciate it. The modernity of Chaucer's English is attested by the number of phrases from his works that have become part of everyday speech: 'Murder will out'; 'The smiler with the knife beneath his cloak'; 'Gladly would he learn and gladly teach', etc.

In any case, when we are really immersed in a tale by Chaucer, his brilliant descriptive gifts and his humour carry us along and make us forget that we are reading a poet who lived more than six hundred years ago. We can clearly see from the *Nun's Priest's Tale* that vigour and swiftness is something new in English poetry.

> ... out at dores sterten they anon
> And syen the fox toward the grove gon,
> And bar upon his bak the cok away,
> And cryden, "Out! Harrow! and weylaway!
> Ha! ha! The fox!" and after hym they ran,
> And eek with staves many another man;
> Ran Colle, oure dogge, and Talbot, and Gerland,
> And Malkyn, with a dystaf in hir hand;
> Ran cow and calf, and eek the verray hogges,
> So fered for the berkyng of the dogges
> And shoutyng of the men and wommen eeke,
> They ronne so hem thoughte hir herte breeke.
> They yolleden as feendes doon in helle;
> The dokes cryden as men wolde hem quelle;
> The gees for feere flowen over the trees;
> Out of the hyve cam the swarm of bees.
> So hydeous was the noyse – a, benedicitee!
> (VII 3377-3393   B^2 4567-4583)

Chaucer's one of the greatest works, *Troilus and Criseyde*, a love-story is taken from the annals of the Trojan War, a war which has provided European writers with innumerable myths. Shakespeare also told the bitter tale of these two wartime lovers. Chaucer's version, with its moral of the faithlessness of women, is not only tragic but also full of humour, and its psychology is so startlingly modern that it reads in some ways like a modern novel. Indeed, it can be called the first full-length piece of English fiction. Of Chaucer's other long works I will say nothing. With some of them, after making a good start, he seems suddenly to have become bored and left them unfinished. But we must not ignore his short love-poems, written in French forms, extolling the beauty of some mythical fair one, full of the convention of courtly love which exaggerated devotion to woman almost into a religion:

> Your eyen two wol slee me sodenly,
> I may the beautee of hem not sustene,
> So woundeth hit throurghout my herte kene.
> (Merciles Beaute 1-3)

But, even in the serious world of love, Chaucer's humour peeps out:

> Sin I fro Love [escaped am so fat,
> I never thenk to ben in his prison lene;
> Sin I am free, I counte him not a bene].
> (Merciles Beaute 37-9)

Unfortunately, however, for Chaucer's work, big changes began to take place in English pronunciation, changes which quite swiftly brought something like the pronunciation of our own times. For instance, the final 'e' of words like 'sonne' and 'sote' was no longer sounded. Henceforward people could find no rhythm in Chaucer's carefully-wrought lines; they regarded him as a crude poet - promising but primitive - and he was classed with dull men like Gower and Hoccleve and Lydgate, men who we remember now only because they catch something of the great light which brazes on their master. However, just as London provided Chaucer with an audience for sophisticated poetry in English, so it also furnished him with the medium in which to compose it. The unique linguistic mixture of fourteenth century London, with its range of variant English forms, its tradition of the exploitation of such variants in literature, and the subordination of language and literature to a higher culture, represented by French, all combined to give Chaucer the historical moment and the material from which to weave original poetry. He did this by blending the English and French traditions he found, and by making an individual language amalgamated from a selection of variants found in London English, made elegant by borrowings from French.[9]

---

9   Cf. Burnley (2002: 235-250); Cooper (2005:253-271); Minkova (2005: 130-157). According to Burnley, modern authors are inclined to summarise Chaucer's debt to French in terms of simple statistics: 51 per cent of his vocabulary is of Romance origin; 1,102 of his Romance

The co-existence of French and English as the twin vernacular languages of England after the Conquest was a very unequal one and the co-existence of two languages in the everyday life of Chaucer's circle would inevitably lead to a certain 'fuzziness' in the demarcation between their two language skills. English was regarded as shifting and various, and the extent of its resources was uncertain; French was often written, at least in technical fields, with a phrasing and syntax owing much to English, whereas English had long ago adopted many of the phrasal idioms of French. In the minds of men with bilingual competence, the boundaries of the languages would be particularly ill-defined, elevation of English style, for they would most naturally be achieved by the importation into it of the words and expressions of prestigious French.

There is little doubt that the ability to use complicated words of Latin, French or even Italian origin was considered by Chaucer, his contemporaries, and more notoriously his fifteenth-century successors, to add dignity and ceremony to literary composition. Ambiguity is of particular interest to Chaucer in English literature but I will not discuss this matter because Prof. Yoshiyuki Nakao (2004) is an authority on this subject which could be fully applicable to the study of the history of English.

If Chaucer was ready to import new French, Latin and Italian loan words in order to lend grandeur to his diction and proclaim his erudition, he was also ready to employ words of a far less estimable kind in the cause of stylistic propriety. Then, what about the result of the language contact in medieval English periods and its effects to the study of the history of English in relation to English literature?

In terms of the language contact-induced change between French and English, the stress system between the two languages coexisted side by side for a long time, and a full reformulation of English stress did not occur until the eighteenth century. There is still some lack of clarity about stress in English, directly resulting from the coexistence of the two systems. In any event, the change in stress patterns was sufficient for English to change from a language that favoured alliteration in verse to one that favoured rhyme.

New influences appeared during the Renaissance, when Latin and Greek achieved unprecedented secular prestige. The following lines from Shakespeare's early play *Love's Labour's Lost* illustrates not only French influence, but also extensive Latin influence(notice there are also some Dutch words; these were borrowed during the late Middle Ages and the sixteenth century, which were times of

---

words are new in the English language. The question of what constitutes a French word is often begged by this kind of study. In any case, such statistics are of limited value in understanding the true nature of Chaucer's language.

extensive trade with Holland): This is clearly an example of multilingualism in English literature.[10]

> And I, forsooth, in love! I, that have been love's whip; ...
> A critic, nay, a night-watch constable;
> A domineering pedant over the boy
> That whom no mortal so magnificent!
> This wimpled, whining, purblind, wayward boy;
> This senior-junior, giant-dwarf, Dan Cupid;
> Regent of love-rhymes, lord of folded arms,
> The anointed sovereign of sighs and groans. (*Love's Labour's Lost*, III, i, 175-84)

Since most borrowings from Latin and especially Greek were at this time academic, they were called "inkhorn terms" and were the subject of much derision in some quarters (including *Love's Labour's Lost*). However, English speakers went on borrowing new terms from whatever languages they came in contact with, giving English its huge vocabulary and its large range of potential stylistic variants. It is borrowing that has given such triplets as *eat* (English), *dine* (French), *ingest* (Latin), or *smack* (Dutch), *kiss* (English), *osculate* (Latin), with their associated ranges from down-to-earth to polite to scholarly or scientific.

In the early days of English literature, if more than one language was used, it was primarily for decorative purposes or to show linguistic virtuosity. For example, some medieval religious lyrics and love lyrics used English, French, and Latin, often switching languages for a refrain. Later, as in the case of dialects, other languages were used in an English context for comic purposes. For example, in Shakespeare's *Henry V*, serious Anglo-French politics are discussed in English without any attempt to represent French in English, but there are several comic scenes in which French is used and misunderstood by English soldiers, and in which a French princess tries to speak English. On the whole, writers before the nineteenth century had a kind of "poetic licence" to overlook the reality of language differences, and to more or less pretend that the whole world spoke English. Under the impetus of making the fictional worlds of literature correspond to the empirical historical world, writers began to feel a need to be specific and plausible about what language was being spoken in a situation, and to explain how characters from different language communities could communicate. Literature itself imposes limits on linguistic realism, in the sense that the more languages one uses in a work, the more one limits the audience that will have access to the work. Moreover, it is rare at least for English writers to know another language well enough to compose in it. Yet, we do not believe this limitation should disqualify a writer from writing about another culture altogether.

---

10 Such words as *critic, magnificent, senior-junior, Cupid,* and *rhymes* are borrowed from Latin; *constable, pedant, mortal, pur* (blind), *giant, Dan, regent, anointed,* and *sovereign* are borrowed from French. The word *domineer* comes from Dutch.

There is no doubt that there was simplification in ME and that contact with Scandinavian and French is the most likely reason for it. Nevertheless, it is doubtful whether we can justify an assumption that there was a stable pidgin or creole English in thirteenth-century households, because we have no real record of the linguistic behaviour of bilingual individuals.

So far I have mentioned to what extent multilingualism has influenced English literature and discussed some of the linguistic changes in the works of some writers due to language contact from the early English times to the medieval English periods, in particular, loan-words and pronunciation and spelling changes during these periods. It is my strong view that we should understand the sociolinguistic situations of language contact among several languages used in the manuscripts or the works of the writers at those times and that an appropriate awareness of stylistic subtlety and elegant verbal manipulation will help understand the overview of the study of the history of the English language as well as English literature in a proper way and of course develop naturally in the sensitive reader from repeated readings, but that awareness can be advanced and encouraged by learning the possibilities inherent in the language, and by discussing particular examples of their literary exploitation.

References

Bailey, C.-j. N. — Karl Maroldt
1977 "The French Lineage of English", In: Jügen Meisel (ed.) *Langues en Contact: Pidgins, Creoles - Languages in Contact*. Tübingen: Verlag Narr, pp. 21-53.

Burnley, D.
1983 *A Guide to Chaucer's Language*. London: The Macmillan Press Ltd.

Cooper, H.
2005 "Literary Contexts", In S. Ellis (ed.) *Chaucer. An Oxford Guide*. Oxford University Press. 253-271.

Craig, H. ed.
1951 *The Complete Works of Shakespeare*. Chicago: Scott, Foreman & Co.

Crystal, David
2004 *Stories of English*. Woodstock & New York: The Overlook Press..

Dobson, Eric J.
1956 *English Pronunciation 1500-1700* (2 vols.). Oxford: Clarendon.

Dekeyser, X.
1986 "Romance loans in Middle English: a re-assessment", In D. Kastovsky and A. Szwedek (eds.) *Linguistics across historical and geographical boundaries*. Berlin: Mouton de Gruyter, 253-65.

Domingue, Nicole Z.
1975 Another creole: Middle English. *Paper presented at the 1975 International Conference on Pidgins and Creoles*, University of Hawaii, Honolulu.
1977 "Middle English: Another Creole?" *Journal of Creole Studies* 1, 89-100.

Ellis, Steve
2005 *Chaucer*: An Oxford Guide. Oxford University Press.

Fisiak, Jacek (ed.)
1995 *Linguistic Change under Contact Conditions*. Trends in Linguistics. Studies and Monographs 81. Mouton de Gruyter.

Healey, A. diPaolo
2005 "The Face of Text: The Dictionary of Old English Project in the Twenty-First Century", In J. Fisiak & H-K Kang (ed.), *Recent Trends in Medieval English Language and Literature in Honour of Young-Bae Park*, Vol I. Seoul: Thaehaksa, 433-480.

Hodges, R.
1984 "The Anglo-Saxon migrations", In L. M. Smith (ed.) *The making of Britain: the dark ages*, 35-47.

Knowles, Gerry
1997 *A Cultural History of the English Language*. London: Arnold.

Kubouchi, T. (ed.)
2006 The Linguistic and Literary Context of the *Ancrene Wisse* Group. *A Symposium Held at the 22nd Congress of the Japan Society for Medieval English Studies*. 9th December 2006. Kyoto: Kyoto Sangyo University

McArthur, Tom
2003 "World English, Euro-English, Nordic English", *English Today*, 19(1), 54-8.

Mesthrie, R.
2006 "World Englishes and the multilingual history of English", *World Englishes*, Vol. 25, No. 3/4, 381-390.

Milroy, J.
1984 "The History of English in the British Isles", In P. Trudgill (ed.), *Language in the British Isles*. Cambridge: University Press, 5-31.

Milroy, J. and Lesley Milroy
    1991   *Authority in Language. Investigating Language Prescription and Standardisation*, 2nd edition. London: Routledge and Kegan Paul.

Minkova, D.
    2005   "Chaucer's language: pronunciation, morphology, metre", In S. Ellis (ed.) *Chaucer. An Oxford Guide*. Oxford University Press. 253-271.

Nakao, Yoshiyuki
    2004   *The Structure of Chaucer's Ambiguity*. Tokyo: Shohakusha [in Japanese].

Ogawa, H.
    2000   *Studies in the History of Old English Prose*. Tokyo: Nan'un-do.

Park, Y-B.
    2000   *A History of the English Language*. Revised Edition. Seoul: Hankuk Publishing Company.

Poussa, P.
    1982   "The Evolution of Early Standard English: The Creolization Hypothesis", *Studia Anglica Posnaniensia* 14, 69-85.

Sebba, Mark
    1997   *Contact Languages. Pidgins and Creoles*. London: Mamillian.

Siegel, Jeff
    1985   "Koines and Koineization", *Language in Society*, 14, 357-78.

Strang, Barbara M. H.
    1970   *A History of English*. London: Methuen.

Sutherland, J. (ed.)
    1953   *The Oxford book of English talk*. Oxford: Clarendon.

Thomason, Sarah Grey — Terence Kaufman
    1988   *Language Contact, Creolization, and Genetic Linguistics*. Berkeley, CA: University of California Press.

Traugott, Elizabeth Closs — Mary Louise Pratt
    1980   *Linguistics for Students of Literature*. New York: Harcourt Brace Jovanovich, Inc.

Wada, Y. (ed.)
    2002   *A Book of Ancrene Wisse*. Suita Osaka: Kansai University Press.

Wallis, J.
    1653   *Grammatica linguæ anglicanæ*. Menston: Scolar Reprint 142.

Wrenn, C. L.
    1967   *A Study of Old English Literature*. London: George G. Harrap.

Wyld, H. C.
    1920   *A history of modern colloquial English*. Oxford: Blackwell.

28 Interjection, Emotion, Grammar, and Literature
Hans Sauer, University of Munich

1. Introduction

How are the terms in my title – interjection, emotion, grammar, literature - connected? The answer is fairly simple: Interjections are a part of grammar; in traditional grammars, they are treated as one of the (usually eight) word-classes or parts of speech - normally the interjection comes last in the list - and traditional grammars also state that it is the particular function of the interjection to express emotion. Moreover, our knowledge of interjections in earlier periods of English (before ca. 1900) rests exclusively on their use in written literature.

Although the interjection is not one of the major word-classes (as opposed to nouns, adjectives, verbs etc.), it nevertheless has its specific function in the system and the use of language in general and the English language in particular – Quirk et al. (1985) are quite wrong in their negative treatment and marginalisation of the interjection. In spite of them it will be interesting to have a somewhat closer look at the structure, the development, and the function of the English interjections.[1]

In any case the interjections should probably be classed among the so-called open (lexical) word-classes, to which new members are frequently added (especially nouns, adjectives, main verbs, secondary i.e. derived adverbs etc.) and not with the closed word-classes, to which new members are rarely added (especially pronouns, prepositions, conjunctions, primary adverbs, and auxiliary verbs). New interjections are certainly added to the English language all the time; for the 20th century the *OED* records, among others: *oops* 1922; *wham* 1923; *bingo* 1927; *okey-doke* 1932; *Sieg Heil* 1940 (probably just as a quotation from Nazi Germany); *yahoo* 1976; *yeek* 1982; *fabbo* (a clipping from *fabulous*) 1984; *feck* (from Irish English) 1992, etc. Of course some of those might have existed in spoken language much earlier, but we can only date them from their first written occurrence.

As the preceding statement implies, interjections are essentially a phenomenon of spoken language, but apart from being treated in grammars they are also used in literature, especially in those types of written literature which imitate spo-

---

[1] The present paper is a revised version of the plenary lecture I gave at the 2nd SHELL Conference in Nagoya in September 2007, and I am very grateful to the organisers of the conference, Professors Masachiyo Amano and Masayuki Okhado, and in particular to Professor Michiko Ogura for inviting me to give this lecture. I also had the opportunity to talk about this topic on other occasions, e.g. in Lviv (Lemberg), at the MESS in Poznan, and at the LIPP symposium in Munich. For help in preparing this printed version, my thanks are due to Julia Hartmann, Susan Bollinger, Wolfgang Mager, Gaby Waxenberger, and I am also grateful to Philip Durkin from the OED for important information, and to Peter Trudgill for encouragement.

ken language or are meant to be recited, e.g. drama, dialogues, epic and narrative texts that include dialogue. Thus the borderlines between written and spoken language are not as narrow as it might seem at first sight. Moreover, electronic recordings of spoken language have only been possible since about 1900; spoken language before that time has to be reconstructed from written sources anyway,[2] and it is perhaps ironic that some Old English interjections have only been preserved in Ælfric's *Grammar*.

In the present article I can just give a very broad overview of the English interjection and its development. I shall deal briefly with questions of definition (2.) and terminology (3.), with the treatment of interjections in grammars and linguistic literature (4.), with the inventory of interjections in Old English, Middle English, Early Modern English, and Present-Day English (5.), with questions of frequency (6.), with the origin of the forms and the development of the system (7.), with the structure of the interjections (8.), their function (9.), and their use in texts (10). Finally, there are a conclusion (11.) and references to the literature cited.[3]

2. Definition

As is the case with most word-classes, the class of interjections is not easy to define, and there are more central and more marginal members. The distinction between interjections and adverbs is especially not always clearcut. Traditional as well as modern grammars often mention three to four characteristics of the interjections, and these cover syntactic, semantic, morphologic and phonologic criteria: They are not syntactically integrated into the sentence in which they occur or which they precede; they express emotions; they are not inflected; some are not integrated into the phonological or morphological system of the language, in our case English – many of these statements are simplifications, however, and I will take up some of them in a little more detail later. As far as their form and origin are concerned, for example, a distinction can be made between primary interjections, which were created as such and are often onomatopoetic or sound-symbolic in origin (e.g. ModE *ah, aha, o/oh, wow*), and secondary interjections, that is members of other word-classes which were then also used as interjections (e.g. ModE *damn, dear me, well*) – but primary interjections are also occasionally used secondarily as nouns etc. Secondary interjections are, of course, normally integrated into the phonological and morphological system. It is often also not easy to pinpoint the exact meaning of an interjection, and many interjections have a broad range of meanings, which sometimes even stand in opposition to each other (i.e. are antonyms). Thus the *OALD* gives the following meanings for Modern English *oh*: 1. 'used to when you are reacting to sth that has been said, especially if you

---

[2] Thomas Edison first invented a phonograph in 1878 (the first word actually recorded was the interjection *hello*), but it took a few more decades of development until this invention and its successor, the record player, could be used for commercial (and scholarly) purposes.

[3] I hope to deal with the phenomenon of interjections in somewhat more detail elsewhere.

did not know it before'; 2. 'used to express surprise, fear, joy, etc.' [the definition under 1. of course also contains the element of surprise]; 3. 'used to attract sb's attention'; 4. 'used when you are thinking of what to say next'. But there are also interjections whose semantic range is narrower; thus *wow* simply expresses great surprise or admiration (cf. the *OALD*).

3. Terminology

As is often the case in linguistics as well as in other disciplines, terminology is by no means uniform. 'Interjection', the term I use here, is the term derived from traditional Latin grammar (*interiectio*), but some modern dictionaries, e.g. the *OALD*, apparently prefer the term 'exclamation'; Mustanoja (1960: 621) seems to use the terms interjection and exclamation more or less as synonyms. Hübler (2007), on the other hand, uses the term 'alternants'.[4] On the term 'inserts', used by Biber et al. (2002), see section 4 below.

All these terms go back to Latin and are relatively recent in English; they were only borrowed into English (either immediately from Latin or via French) in the 14th to 16th centuries: *interjection* < *interjectio* (literally 'something thrown in between') < *intericere*; *exclamation* < *exclamatio* < *exclamare*; *alternants* < *alternare*. Ælfric in his Latin-Old English grammar, written around 1000, translated *interjectio* as *betwuxaworpennyss* or *betwuxalegednyss*, literally 'something thrown in between' or 'something laid in between', but whether these loan-translations were used outside his grammar or outside the classroom is impossible to say – certainly they did not survive the Old English period.

'Emotion' is a relatively recent term, too; it was borrowed from French *émotion* in the 16th century, but it acquired its present meaning 'a strong feeling such as love, fear or anger' (*OALD*) still later. *Roget's Thesaurus*, which structures the English vocabulary according to word-fields (semantic fields) and was first published in 1852,[5] uses 'affections' and not 'emotions' as the superordinate term (hyperonym) for feelings such as love, hate, fear, hope etc. Today, the meaning of *affection* is mainly restricted to positive feelings, i.e. 'the feeling of liking or loving sb/sth very much and caring about them', 'a person's feelings of love' (*OALD*). A native synonym of *emotion* is *feeling*, defined by the *OALD* as (among other meanings) 'a person's emotions rather than their thoughts or ideas', 'strong emotion', but since *feeling* has other meanings, too, *emotion* is probably the more unambigous term. In any case it is noticeable that dictionaries such as the *OALD* and the *LDCE* define *emotion* with the help of *feeling*, and *feeling* with the help of *emotion*.

Of course the phenomenon of emotion is much older than the term. The traditional Latin grammars used terms such as *affectus mentis* or *affectus animi* or

---

4 Apparently he adopted this term from Poyatos (1993).
5 Here used in the edition by Dutch (1962).

affectus commoti animi, and Ælfric in his grammar translated this as *modes styrung* 'agitation of the mind' – again we do not know whether this was a common Old English term for the phenomenon under discussion or whether it was only employed by Ælfric and other 11th century teachers who used his grammar.

4. The treatment of interjections in grammar and linguistic literature

The first Western grammar was the *Technê grammatikê* by Dionysius Thrax (1st century B.C.), which established the pattern of word-classes that (with modifications) is the backbone of most grammars still today. Dionysius distinguished eight parts of speech, namely noun (nomen), verb, participle, article, pronoun, preposition, adverb, conjunction.[6] He did not yet list the interjection separately, but treated it as part of the adverb. The first author to recognise the interjection as an independent word-class was apparently Quintilian (ca. 35 – 100 A.D.) in his *Institutio oratoria*.

After Quintilian, the interjection was regularly included in grammars. Isidore of Seville (ca. 570 - 636) in his influential *Etymologiae* also mentions it (I.xiv, ed. Lindsay):

> DE INTERIECTIONE. Interiectio vocata, quia sermonibus interiecta, id est interposita, affectum commoti animi exprimit, sicut cum dicitur ab exultante 'vah', a dolente 'heu', ab irascente 'hem', a timente 'ei'. Quae voces quarumcumque linguarum propriae sunt, nec in aliam linguam facile transferuntur.

Around 1000 A.D. Ælfric in his Latin-Old English grammar (i.e. a grammar of Latin, but largely written in Old English) also deals with the interjection and translates the terminology into Old English, see the examples given above.

Another of the many sources is Hugo of St Victor (ca. 1096 - 1141), who writes[7]

> Pars orationis qua interiecta aliis partibus orationis animi tantum exprimit affectus voce incondita quae ex natura magis quam institutione profecta videtur.

These quotations show that in the late antique, the medieval and the early modern grammars three characteristics of the interjection were regarded as particularly noteworthy:

> (1) Morphologic and phonologic: The interjection is used *voce incondita*, often translated as 'rude' or 'imperfect' voice. For the ancient and medieval grammarians this apparently meant "that it has no formal relation to other words" (Michael 1970: 77) and is not in-

---

6 From a modern point of view it is noticeable that the adjective is not yet recognised as a separate word-class (but treated as part of the noun), whereas the participle is listed as a separate word-class (and not as an inflected form of the verb).
7 Quoted from Michael (1970: 78), who also gives a useful survey of early grammars.

flected; from a modern point of view it could also mean that it is not necessarily integrated into the phonological system.
(2) Syntactic: It is *interiecta* or *interposita*, i.e. it is not integrated in construction with other words.
(3) Semantic or psychological: *Animi affectum significat* or *affectum commoti animi exprimit*, that is, it expresses the emotion (of an agitated mind).
Other features sometimes mentioned are:
(4) Interjections are sometimes difficult to translate from one language into another, see the quotation from Isidore given above. Ælfric also mentions this, although when giving examples he states, e.g., that for laughter *haha/hehe* is used in Latin as well as in English (279/14-16).
(5) A further point that was discussed in grammars is whether interjections are words or one-word sentences. According to Mustanoja, who is endorsed by Mitchell, they are both, i.e. words and one-word sentences; they play "no part in the syntax of the sentence" in which they are included, but are simultaneously "functionally equivalent to a whole sentence, i.e. [they] express an idea which is complete in itself" (Mustanoja (1960: 621), also quoted by Mitchell (1985: § 1234)). Thus an exclamation like Modern English *oh* can express meanings such as 'I am surprised' or 'I am disappointed' etc.

Whereas the interjection is thus regularly treated in the earlier grammars, it is often held in low esteem, regarded as marginal or entirely ignored in later grammars, especially of the 20th century. If it is mentioned at all, the attitude is sometimes rather negative. The influential grammar by Quirk et al. (1985), which is called "comprehensive" by its authors, devotes less than two of its 1779 pages to the interjection, and what the authors have to say is even slightly hostile: interjections are a "marginal and anomalous class" (1985: 67), "they are grammatically peripheral" as well as "peripheral to the language system itself" (1985: 74), they "are purely emotive words which do not enter into syntactic relations" (1985: 853), and "Some of them have phonological features which lie outside the regular system of the language" (1985: 853). The implication seems to be that "purely emotive words" do not really have a place in the grammatical description of a language. Thus Quirk et al. represent rather a step backwards as compared to the medieval and early modern grammars. Interjections are apparently seen as something that disturbs the neat structure of the language system or at least the grammarians' idea about language structure.[8]

Fortunately this negative attitude is no longer up-to-date. The *Longman Grammar of Spoken and Written English* by Biber et al., here used in its condensed version, the *Longman Student Grammar of Spoken and Written English* by Biber et al. (2002), and ironically published by the same publisher as Quirk et al. (1985), namely Longman, has a much more positive attitude.

Biber et al. (2002: 15-16), group the word-classes (parts of speech) into three "major families of words": in addition to the well-known concepts of (1) lexical

---

8   Of course Quirk et al. (1985) was in many ways a pioneering work and has a lot of merits and I do not wish to denigrate it here – I am just talking about their treatment of interjections.

words forming open classes, and (2) function words forming closed classes, they introduce the concept of (3) 'inserts', and they regard interjections as a subgroup of the inserts. Although they reiterate familiar remarks such as "inserts do not form an integral part of a syntactic structure" (in spoken language there is often a break in intonation) and that "they often have an atypical pronunciation" (Biber et al. (2002: 16)), they nevertheless stress that inserts not only often carry emotional meaning, but also "make an important contribution to the interactive character of speech, because they signal relations between speaker, hearer(s) and discourse" (2002: 449). They also point out that inserts occur mainly in the initial position of an utterance, apart from the hesitators, which typically occur in the middle.

They distinguish between ca. nine types of inserts (2002: 450-453):

(1) interjections in the stricter sense, e.g. *oh*;
(2) greetings and farewells, e.g. *hi, hello, good morning, bye, bye bye, goodbye*;
(3) discourse markers, e.g. *well, right, now*;
(4) attention-getters, e.g. *hey, say*;
(5) response-getters, e.g. *okay, huh* /hʌ/, *eh* /eɪ/, *right*;
(6) response forms, e.g. *right, yes, yeah, okay, no, nope, mhm, uh-huh* /'əhə/;
(7) hesitators, e.g. *um* or *erm* /əm/, *uh* or *er* /ə/;
(8) polite formulae, e.g. *please, thank you, thanks, sorry, beg your pardon, pardon me*;
(9) expletives (swear words), e.g. *gosh, geez, gee, God, Jesus, Christ, good heavens, damn, goddamit, heck, bloody hell, fuck*.

Thus the treatment by Biber et al. certainly marks some progress in linguistic description, although they just give a survey and do not go into much detail. Of course classifications as this can probably never be entirely complete or a hundred percent satisfactory; to the list could be added, for example, (10) emphasisers (related to expletives) and corroborative phrases; (11) commands and exhortations; (12) commands given to animals; (13) hunting cries; (14) drinking formulae, e.g. *cheers*; (15) imitation of sounds, etc. – commands given to animals and hunting cries are mainly used by members of certain professions or practitioners of certain pastimes, thus they belong to language for specific purposes (*Fachsprachen*). As the examples also make clear, some exclamations belong to several categories (e.g. *right*). In the following, I shall continue to use the more traditional term 'interjection' to cover all types of inserts just mentioned, and I regard interjections in the narrower sense as a subgroup.

Just as many modern grammars, histories of English and historical grammars also usually treat the interjection as a marginal phenomenon, if at all. Thus the terms 'interjection' and 'exclamation' do not occur in the indices of the first two, voluminous volumes of the largest history of the English language, the *CHEL* (*The Cambridge History of the English Language*), which between them have more than 1300 pages. In grammars of Old and Middle English, a chapter on the interjection is also the exception rather than the rule. Old English interjections are dealt with fairly briefly by Mitchell (1985, I: 526 – 528, esp. §§ 1234-1239), Middle English interjections are treated in somewhat greater detail by Mustanoja (1960), and some Early Modern English interjections are listed by Hübler (2007); Shakespeare's interjections in particular have been collected by Franz (1939: 230-235). There has also been a number of recent articles on specific interjections or periods or text-types, e.g. Brinton (1996), Hiltunen (2006), Stanley (2000), Taavitsainen (1998), but as far as I know there is no general survey of the history and development of the English interjections.

5. The changing corpus of English interjections
5.1. General considerations

Just as the English vocabulary in general, the number of interjections has also grown significantly during the history of the English language. Whereas ca. 35 - 40 interjections are attested from Old English, a manual count of the *OALD* yielded ca. 170 interjections (labelled exclamations in the *OALD*) which according to the *OALD*'s title are current in Present-Day English. An electronic search of the materials of the *Oxford English Dictionary* conducted in the offices of the *OED* in Oxford in August 2007 even yielded the much higher number of 1379 English interjections attested between ca. 670 and 1992.[9] This number is, however, to be used with caution and difficult to interpret in several respects: Not all of those 1379 interjections are still used in Modern English, and many of them are secondary interjections – if only those primary interjections that are still used today were taken into account, the number would certainly be much smaller.

For several reasons it is, however, impossible to give precise numbers for any period of English: For one thing, it is not always clear which forms should be regarded as separate interjections and which as variant forms (allomorphs) of the same interjection; for another, it is sometimes not clear whether combinations of interjections should be listed separately as new interjections, or just under their parts. Thus Modern English *o* and *oh* are simply spelling variants of the interjection BrE /əu/, AmE /ou/, and *ha* and *hah* are spelling variants of the interjection /ha:/; on the other hand, Old English *nese la nese* 'no oh no' should probably be regarded as a combination of *nese* and *la*, and not as a separate interjection. Whereas *haha/hehe* is given as one interjection in Old English by Ælfric, its Modern English continuation *ha! ha!* is simply listed as a repetition of the interjection *ha* by the *OALD*, s.v. *ha* - for Old English, however, the element *ha* is not attested independently.

---

9   My thanks are due to Philip Durkin from the *OED* for conducting this research for me.

5.2. The inventory of Old English interjections (i.e. ca. 700 – ca. 1100)[10]

Keeping the above-mentioned caveats in mind, ca. 35 – 40 interjections are attested for Old English, about eight of them are mentioned in Ælfric's *Grammar*, others in other sources (cf. Mitchell (1985, I: 526-528), Sauer (2006: 46)): *afæstla, buf, ea, eala, ealswsa, efne* (plus the combination *efne nu*), *egla, enu, eow, gea, georstu, gese, haha/hehe, henu, hig, higla, higlahig, hui(g), hu, hula, huru, hwæt, la* (plus combinations with *la*, e.g. *gea la gea, nese la nese, do la do, swuga la swuga* etc.), *lahu, na, nese, nic, nu, nula, sehde, tæg tæg, uton, wa* (plus combinations: *wa is me, wamme*), *wala, walawa, wegla, weglaweg/weilawei, wel, wella, wellawell*.

5.3. The inventory of Middle English interjections (i.e. ca. 1100 – ca. 1500)

If we follow Mustanoja (1960: 620ff.), we get a list of ca. 25 primary and secondary Middle English interjections: *a, aha, alas, alack, alarm, away/awei, benedicite, ei, eiei, fie (fi, fy), ha, haha, harrow, hay (hey, hi), heyho, hohey, ho (how), lo (la), me, now, o (ow), owe, way (wey, we), weila (welo, wale), wi (we, wo (wa), wolawo (weilawo, weilawei)*. This list is shorter than the list for Old English given above; it is not complete, however: Chaucer's *tehee*, for example, is missing. Moreover, Mustanoja himself points out that in Middle English religious names were often used as secondary interjections (*God, Christ, Mary, Peter* etc.), that there were commands and exhortations (*abyd, come, go, help* etc.), salutations (*hail, well wurthe, welcome* etc.), drinking formulas (*wassail*), "corroborative phrases, oaths and imprecations" (once more: *God, Christ, Mary* etc., but also the devil, furthermore *goddamn* etc.).

5.4. Early Modern English interjections (i.e. ca. 1500 – ca. 1700)

I shall not attempt to give a complete list of Early Modern English interjections here; I only mention ca. 40 of those which are for the first time attested in the Early Modern English period (see Hübler (2007: 203-208)): *ahem, bah, bo-peep, boohoo, gee, golly, hem, holla, huh, hm, hum, humph, hush, hullo, nonny-nonny, oh, pah, pish, plash, pluff, phew, pooh, peekaboo, prithee, phoo, presto, pshaw, swash, shoo, taha, thwack, thud, tut, ugh, uh, um, whoa, whack, whoo, wow* etc.

5.5. Modern English and present-day English interjections (i.e. ca. 1700 – 2008)

Once again, limitations of space prevent me from listing all the ca. 170 interjections (exclamations) which are current in Present-Day English according to the *OALD*. Under <b>, for example, we get nine exclamations: *bah, bam, beaut, begad, bingo, boo, boy, brrr, bye*. With other letters, there is often a discrepancy

---

10 It is usually assumed that Old English began around 450 A.D.; 700 is the date of the earliest (non-runic) written records.

between spelling and pronunciation. Thus, if we take the end of the alphabet (from <u> to <z>), the *OALD* lists seven interjections under <y> /j/ (*yea, yeah, yep, yes, yo, yuck, yum*), six under <u> (*ugh* /ɜː, ʊx/, *uh* /ʌ, ɜː/, *uh-huh* /ˈʌhʌ/, *uh-oh* /ˈʌəʊ/, *uh-uh* /ˈʌʌ/, *um* /ʌm, əm/), one under <w> /w/ (*wow*), and none under <v>, <x> and <z>. *Yea, yeah, yep* and *yes* are different forms of 'yes', distinguished mainly stylistically: *yea* (old use), *yeah* and *yep* (informal), *yes* (neutral), and they show once more the problems of classification and the difficulty of being consistent: Whereas the *OALD* labels *yep* as exclamation and *yes* as exclamation and noun, it labels *yea* as adverb and noun, and *yeah* as adverb – this different categorisation, however, does not seem to be justified; all four forms should primarily be labelled as exclamations (or interjections).

6. Frequency

During all the periods of English, some interjections were (or are) attested frequently, whereas others are attested rarely or just once. While the frequently attested interjections were probably also used frequently, the question of frequency is harder to decide for the rarely attested interjections. Some of those may actually seldom have been used, but with others their rare attestation seems rather to be due to the peculiarities of written transmission. Thus it is hard to say whether Ælfric's *afæstla* (*ÆGram* 280/13) was confined to his grammar or whether it was used in other contexts, too; *haha/hehe*, also attested only in his grammar (279/15), on the other hand, must have been a common interjection, since it occurs in Modern English as well as in many other languages (cf., e.g., German *haha/hehe/hihi/hoho*), and probably goes back to Indo-European (cf. Latin *hahahe*). Similarly, Middle English *tehee* is only attested in Chaucer's *Miller's Tale* (3740), but since it is also recorded in the *EDD* from 19th century English dialects, it must have been more widespread.

In Middle English, *alas* was apparently one of the most frequently used interjections; the most frequent Modern English interjection seems to be *oh*.

7. Origin of the interjections and development of the system

As the lists given under 5.2. – 5.5. above make clear, the inventory of English interjections has changed considerably from Old English to Modern English, with the most dramatic changes occurring during the Middle English period. Many of the earlier interjections died out, whereas new interjections entered the language at all times. It is particularly striking that a number of the Middle English interjections (many of which live on in ModE) were taken over as loan-words from French (or Anglo-Norman) – some of them ultimately go back to Latin.

But to begin at the beginning: Some of the Old English interjections were probably inherited from Indo-European (via Germanic), e.g. *ēa* < *au* (cf. German *au, aua*; L *au, hau*); *haha/hehe* (see above); *wā* < **wai* (cf. G *weh, wehe*, L *vae*).[11] At least one goes back to Germanic, i.e. *gea* (cf. German *ja*). Many are Old English formations, especially those formed with *lā*, see the next section.

The fact that some interjections were affected by regular sound changes shows that at least those were integrated into the phonological system of Old English, which weakens the claim to the contrary by Quirk et al. (1985). OE *ēa* exhibits the regular sound change from Gmc *au* to OE *ēa*, and OE *wā* exhibits the regular sound change of Gmc *ai* to OE *ā* - later it changed regularly to *wō* and then to *woe* /əu/. Another example of an interjection that was affected by regular sound-changes is OE *lā* > ME *lō* > ModE *lo* /ləu/.

Some of the Old English interjections survived in later periods, e.g. *haha, what* < *hwæt, lo* /ləu/ < *lā, weila* < *wegla, wolawo* < *walawa, yea*, etc. Many of the Old English interjections died out, however, whereas many new exclamations are attested in Middle English (and in later periods). Although many of those were originally onomatopoetic, at the same time many also are loan-words from French (and ultimately from Latin), e.g. *a, ha, harrow, o, alas, alarme* (ultimately from Italian *all' arme* 'to the arms'), etc. It may seem strange at first sight that simple and onomatopoetic interjections should be loan-words, but this simply mirrors the general development of English, which was characterised by a massive influx of loan-words from French (and Anglo-Norman) during the Middle-English period. This shows that the interjections are (or at least were at that time) affected by the general development of the language and do not stand outside it, which is another argument against the claim made by Quirk et al. (1985) that interjections are outside the language system. It seems hard to imagine that interjections such as *ah, oh* etc. should not have existed in Old English, but certainly they are not attested in the written documents that have survived. The poet (or translator) of *Christ I* (= *The Advent Lyrics*), for example, regularly rendered the *O* of his Latin source as *eala*; obviously he did not want to use *O*.

The Middle English inventory of interjections is more recognisably English, and many of the Middle English interjections lived on in Early Modern English and are still current in Modern English. In the Early Modern English period also a large number of new interjections entered the English language.

8. Structure of the interjections

Earlier we mentioned the distinction between primary and secondary interjections. More important for the present discussion is another distinction, namely between morphologically simple and morphologically complex interjections, which cuts across the distinction mentioned between primary and secondary interjections. Many of the simple primary interjections apparently originated through onomato-

---

11 See the *AEW*, e.g. s.v. *ēa, gea, wā*.

poetic or sound-symbolic processes. For the formation of complex interjections, combination of elements, reduplication, and phrases play a role.

(1) Simple interjections: Some of the Old English interjections were apparently primary and morphologically simple, e.g. *se, buf, ea, gea, hig, la, na, wa* (*wa* as a noun is probably secondary), their origin was probably onomatopoetic, although some were affected by earlier or later sound-changes (e.g. *ea, wa, la, na*) and thus lost their onomatopoetic force; a few were probably secondary (and also morphologically simple), especially *hwæt* (< interrogative pronoun) and *wel* (< adverb of *god* 'good'). Many of the Middle English interjections were also simple (simplexes), among them many of the loan-words, e.g. *a, ei, fie, ha, harrow, hay, ho, o; alas* and *alarm* were complex in the donor language, but probably obscured and simple in English. Simplexes among the Early Modern English interjections are, e.g., *bah, gee, hem, huh, hum, pah, pish, plash, tut, ugh, uh, um, wow* etc.; once more, many of them are probably of onomatopoetic or sound-symbolic origin. Among the loan-words is *presto* (from Italian).

(2) Combinations: In Old English, the most frequently used element for forming complex interjections was apparently *la*. Sometimes *la* was added to other elements (often to other interjections), possibly as an intensifier, e.g. *æwfæst* (adj.) – *afæstla; ea* (interj.) – *eala; hig – higla; hu – hula; hwæt – hwætla; nu – nula; wa – wala; wegla; wel –wella*; occasionally *la* was inserted between reduplicated elements, e.g. *higlahig, hilahi, walawa, weglaweg, weilawei, do la do, swuga la swuga*. In Middle English, *la* was apparently no longer used for forming interjections (survivals from Old English were *weilawei, wolawo*), while a number of combinations were formed with *a-* in Middle English, e.g. *aha, away, a mercy* etc.; another example for a combination is *heyho*. A complex Early Modern English interjection seems to be *peekaboo*.

(3) Reduplication: Pure reduplication seems to have been relatively rare with Old English interjections, e.g. *haha/hehe; tæg tæg*, nor was it frequent with Middle English interjections, e.g. *eiei* (cf. Mustanoja (1960: 622)) – *haha* was inherited from Old English. Among the Early Modern English examples of reduplication is *nonny-nonny*; an example of a rhyme-formation is *boohoo*. On Old English reduplication with *la* inserted, which was apparently more frequent, see above.

(4) Phrases: Some Old English interjections are full or condensed phrases, e.g. *wa is me* and shortened *wamme* (mentioned in Ælfric's *Grammar*); *georstu*, apparently from *geheres þu; gese* perhaps from *ges, si* 'yes, it be', and *nese* probably from **ni si* 'may it not be, it should not be'.[12] An Early Modern English example is *prithee* from the phrase *I pray thee*.

9. Function

If we follow the distinction of functional types of interjections (or inserts) mentioned above, the following – once more very preliminary – picture emerges; it shows that some functions were expressed by interjections as early as the Old English period (and probably even before); for others, interjections were used later, or at least the use of interjections for some functions was only recorded in writing or print later.

---

12 For some of the forms, see *AEW*.

(1) Interjections in the stricter sense and for the purpose of expressing emotions have been attested at all periods, although not all kinds of emotions were attested at all periods. For example there have always been interjections expressing grief, sadness, lament etc. (and wonder, surprise), e.g. OE *ea, eala, wa, wala, weglaweg* etc.; ME *alas, weila(wei)* etc.; EModE *boohoo* etc. Interjections expressing reproach and reprimand (*fie*) or triumph and contempt ('Schadenfreude') (*tehee*), on the other hand, seem to have been new in Middle English. Of course these emotions could also be described in sentences, e.g. "He wepeth, weyleth, maketh sory chere, He siketh with ful many a sory swogh" (Chaucer, *Canterbury Tales*, "The Miller's Tale", 3618).
(2) Greetings and farewells: In Old English, greetings and farewells were apparently expressed with sentences or phrases, e.g. "Wæs þu, Hroðgar, hal!" (*Beowulf* 407); "Ælfred kyning hateð gretan ...."(King Alfred's Preface to the *Pastoral Care*). Interjections as greetings have been attested from Middle English, e.g. *hayl, benedicite*.
(3) Discourse markers: Attested from Old English, e.g. *huru* 'yet, even, truly ...'.
(4) Attention getters: Also attested from Old English, e.g. *hwæt, efne, enu, georstu, henu* etc.; cf. ME *what, why, how, lo*, as in Chaucer, *Canterbury Tales*, "The Miller's Tale" "What! Nicholay! What, how! What, looke adoun!" (3477); "Thanne wol I clepe 'How, Alison! How John!' ... And thou wolt seyn 'Hayl, maister Nicholay'" (3577 – 3579).
(5) Response getters: Probably some of the interjections mentioned under (4) also served as response getters.
(6) Response forms: Attested from Old English onwards, e.g. OE *afæstla, gea, gese; ne, nese, nic*; ME *ywis, yis, ye, nay, ne*, etc.
(7) Hesitators are apparently only recorded from Early Modern English onwards; during the Old and Middle English period literature was apparently not realistic enough to record them in writing.
(8) Polite formulas are probably attested from Middle English onwards.
(9) Expletives are apparently attested from Middle English onwards, e.g. *certes, certeyn, parfay, By armes and by blod and bones, By Goddes soule, a devel way, a twenty devel way*.

10. The use of interjections in texts

Many literary texts from the Old English period until the present day provide examples of the use of interjections. Often they are used to imitate spoken language but simultaneously also to create narrative effects; again, only a sketch can be given here. I briefly discuss examples from *Beowulf* and from Chaucer; I skip Shakespeare, but I mention the comics, a text-type that (apart from some precursors) began in the late 19th century and has been flourishing for quite some time now.

(1) *Beowulf*

Beowulf as well as several other Old English poems open with the exclamation *Hwæt*, which has been the object of at least two recent lengthy discussions.[13] In *Beowulf* (and probably in some of the other poems, too) it is used as a pragmatic or discourse marker, or, in the terminology used above, as an attention getter: It evokes the world of oral poetry and conjures up the image of the warriors who are

---

13 Brinton (1996: ch.7); Stanley (2000); cf. also Milfull and Sauer (2003).

noisy during their feast in the hall, and of the singer, the *scop*, who wants to tell his story, but has to get their attention first and to ensure that they are quiet. In all the poems concerned, *Hwæt* is also followed by the narrator's indication that he is just retelling an old story or song which he heard a long time ago, and with which his audience is also familiar. Brinton (1996) therefore labels *Hwæt* as a marker of common knowledge. One of the problems of its use in *Beowulf* is that it adds an additional stressed syllable.[14] To render the meaning of *Hwæt*, a large number of translations have been suggested, ranging from archaic and old-fashioned ones such as *Lo! Hark! Behold!* to more colloquial ones such as *Hear! Listen! Indeed!* Seamus Heaney was apparently the first translator to use *So*, and in the introduction to his translation he connects this to the Irish tinge of his translation.

(2) Chaucer

For Middle English, Chaucer provides a wealth of examples of interjections and their use. In his *Canterbury Tales* in "The Miller's Tale" alone, he uses more than twenty different interjections: *allas, benedicite, certes, certeyn, ei, fy, harrow, hayl, help, how, lo, nay, ne, out, parfay, tehee, weylawey, what, why, ye, yis, ywis. Allas* (a loan-word!) occurs most frequently (12 instances), followed by *what* (nine instances); the others are rarer. Often they are used in combination, e.g. "What! Nicholay! What, how! What, looke adoun!" (3477), or "or I wol crie: out, harrow, and alas" (3286), or in the dialogue between Absolon and Alisoun: "Fy! allas! What have I do?" / "Tehee! Quod she, and clapte the window to." (3739 - 3740). This creates the impression of colloquial speech, but nevertheless it is integrated into the metre (iambic pentameters) and is thus one of the many examples of Chaucer's narrative art. Chaucer also employs his interjections in a number of different functions, e.g. interjections in the narrower sense to express grief, sorrow and lament (*allas, weylawey*), or anger and regret (*fy*), or triumphant scorn and contempt (*tehee*); furthermore there are greetings (*hayl!*), attention and response getters (*what, how*), emphasisers and expletives (*certes, certeyn, parfay, a devel way, a twenty devel way*; some expletives are phrases: *By armes and by blod and bones, By Goddes soule*), commands and exhortations (*out, harrow*). With Chaucer it might even be possible to discern sociolinguistic differences, although this would require further investigation.

(3) Comics

When I said at the beginning of this essay that interjections are not one of the major word-classes, this is not quite true of the text-type 'comics', where interjections play a much larger role than in other and more traditional text-types. Comics are basically stories that consist of a combination of words and pictures, and that are divided into a sequence of frames. They are also basically a phenomenon of the 20th and 21st century, and they seem to be hugely popular, in the USA and in Europe as well as in Japan and in other countries. In comics, several frames in

---

14 A possible solution is to regard it as outside the metrical scheme of the first line.

sequence often consist of interjections only. A distinction has to be made, however, between interjections that imitate sounds, and interjections that are uttered by the characters.

In one of the Simpsons Comics ("How the Vest [sic!] was Won!"), in a sequence where a dog attacks Bart Simpson the sounds are imitated as "Barrk Barrk Snarrl Snap Bark Grrrrrrrr", or "Grrrr! Growl! Snap! Chew! Rend!". At least two things are noticeable here: (a) The majority of interjections used in this specific example are secondary interjections, i.e. ordinary words used as interjections – but this is not the case in other examples. (b) Spelling is used in an iconic way: The doubling or multiplying of letters is intended to imitate the intensity of the noise. I also have the impression that the relation between spoken and written language is here almost reversed: Whereas interjections are basically oral phenomena and are written down to give texts the character of spoken language, in comics sequences as the one cited above we basically have to do with written language that forms a kind of visual carpet – nobody would pronounce such sequences. To be fair, they are not uttered by one of the characters, but imitate sounds, specifically sounds connected with the dog's barking and biting.

11. Conclusion
Although I have only been able to give a brief sketch here, I hope to have shown that interjections are an interesting subject that can be approached from many different angles and that merits closer attention. From an historical point of view one insight has been that interjections form part of the system of the language in many ways (contrary to what Quirk et al. (1985) claim): Although many start as onomatopoetic or sound-symbolic formations, they are then often integrated into the phonological system of the language and are affected by ordinary sound-changes, thus also losing their original onomatopoetic force. Interjections can also be borrowed from other languages, and a number of the Modern English interjections are in fact loan-words from French (ultimately from Latin etc., e.g. *alas, oh*). Poets often integrated interjections into the metrical scheme. Another insight has been that the system of English interjections has changed quite considerably from Old English to the present day, with the most decisive break probably occurring during the Middle English period – this is in accordance with the general development of the English vocabulary. From a functional and pragmatic point of view it is important that interjections not only express emotions, but are also used for other purposes, e. g. as greetings and farewells, as attention and response getters, as hesitators, as polite formulas, as emphasisers and expletives (shading off into swear words), as commands, etc. For some of these functions, interjections have been attested since the Old English period, for others, interjections have only been attested since Middle English or Early Modern English.

References

Texts

ÆGram *Aelfrics Grammatik und Glossar*, ed. Julius Zupitza (Berlin: Weidmann, 1880; 4th ed. with a new introduction by Helmut Gneuss (Hildesheim: Weidmann, 2003)).
Beowulf Heaney, Seamus, *Beowulf* (London: Faber & Faber, 1999) [many reprints].
Chaucer *The Riverside Chaucer*, 3rd ed., gen. ed. Larry D. Benson (Oxford: Oxford University Press 1988).
Isidore *Isidori Hispalensis Episcopi Etymologiarum sive originum libri XX*, ed. W.M. Lindsay (Oxford: Oxford University Press, 1911 [many reprints]).

Dictionaries

AEW F[erdinand] Holthausen, *Altenglisches etymologisches Wörterbuch* (Heidelberg: Winter, 1934 [3rd ed. 1974]).
EDD Joseph Wright, *The English Dialect Dictionary*, 6 vols. (Oxford: Oxford University Press, 1898-1905).
LDCE *Longman Dictionary of Contemporary English*, 4th ed., gen.ed. Della Summers (Harlow,Essex: Pearson Education, 2003).
OALD *Oxford Advanced Learner's Dictionary of Current English*, by A.S. Hornby, 6th ed. ed. by Sally Wehmeier (Oxford: Oxford University Press, 2000).
OED *The Oxford English Dictionary*, ed. by J.A.H. Murray et al., 2nd ed. by J.A. Simpson and E.S.C. Weiner (Oxford: Oxford University Press, 1989).
Roget *Roget's Thesaurus of English Words and Phrases*, new edition by Robert A. Dutch (London: Longmans; Harmondsworth: Penguin, 1962 [many reprints]).

Handbooks and literature

Biber, Douglas, et al.
    2002   *Longman Student Grammar of Spoken and Written English*. Harlow, Essex: Pearson Education.
Brinton, Laurel J.
    1996   *Pragmatic Markers in English: Grammaticalization and Discourse Functions*. Berlin: Mouton de Gruyter.

CHEL *The Cambridge History of the English Language*, 6 vols., gen. ed. Richard M. Hogg (Cambridge: Cambridge University Press, 1992 ff.).

Ehlich, Konrad
1986 *Interjektionen*. Tübingen: Niemeyer.

Franz, Wilhelm
1939 *Shakespeare-Grammatik: Die Sprache Shakespeares in Vers und Prosa*, repr. 1986. Tübingen: Niemeyer.

Hiltunen, Risto
2006 "Eala, geferan and gode wyrhtan: On Interjections in Old English", in: *Essays in Honour of Bruce Mitchell*, ed. John Walmsley. Oxford:Blackwell, 91-116.

Hübler, Axel
2007 *The Nonverbal Shift in Early Modern English Conversation*. Amsterdam: Benjamins.

Michael, Ian
1970 *English Grammatical Categories and the Tradition to 1800*. Cambridge: Cambridge University Press.

Milfull, Inge B. — Hans Sauer
2003 "Seamus Heaney: Ulster, Old English, and *Beowulf*", in: *Bookmarks from the Past: Studies in Early English Language and Literature in Honour of Helmut Gneuss*. Edd. L. Kornexl and U. Lenker. Frankfurt am Main: Lang, 81-141.

Mitchell, Bruce
1985 *Old English Syntax*. 2 vols. Oxford: Oxford University Press.

Mustanoja, Tauno F.
1960 *A Middle English Syntax. Part I: Parts of Speech*. Helsinki: Société Néophilologique.

Poyatos, Fernando
1993 *Paralanguage: A linguistic and interdisciplinary approach to interactive speech and sound*. Amsterdam: Benjamins.

Quirk, Randolph, et al.
1985 *A Comprehensive Grammar of the English Language*. London: Longman [many reprints].

Sauer, Hans
2006 "Ælfric and Emotion", *Poetica* [Tokyo] 66: 37-52.

Stanley, Eric Gerald
2000 "Hwæt", in: *Essays on Anglo-Saxon and Related Themes in Memory of Lynne Grundy*. Edd. J. Roberts & J. Nelson. London: King's College Centre for Late Antique & Medieval Studies, 525-556.

Taavitsainen, Irma
1998 "Interjections in Early Modern English ...", in: *Historical Pragmatics*, ed. Andreas Jucker. Amsterdam: Benjamins, 439-465.

Studies in English Medieval Language and Literature

Edited by Jacek Fisiak

Vol. 1 Dieter Kastovsky / Arthur Mettinger (eds.): Language Contact in the History of English. 2nd, revised edition. 2003.

Vol. 2 Studies in English Historical Linguistics and Philology. A Festschrift for Akio Oizumi. Edited by Jacek Fisiak. 2002.

Vol. 3 Liliana Sikorska: *In a Manner Morall Playe*: Social Ideologies in English Moralities and Interludes (1350-1517). 2002.

Vol. 4 Peter J. Lucas / Angela M. Lucas (eds.): Middle English from Tongue to Text. Selected Papers from the Third International Conference on Middle English: Language and Text, held at Dublin, Ireland, 1-4 July 1999. 2002.

Vol. 5 Chaucer and the Challenges of Medievalism. Studies in Honor of H. A. Kelly. Edited by Donka Minkova and Theresa Tinkle. 2003.

Vol. 6 Hanna Rutkowska: Graphemics and Morphosyntax in the *Cely Letters* (1472-88). 2003.

Vol. 7 The *Ancrene Wisse*. A Four-Manuscript Parallel Text. Preface and Parts 1-4. Edited by Tadao Kubouchi and Keiko Ikegami with John Scahill, Shoko Ono, Harumi Tanabe, Yoshiko Ota, Ayako Kobayashi and Koichi Nakamura. 2003.

Vol. 8 Joanna Bugaj: Middle Scots Inflectional System in the South-west of Scotland. 2004.

Vol. 9 Rafal Boryslawski: The Old English Riddles and the Riddlic Elements of Old English Poetry. 2004.

Vol. 10 Nikolaus Ritt / Herbert Schendl (eds.): Rethinking Middle English. Linguistic and Literary Approaches. 2005.

Vol. 11 The *Ancrene Wisse*. A Four-Manuscript Parallel Text. Parts 5–8 with Wordlists. Edited by Tadao Kubouchi and Keiko Ikegami with John Scahill, Shoko Ono, Harumi Tanabe, Yoshiko Ota, Ayako Kobayashi, Koichi Nakamura. 2005.

Vol. 12 Text and Language in Medieval English Prose. A Festschrift for Tadao Kubouchi. Edited by Akio Oizumi, Jacek Fisiak and John Scahill. 2005.

Vol. 13 Michiko Ogura (ed.): Textual and Contextual Studies in Medieval English. Towards the Reunion of Linguistics and Philology. 2006.

Vol. 14 Keiko Hamaguchi: Non-European Women in Chaucer. A Postcolonial Study. 2006.

Vol. 15 Ursula Schaefer (ed.): The Beginnings of Standardization. Language and Culture in Fourteenth-Century England. 2006.

Vol. 16 Nikolaus Ritt / Herbert Schendl / Christiane Dalton-Puffer / Dieter Kastovsky (eds): Medieval English and its Heritage. Structure, Meaning and Mechanisms of Change. 2006.

Vol. 17 Matylda Włodarczyk: Pragmatic Aspects of Reported Speech. The Case of Early Modern English Courtroom Discourse. 2007.

Vol. 18 Hans Sauer / Renate Bauer (eds.): *Beowulf* and Beyond. 2007.

Vol. 19 Gabriella Mazzon (ed.): Studies in Middle English Forms and Meanings. 2007.

Vol. 20 Alexander Bergs / Janne Skaffari (eds.): The Language of the Peterborough Chronicle. 2007.

Vol. 21 Liliana Sikorska (ed.). With the assistance of Joanna Maciulewicz: Medievalisms. The Poetics of Literary Re-Reading. 2008.

Vol. 22 Masachiyo Amano / Michiko Ogura / Masayuki Ohkado (eds.): Historical Englishes in Varieties of Texts and Contexts. The Global COE Programme, International Conference 2007. 2008.

www.peterlang.de

Gabriella Mazzon (ed.)

Studies in Middle English Forms and Meanings

Frankfurt am Main, Berlin, Bern, Bruxelles, New York, Oxford, Wien, 2007.
292 pp., num. tab. and graph.
Studies in English Medieval Language and Literature. Edited by Jacek Fisiak.
Vol. 19
ISBN 978-3-631-55951-2 · pb. € 53.–*

The Volume contains written versions of some contributions to the Fifth International Conference on Middle English (ICOME 5), held at the University of Naples in 2005. Most of the papers concentrate on individual aspects of grammar and semantics, although some focus on dialectal fragmentation, and others adopt a pragmatic perspective. There is still a lot to be done in the study of the Middle English lexicon, in the same way as there are many aspects of grammar that have not been fully studied yet. The volume aims at providing contributions that can further the knowledge of these subfields of English historical linguistics, through state-of-the-art case studies that also exploit all modern resources such as computerised corpora and electronically tagged texts.

Contents: Morphology · Word formation · Semantics · Pragmatics · Text types · Dialectal distribution of forms · Document sources

---

Frankfurt am Main · Berlin · Bern · Bruxelles · New York · Oxford · Wien
Distribution: Verlag Peter Lang AG
Moosstr. 1, CH-2542 Pieterlen
Telefax 00 41 (0)32/376 17 27

*The €-price includes German tax rate
Prices are subject to change without notice
Homepage http://www.peterlang.de